D1296893

THE ARCHITECTURE OF CONCEPTS

The Architecture of Concepts

THE HISTORICAL FORMATION OF HUMAN RIGHTS

PETER DE BOLLA

FORDHAM UNIVERSITY PRESS

New York 2013

Copyright © 2013 Fordham University Press

All rights reserved. No part of this publication may be
reproduced, stored in a retrieval system, or transmitted
in any form or by any means—electronic, mechanical,
photocopy, recording, or any other—except for brief
quotations in printed reviews, without the prior
permission of the publisher.

Fordham University Press has no responsibility for the
persistence or accuracy of URLs for external or third-party
Internet websites referred to in this publication and does
not guarantee that any content on such websites is, or will
remain, accurate or appropriate.

Fordham University Press also publishes its books in a
variety of electronic formats. Some content that appears in
print may not be available in electronic books.

Library of Congress Cataloging-in-Publication Data

De Bolla, Peter, 1957–
    The architecture of concepts : the historical formation of
human rights / Peter de Bolla.
        pages cm
    Summary: "The Architecture of Concepts presents a
new history of ideas. Using digital archives to track the
historical formation of the concept of human rights across
the Anglophone eighteenth century, it argues that a better
understanding of the architecture of the concept will enable
us to deliver on its universal aspirations" — Provided by
publisher.
    Includes bibliographical references and index.
    ISBN 978-0-8232-5438-5 (hardback) — ISBN 978-0-8232-
5439-2 (paper)
    1. Human rights—History.   2. Civil rights—History.
3. Liberty. I. Title.
    JC571.D3328 2013
    323—dc23

                                        2013021233

Printed in the United States of America
15 14 13   5 4 3 2 1
First edition

In memoriam
Gregory T. Polletta

CONTENTS

This book has been made possible by the Leverhulme Foundation. Without the award of a Major Research Fellowship (2007–2010), the tooling up required to carry out this project would have been impossible. I am grateful to the director of the Leverhulme and its awards committee for providing the grant that gave me the unencumbered time that any major research project needs. I am also grateful to the University of Cambridge for accepting the terms of the award, something that increasingly one may not be able to take for granted. My faculty colleagues and the University committee overseeing leave entitlement also provided the opportunity for completing the manuscript by granting additional leave in 2011–2012.

Many friends, colleagues, and members of a large number of audiences helped me shape and refine the project. It gives me enormous pleasure to thank the following who were instrumental in providing occasions on which I had the opportunity to present my ideas in public: Amanda Anderson, John Barrell, John Bender, Jay Clayton, Maud Ellmann, Frances Ferguson, Harriet Guest, Ewan Jones, Jonathan Lamb, James Raven, Bruce Robbins, David Simpson, Cliff Siskin, and John Wilkinson.

The years spent on this project have almost precisely overlapped with my participation in the Re:Enlightenment Project, directed by Cliff Siskin at NYU. My colleagues in that project, William St Clair, Leslie Santee Siskin, Kim Sloan, and Bill Warner, have been exposed to the development of my thinking about concepts more than they might have wished. I thank them for providing excellent company and invigorating discussion. I would particularly like to acknowledge the importance of a three-way collaborative venture within the Re:Enlightenment group for testing some of the most challenging ideas presented in this book. Thanks to Cliff Siskin and Bill Warner for engaging in a truly collective enterprise.

Books are written in lived contexts. It would be fraudulent not to acknowledge the very privileged environment in which I have been lucky enough to carry out my professional life. The peculiar and often peculiarly absorbing environment of collegiate Cambridge has both generated the intellectual milieu I consider to be my home and at the same time given definition to what I have from time to time needed to escape. But whether at home or abroad, my intellectual companions have been constantly in the background as the project took shape. This book has not been written for them, but they have been my imagined interlocutors on many more occasions than they might care to know.

The pleasures and accidents of daily life also provide the backdrop for any research project, and they have had more of a determining effect on both its progress and shape than I am able to fully know. In this case, the lived context within which this book has been written has just one companion. It has not been written for her, but it has been my great good luck to count on her companionship throughout its writing.

It is a great sadness to me that another companion, the person who read the penultimate draft of this book with extraordinary care and generosity, did not live to see it in print. It is dedicated to his memory.

Shepreth, November 2012

Introduction

This book has three distinct aims. First, it seeks to contribute to our understanding of concepts. Such a contribution is doubtless fraught with difficulty since even a cursory inspection of the very wide range of disciplines and even more disparate discursive locales in which the word *concept* is used leads to the conclusion that we do not seem to have a very clear sense of what concepts are, or might be. Once one begins, say, to compare how literary or social studies work with the term, or attempts to find a common thread in how philosophy, across its various subdisciplines and areas of inquiry, deploys the word, it rapidly becomes clear that we are a very long way away from something like a general—and certainly generally accepted—theory of concepts. For many, this would seem to cause few problems. *Concept*, like its close cognates *idea* or *notion*, appears to do the work we ask of it while remaining poorly delineated conceptually. But if one is interested in the history of ideas, of how we come to think of certain things the way we do, where *things* refers not to concrete objects but to abstractions, a theory of concepts, or at least a more detailed account of how concepts are formed and operate over time and how they function in particular local instances of thinking, would be useful. Although in its most general formulation the question "Where do ideas come from?" is unlikely to generate much excitement, the more specific question "Where does the idea of universal human rights come from?" seems worth asking. And in its wake some follow up questions, "How did such an idea get credence?," "What ideas are associated with or distinguished from it?," "Have such associations or differentiations been the same over time?" also seem worthwhile. While the following study does not propose a general theory of concepts, it does suggest ways in which the questions I have just raised might be answered with clarity and detail. More specifically, it offers a particular way of understanding the history of ideas that is sensitive to how concepts are structured and operate in historically determined networks of linked conceptual forms. That internal structure—call it the disposition of its elements—coupled to its connections within and across networks of associated and differentiated concepts is what I call the "architecture" of a concept. The book's first aim, then, is to provide a more detailed and supple account of concepts as historical forms than is currently available.

Its second aim is to provide an exemplification of a specific methodology for tracking both the history of conceptual forms and their architectures by using data derived from digital archives. It is my hope that scholars will take this methodology, no doubt refining it along the way, and apply it to different conceptual examples. Since the history and shape of conceptual forms may have relevance for many researchers whose interest and expertise does not lie exclusively in the Anglophone eighteenth century or the history of ideas, I hope that the uses to which I put digital archives will provoke new kinds of inquiry in a wide range of disciplines.

Its third aim is announced in my subtitle: human rights. I intend this book to offer a contribution to the history of the concept of human rights. More narrowly, my argument outlines how current conceptions of international human rights are built upon a particular conceptual architecture that has deep roots in the Enlightenment. Unfortunately, that conceptual architecture is unfit for purpose, at least if what one wants it to do is provide the means for understanding human rights as universal, or, if not necessarily understand this concept, then put into practice the most efficacious way of realizing so-called universal human rights. In addition I shall argue that, whether or not the history of this conceptual form, or its history of formation, is decisively damaging (as the following will suggest to be the case), the current conceptual structure of "human rights"—that is, rights one holds by dint of being human—will not allow one to think universal rights in the ways we aspire to. My argument in detail, which follows, suggests that the concept is effectively constructed from the wrong supports. This is to say it will not enable one to think universal rights in something like the mood or tense that is required. It will take much of this book to explain that observation, but by the concluding chapter this third ambition—to say something of measure about how we think human rights in the contemporary moment—will be very clear.

It needs to be highlighted that this study is concerned with the concept of human rights in the English language. Whenever I speak of rights in this book, whether or not I insert the qualifier *English language*, I am referring to the specific case of a concept deployed in Anglophone culture for the most part during the eighteenth century. Concepts are, for sure, ineradicably linguistic even if, as the first chapter explains, they are not identical to words; consequently, the specific natural language in which any conceptual architecture is articulated has a determining effect on its operation, cognitive range, and reach. The difference of language cannot be easily negotiated, still less evaded. This means that one should respect the fact that the concept *droits* in French is not identical to *rights* in English. Although the uses of these two words may overlap a great deal, and the discursive environments in which they occur may be highly compatible, they do not and cannot share the same conceptual architecture. The consequences of this have been poorly understood in the now-large literature on human rights across fields and disciplines, from philosophy, international relations and politics to legal, historical or literary approaches to the topic. Moreover, as this nonnegotiability of the difference of language implies, a "universal" concept in the sense of a singular entity available to all cultures is conceptually incoherent.[1]

It should also be noted that my focus on concept rather than "discourse" seeks to do something new. Scholars working in the humanities, be their interests philosophical, literary, sociological, or historical, have become so familiar with what three or four decades ago seemed so challenging, the so-called linguistic turn, that we take for granted the idea that the close study of discourse will provide (adequate, perhaps compelling) answers to the questions we pose. There are so many accounts of this revolution (in the quiet sense) in social and cultural history, literary studies, or anthropology that even a brief sketch is unnecessary here, but I wonder if the time has

---

1. This suggests that something like "comparative conceptual history" would be a very useful tool for understanding how one might begin to get further along in the construction of conceptual forms that are both open in the sense that Morris Weitz suggested and at the same time "open" with respect to the translation of concepts across natural languages. On Weitz, see below, p. 37.

come to move below the level of the statement, as Foucault termed it, or augment our understanding of the supra-sentential discursive. My thought is this: Have we become so familiar within the habitus of discourse, so well trained to focus on both its meanderings into the unsayable and policings of the sayable that we have forgotten about its substrate? For what lies below the level of the discursive surely has as much a role to play in how and why we construct our understandings of the world as the words, phrases, sentences, and statements that we use and use us. Perhaps the time is ripe for a conceptual turn.

As I have already had occasion to remark, what we commonly, and frequently very loosely, refer to as concepts are, for the most part, what thirty years ago we would have called undertheorized. There is no widely applied "theory of the concept," no specific description of the kinds or types of conceptual form, no systematic account of conceptual structure. Although some of these things are objects of inquiry in some domains of research, by and large the idea of the concept remains very rudimentary. So much so, in fact, that for all intents and purposes one can assume that concepts are simply words. But what if we begin to develop a far more detailed and rigorous account of conceptuality? What might be gained in respect to our understanding of how we arrive at understanding? This book asks that question and proposes some preliminary answers to it. By its close, what is at stake in a "conceptual turn" should be very evident.

To begin here requires one to have at the very least a working description of the term *concept*. My first chapter elaborates such a description, which I can preempt by providing a provisional definition: Concepts activate and support cognitive processing and enable us to sense that we have arrived at understanding. They are "ways of thinking" whose identified or identifiable labels provide in shorthand the names we give to particular routes for thinking such and such, and for getting from one thought to another. Although some are far more so than others, concepts are like subway or tube maps projected into multiple dimensions, consequently their geometry is complex. It is both the disposition and arrangement of their internal elements and their external connections that comprise the ports and wiring that allow or enable those complex geometries to be created. We need to understand these internal configurations and external connections in order to get a better purchase on why a particular concept helps us to think *this* rather than that. And, perhaps as importantly, we need to be aware of a concept's architecture, its internal structure and network connections, in order to understand why we are *unable* to think otherwise. By tracing the histories of these forms, unearthing their complex geometries over time, we will better understand what there might be within a conceptual form that prevents us from thinking what we deem it important, even necessary, to think. This book argues that a more substantial account of the history of the formation of the concept "human rights" allows us to see its architecture in these ways: both enabling and disabling thinking *that*.

The distinctive contribution the book intends to make to the current discussion about and understanding of "human rights" cannot be cut loose from the particular way I see conceptual forms in general. This is because one of the consequences of moving from the discursive to the conceptual is a difference in the level of explanation which throws into relief heretofore hardly noticed or observable features of the history of ideas, the history of thinking. That difference in level requires a different forensics that is sensitive to the fact that concepts are cultural as well as mental entities. And the consequence of that, awkward or strange as it undoubtedly will seem, is the thought that culture thinks, or that the sense of arriving at understanding is not the exclusive preserve of an individual mind. Furthermore, although human agents undoubtedly generate compelling pictures of how they themselves imagine thinking—compelling certainly to them—the proposition that concepts are also cultural entities is intended to underline the fact that these same agents are inserted in supra-agential cognitive strategies. The history of ideas, as customarily practiced, operates under the rubric of the first of these observations: It assumes that ideas are held, proposed—originated even—by human agents. I do not doubt that this way of thinking has benefits and conveys what we have long taken to be a truth about how ideas in history are transmitted, connect to each other and generally create the "worldviews" that enabled historical agents to arrive at understanding. But a different way of seeing such a history of ideas, the way proposed by this book, would seek to temper that observation with another: We inherit the concepts we live by. We are inserted into variously commonly held conceptual networks that in effect think for us, or at least provide the enclosures within which thinking takes place. In order to understand how such an observation might lead to another, albeit complementary, way of tracing the history of ideas, one needs to see the difference that the conceptual turn makes. For that to become legible, the term *concept* must itself be subjected to close scrutiny. The first chapter proposes to do just that.

My second chapter sets out an innovative method for identifying the construction of concepts based on the evidence of word use across the eighteenth century. I derive this evidence from the text base of eighteenth-century printed materials, Eighteenth Century Collections

Online (ECCO), which contains over thirty-three million pages of text. Although this does not comprise a complete record of the culture at large of the English-language eighteenth century (of course there could never be such a thing) it is the best we currently have.[2] It is incontrovertibly the case, however, that these new digital archives allow us to see language use across very large communities—effectively across the print culture of the English-language eighteenth century. This is a very large corpus.

The third chapter shifts gears by turning to the historical actors who began to "culture" a new conceptual form for rights. It presents a narrative that seeks to show how a concept was constructed by collective sociality—how a linguistic community altered a conceptual architecture so that a concept might better do the work then required of it. Taking the First Continental Congress as an experimental "black box," I show how during the early 1770s the colonists made an intervention into the long history of the English-language concept of rights. It is important to register the connections between this chapter and the previous. The data presented in the second chapter help one identify where particular stresses and pressures built up over the length of the century with respect to the architecture of the concept of rights. This is why my study places particular emphasis on the period 1760–1770 and the early 1790s. The major preoccupation of the third chapter is to provide a detailed account of how a transformation in conceptual architecture became common currency in a community. It pushes very hard on the consequences of my suggestion that concepts be understood as cultural entities, and that their environment for circulation is a "common unshareable" domain, held simultaneously by one on behalf of the many and by the collective on behalf of the individual.

The fourth chapter changes tack once again. In this case, the findings of the second chapter are set against a narrative that explores the vicissitudes of a conceptual form entering the culture at large. The data clearly show a substantial upswing in the presence of "rights talk" at the end of the eighteenth century. One can hardly imagine that anyone even dimly acquainted with the period would find that surprising. Nor would the immediate cause of the spike in circulation of the word *rights* in the 1790s be news to many: the widespread public attention given to the publication of

2. ECCO remains incomplete with respect to all printed materials in English: Its inclusion of texts printed outside Britain is spotty, and even within the British isles its inclusiveness might yet be improved so as to hold parliamentary papers, court records, and so forth. It is perhaps less likely that one day it might also include manuscript materials, letters, and other handwritten ephemera.

Thomas Paine's *Rights of Man* and the attendant governmental attempts to control its circulation. But caution is required here: This does not necessarily indicate that the *concept* of human rights was by this moment well established or put into wide circulation. As this fourth chapter demonstrates, the common assumption that "human rights" were invented in the eighteenth century needs at the very least considerable revision. Of course, it needs to be said that everything here depends on what one takes the *concept* of "human rights" to be. The two previous chapters present in detail a form of conceptual analysis that is intended to make that very clear.

My conclusion draws together the various historical and theoretical strands of the argument in order to cast a different light on our uses and understanding of contemporary human rights. It suggests that our dissatisfaction with the concept can best be understood by attending to its architecture and its historical formation. The three central chapters present three different ways of doing that. To some extent, then, this book deliberately develops a hybrid form of conceptual history: It sets out to show how digital procedures can bring new facts to light while at the same time testing these new observations by using older, more familiar methods. If the book's conclusion suggests that a missed opportunity occurred in the historical formation of human rights, it does not regard that as decisive. A clear understanding of the conceptual architecture of rights, both then and now, provides a crucial first step in enabling us to think better about the inequalities that are inherent in being human. With luck, there will be future human rights.

A Note on Methodology

This study is based upon the use of digital archives, most especially Eighteenth Century Collections Online (ECCO), for constructing data-dependent descriptions of conceptual architectures. These data represent the frequencies of word use, taken both as singular terms and as concatenations in phrases. Counts are given not for the number of times a word or a phrase appears across the century but for the number of texts within which a search item appears. These frequencies of appearance in texts have been tracked in twenty-year segments, presenting the data in the manner shown in table 1.

The search operator N finds uses of the two terms in either order; the search operator W searches for the terms in the order specified. Searches for exact phrases use quotation marks: Thus, "rights of man" searches for

Table 1. Number of eighteeth-century texts containing the word *rights* within five words of *duties*.

	1700–1720	1720–1740	1740–1760	1760–1780	1780–1800
rights N5↓ duties	140	157	175	349	1136

Source: Eighteenh Century Collections Online (ECCO),
http://galenet.galegroup.com/servlet/ECCO

the exact phrase. The numerical-values count reprints of specific texts or multiple editions. Since my aim is to assess the dispersal of a concept across the culture at large (here accessed through the database of printed texts) the "noise" (insofar as it is noise) that is in these figures does not concern me. I am not proposing to compare how many times a word or phrase was used; rather, I am seeking to assess how widely a word or phrase circulated across and within the text base. And I am most interested in the appearance of words within proximate ranges of other words since this provides the basis for identifying a conceptual network. In this case it does not matter if the words are syntactically or grammatically coherent, that is used in the same sentence. For similar reasons, I am not concerned about the dissemination of specific texts or about the size of a putative readership since the methodology aims to construct a picture of a culture-wide conceptual network. It does not matter for the purposes of my argument—at least until the fourth chapter—whether many or few historic actors availed themselves of the concepts whose architectures I describe.

The extraction of these data from the archive is beset with problems that will be familiar to anyone who has explored ECCO. As is now well known, the optical character recognition (OCR) software used by Gale, the publisher, compromises the reliability of the data extracted. Although this is regrettable, the following study is intended to be exemplary of a new kind of conceptual history. When in the not-too-distant future the glitches in the software no longer cause these problems, the compilation of more secure data will be possible. But since I doubt that there will be significant changes to the profiles I have created for the concepts here studied, the revision of precise numerical values will be unlikely to lead to different conclusions. I am, nevertheless, confident that at the time of carrying out the searches (for the most part in 2009–2010) all of the data presented are accurate.

It is important to understand the ways in which this methodology has been used. The numerical data provide a first glimpse of the components of the object of my study: the architecture of conceptual forms. These data help in the reconstruction of a conceptual network and enable one to begin plotting connectivities within networks. These preliminary accounts of a conceptual architecture are then subject to scrutiny by reading into specific cases.

Something also needs to be said about the presentation of the data as raw numbers. My aim in compiling these data has been to create more precise descriptions of the architecture of the concept of rights than has been possible in the past. The raw numbers enable one to generate a picture of a concept's multiple connections and supports: They enable the construction of something like an architectural diagram or plan. When these numbers are manipulated, either through presentation in other forms, such as graphs or charts, or through statistical extrapolation, the lineaments of these architectural elements become less legible. In the case of statistical extrapolation, say the expression of frequencies of use as a percentage, the purpose of the data is distorted. This is because I am not suggesting that a set of choices presented themselves in respect to the precise connections a concept may have made within a network at a particular time, choices that could be expressed as greater or lesser likelihood for a specific connection (say, "rights-privileges" in 20% of all texts published in the twenty-year period 1700–1720); rather, I am attempting to allow a view onto the rough and ready cultural terrain within which a concept's connections to a network were multiple and inconsistent. This complex and often messy picture would have been obscured had I not presented the data simply as raw numbers. Although at certain points I depart from this, most commonly, though not exclusively, where I move from the full text base to disaggregated segments of it, this is intended to reinforce the interpretation of the raw data.

It should also be pointed out that the long lists of terms that are presented in the second chapter are exemplary rather than exhaustive. I have included both terms which on initial inspection might have been assumed to be within the orbit of rights and those which after hundreds of hours searching appeared with the greatest frequency (and, in some interesting cases, were not predicted). These lists, then, do not present *all* terms. Of course some interpretive decisions have been made with respect to inclusion, and they have been based on my own observation of how the term *rights* dragged other terms in its wake. It would be useful to learn whether these impressions would be significantly altered were one able to computationally generate a complete list of all terms. At present, the rights holder to the database will not enable such a search. Here once again my methodology is offered as a prototype: I have every expectation that future scholars will both refine it and have access to deeper computational search protocols that will develop this new way of thinking concepts in history. If this book prompts that, it will have done its work splendidly.

CHAPTER I

On Concepts as Cultural Entities

This book proposes a new way of understanding the historical formation of the concept of human rights. It has both a specific and a general target: in the case of the former it seeks to contribute to a history of political concepts, even if, as shall become clear, some of its ways of doing history may be eccentric, and in the latter it intends to test a methodology for analyzing the structuration or architecture of concepts in general. In order to make sense of these aims, it will be necessary to establish the distinctive way in which I am thinking about concepts before outlining how, in my view, they are amenable to the historical analysis of their structuration. This opening chapter seeks to do both of these things.

From such a general perspective it might look as if this project intends to find natural company within the long tradition of Western philosophical inquiry, sharing its aims or objectives, perhaps, with certain streams of speculation into epistemology or, more recently, with the philosophy of mind or even cognitive science. But, as this first chapter seeks to explain, I have come to see its contribution lying elsewhere. In fact in a certain light this project may look like an alternative, if complementary, way of understanding conceptual forms, since the account of concepts I shall try to develop, and certainly the kinds of analytic attention I shall bring to bear on concepts, leads me to suppose that the object of my inquiry—the concept of human rights—is perhaps best understood as held within culture in its largest sense.[1] By the final chapter it will have become clear what is at stake here: The structure of the concept of universal human rights is weakened—perhaps to the extent of dissolution—when rights are considered as subjective properties. If the universal is to have any purchase on how the *human* in human rights is thought, made intelligible, the concept can only be applied or operated in the supra-agential. In the common unshareable of culture. Or, to put that another way, that concept, universal human rights, finds its support in the common unshareable. This leads to the observation that, for reasons outlined in this book, contemporary attempts to operate the concept of rights in a universal register are bound to fail because the structure of the concept renders "universal human rights" incoherent: One cannot think such universal human rights with a concept of rights understood as individual or subjective claims.

It is of course the case that one might prefer to characterize human rights in terms of ideology, or seek to explore and explain those rights in terms of the language or discourse used to determine or convey them.[2] In all these cases, one might find little of note in the claim that language, discourse, or ideology are singly and severally cultural forms.[3] But the claim that the *concept* of human rights is not only a property of mind but also a property of culture is more unusual, and the distinction it upholds—

1. I do not wish to imply that this way of thinking about ideas, their generation and dissemination, is completely without precedent, although, as will become apparent, I do think that the move from the analog to the digital with respect to archival resources is game changing in terms of our ability to assess the penetration and dissemination of specific ideas within particular cultures. In some ways the current project could be seen as very old fashioned, as drawing on what Arthur Lovejoy considered to be the history of ideas that was "especially concerned with the manifestation of specific unit-ideas in the collective thought of large numbers of persons, not merely in the doctrines of or opinions of a small number of profound thinkers or eminent writers . . . It is, in short, most interested in ideas which attain a wide diffusion, which become a part of the stock of many minds." Arthur O. Lovejoy, *The Great Chain of Being* (Cambridge, Mass.: Harvard University Press, 1948), 19.

2. Much recent work of a philosophical character on international human rights seeks to clarify the language within which rights claims are made and justified. For a good account from the domain of political philosophy, see Charles R. Beitz, *The Idea of Human Rights* (Oxford: Oxford University Press, 2009).

3. Lynn Hunt, in her recent *Inventing Human Rights: A History* (New York: W. W. Norton & Company, 2007), essentially sees the issue in terms of language or discourse.

between concepts as, on the one hand, mental and, on the other, cultural entities—will be central to the investigation following. The present study, then, is less interested in how or why an individual may have had, possessed, or used a specific concept than in the recovery of a specific culture's conceptual resources. Or, more accurately, a recovery of the historical construction of a particular concept within Anglophone culture. This way of thinking about concepts is based upon the observation that the forms in and with which we think are not entirely—or even in some cases at all—of our own making or possession. We inhabit those forms presented to us, made available within the culture that feeds, polices, and sustains our interactions as persons, and it is those interpersonal communications that provide evidence for our sharing conceptual lexicons. Such interactions also, crucially, constitute the contestable space that gives definition to our senses of selfhood and thereby impact—perhaps decisively—what can be understood under the rubric of the human. How that observation impacts putative "human rights" is addressed in the concluding chapter.

Recent inquiries into the realm of the conceptual have placed considerable weight on the linguistic, supposing language to provide the aperture that gives access to the object of inquiry, concepts. It is difficult to imagine any other way of breaking in upon conceptual form unless one were to hold a radically materialist account of thought and thinking and to believe that neuroscience might one day be able to furnish the technology for inspecting those material objects within the brain that correspond without remainder to concepts. Leaving this aside, it seems to me that the focus on language may provide resources that have yet to be substantially exploited: There may be more than one way of using the aperture that language provides. Cognitive science tends to see the human subject as a language-processing machine and to portray concepts as mental counters that operate within a computational model of human cognition. The basis for this account lies in both empirical observation of language use and long-standing theories of psychology; in joining both together it provides a powerful account of how we make sense of the world and ourselves by attending to subjective linguistic behavior. According to this view, when a person uses a particular lexical item correctly, that person is said to posses the concept designated by the word. But what would this picture look like if the linguistic behavior attended to was not individual or subjective but cultural and historical?[4] Once one begins to press the aperture of language

---

4. Not all philosophers of mind share this emphasis, which provides one of the building blocks of cognitive science. Jerry Fodor, for example, perhaps the fiercest critic

changing
definition

in this different way, it begins to make sense to think about concepts as also counters in the world at large, as being held in the larger linguistic communities that are given shape by time and history, social and political praxis.

This study exploits the current situation in which the move from the analogue to the digital provides one with an opportunity for exploring the largest possible contexts for language use. This, coupled with the vast storage potential of the digital archive and the continuously evolving means for searching and analyzing the data held within it, is already opening up new ways of knowing the past. Although the current inquiry uses but a fraction of this powerful technology, it does, I hope, provide an example of some of the new methods that in the future will become far more sophisticated and attuned to newly minted specific areas of study and the questions prompted by and within them. In any event I hope that, as the present study advances, a second strand to the story above begins to emerge: If concepts can be thought about as mental entities, as held within the internal cognitive processes that human beings engage in, then they can also be thought about as cultural entities. By this I mean that concepts can be understood as inhabiting the common unshareable space of culture. This book sets out to explore that observation, testing it along the way, through the optic of a singular conceptual form, which today goes under the rubric of "human rights."

If these general remarks more or less successfully set the scene for what follows, it leaves hanging a crucial question that will be addressed at length in this introductory chapter: How is the term *concept* to be understood in this study? If, as I claim, the move from the discursive to the conceptual creates the distinctiveness of the present study, that innovation will only be legible if a more robust account of conceptuality than is currently available is provided. It is this that will enable one to assess the pay-off of my putative "conceptual turn." The first part of this chapter, therefore, will try to clear some space for thinking conceptuality in ways that might advance how we understand both how conceptual forms function and the manner in which they are connected historically to other concepts. One might imagine that a good place to begin, then, is the vast literature across many fields that inquires into this troublesome aspect of how we think (or at the very least commonly speak) about thinking.[5] This, at least, was where

---

of the cognitive science model of mind, prefers to see concepts not simply as items in a subjective mental universe but also as shareable and public. See below, note 22.

5. Another way of putting this would be to say that I will need to establish what I want the term *concept* to do. The troublesome nature of the concept is well described

I began, but it soon became apparent that this would be unlikely to yield much of any use. As the philosopher George Rey has noted, "the word 'concept' . . . is applied to a bewildering assortment of phenomena commonly thought to be constituents of thought."[6] Furthermore, definitions in this matter are notoriously vague as a cursory inspection of the dictionary illustrates.[7] Notwithstanding such difficulty, this introduction aims to negotiate some current uses of the term *concept* in order to reveal as clearly as I can what will constitute the center of attention in the rest of this book. And, perhaps more crucially, it aims to establish a difference in kind or type between conceptual forms.

Within the philosophical tradition of speculation called epistemology, the question "What is a concept?" does not necessarily take center stage, but it would be difficult to imagine an epistemology innocent of a more or less rigorous attempt to define one or other of the following: *concepts, ideas, notions,* or *mental representations.*[8] The very nature of this list and its implied distinctions or clarifications ought to be enough to warn one that this territory is full of rocks and stones ready to trip one up. Not all of the inquiries that might be called to mind here—a list of proper names will be enough to indicate the range and diversity of the tradition, from Plato through Augustine, Bacon to Descartes and Hume, from Kant through Davidson, Aquinas to Ricoeur—take the question "What is a concept?" to be foundational. There are indeed some philosophers within this wide and incoherent grouping who might have expressed a preference for beginning with an alternative query "What do concepts do?" Notwithstanding this qualification, the Western philosophical tradition of epistemology can

by Ray Jackendoff, who has noted, "Asking a psychologist, a philosopher, or a linguist what a concept is is much like asking a physicist what mass is." See "What Is a Concept, That a Person May Grasp It?," in *Concepts: Core Readings,* ed. Eric Margolis and Stephen Laurence (Cambridge, Mass.: MIT Press, 1999), 305–33.

6. See the entry for *concepts* in Samuel Guttenplan, ed., *A Companion to the Philosophy of Mind* (Oxford: Blackwell, 1994), 185.

7. The *OED* includes the following definitions: "a general idea covering many similar things derived from study of particular instances" and "something conceived in the mind."

8. If this is an accurate depiction of one of the core concerns for epistemology, it is perhaps surprising that so few histories of how Western philosophy has gone about theorizing concepts exist. This, indeed, was the reaction of Morris Weitz late in his career when he set about to write "the first" history of the theory of concepts. See the preface to his *Theories of Concepts* (London: Routledge, 1988), which remains a valuable resource.

be said to be necessarily implicated one way or another in the establishment of the concept of *concept*.[9] Be these inquiries aimed at breaking in
upon the relations between mind and world, perception and cognition, or
knowledge and belief they need at the very least a working hypothesis of
what it might be to operate with concepts in the most general sense—self-
evidently enough, one might suppose, since concepts, as the philosopher of
mind Christopher Peacocke notes, are ways of thinking something.[10]

Concepts feature, of course, in more than one branch of philosophy, and
each requires the term to do different kinds of work: Within aesthetics, for
example, conceptual coherence whereby the necessary and sufficient conditions for something to be classed under the rubric of a specific concept
(say "beauty") is often said to be inachievable or inappropriate.[11] But it is
the philosophy of mind, and especially its most recent interface with cognitive science, that provides the most striking, coherent, and substantially
developed way of thinking about concepts as mental entities. Concepts
within this tradition of investigation that has developed out of psychology
are most commonly taken to be mental particulars.[12] I shall, therefore, use

9. Although the contemporary Anglophone philosophical tradition often sets itself
against the work of Jacques Derrida, in this respect at least they share a common goal:
the elucidation of what it means to say "I know." From his early book on Condillac to
the posthumously published last works, Derrida never stopped probing the foundations
of thought and the protocols for thinking. In a late comment that will have proleptic
force in regard to my own attempts to outline the structure of the concept of human
rights, Derrida writes: "The list of 'what is proper to man' always forms a configuration, from the first moment. For that very reason, it can never be limited to a single
trait and it is never closed; structurally speaking it can attract a nonfinite number of
other concepts, beginning with the concept of a concept." Jacques Derrida, *The Animal
That Therefore I Am*, ed. Marie-Louise Mallet, trans. David Wills (New York: Fordham
University Press, 2008), 5.

10. See Christopher Peacocke, "Concepts," in *A Companion to Epistemology*, ed. Jonathan Dancy and Ernest Sosa (Oxford: Basil Blackwell, 1992), 74.

11. See, for example, Frank Sibley's now-classic essay "Aesthetic Concepts," first
published in 1959 and reprinted in Frank Sibley, *Approach to Aesthetics: Collected Papers
on Philosophical Aesthetics*, ed. John Benson, Betty Redfern, and Jeremy Roxbee Cox (Oxford: Clarendon Press, 2001), 1–23.

12. Some philosophers, however, do not start from this assumption, preferring
to see concepts as abstract entities. And another view sees them as behavioral or psychological abilities. For a good account of these differences in starting positions, see
Stephen Laurence and Eric Margolis, "Concepts and Cognitive Science," in *Concepts:
Core Readings*, ed. Eric Margolis and Stephen Laurence (Cambridge Mass.: MIT Press,
1999), 3–81; esp. 5–6.

this as my first lever for opening up an exploration of the most general question: "What is a concept?" As will become clear, this lever has helped me to identify what I think is lacking in our attempts to think about conceptual form.

Since the general orientation of this study is historical, it seeks to provide detailed accounts of the changing networked connections of "rights" over the course of the Anglophone eighteenth century, the first part of this chapter will also draw upon a very different genre of inquiry—developed in the Anglophone context to a large extent out of the history of political thought—that inquires into the historicity of concepts.[13] Commonly referred to as the Cambridge school of intellectual history, this field of inquiry is less interested in the question "What is a concept?" than in how or why concepts change over time. Once again I shall use the following sketch of a substantial tradition of intellectual inquiry as a lever for identifying with greater precision what this study proposes to address.

The Cambridge school of intellectual history sees concepts as having extension, and it is this that generates the area of interest for its practitioners. Thus, although there is no particular reason to dissent from the view that concepts are held within the mind and its processes of intellection, that is no reason to suppose that concepts are not mental entities; there is nevertheless a further aspect of conceptuality that requires examination. Concepts are things to be "grasped" from somewhere other than the recesses of the mind in order to make sense of both the world and an interior mental universe. The concept of patriotism, for example, has a long history from the ancient Greeks to our own era: It is a counter in the languages of politics that have shaped distinct periods and sociopolitical communities; it exists within the negotiated spaces that comprise the practices of everyday political life and, as such, it is often contested.[14] Although one may feel oneself to be a patriot and therefore have the sensation of possessing

13. See Terence Ball, *Transforming Political Discourse: Political Theory and Critical Conceptual History* (Oxford: Oxford University Press, 1988). Within the context of German history a slightly different project has been established, commented upon below, and most often associated with Reinhart Koselleck and his collaborators in *Begriffsgeschichte*. For a good overview, see *The Meaning of Historical Terms and Concepts: New Studies on Begriffsgeschichte*, German Historical Institute Occasional Papers no. 15, ed. Hartmut Lehmann and Melvin Richter (Washington, D.C.: German Historical Institute, 1992).

14. See Mary G. Dietz, "Patriotism," in *Political Innovation and Conceptual Change*, ed. Terence Ball, James Farr, and Russell L. Hanson (Cambridge: Cambridge University Press, 1989), 177–93.

or owning such a concept, in applying it to an aspect of one's identity it also has an external life: The concept of patriotism is a common (if malleable and contested) property.[15] Concepts, according to this way of seeing things, also exist in the *sensus communis*.

It should be noted that my second exemplary field of inquiry is not particularly interested in conceptuality in its most general forms. This helps in my preliminary attempt to characterize differences in type between conceptual entities. As its rubric indicates, the history of political thought sets its sights on what we most commonly refer to as political concepts.[16] Furthermore, this second genre of inquiry is not as coherent or consistent as the first in its adoption of a common disciplinary understanding of the nature of conceptuality.[17] For example, some working within this tradition remain skeptical as to whether concepts can in fact be said to be historical forms, as "having history" (in these cases much hangs on how one understands historicity), while others have gone on to develop a very substantial literature that seeks to trace the alteration of concepts over time.[18]

15. It is important to note that this kind of concept—what might be unproblematically taken as a political concept—does not behave in quite the same way as those concepts naming natural kinds. One could not, for example, make the same observation about the concept "bird," even if the symbolic articulation of birds and the meanings attached to specific birds clearly changes over time according to the varied cultural contexts in which the term is used. The issue here is over the shape or structure of specific conceptual forms, discussed in detail below.

16. This begs a question about the coherence of politics as a qualifier of conceptual form. Are political concepts, for example, easily and consistently differentiated from ethical concepts? For the most part I shall not be concerned to address this issue since little will hang on whether or not "human rights" belongs to a specific class of concept understood in these broad terms, while everything will hang on whether the structure of the concept "human rights" is identical to the structure of the concept "rights of man." If, as I argue at some length in the following chapter, these two conceptual forms are structured in different ways, the standard readings of the history of political thought throughout the Anglophone eighteenth century need at the very least some attenuation. More precisely, the conceptual analyses proposed by this book indicate that an error has been made with regard to the genealogy of "human rights" that sits at the center of both historical and contemporary theoretical accounts of this concept.

17. To some cognitive scientists and philosophers of mind, this will doubtless appear to be an exaggerated claim: The recent history of cognitive science is littered with disputes that appear to have small chance of resolution. Even so, the majority of cognitive scientists would accept that the central objects of inquiry for their discipline, lexical concepts, are structured mental representations.

18. See, for example, Anthony Pagden, ed., *The Languages of Political Theory in Early Modern Europe* (Cambridge: Cambridge University Press, 1987); Terrence Ball and

One could quite reasonably object that both of these traditions of inquiry—the philosophy of mind, with its outworking into cognitive science, and the Anglophone tradition of the history of political thought—are far more varied than I here suggest. I shall nevertheless leave my sketch at this rather gross level of resolution in order to preserve the hardest outlines of a distinction that provides the foundation for my own way of thinking about concepts: the difference between words and concepts.[19]

Word and Concept

Answers to the question with which I began, "What is a concept?," will to a great extent be determined by the uses to which a specific discipline wishes to put the category "concept."[20] Contemporary cognitive science, for example, is by and large uninterested in the kind of mental operations that are associated with complex thoughts since its primary focus is on

---

J. G. A. Pocock, eds., *Conceptual Change and the Constitution*, (Lawrence: University of Kansas Press, 1988); Terence Ball, James Farr and Russell L, Hanson, eds., *Political Innovation and Conceptual Change* (Cambridge: Cambridge University Press, 1989); Gordon J. Schochet, ed., *Proceedings for the Center for the Study of the History of British Political Thought*, 5 vols. (Washington D.C., 1990–1993); and J. G. A. Pocock, Gordon J. Schochet and Lois G. Schwoerer, eds., *Varieties of British Political Thought 1500–1800* (Cambridge: Cambridge University Press, 1991). As will become clear below, the alteration that most of these scholars are interested in is the *meaning* of particular concepts. My own interest is slightly adjacent to this and commented upon below.

19. For an outline of the philosophy of mind, see Samuel Guttenplan, ed., *A Companion to the Philosophy of Mind*, (Oxford: Blackwell, 1994) and for the historical traditions I refer to, see Iain Hampsher-Monk, "Speech Acts, Languages or Conceptual History?," in *History of Concepts: Comparative Perspectives*, ed. Iain Hampsher-Monk, Karin Tilmans and Frank van Tree (Amsterdam: Amsterdam University Press, 1998), 37–50; and Melvin Richter, *The History of Political and Social Concepts: A Critical Introduction* (Oxford: Oxford University Press, 1995), esp. ch. 6.

20. And even within particular disciplines there may be very divergent and competing claims about the nature of conceptuality. As Morris Weitz notes, "The history of philosophical theories of concepts, from Plato to Gilbert Ryle and Peter Geach, reveals an indisputable variety of explicit theories that range from concepts as supersensible entities (universal, meanings, abstract objects, definitions, predicates, and relations), mental entities (innate ideas, images, thoughts, or conceptions), neutral intermediaries between words and things, and abstractable items, ranging from families of sentences to an assortment of mental abilities or capacities." *The Opening Mind: A Philosophical Study of Humanistic Concepts* (Chicago: University of Chicago Press, 1977), 3.

subpropositional mental representations.[21] Within this area of inquiry, the distinction between words and concepts carries little weight; indeed classical cognitive science operates with a category "lexical concept"—examples are *bird* and *bachelor*—which happily blurs the boundary between word and concept.[22] In contrast, many anthropological accounts of conceptual acquisition use the distinction between word and concept as axiomatic.[23] For the Cambridge school historian of political ideas Quentin Skinner, the distinction is not quite so rigidly adhered to, but the stakes in holding to a difference between words and concepts is nevertheless admirably clearly spelled out. Perhaps the account of the interrelations between words and concepts closest to my own working hypothesis is that offered by Reinhart Koselleck: "A word," he notes, "becomes a concept if [the] context of meaning in which—and for which—the word is used, is entirely incorporated into the word itself." In this way words and concepts are never completely

21. Here I mean to refer to both "prototype" and "classical" accounts of concepts as described by Margolis and Laurence. See Eric Margolis and Stephen Laurence, "Concepts and Cognitive Science," in *Concepts: Core Readings*, ed. Eric Margolis and Stephen Laurence (Cambridge, Mass.: MIT Press, 1999), 3–81; esp. 8–43. The account of concepts I shall go on to develop has more affinity with what Margolis and Laurence call the "theory-theory of concepts," which understands concepts as being like theories or similar to theoretical terms; they are "representations whose structure consists in their relations to other concepts as specified by a mental theory" (47). The theory-theory view has also been used to throw light on both how and why scientific theories change over time, and on how they are generated. On this, see Susan Carey, *Conceptual Change in Childhood* (Cambridge, Mass.: MIT Press, 1985), and her more recent *The Origin of Concepts* (Oxford: Oxford University Press, 2009).

22. See Eric Margolis and Stephen Laurence, "Concepts and Cognitive Science," in *Concepts: Core Readings*, ed. Eric Margolis and Stephen Laurence (Cambridge, Mass.: MIT Press, 1999), 4–5. This should not be taken to indicate that cognitive science is only interested in what are called primitive concepts; indeed, Jerry Fodor lays great stress on a coherent account of "complex" concepts and their basis in what is called compositionality, that is, the process by which lexical items are coherently arranged into phrases in natural languages. Fodor is also committed to the view that concepts are public and shared by other people, a way of thinking about conceptuality that will be developed in a slightly different direction below. The most succinct account of his position is *Concepts: Where Cognitive Science Went Wrong* (Oxford: Clarendon Press, 1998). For a good critical account of Fodor's view, see Susan Carey, *The Origin of Concepts* (Oxford: Oxford University Press, 2009), 510–26.

23. See Pascal Boyer, *The Naturalness of Religious Ideas: A Cognitive Theory of Religion* (Berkeley: University of California Press, 1994), 61: ". . . accounts of concepts and conceptual structures should not be confused with accounts of *word-meanings*. . . ."

separable even if, as Koselleck claims, "the concept is fixed to the word, but at the same time it is more than the word."[24] In this book I too shall hold fast to the observation that words are not concepts even if concepts are expressed in words.[25] This has a common-sense feel to it: it is self-evidently the case that one cannot refer to a putative concept without using language, but it is not this unavoidable fact of linguistic representation that provides cause for reflection. It is the phenomenology of thinking. Although we evidently use words to express our thoughts, it does not feel as if we think (certainly not exclusively) in words. This sensation of something happening "in our heads" provides one of the prompts, of course, for the Western tradition's attempts to understand mind and consciousness.[26]

24. This is quoted by Hans Erich Bödeker in "Concept—Meaning—Discourse: Begriffsgeschicte Reconsidered," in *History of Concepts: Comparative Perspectives*, ed. Iain Hampsher-Monk, Karl Tilmans and Frank van Vree (Amsterdam: Amsterdam University Press, 1998), 54. Bödeker is quoting from Koselleck, *Archiv für Begriffsgeschicte*, (1967), 86.

25. Twentieth-century philosophical treatments of this issue range from the reduction of concepts to words (according to W. V. O. Quine, all talk about concepts is paraphrasable into talk about words, which leads him to conclude that there are no concepts) to the promotion of the essential difference between words and concepts. As Morris Weitz states emphatically, ". . . there are concepts . . . they are not reducible to words, things, paraphrases, contextual definitions, uses of words, or abilities to wield words or perform other tasks." *The Opening Mind: A Philosophical Study of Humanistic Concepts* (Chicago: University of Chicago Press, 1977), 17. The best succinct account of the ways in which twentieth-century philosophers approached this problem is to be found in the first chapter of Weitz's book.

26. A perfectly rational response to this observation would be to investigate with whatever means we might have at our disposal what precisely does happen "in our heads." The difficulties in doing so, however, should not be passed over lightly. Since what happens in our heads does not, in most cases, mean "what happens in our brains," we are required to first establish what mind or consciousness might be and then, having done so, invent some methods for probing the interior workings of such things. Although I have no expertise here, it seems to me that neuroscience has increasingly opened out this territory for inquiry, but it would be premature to claim that this approach—even when coupled to advances in cognitive science—will eventually reveal the secrets of mind, unless, of course, one holds (as some cognitive scientists do) that mind and brain are essentially collapsible into each other. This is to say I cannot convince myself that mind is reducible to brain without remainder, even if it seems increasingly clear to me that the complex parallel processing of the brain is the cause of my belief in mind. A recent book by a psychologist who does claim some expertise in this matter puts it in the following way: "It may represent an intractable problem that neither new measuring

That tradition—contemporary neuroscience notwithstanding—finds no difficulty in agreeing with the proposition that concepts, whatever they may be, are not identical to words. This distinction, vague though it remains, seems natural to us.[27] Or, to put that another way, we seem to want this distinction to do some work for us: We want to be able to say that the concept of the museum is not the same thing as the meaning of the word *museum.* Or we want to deny that the thing designated by the word (say, the physical building) is in some sense the instantiation of everything we take to be articulated by or within the concept "museum."[28]

A further example may help clarify what is at stake: If one were to ask whether the ancient Greeks had a concept of tourism, one would not be asking whether they had a *theory* of tourism but whether tourism was included within their mental landscape. Would they have been able to grasp the notion or idea of "tourism"? Some would wish to answer that question by posing a follow-up: "Did the ancient Greeks have a word for tourism?" And if the answer is yes, this would be taken to indicate that the concept was available to them.[29] Here, immediately, one begins to see the deep

---

devices nor computational engines could ever begin to unravel. There are too many uncertainties, too many neurons, too many idiosyncratic connections (e.g., the brain is not really organized as a simple crystalline structure) for us ever to be able to understand its detailed organization and how, specifically, this complex information pattern produces the reality we call mind." William R. Uttal, preface to *Mind and Brain: A Critical Appraisal of Cognitive Neuroscience* (Cambridge, Mass.: MIT Press, 2011), xvi.

27. It is the same division that we find in talk about concepts as being both internal, the counters of a subjective mental process, and external, something not ours that we need to "grasp" in order to arrive at understanding.

28. Putting it this way immediately opens up the gap between words and their designations, on the one hand, and concepts. The word *museum* designates both the physical building and a nonphysical set of practices, an institution that is culturally and historically determined, but even if we take the primary reference to be the second sense, the institution, we would still want to reserve the position outlined: the concept of the museum cannot be collapsed without remainder into this second meaning, the museum as institution. The concept "museum," then, can be operated in making sense of a set of practices, an institution (that is the primary locale for those practices), and a physical building. If, in operating this concept, a designatory function occurs it can quite easily comprise all three at once. This suggests that in using concepts we are quite comfortable with "fuzzy" counters (lacking precise definition) or with multiple parallel designations.

29. The converse is often taken to be less decisive: If the answer is no, the retort often follows, "but the absence of the word does not imply the absence of the concept."

entrenchment of our commitment to the conflation of words and concepts.[30] It is this, perhaps, that seems to create an inevitable drag toward the orbit of meaning. This is evident from noting that, in the example above, if the ancient Greeks did have a word for tourism it would naturally be assumed that they knew what it meant, and that the meaning of the word conveyed the content of the concept. Thus we arrive at the common view that concepts are the meanings of the words that convey them.[31] Since there can be no concepts available to inspection that do not come in the form of words, a semantic account of concepts begins to seem most plausible.

This answer to the question "What is a concept?" underpins a range of contemporary inquiries from different disciplinary traditions. In a collection of essays drawing on the protocols of cognitive science and linguistics edited by Philip van Loocke, *The Nature of Concepts: Evolution, Structure and Representation*, Andy Clark's essay entitled "Is 'Mind' a Scientific Kind?" proposes:

> Thus suppose that learning to use the word "dog" in a way that meets public criteria involves training several disparate and internally disunified cognitive resources. What the training results in is thus a kind of tuning of many different parts of an overall system. Upon successful completion of such training, we say of someone that he has mastered the concept.[32]

Although the issue here, what it might be to "have" or "possess" a concept, is not precisely that of essence—what *is* a concept?—it is nevertheless dependent upon the collapse of "concept" into meaning. If the word *dog* is

---

30. Morris Weitz puts this well: "Concepts, however, are not words, even if they turn out to be harmful or harmless substitutes for words; nor do concepts imply words. And the use of concepts is not the same as the use of words; nor does the use of concepts imply the use of words. My contention is only that talk about concepts (including talk about theories of concepts) implies corresponding theories of uses of words. But this entailment does not render equivalent the having of concepts and the correct employment of certain expressions . . ." See Morris Weitz, *The Opening Mind: A Philosophical Study of Humanistic Concepts* (Chicago: The University of Chicago Press, 1977), 4.

31. As Ray Jackendoff states: "The expression *concept*" is used to mean essentially "a mental representation that can serve as the meaning of a linguistic expression." "What Is a Concept, That a Person May Grasp it?," in *Concepts: Core Readings*, ed. Eric Margolis and Stephen Laurence (Cambridge, Mass.: MIT Press, 1999), 309.

32. Andy Clark, "Is 'Mind' a Scientific Kind," in *The Nature of Concepts: Evolution, Structure and Representation*, ed. Philip van Loocke (London: Routledge, 1999), 157.

used correctly, according to its meaning in English, then the user may be
said to be in possession of the concept "dog."[33] Although word and concept
may be considered to be distinct they are, nevertheless, soldered together
by meaning. It would seem, therefore, that one can almost do away with
concepts altogether since it is possible to get along fine simply by turning
to pragmatics. It is perhaps strange, given this significant gravitational pull
toward the semantic account, that the proposition that words are distinct
from concepts retains currency. To some extent this can be explained in
historical terms: At least since Descartes the Western philosophical tradition found it natural to suppose a mentalistic account of concept use—
mind, not language, was taken to be the primary locus for the application
of concepts. But since Kant this tradition has increasingly been concerned
to weight explanatory models for thinking against mind and in favor of
language. Where the first sees language as merely a convenient tool for expressing thought, the second gives to language its own coherence and autonomy. This has resulted in late twentieth-century philosophers of mind
reversing the relation between mind and language: According to the now
prevailing view, mental events are to be understood as merely internaliza-
tions of external acts of assertion. In this scenario words do not express
thoughts; thoughts make sense of utterances. Notwithstanding this rever-
sal, a residual attachment to the distinction between words and concepts
persists, whether concepts be described as "mental entities" (cognitive science), "mental representations" (Leibniz, Wolff), or "notions" (Berkeley).
The philosopher Arnold Davidson, for example, writing about the concept
of sexuality in his book *The Emergence of Sexuality*, states: "The very word
'sexuality,' as well as our concept of sexuality, first appears, according to the
Oxford English Dictionary, in the late nineteenth century."[34] The cultural
critic and theorist Mieke Bal in a book entirely devoted to the topic of concepts writes that "concepts are not ordinary words, even if words are used

33. From the perspective of cognitive science, there are a number of problems with
this "classical" view. It turns out that on closer scrutiny most concepts lack definitional
structure: We cannot say *exactly* what a concept means. Furthermore, both ignorance
and error may play a role in our using concepts (that is to say we may believe in error
that a concept means *x*), or we may only have a partial sense of the meaning of a concept
yet nevertheless use it perfectly well. For a good account of these difficulties, see the
jointly authored introduction to Eric Margolis and Stephen Laurence, eds., *Concepts:
Core Readings*, (Cambridge, Mass.: MIT Press, 1999).

34. Arnold Davidson, *The Emergence of Sexuality* (Cambridge, Mass.: Harvard University Press, 2001), 37.

to speak (of) them."[35] And the historian of political thought Quentin Skinner, making the same point in perhaps the clearest outline, notes: "If we wish to grasp how someone sees the world—what distinctions he draws, what classifications he accepts—what we need to know is not what words he uses but rather what concepts he possesses."[36] In all these and countless more cases the distinction between a word and concept silently operates. Small wonder, perhaps, that it seems to have the ring of truth about it: It seems to express a solid and certain truth. Yet, notwithstanding this common sense to the matter, there is no standard resource which makes clear the basis for this difference, or still less a repository of concepts, an encyclopedia or dictionary to which one might refer for guidance.[37] Part of the problem lies in the fact that, as Morris Weitz noted in 1977, an answer to the question "'what are concepts?' seems as remote today as ever."[38]

I doubt that my narrow focus on a single concept throughout this study will make much progress with respect to this most general account of what concepts are, but its insistence on the difference between words and concepts, essentially its refusal to elide concept, word, and meaning—the elision that both cognitive science in its classical guise and *Begriffsgeschichte* make—is adhered to in order to allow the architecture of a conceptual form to become visible. I mean, therefore, to direct attention toward the structural elements that determine how concepts are connected to other concepts in historically defined networks. I see this as building upon, even as it moves a few steps beyond or beside, the work of the Cambridge school, which will be addressed in the following section. It is useful to cantilever this historical account of conceptuality with the cognitive-science approach because the two intellectual traditions cast very different lights on my object of inquiry. In turning to the work of Quentin Skinner, for ex-

35. Mieke Bal, *Travelling Concepts in the Humanities: A Rough Guide* (Toronto: University of Toronto Press, 2002), 23.

36. Quentin Skinner, "Language and Social Change," in *Meaning and Context: Quentin Skinner and His Critics*, ed. James Tully (Cambridge: Polity Press, 1988), 120.

37. Such dictionaries or encyclopedias do, of course exist, but they commonly sidestep the issue of the distinction between words and concepts in their desire to provide a template for a specific field. Examples are legion, but see for example George P. Fletcher, *Basic Concepts of Legal Thought* (Oxford: Oxford University Press, 1996); Robert H. Lavanda, *Core Concepts in Cultural Anthropology* (Boston: McGraw Hill, 2003); John Lechete, *Key Contemporary Concepts* (London: Sage, 2003); Gregory L. Murphy, *The Big Book of Concepts* (Cambridge, Mass.: MIT Press, 2002).

38. See Morris Weitz, *The Opening Mind: A Philosophical Study of Humanistic Concepts* (Chicago: University of Chicago Press, 1977), 17.

ample, the question "What is a concept?" falls away into the background as another, perhaps more answerable, question hoves into view: "What does *this* concept *do?*"

Conceptual History

Do concepts have histories? There are at least two quite distinct questions wrapped up together in this formulation. First, it asks: Are conceptual forms historical in character? Did the Middle Ages work with some or indeed an entire set of concepts that were constructed in ways different from, say, the early modern period? Second, it asks: Are the meanings of concepts historically contingent? As will become clear, most of what I have to say about "human rights" in the Anglophone eighteenth century assumes that concepts are amenable to historical description, but in order to understand the specificity of the descriptions I offer, I must first establish how one might begin to describe and analyze the structuration of concepts.[39] A good way to begin is by looking at how the second question raised above, "Do the meanings of concepts change over time?" has been addressed.[40] It is this question that has primarily occupied those historians, in both the Anglophone school of intellectual history and the German school of *Begriffsgeschichte*, who have tried to map specific conceptual histories. I am going to turn to Skinner for my example here, while bearing in mind that his own project is distinct from those of his colleagues in the "Cambridge school," as it is also from that of Koselleck and his collaborators, because his consistent address to this question is exemplary. In many ways his considerable achievement over a long and productive career provides the clearest account of how one might think about the meanings of concepts contextually.

Skinner is committed to the notion that the conceptual armory of actors in the past may not be identical to our own; this is why he is keen to

39. Within linguistics and cognitive science, concepts are spoken about in terms of lacking "definitional structure" since the formulation of tight definitions for lexical concepts is very troublesome. I have in mind something slightly different from a definition when speaking about the structuration of concepts, outlined below.

40. A good and succinct overview of the ways in which this question has preoccupied conceptual historians can be found in Terrence Ball, "Conceptual History and the History of Political Thought," in *History of Concepts: Comparative Perspectives*, ed. Iain Hampsher-Monk, Karin Tilmans, and Frank van Vree (Amsterdam: Amsterdam University Press, 1998), 75–86; Ball notes, for example, that "in an important sense, then, words do not have histories but concepts do" (82).

insist that in describing and explaining how historical actors made sense of their worlds the historian use the same language as those actors. Consequently, to the extent that history may be said to exert some influence in respect to the components of the lexicon of concepts active at any one time, he believes that concepts are historical in nature. One should note, however, that this is not the same thing as claiming that a specific concept has a history, nor that its *conceptuality* is historical. While the uses to which a concept might be put can change—in different circumstances, historical or not—Skinner is less certain that concepts as such are historical forms. As he remarks in relation to the project of *Begriffsgeschichte*, he is prepared to accept that there is "evidence in favour of the claim that concepts have history," but, immediately qualifying his statement, he adds: "or rather, that the terms we use to express our concepts have a history."[41]

In the same essay he comes up with a slightly different—perhaps surprising—formulation that would seem to retract the position I have just outlined. He writes: "My almost paradoxical contention is that the various transformations we can hope to chart will not strictly speaking be changes in concepts at all. They will be transformations in the applications of the terms by which our concepts are expressed."[42] Here one can see that the immense force that ties words to concepts makes it very difficult to distinguish between whatever may happen to concepts over time and what happens to words. Indeed, according to Skinner, although we quite correctly need to insist that concepts be distinguished from words, it is the *relation* between words and concepts that is more obviously susceptible of historical analysis. As he puts it in an essay he first published in 1979 on Raymond Williams's *Keywords*:

> What then is the relationship between concepts and words? We can scarcely hope to capture the answer in a single formula, but at least the following can be said. The surest sign that a group or society has entered

41. Quentin Skinner, "Retrospect: Studying Rhetoric and Conceptual Change," in *Visions of Politics* (Cambridge: Cambridge University Press, 2002), 1:180. Skinner here seems to be operating an internalist or mentalistic account of conceptual use.

42. Ibid., 1:179. This seems to be a riff on his position of ten years earlier when in a reply to his critics he notes: "To understand a concept, it is necessary to grasp not merely the meanings of the terms used to express it, but also the range of things that can be done with it. This is why in spite of the long continuities that have undoubtedly marked our inherent patterns of thought, I remain unrepentant in my belief that there can be no histories of concepts; there can only be histories of their uses in arguments." *Meaning and Context: Quentin Skinner and His Critics*, ed. James Tully (Cambridge: Polity Press, 1988), 283.

into the self-conscious possession of a new concept is that a corresponding vocabulary will be developed, a vocabulary which can then be used to pick out and discuss the concept in question with consistency. This suggests that, while we certainly need to exercise more caution than Williams does in making inferences from the use of words to the understanding of concepts and back again, there is nevertheless a systematic relationship between words and concepts to be explored.[43]

If one were to hold a strict mentalistic theory of concepts—the processes and procedures of conceptual application are independent of language— such a systematic relationship between words and concepts gives pause for reflection. This is where Skinner's more nuanced sense of the shuttling back and forth between concepts and words in the praxis of social interaction opens up a rich field for inquiry. The *relations* between words and concepts are multiform, or at least susceptible of calibration. If one holds to this view the forensic utility of the "meaning test" (whereby one infers that a concept is possessed by a speaker when she or he uses a word correctly) diminishes since a necessary and sufficient condition for our being said to "possess" a concept, that is, our using a word correctly, loses its precision as the variety of ways of using words moves to the center of attention.[44] Consequently, if one is committed to the notion that the evidence for the presence of a concept cannot be merely a word, since concepts are not identical to words, then one has to confront the thought that a concept may be present at a particular time even though no word for that concept yet existed.[45] What I take away from this way of thinking the issue is the

43. Reprinted in *Visions of Politics* (Cambridge: Cambridge University Press, 2002), 1:160.

44. Thus, as Skinner insists, we should respect "the deep truth that concepts must not be viewed simply as propositions with meanings attached to them; they must also be thought of as weapons (Heidegger's suggestion) or as tools (Wittgenstein's term)." "What Is Intellectual History," *History Today* 35 (1985): 51.

45. This is the point that Quentin Skinner makes: ". . . it cannot be a necessary condition of my possessing a concept that I need to understand the correct application of a corresponding term. Suppose, for example, that I am studying Milton's thought, and want to know whether Milton considered it important that a poet should display a high degree of originality. The answer seems to be that he felt it to be of the greatest importance. When he spoke of his own aspirations at the beginning of *Paradise Lost*, what he particularly emphasized was his decision to deal with 'things yet unattempted in prose or rhyme.' But I could never have arrived at this conclusion by examining Milton's use of the word *originality*. For while the concept is clearly central to his thought, the word did not enter the language until a century or more after his death. Although a history

possibility that a concept may be stretched across a number of words, or between words. Or that concepts are units of "thinking" that cannot be expressed in words without remainder: Their modalities of intellection are not identical to the grammar, syntax, or lexis of a natural language.

Skinner's response to this has been to investigate, with extraordinary tenacity and dazzling intellectual vivacity, the precise conditions in which historical actors used both words and conceptual landscapes to do specific things. Although often misunderstood in his aims or procedures by many of his critics, he has never departed from the observation, made early on in his career, that if, as Wittgenstein remarked "words are also deeds,"[46] then historical intention (what one intends *to do*, not what one intends *to mean*) is recoverable from our patient exploration of how actors in the past used words. Since their use is, under one rubric, the safest route to ascertaining their meaning, it is inevitable that concept, word, meaning, and use will constitute a manifold that often cannot be seen in any way except as linked together: You always get the full panoply of terms even if you are attempting to direct attention to only one of them. This is why Skinner is unconcerned about the fact that, by directing attention to language and rhetoric, the mutual attraction or welding together of word and concept is inevitably only a short way down the road. For Skinner, this does not matter to any degree since his aim is to find coherent and convincing ways of answering the question "How can we make sense of what authors were doing by writing in the past?" How, as Skinner puts it, "can we see things their way," that is, "grasp their concepts, appreciate their beliefs, follow their distinctions"?[47] His is a history of uses, of either words or concepts or both, that sets out to get straight the distances between our own worldview and those of actors in the past. This helps me identify what in the present inquiry fails to find a comfortable fit with Skinner's project. Throughout this study I attempt to go past or see beyond what one might take to be the

---

of the word *originality* and its various uses could undoubtedly be written such a survey would by no means be the same as a history of the concept of originality—a consideration often ignored in practice by historians of ideas." Quentin Skinner, "Language and Social Change," in *Meaning and Context: Quentin Skinner and His Critics,* ed. James Tully (Cambridge: Polity Press, 1988), 120. The crux of this extremely acute observation lays in Skinner's characterization of the presence of a concept with the correct use of *its corresponding term.*

46. Quoted in Skinner, *Visions of Politics* (Cambridge: Cambridge University Press, 2002), 1:4.

47. Quentin Skinner, *Visions of Politics* (Cambridge: Cambridge University Press, 2002), 1:3.

mental landscape of an agent in the past in order to recreate the cultural terrain that provided historical actors with a conceptual lexicon for playing out their roles, making sense of their worlds and to each other. I take this direction because I am committed to the hypothesis that concepts can be parsed historically within the *langue* of culture. From within this project, insofar as one might speak of concepts being "possessed" they are possessed by culture at large. Consequently, I am interested less in how, say, Thomas Paine saw things than in how the radical culture of the 1790s in Britain allowed him to see things.

I imagine that Skinner would have no difficulty in accepting such a hypothesis; in one sense his entire career has been spent painstakingly recovering (perhaps not the best word since it implies that one might be able to completely erase the distance of time, something Skinner would find untenable) the intellectual contexts within which historical actors played out their lives. The present study, however, not only aims to open up these intellectual contexts to the parsing of their conceptual networks; it also seeks to provide the means for inspecting the specific architectures of conceptual forms. As the following sections of this introduction argue, this requires one to think about conceptuality in new ways, or at least develop what is latent in some contemporary conceptualizations of conceptuality.

Stated thus, these aims and objectives would hardly seem novel to anyone signed up to the so-called Cambridge school of intellectual history; certainly J. G. A. Pocock's use of the term *discourse* to refer to the habitat, as it were, of what he seeks to understand would seem to be operating with the same observation.[48] Yet the emphasis I wish to place on concepts being held within culture leads me to explore something slightly different from, even if compatible with, the objects of inquiry in the work of both Pocock and Skinner. Most especially, it downplays the sense that concepts might be mental counters (they are that, for sure, but the claim is that they are also something else) in order to highlight the ways in which concepts may be said to have a kind of non-agential extension. Although *discourse*, certainly as that term was developed in the work of Michel Foucault, might cover similar territory, I see the move from language to concept as foundational for this study: I have set out to explore how the distinctive form

48. Melvin Richter argues that Pocock's histories "are for the most part linguistic," but this should not be taken to imply that he uses a consistent approach—his method, Richter thinks, is more eclectic. See Melvin Richter, *The History of Political and Social Concepts: A Critical Introduction* (Oxford: Oxford University Press, 1995), 128–29.

of conceptual analysis deployed herein opens up a very different way of understanding the history of thinking and the thinkable.

Perhaps the most useful contribution this "conceptual turn" might make to the history of ideas is the redirection of attention to culture as one of the locales in which concepts find coherence. This will, for sure, entail a slackening of attention directed toward human agents in the past whom we standardly think of as "having ideas." Although I see no good reason to suppose tht such agents, then as now, did not possess a lexicon of concepts that enabled them to make sense in and of the world, and therefore merit in asking what an historical actor meant by using a particular term in a specific context at a designated moment, such an approach furthers a history of ideas only so far. It seems to me that there is another dimension, the cultural, that can provide evidence of another kind. This is to take seriously the notion that culture has ways of thinking. The realm of culture—the largest unit of linguistic praxis—has etched onto its surface the tracks left behind by the most general operations of past conceptual compendia. By learning to read those traces, we can begin to uncover how specific concepts were used in the past, begin to reconstruct their grammar and syntax. This does not imply that specific language users, actors in the past, no longer have a role to play in our attempts to understand how ideas are formed and used, transmitted and transformed. On the contrary, the inclusion of the wider cultural analysis will only serve to enhance our understanding of the delimited confines, the common unshareable of culture, within which they acted and brought sense to bear upon and for themselves and their worlds. This in turn will lead to a far more complex picture of the relations between agency and culture, individuated ideas and the commonwealth of knowledge. This study is built upon the fact that the circulation of concepts in past cultural environments is increasingly open to inspection as the digitization of vast archives carries on apace. We are beginning to be able to discern patterns of linguistic behavior that can be said to be supra-agential: cultural all the way down. This will, for sure, redraw our maps that chart the transmission, construction, and adoption of ideas over time.

Conceptual Kinds

The two preceding sections have set out in very broad terms some ways in which answers to two separate questions—"Are concepts distinct from words?" and "Do concepts have histories?"—have been sought. Although an answer to the first seems to be yes, it turns out that the distinction is too porous to be of much use. Furthermore, that porosity infects any attempt to answer the second. In order to make some headway in this matter, the following section proposes a typology of conceptual kinds. As I hope to demonstrate, once one distinguishes between types of concepts, these questions take on different complexions. I propose five categories for this typology: kind, function, structure, modality, and phase. In addition in the following chapter, I also outline three architectural elements that enable different ways of connecting concepts in a network: the hinge, the deposit, and the platform. I recognize that this typology is both unfamiliar and relatively complicated, so I shall spend the rest of this first chapter slowly elaborating it. Before I begin in earnest, however, it is important to recall that the concepts providing the focus for this study do not often figure in the work of linguists or cognitive scientists.[49] I have almost nothing to say about what some linguists call "simple,"[50] and some cognitive scientists call "lexical," concepts.[51] This is because my interest is firmly historical.

49. The standard distinction made by linguists between object concepts—plants, animals, etc.—and abstract concepts—love, dignity—commonly relegates the latter to the realm of the other disciplines (say literary studies or ethics) on account of the difficulty in applying tight criteria to their definition. As E. E. Smith and Douglas L. Medin comment, "no mathematician or metaphysician has come even close to constructing a classical-view description of such [abstract] concepts." See E. E. Smith and Douglas L. Medin, *Categories and Concepts* (Cambridge, Mass.: Harvard University Press, 1981), 5. The way I see things this indicates why a different approach is required if one is to make much headway in understanding the historical formation of political concepts like rights.

50. Within the prototype tradition of cognitive science, "simple" concepts are denoted by single words, and they are distinguished from "composite" concepts. On this, see Edward E. Smith, Daniel N. Osherson, Lance J. Rips, and Margaret Keane, "Combining Prototypes: A Selective Modification Model," in *Concepts: Core Readings*, ed. Eric Margolis and Stephen Laurence (Cambridge, Mass.: MIT Press, 1999), 355.

51. The distinction between *classical* and *prototype* categories made by many linguists (where "classical" categories are defined as possessing necessary and sufficient criteria for membership and "prototype" or "family resemblance"—following Wittgenstein—as lacking such conditions) is also useful in discriminating between types of concept that I call reificational, for which see the discussion on p. 35. On the merits of the prototype theory, see G. Lakoff, *Women, Fire, and Dangerous Things: What Categories Reveal about the Mind* (Chicago: University of Chicago Press, 1987); E. E. Smith and D. L. Medin, *Categories and Concepts* (Cambridge, Mass: Harvard University Press, 1981); and on the merits of the classical view, see G. Rey, "Concepts and Stereotypes," *Cognition* 15 (1981): 237–62; S. L. Armstrong, L. R. Gleitman, H. Gleitman, "What Some Concepts Might Not Be," *Cognition* 13 (1979): 262–308; and for a good review of the debate, see

Not much, it seems to me, can be gained by inquiring into the historical variance of the structure of the concept "cat" (here taken to be a "simple" or lexical concept). In contrast, inquiring into the historical sensitivity of the structuration of the concept "justice" may well pay dividends. Not only will this approach help one delimit the field of conceptuality in ways that make the differences in kind or type of concept bite, it may also shed light on how past cultures operated with concepts whose names appear to be held in common over large expanses of time. That apparent invariance, however, may belie quite significant alterations in either a concept's internal structuration or its external connections, or both. Much will hang, then, on a more accurate description of what I call the "architecture" of conceptual forms. It is this that makes possible an identification of those aspects of a concept that enable and disable our thinking-this-way. The following typology, essentially built upon the observation made by Christopher Peacocke that concepts are "ways of thinking something," is intended to do just that.

In order to make sense of the typology of concepts I am going to present, it is first necessary to create some distinctions in kind between conceptual forms. I shall begin, then, by returning to a very basic or pretty rudimentary account of conceptuality. Thus, notwithstanding the observation about the historical variance of the concept "cat," there is some benefit to starting with what might on initial inspection seem to be "simple concepts" and proceeding at a relatively slow pace.[52] This, I hope, will render intelligible the more fine-grained picture of conceptual form that emerges. The concept "cat," for example, can be taken as a "way of thinking something." Such a concept, in common with all concepts delineating natural kinds, can be said to enable one to think the species of animal called cats and to distinguish exemplars of this concept (my fluffy Persian) from other animals (my sleek Saluki). Thinking this way essentially constructs a comparative framework in which the thing designated by the concept is matched (or not) with another object—a procedure sometimes known

---

Steven Pinker and Alan Price, "The Nature of Human Concepts: Evidence from an Unusual Source," in *The Nature of Concepts*, ed. Philip van Loocke (London: Routledge, 1999), 8–51.

52. This already raises a good number of questions, such as: What are the criteria for "simple" or "complex"? Does such an account immediately install a relation between these two types, and if so is that relation to be understood as a "metaconceptual" aspect or as merely a hierarchical and therefore value-derived observation in regard to mental processing? As Derrida might have observed, is conceptuality itself a simple or complex concept? And what, as a rider, would enable one to phrase an answer to this question?

as "similarity" switching in cognitive science—thereby providing support for the hypothesis that lexical concepts are best understood in relation to "prototypes."[53] "Thinking cat," in this example, to all intents and purposes is the application of the lexical item *cat* to either an object in the world or to a mental representation. It shares features with the process of naming objects and with the correct use of words in a natural language. Its simplicity may be said to lay in the assumed ease with which we use nouns to designate things in the world.[54]

If concepts are "ways of thinking something," then one model of the understanding that seems to have persuasive force imagines our minds to be full of a large number of these lexical concepts and their matching prototypes. The process of cognition is one in which the names of the manifold things there are both in the world and in our own mental universes are connected to specific items in our storehouses of concepts. As has been pointed out above, this way of seeing things effectively finds no difference between words and concepts. Thus, according to a linguist or a cognitive scientist, evidence for our "possessing" a concept is provided by our using a word correctly. If, for example, I do not know the word *arachnid* and have never encountered a spider, I am unable to assign this creature to its species and can be said, therefore, to lack the concept "arachnid." Concepts considered in this way are said to be mental representations that have nonshareable instantiations, called tokens. This accounts for the fact that although two people may share the same concept of cat, they cannot "token" cat identically: Each has a singular mental representation with features that are not necessarily (and do not need to be) held in common. Mental representations according to this view are subjective in the sense that each token is uniquely possessed, belonging to only one subject.[55]

53. See Eleanor Rosch, "Principles of Categorization," in *Concepts: Core Readings*, ed. Eric Margolis and Stephen Laurence (Cambridge, Mass.: MIT Press, 1999), 189–206.

54. This begs the question as to whether naming is a "simple" cognitive process. Within linguistics and cognitive science the so-called prototype tradition for understanding what concepts are sees simple concepts as those denoted by single words. Composite concepts are denoted by more than one word, e.g., "literary politician." On the theory of the prototype, see Edward E Smith, Daniel N. Osherson, Lance J Rips and Margaret Keane, "Combining Prototypes: A Selective Modification Model," in *Concepts: Core Readings*, ed. Eric Margolis and Stephen Laurence (Cambridge, Mass.: MIT Press, 1999), 355–90.

55. See Stephen Laurence and Eric Margolis, "Concepts and Cognitive Science," in *Concepts: Core Readings*, ed. Eric Margolis and Stephen Laurence (Cambridge, Mass.: MIT Press, 1999), 7.

In this example to hand, the so called "simple" concept that functions primarily as a designator for something in the world, concepts operate in a structured environment—call it a mental universe—that enables the distinction of one from another according to semantic value. When all these items are collected together, they begin to form a lexicon, a set of terms that helps in making sense of the world. What some might refer to as a "mental universe" or a conceptual toolbox can just as effectively be called a dictionary, and each person constructs and curates her own singular lexicon of items that may be called upon in processing her own individual experiences. If this is a convincing enough sketch of the very elementary uses to which we put simple concepts (or how such concepts function within cognitive processing) it can immediately be seen that the word/concept distinction is very weak: One can get to pretty much the same place by substituting the word *word* for *concept*. This helps me identify what is of no interest for this inquiry: simple concepts that effectively elide the distinction between word and concept. As is immediately clear, the mental universe referred to above is essentially a language, and the simple concepts in its lexicon consist in a set of nouns.[56] In what follows I shall assign such simple concepts to the "kind" I call *reificational* and to the "function" *nominal* since their primary purpose is to name or designate something.[57] Although this book is concerned with very different kinds of

56. According to the "classical theory of concepts," most concepts and all lexical concepts are defined as structured mental representations that encode a set of necessary and sufficient conditions for their application. This provides a way of understanding how and why a particular concept is applied to its extension, say to an object of perception. I take that to be a description of the function of naming. For a good account of this, see Stephen Laurence and Eric Margolis, "Concepts and Cognitive Science," in *Concepts: Core Readings*, ed. Eric Margolis and Stephen Laurence (Cambridge, Mass.: MIT Press, 1999), 3–81.

57. I mean to make a distinction here between the mental process of naming and the definition of a word. The function of a concept—here, naming—need not result in our being able to give a definition of the word that expresses the concept, which is to note that a concept's extension (what it names) can sometimes remain fuzzy. This is the point that Wittgenstein makes in respect to a concept like "game," for which we may lack a precise definition while getting along just fine with an open set of properties. See Ludwig Wittgenstein, *Philosophical Investigations*, trans. G. E. M. Amscombe (Oxford: Basil Blackwell, 1958), esp. § 65–76. For a good account of Wittgenstein's notion of "family resemblance concepts" see Hans-Johann Glock, "Wittgenstein on Concepts," in *Wittgenstein's "Philosophical Investigations": A Critical Guide*, ed. Arif Ahmed (Cambridge: Cambridge University Press, 2010), 88–108, and in particular his comments at 104: ". . . Wittgenstein's suggestive remarks go astray, since they tie concepts too closely

concepts, it is useful to begin here since I take this nominal function to be common to all conceptual forms.

By no means all concepts are like this. Things become more complicated, moreover, once one moves away from concepts whose primary function is to name natural kinds. Size, for example, is not a thing in the world as a cat is, even if it is, of course, a property of things in the world. It can be said to name an idea, the quality of objects we associate with the amount of space that they occupy, and it brings in its wake a relative scale with designators for points along it. Although one cannot point to size in the same way as one can to a cat, it is a simple matter to point to an object that is large. But the cognitive processing that is set in motion in this case is not quite as simple as the first. I call such modes of processing a conceptual "modality." Returning for a moment to the most basic form of concept exemplified by 'cat' above, reificational concepts set in motion a relatively uncomplicated process of cognition by which something is compared to something else—an apple, say, to a tree.[58] I call this modality *isogetic*.[59] It is not quite like this with my second example, where a slightly more complicated set of mental procedures is set in motion. This is partly because, unlike the first case where the concept "cat" can only be used in respect of those animals belonging to the species cat, the concept "size" can be used as a way of thinking the scale of all manner of things, and not only those things that have material form. Concepts like size I assign to the "kind" I call *ideational*. They allow us to make sense of phrases such as "Marxism is a big idea." There is also a difference in conceptual "structure." In the first case, a reificational concept essentially has a *rigid* structure: It operates by identifying or fabricating (in this instance it does not matter which) a homology. The concept "cat" can only be applied to those things that are correctly named as cats unless one invokes the special case of figurative uses. In the second case, of "size," the concept has a more pliable structure since it can be used for making sense of a variety of things in the world, both material and immaterial. Its structure, then, can be said to be *plastic*.

---

to language. . . . [His] proposal can easily be given a Kantian twist, however, which ties concepts in the first instance to thought or understanding rather than language. Concepts are techniques not just for using words, but for mental acts or operations."

58. This begs the question as to the complexity of nominalization: How do I know how to assign lexical concepts to objects in the world or to mental representations? Is the performative act of naming "natural," without ambiguity or anything other than provisional? These issues are harder to resolve than might at first appear.

59. And, once again, the process and procedures of "comparison" ought not be assumed to be unproblematic.

In the foregoing I have characterized "ways of thinking," the process of intellection, or the kinds of mental activity set in motion by a specific concept, as the modality of a concept. In the case of my first example, the concept "cat" can be invoked correctly when thinking about very many kinds of cat, but, notwithstanding this range of application, it can only be invoked correctly with reference to animals that are within the species.[60] The modality of thinking this way I call *isogetic* because it uses the operator "similarity" in order to arrive at a correct linkage of the items in play: concept to perceived object, or mental representation to concept. And it operates in a *single* "phase": Once the match has been made, the process of cognition is complete. In the case of the second kind of concept, "size," the modality of thinking set in train by reaching toward this concept involves at least two quite distinct phases. First, one must be able to reach for the abstraction "size" without recourse to any specific mental representation (one does not need to "token" this abstraction) before operating a set of matches between tokens for the object to which the qualifier of size is to be applied. Second, since "size" always brings with it a relative scale, one must match the object and its token to other objects and their tokens. The second phase of this cognitive process assigns an appropriate word for the point along a relative scale, either with reference to objects that fall within the same class or with reference to other objects. An orange, for example, can be understood as being small with respect to both other oranges and to motor cars and buildings.

In the first phase, the grasp of an abstraction, the concept 'size' does not function nominally, rather it provides a way of thinking the quality of something. Its function is what I call "containing" since it provides a repository in which different things can be placed. And its modality is "schematic" since the abstraction is used to order the different things to which it is applied by a measure. In its second phase, whereby a designator of size is applied, the function is nominal. Like other terms of measurement, there are a number of terms used for relative size: minuscule, small, huge, enormous, and so forth. The modality of thinking in this second phase is isogetic since, in order to locate the right term, one must operate with a

60. Some linguists and philosophers would say that "cat" in this example is a closed concept since it is used correctly when the necessary and sufficient conditions for being a member of its class are met. The alternative, an open concept, can operate perfectly well without such definitional coherence. On this, see Morris Weitz, *Theories of Concepts* (London: Routledge, 1988); Paul Thagard, *Conceptual Revolutions* (Princeton, N.J.: Princeton University Press, 1992), 17–19.

comparative mode. These examples are intended to describe how concepts activate different ways of thinking: This is my first attempt to discriminate between kinds or types of concept. Thus, simple designatory concepts like cat have a rigid structure (they can only be applied correctly to the things they designate) and set in motion a single phase of cognitive processing. In contrast, ideational concepts like size have plastic structure (they can be applied to many different things) and operate in a dual phase.[61]

Most concepts fall into the kinds I call reificational and ideational, and they can be considered as the basic tools we use for making sense. Of course tools can be used in different ways and for different purposes, both effectively and appropriately as well as inappropriately (as Wittgenstein noted). But there is a third kind, a particular type of ideational concept I call "noetic" that is better understood as a map or blueprint. Although far fewer in number, these concepts set in motion more complex ways of thinking because their coherence is established by the tension that connects them in a network with other concepts. These networked connections are in turn determined by a grammar and syntax that together create very complex geometries. The modality most commonly set in motion by these noetic concepts is "axiomatic" since they provide structures for making sense of things other than what they name. They provide maps or blueprints for enabling comprehension of large items of cognition, sitting, as it were, in the background of mental processing. When they operate in this fashion,

61. Classical accounts of conceptuality within cognitive science essentially model cognition as a sequential process, as if the brain functions through a series of discrete operations. Since the late 1980s, the classical view that promotes the representational theory of mind (RTM) that has substantially attracted the majority support of cognitive scientists has been challenged by so-called connectionism, which sees brain functionality as a parallel processing operation. According to this view, the brain simultaneously carries out a large number of cognitive activities. Recent work has tried to combine these two accounts under the pressure of a particularly challenging criticism—mounted most impressively by Jerry Fodor—of connectionism. Since, as Fodor notes, two of the most salient features of thinking, its productivity and systematicity, are not compatible with connectionist accounts of cognition, at the very least the classical view needs to be revisited. Insofar as the present account of conceptual forms can be understood with reference to this more recent work in cognitive science, it seems to me suggestive to note that my own account of conceptual networks shares some vocabulary (perhaps unwittingly) with connectionism. For a good introduction, see Andre Kukla and Joel Walmsley, *Mind: A Historical and Philosophical Introduction to the Major Theories* (Indianapolis, Ind.: Hackett, 2006), esp. ch. 8. For a good guide to the pros and cons of the classical account, see Jerry Fodor, *The Mind Doesn't Work That Way* (Cambridge, Mass.: MIT Press, 2000).

their phase is what I call "continuous" and their structure "adaptive" since their application is open ended.

The concept "time," for example, sits in the background when we operate a large number of concepts with which it connected. Concepts such as history, age, and memory would be unintelligible without the concept of time working in an axiomatic modality. Faith is another example of this kind of ideational conceptual form. Unlike time, however, its modality is not restricted to one type. One can see this by noting that the way of thinking prompted by faith can be isogetic (used as a comparator to distinguish between kinds of faith), schematic (used to provide a grid for making distinctions between kinds of belief), or axiomatic (used as a self-evident theorem). Furthermore, its phase can also be any of the three types: single, dual, or continuous. When it operates under the rubric of the third type, continuous, something noteworthy occurs in cognitive processing: Reaching for the concept is like turning to a map or plan for guidance in the sequence of thinking. The concept provides the routes for moving thought along, thereby enabling one to understand complex interpretive phenomena, such as why someone acts in the ways that they do, or why a person might believe in resurrection. When operating with noetic concepts, we do not necessarily need to call to mind the meaning of the word that gives its outline to the concept. We do not require an answer to the question "What does this term designate?" because it can operate in the background, providing a mini-theory that enables one to arrive at a sense of understanding something other than faith itself.

In order to facilitate the use of these terms, the accompanying schematic diagram is offered. It should be noted that, although the terms are set out in a fashion that organizes them both vertically and horizontally, I do not intend this organization to imply that the conceptual kinds are always aligned with the function, structure, modality, and phase in the vertical axis. This is to say that, for example, ideational concepts may function in any of the three ways or operate with any of the three modalities.

Conceptual Kind	reificational	ideational	noetic
Conceptual Function	nominal	containing	load bearing
Conceptual Structure	rigid	plastic	adaptive
Conceptual Modality	isogetic	schematic	axiomatic
Conceptual Phase	single	dual	continuous

This schema will be invoked on a number of occasions throughout the rest of this book as a kind of *aide memoire* for what I recognize to be an unfamiliar set of terms.

The Architecture of Concepts

The foregoing has set out a typology of concepts considered as mental entities. This typology seeks to build upon Peacocke's "ways of thinking" in order to generate a means for differentiating between kinds of concept. Although the focus for the chapters following is on one ideational concept, rights, I do not only wish to differentiate types of concept when understood as mental entities: I also intend to demonstrate how a particular form of conceptual analysis, what I call a forensics, enables one to understand how concepts are structured when considered as cultural entities embedded in history. Each of the following chapters will take a slightly different approach to writing a conceptual history, but my intention in all three is to open out the observation that the exemplary concept of rights operates in the common unshareable of culture. When seen this way, one can begin to note how concepts operate according to a specific grammar and syntax that situates them in a network of linked concepts. That grammar and syntax becomes legible by tracking the use of words over time, as do the networks within which they were historically suspended. In order to be linked together, concepts have to present themselves as variously open or closed; this "fit" depends upon the shape or format of a concept's edges, which permit more or less compatible interconnections. That shape is determined by the internal configuration of each concept. Taken together, the network connections and the internal structure comprise the architecture of a concept. The following chapters set out to demonstrate that such architectures are susceptible of historical inquiry.

In claiming that concepts are cultural entities, I do not mean to suggest that the distinctions between subjective and objective, individual and collective, or private and public determine the differences between mental and cultural forms. Nor, when I use the term *cultural* with respect to concepts, am I thinking of the ways in which the meanings of words have common, collective, or cultural significance.[62] My focus is entirely on how an epistemic architecture was deployed by and constructed in the largest cognitive community open to inspection: a culture at large represented in the traces left by its uses of words. As outlined above, although both reificational and ideational concepts may be historically variant in respect

62. The most extensive account along these lines is to be found in the German project of *Begriffsgeschicte*. See Joachim Ritter and Karlfried Gründer, eds., *Historisches Wörtebuch der Philosophie*, 8 vols. (Basel: Verlag Schwabe, 1971).

to their functionality and modality, it is the variance in the second type that is more likely to tell us something useful about how actors in the past made sense of their world. If one can get a fix on that, it becomes possible to make convincing arguments about the overlap between the conceptual universes we inhabit in our own time and those inhabited by actors in the past. This is to make the difference in kind between concepts bite. Thus, one should note that the architectures of most reificational concepts are likely to be chrono-invariant, even if the history of science and empiricism in general indicate that names for material kinds do change or new objects are discovered for which names are furnished.[63] If one compares this with an ideational concept such as justice, one immediately perceives the difference. Over time and in different locales, justice has been linked with neighboring concepts in a variety of ways and with varying strengths of connection. Its relations to the concepts of retribution or punishment, for example, have not been singular over the course of human history. Once one begins to exhume a history of those relations, it becomes apparent that its sitedness within conceptual networks is culturally variant. The Judeo-Christian tradition, for example, builds a network of related ethical concepts that, taken as whole, have provided a road map for morally sanctioned human behavior. Furthermore, within that tradition, the network connections between justice and retribution have varied. Although these observations could be equally well made by attending to the *meanings* of these words, it is not semantics that I wish to call to mind. My purpose is to draw attention to the edges between concepts in order to expose historical variation in a concept's architecture. This leads me to pose some follow-up questions, such as "What alters a connective interface?" "What is within the architecture of a specific concept that allows or enables it to be networked in different ways over time?" The rest of this book sets out to answer these questions with respect to human rights.

One can think of a network of concepts in its simplest form as a lexicon of nouns.[64] Reificational concepts name distinct objects, and they preserve

63. Here the distinction between the meanings of words and concepts and a concept's architecture bites. Even if this distinction is complex since the internal structure of a concept is not indifferent to how it is used or deployed—and therefore not indifferent to its meanings—it remains the case that reificational concepts are most likely to have very long half-lives in terms of their internal structuration.

64. Within the diverse traditions that have attended to conceptual forms from a philosophical perspective, the work of both Hobbes and Wittgenstein is commonly said

and respect those distinctions.[65] In this sense, the network of connections between such concepts can be visualized as stretching out across a planar surface, each concept marking its similarity and difference from every other concept on the plane. Ideational concepts may also be networked across a single planar surface, but they can also be networked in complex figurations that link across planes or surfaces. An ideational concept like motion, for example, in English can be connected via opposition to stasis.[66] This horizontal connection via polarity occurs on a common planar surface, but more complex vertical connections can be made across planar surfaces. Arrested movement, stasis, stillness, stagnation, or immobility are connected to motion in a conceptual network. Here I am thinking not of the shades and differences in meaning that pertain between these terms but

---

to model concepts as linguistic entities. On this, see Morris Weitz, *Theories of Concepts* (London: Routledge, 1988).

65. This chimes with the classical view of concepts, which understands lexical concepts as meeting necessary and sufficient conditions for coherence. But, as critics of the classical view have been quick to point out, the tightness of such conditions often varies to such an extent that partial observance of the criteria often seems to work just fine or, in other, more extreme cases, definitional structure is entirely lacking. This criticism does not seem to allow for the temporality of conceptual operation: Our application of reificational concepts needs only to work *in this case*—which is to say that the distinctions it upholds and respects need only be applied in the moment of cognitive processing. It does not matter for the sake of this argument that those distinctions may blur or dissolve in the next moment, or indeed that one might mistakenly apply an inappropriate concept.

66. This raises the issue of cultural difference: Are there cultures in which the concept of motion is redundant, or unavailable—or which have a concept of stasis but no corresponding polar opposite? Here the fact that this study is based on a monolinguistic archive needs to be highlighted: In moving across linguistic boundaries, the issue over the binding between words and concepts is immediately raised. This study is predicated upon the assumption that different languages necessarily work with different concepts: Although the word *chat* might be networked in French in very similar ways to the word *cat* in English, thereby suggesting that reificational concepts might be held in common across linguistic contexts, this similarity weakens considerably when one turns to ideational concepts. Insofar as this study is concerned, then, the restriction to "rights" in the English language is necessary if one is to gain clarity with respect to a conceptual architecture: "Droits" must be, according to this view, structured differently as a concept. This is not intended to imply, however, that very interesting areas of overlap or intercalation may pertain. With respect to the rights of man and Paine's adoption and promotion of this phrase, the biographical facts alone suggest that miscegenation between cultural contexts must have occurred. This very rich and extensive field of cross- and intercultural conceptual formation remains to be mined in further studies.

of the rules of connection and binding that determine a specific set of connections. Those rules must correlate with the meanings of the terms, but they also apply to and determine conceptual geometries. Moreover, they determine the shape of such geometries over time.

When concepts are considered as cultural entities, it becomes possible to discern how "ways of thinking something" are not only determined by an agent who thinks. While, on the one hand, it makes good sense to suppose that a thinking being possesses a set of concepts in order to arrive at coherent understanding, those concepts are not, for the most part, made up or invented by her. This is to note that we are inserted into commonly held practices of making sense, and the concepts we deploy are more like things we inherit or accept. Take the example of "democracy," an example of the kind of concept I call noetic. One can speak about and make sense of current international relations by using this concept without needing or indeed being able to say what such a concept means,[67] let alone parsing its grammar.[68] Because the concept is operated through the modality I call axiomatic, it is taken as a given, its "way of thinking something" is common currency, held, as it were, in the ether of the social processes of communication, in the *sensus communis*. And, perhaps more importantly for the argument set out in the following chapters, the understanding arrived at by using this concept is determined by its architecture. It is this that determines the conditions of possibility both for making sense in this matter and for any interlocutor making sense of what is said: Its grammar determines what can be understood *in this case*.

67. Some philosophers and cognitive scientists account for this kind of concept as requiring only partial definition. On this, see Christopher Peacocke, "Implicit Conceptions, Understanding and Rationality," (paper, Sociedad Filosofica Ibero Americana (SOFIA), 10th Annual Conference, Barcelona, Spain, June 1997). Such accounts of conceptuality are labeled neoclassical by Laurence and Margolis. See their "Concepts and Cognitive Science." in *Concepts: Core Readings*, ed. Eric Margolis and Stephen Laurence (Cambridge, Mass.: MIT Press, 1999), 52–59.

68. This raises a question that bears upon Wittgenstein's critique of the classical analysis of concepts (the elucidation of the necessary and sufficient conditions for membership of the class). In his proposal of "fuzzy concepts," that is, those we use perfectly competently without possessing a definition of them according to the strict criteria of classical analysis, the so-called "game" resolution whereby a concept only needs to recognize a set, or overlapping set, of "family resemblances" nevertheless needs "rules" or a grammar. By attending to how such concepts are used, one can construct those rules or grammar that pertain in this case. My historical point is that this grammar need not be conspicuous to an historic agent and that it is chrono-variant.

Concepts seen from the side of the social or cultural come bound in a set of relations with other concepts.[69] In the foregoing example, when reaching to the concept of democracy, one necessarily activates, to varying strengths, other epistemic architectures: Concepts are held within the web of cultural praxis. In most cases, certainly with reificational concepts, the web of connection is easily perceived and very rudimentary (a reificational concept marks its difference from all other concepts, thereby being connected by negation). What is called competence in a natural language is predicated upon our being able to notice and respect these connections. But in some cases the connections are harder to work out and may operate in far more complex ways. Often the complexity of connection and geometry of a network effectively means that these concepts work under the radar, as it were. We do not notice that by using one concept we are caught within its web of connection. This is why it is important to develop a more sophisticated account of conceptual forms; by doing so we are less likely to be trapped into situations in which concepts do our thinking for us in ways we might find surprising or even counter to our intentions. This observation will be pressed hard in the chapters that follow, where I develop a way of generating data that throw light on the strength of attraction one concept may have had to another. I call this the orbital drag that accompanies a specific ideational concept, which connects it in sometimes very complex geometries to other concepts. One can see the force of this way of thinking by noting that, over a long period of time in the English language context, "democracy" pulls within its orbit "liberty." In operating the first concept, one cannot but be operating the second. This tells us something about the range and enclosures of thinking with the concept of democracy.[70] It identifies the reason for our thinking that liberty is best protected and guaranteed by democracy, even if in fact democracy has itself been thought

69. This is close to how Koselleck understands the connections between concepts. See, for example, Hans Erich Bödeker's commentary on *Begriffsgeschicte*: "*Begriffsgeschicte* views a concept as a collection of experiences and expectations, perspectives and explanations, of historical reality. Therefore, from the outset, a concept exists within a theoretical constellation or conceptual diagram. A single concept can hardly be understood without reference to other concepts." "Concept—Meaning—Discourse," in *History of Concepts: Comparative Perspectives*, ed. Iain Hampsher-Monk, Karl Tilmans and Frank van Vree (Amsterdam: Amsterdam University Press, 1998), 55.

70. This is not to suggest that its range is a constant over time. For an account of the various fortunes of the concept of democracy, see John Dunn, *Setting the People Free: The Story of Democracy* (London: Atlantic Books, 2005).

variously over time—and in some of its guises might appear—to have a rather awkward fit with liberty.

The rate of change in any one conceptual network may vary considerably; some noetic concepts may have very stable and long-standing network connections. One can see this by taking some examples. "Honor," "duty," "pride," and "guilt" are suspended in a network in the English language that has hardly changed over long stretches of human history. Indeed we commonly think of these moral concepts as embedded in our deep past without the need to respect the difference that linguistic specificity makes: They are present from the beginning of Western civilization's efforts at regulating behavior. When looked at from this angle, since these words would seem to have been used in the same way over long stretches of time, we can say that their network connections have remained by and large historically invariant.[71] They may be said to be chrono-invariant noetic concepts. In contrast, both the internal structuration and the networked connections of a concept like "person" or "self" seem much more amenable to being plotted historically. Concepts of this kind can be said to be chrono-variant noetic concepts.

One might legitimately wonder if this schematic account of a putative typology of concepts and their networked relations within the *sensus communis* is no more than a redescription of some differences between kinds of noun. Might the above merely be another way of noticing that the contexts in which words are used change over time and, given that a use context determines the meaning of words, that some meanings have very long half-lives while others change quite rapidly? Moreover, if the focus of attention is primarily on the diachronic, would it not be sensible to turn first to etymology or historical semantics? If one were attending to words and meanings I think these would be very germane objections, but in what follows I shall be attending to something else: to both the ways in which concepts are internally structured and how, over time, those internal structures enable and disable connections within a conceptual network.

71. I do not want to claim here absolutely that these concepts could have no variance over time, or that they must be completely impervious to historical inflection; it may well be that they simply have very long and stable careers in our thinking about morality. The question to pose here is: Under what conditions would such concepts feel the pressure of history? Or, as problematic for a history of *invariant* concepts, what are the protocols and procedures for resisting conceptual change? What are the motivations for accepting and promoting invariance in how we make sense of "core" human values?

One way of beginning to see the force of this distinction would be to take the argument put forward by Thomas Dixon in his book *From Passions to Emotions*: that the concept of emotion was only invented in the early nineteenth century.[72] If one takes this as a coherent account, a number of questions need to be addressed. How did persons alive before this date get by without such a concept? Why did it emerge at the specific moment Dixon claims that it did? Is the concept built up from elements of previously operative concepts, or from parts of those concepts? Did an earlier conceptual form, say the concept of the passions, mutate into this new concept "emotion"? If so what are the processes or procedures by which one concept mutates into another? Did the invention of "emotion," which must also have been an insertion into a network of previously extant concepts, leave that network unchanged, the relations between concepts unaltered? And, in back of all these questions is the set that I wish to highlight in the rest of this study: How is an ideational concept built or structured? What were the grammar and syntax of its networked connections? What was its architecture?

To put some flesh on this abstract sketch: During the eighteenth century one may, for example, in English have spoken of divine right but not of mortal right, even though the *rights of man* became, by the early 1790s, a widely disseminated phrase. I take this to indicate that the semantic opposition "divine/mortal" did not figure in the architecture of the concept of "right" for the length of the century. It was not a node in the conceptual network within which "rights" was suspended. By the 1790s, however, the concept of rights had become much more strenuously connected to "personhood" as the legitimacy for universal rights claims began to be ex-

---

72. Dixon calls emotion a "category": "In this book I investigate the creation of 'the emotions' as a psychological category," Thomas Dixon, *From Passions to Emotions: The Creation of a Secular Psychological Category* (Cambridge: Cambridge University Press, 2003), 1. His use of this term, however, is very close to how I conceive of concepts. He writes, "'Emotions,' unlike 'affections,' 'passions,' 'desires,' and 'lusts' did not appear in any English translation of the Bible. These simple observations highlight an important fact about the way that these terms derived their meanings from networks of related concepts. The words 'passions' and 'affections' belonged to a network of words such as 'of the soul,' 'conscience,' 'fall,' 'sin,' 'grace,' 'Spirit,' 'Satan,' 'will,' 'lower appetite,' 'self-love' and so on. The word 'emotions' was, from the outset, part of a different network of terms such as 'psychology,' 'law,' 'observation,' 'evolution,' 'organism,' 'brain,' 'nerves,' 'expression,' 'behaviour' and 'viscera'" (4–5). Note here the perennial problem in distinguishing with any real force the difference between words or terms and concepts or categories.

plored. This necessitated a recalibration of the orders of rights claims that was dependent upon a relaxation of the grip the distinction between the human and the divine had theretofore exercised with respect to rights. This could only be achieved in and by a culture that was prepared to give up on its long-standing commitments to Christian orthodoxy and accept as legitimate a newly structured concept: rights of man. How, for the most part, that failed to happen is the story this book tells.

CHAPTER 2

"... the Fundamental Rights and Liberties of Mankind ...": The Architecture of the Rights of Mankind

It is, by now, almost a commonplace to state that "human rights" were invented in the eighteenth century.[1] Although it is not immediately clear what

---

1. A recent book by James Griffin begins: "Use of the term 'human rights' began at the end of the eighteenth century ..." See *On Human Rights* (Oxford: Oxford University Press, 2008), 9. Although, as I shall comment on below, Griffin does not make an elision between "human rights" and the "rights of man," many writers within the traditions of scholarship concerned with the history and philosophy of political concepts turn to the Enlightenment as the most obvious source for contemporary ideas of universal rights. See, for example, the following taken from a student guide: "The concept of rights first became unmistakably prominent during the period of modern intellectual history known as the Enlightenment ..." William A. Edmundson, *An Introduction to Rights* (Cambridge: Cambridge University Press, 2004), 15. Lynn Hunt, in her history of the concept entitled *Inventing Human Rights*, is careful to distinguish the different locutions used in the historical period of the Enlightenment, noting that "eighteenth century people did not often use the expression 'human rights,' and when they did they usually meant something different by it than what we mean," but her general thesis remains that the "moment of emergence of human rights" is the Enlightenment. See Lynn Hunt, *Inventing Human Rights* (New York: W. W. Norton, 2007), 22. Samuel Moyn, in his *The Last Utopia: Human Rights in History* (Cambridge, Mass.: Belknap Press

Table 2. Number of eighteenth-century texts containing *human rights*

	1700–1720	1720–1740	1740–1760	1760–1780	1780–1800
human rights	20	22	25	51	254

Source: Eighteenth Century Collections Online (ECCO), http://galenet.galegroup .com/servlet/ECCO.

it might mean to say that a concept was "invented" at a particular moment in time (or over a particular stretch of time, say the eighteenth century), I shall leave this hanging since I want to begin with a more simple-minded examination of the validity of this statement.[2] If one searches the database of eighteenth-century printed materials in English (ECCO) for use of the term *human rights*, one finds that the century was almost entirely innocent of this locution.[3]

---

of Harvard University Press, 2010), is unusual in his careful discrimination between the early modern discussion of rights and its extension into the eighteenth century and our own contemporary understanding of the concept of international human rights, which he dates to the 1970s. In an afterword to a recent collection of Amnesty lectures, he makes the point more forcefully: "it is ultimately misleading to claim that there ever existed 'human rights' in the Enlightenment—at least in the sense they have now and with which the phrase entered the English language." Much of the following explores that observation with detailed analyses of the construction of the historical concept "rights of mankind." Samuel Moyn, "Afterword: The Self-Evidence of Human Rights," in *Self-Evident Truths? Human Rights and the Enlightenment*, ed. Kate E. Tunstall (New York: Continuum, 2012), 258.

2. Objections to the dating in the previous sentence clearly raise the issue that is at the center of this book: How is the concept "human rights" constructed? Some might argue in respect to the moment of origin that universal rights have been a feature of human society from its inception, others that the concept is distinctively Western in origin. The ancient Greeks—as in all things connected to human culture—are said by some to have invented rights discourse (this view is also contested), but a more common contender for the origin of modern rights is Roman law. All of these beg the question raised above: Although the concept of rights may have been available to a wide range of cultures and societies before the eighteenth century, does that mean the concept of universal human rights was also in circulation? As will quickly become clear, I believe that question can only be answered by attending to the specific structure of conceptual forms.

3. The significance of these numerical values will become more evident as further data is presented. See, for example, the larger run of data in table 3 below. A good start-

A similar search for the phrase *rights of man* indicates an even lower frequency up to 1760 (twenty-five occurrences to this date), although by the last twenty years the term had become firmly established, in no small part due to the political storm prompted by the publication of Part I of Thomas Paine's *Rights of Man* in 1791.[4] Of course an immediate retort to this observation would be that the period simply used a different word or phrase for referring to what we call human rights, and, as will become clear below, a possible contender would certainly be *rights of mankind*.[5] I begin here in order to underline one of the observations made in the previous chapter about the nature of conceptuality and the relations of words to concepts. If one intends to write a history of the *concept* of human rights rather than a history of the uses of the phrase, the difference—howsoever that might be drawn—between words and concepts needs to be respected. At the very least, then, one must endeavor to hold on to the distinctiveness of conceptuality. This, it seems to me, will only pay dividends if, inter alia, one generates a model for conceptual form. The following certainly sets out to respect this minimal protocol. Furthermore, if one holds to the view that concepts are not identical to words and that it is possible to think with concepts that lack lexical consistency, or that do not have precise nominal values, then two areas of linguistic behavior require attention. On the one hand, candidates for alternative labels for the concept in question must be tested (e.g., the eighteenth century had a concept of human rights but referred to this concept as the "rights of mankind") while, on the other,

---

ing observation, however, might be that these values, representing as they do sweeps across the entire text base for each twenty-year segment, are very low given that the term *rights* appears in 8,949 texts in the first twenty years of the century.

4. Searching for the term *rights of man* runs into the optical character recognition problems adverted to in the introduction: The search engine finds both the exact phrase and those instances where *man* is linked by a hyphen, most commonly to *kind*. A visual check of the search results indicates that the phrase *rights of man* appears in two texts in the first twenty years of the century, in three in the years 1720–1740, and in twenty texts in the next twenty years. Thereafter, the number of incidences begins to get more substantial (including the noise). By the last decade of the century, the search engine returns 2,757 instances.

5. The incidence for *rights of mankind* is 229 (1700–1720); 338 (1720–1740); 544 (1740–1760); 1,344 (1760–1780); 2,171 (1780–1800)—clearly a far higher incidence for most of the century than for either of the previous two, but still for most of the century a relatively low incidence in the archive as a whole. The level of incidence, of course, does not address the issue over whether the concepts "human rights" and "rights of mankind" are identical, or indeed if they overlap in any way. This will be taken up below.

the matrices of verbal usage that may have enveloped, activated, or contained a specific concept without giving it a name, or nominal value, need to be ascertained.[6] The first of these tasks is relatively easy to perform, whereas the second requires a considerable scaffold of methodology in order to reveal how concepts may lie in between or outside nominal values or may be given shape or form in nonstandard lexical uses or behaviors. And this second hypothesis has a further, perhaps more intriguing, extension: It may well be that these nonstandard areas of linguistic behavior in which singular or precise nominal values for concepts do not pertain are, in fact, pretty common (and therefore more "standard" than we might at first assume).[7] One might very well be able to negotiate the world and one's self with a conceptual lexicon that contains a proportion of "fuzzy" concepts, those that lack coherence or consistency. This observation can be taken in a number of directions with respect to my initiating question about the "invention" of human rights: It may have been the case that the period may not have had access to a fully formed concept of human rights, or perhaps it created a kind of concept *in potentia*, an as yet to be fully formed or coherent conceptual entity. But, then again, perhaps it simply failed to identify a need for such a concept of human rights.[8] Or, having identified a

6. This alternative way of thinking conceptuality is relatively common, even if the consequences of holding such a view led to some of the difficulties explored below. See, for example, the work of the anthropologist Pascal Boyer: "Although concepts provide the basis of language use, there is not a perfect congruence between concepts and words in natural languages. There are many examples of concepts which are certainly represented even though there is no word to label them, and conversely there are many cases in which a variety of words can be used without a corresponding variety of concepts." *The Naturalness of Religious Ideas: A Cognitive Theory of Religion* (Berkeley: University of California Press, 1994), 61–62.

7. This is the point that Alan Gerwith makes when he notes that "it is important to distinguish between having or using a concept and the clear or explicit elucidation of it. . . . Thus persons might have and use the concept of a right without explicitly having a single word for it." *Reason and Morality* (Chicago: University of Chicago Press, 1978), 99.

8. If this notion of conceptual forms as emergent, as being *in potentia*, carries conviction, it generates some further lines of inquiry. If the concept of human rights were there in potential, why did the eighteenth century not fully realize it? Is it possible to identify impediments to its full realization? What might enable or prompt conceptual potentialities into making the last step toward fully formed coherence? Already one can see from the tenor of these questions that they imply or are constructed upon a specific model of conceptuality that would enable one to inspect the internal layout of a conceptual form. This will be developed below.

need, it found greater use for a fuzzy concept of the rights of mankind, say, than it did for a coherent and well-defined concept of human rights.[9]

This way of thinking needs the considerable support of what I shall call "conceptual analysis," with its particular forensics and modes of analysis, and only with that support will it become possible to patiently build a convincing set of observations about the formation of concepts in general. It will, then, take most of this book to make sense of the hypothesis just raised, that the period was unable to reach to a coherent concept of human rights where that coherence was provided by nominal values ("human rights" are to be distinguished from other rights, say the rights of the citizen). Put in its most succinct form, the hypothesis states that an eighteenth-century person would have failed to operate the concept "human rights," at least insofar as the contemporary concept is assumed to enable us to think universal human rights, that is, applicable to and held by all persons howsoever inflected—person, citizen, agent, biological entity.[10] Perhaps even more disturbing to the standard historical accounts of the political ideologies of the period, as the following demonstrates, this lack with respect to what is commonly assumed to be our contemporary configurations of the concept of universal human rights was not simply compensated for by the use and exfoliation of *another* (earlier, or less tractable or universal) conceptual structure, the rights of man. It is not the case that where we aspire to reach to the concept "universal human rights" our eighteenth-century forebears grasped that same concept under the rubric of "rights of man."[11] The fact is more complicated: The period operated or

9. This implies that thinking may be efficaciously enabled by "fuzzy" as well as coherent concepts. In fact in some cases the lack of coherence may be advantageous. A contender here would be "deconstruction" in its strict Derridean sense.

10. The standard formulation for universal human rights is those rights one has by dint of being human. Many have pointed out, however, that this claim is merely a belief and not susceptible of rational elaboration. It is particularly difficult to find reasons for claiming that some of the rights outlined in the Universal Declaration of 1948 and its subsequent codicils and extensions—say, certain economic and social rights—are universal, held equally by all. On this see Michael Freeman, *Human Rights* (Cambridge: Polity Press, 2011), 61–68. Moreover, much hangs on the assumption that our contemporary concept does indeed enable us to think rights in the register of the universal. In fact, as will become clearer as my argument progresses, that assumption rests on very fragile foundations.

11. Care is needed here with respect to the longer reach of this argument: As will become clear, there are similarities, even continuities between eighteenth-century conceptions of rights and contemporary human rights. This overlap or continuous tradition is evident in the use we currently find for thinking "human rights" with the concept

had access to two quite distinct concepts that enabled eighteenth-century persons to make sense of rights when applied to "man." In the case of the first of these concepts, it was nigh impossible to think rights as universal. In the case of the second, although rights might have, with some imaginative exercise, been capable of universal extension, the pressure that this applied to the concept "man" made such an extension problematic.

The upshot of this is that in neither case was anything like our own contemporary aspiration for a conception of universal human rights in reach. This, it seems to me, has largely gone unnoticed in the vast literature commenting on rights in the Enlightenment, still less have the consequences of this observation been explored in respect to how we might begin to understand concepts in history and as historical forms. The standard story, then, which plots the gradual emergence of "the rights of man" over the course of the eighteenth century, finding its terminus in their extensive popular proclamation during the early the 1790s, is at best very partial and at worst a grossly misleading account. This chapter begins the task of explaining both why that is so and how this observation does not simply challenge a received *history* of ideas but also the basis upon which such histories might be constructed.

As perhaps is immediately obvious, this is a strong hypothesis that will need to be hedged with a number of qualifications—to begin with, as has been noted above, the period is not entirely innocent of the locution *human rights*—but the utility of its strength lies in the fact that it gives a very clear outline to the shape of the following inquiry. In what ways does our contemporary concept of human rights, with all its difficulties for international politics, draw upon a long tradition of rights discourse for its structuration? I do not think an adequate answer to this question can be found by simply looking toward the discursive: Comparative descriptions intending to show the differences and similarities between eighteenth-century uses of the term *human rights* and our own contemporary uses only get one so far (and in fact not very far at all). For this reason, the current study does not seek to clarify the meaning of the term *human rights*, either then or now. Nor does it place great emphasis on a sequential account of the long Western tradition of rights discourse, on the key texts or debates on

---

"right(s)" as outlined below. My point is that the conceptual architecture of "right(s)" will not allow one to think rights as universal either now or in the eighteenth century, so the continuity that persists is in fact the difficulty or even impossibility of thinking rights as universal. This is not quite the point that is made by those who propose a genealogy of contemporary rights as a form of legitimation.

and about rights.[12] Although I shall certainly pass by or through some of those debates and texts, my concerns are focused on something else. This is because the following asks a different question: To what extent is the architecture of our contemporary concept of international human rights derived from or compatible with the various ways in which the concepts of rights of man or of mankind were structured in the eighteenth century? I am, then, less interested in discursive forms or practices than in the architecture of conceptual entities and their historical valences. The best way of putting this is: The aim of the project is to recover how the eighteenth century thought with and through two distinct concepts, "right(s)," as applied to or conjugated with mankind, and "rights of man." The impersonality of that formulation is intended to highlight what is at stake in thinking about concepts as cultural entities.

Notwithstanding these methodological difficulties, it may be possible to begin with a more modest and common-sense approach. If one must for the moment hold off claiming that human rights were invented during the eighteenth century, perhaps one can, nevertheless, find the foundations for the rights of man within the Enlightenment. Even if the period for all intents and purposes did not use the phrase, surely, one might observe, it was inward with at least some elements of the concept as it is currently structured and deployed. The Enlightenment, it is commonly held, made significant progress in respect to political enfranchisement (even if in Britain universal suffrage would take another century or more to become law), and its "revolution in ideas" resulted in what most would regard as a liberation for the human subject.[13] No longer tied to the restrictive conventions of courtly society, freed from the yoke of economic servitude, and increasingly (though far from universally) liberated from certain religious ortho-

12. As shall become clear below, I mean to contrast a linear narrative account of the history of ideas derived from the great texts and authors of the perceived, accepted, and accredited tradition with a data-driven analysis that shows how ideas coalesce at particular moments, creating stability sometimes over long periods of time, sometimes over remarkably short periods.

13. If one reads this in terms of a Lockean description of political power that gives to man in society "a *Right* of making laws . . . for the Publick Good," there can be no doubting the sense of liberation both from the Filmerian notion of divine right that applied to an hereditary monarchy and from the Hobbesian violence of society founded on "might is right." See John Locke, *Two Treatises on Government and a Letter Concerning Toleration*, ed. Ian Shapiro (New Haven, Conn.: Yale University Press, 2003), Treatise 2, ch. 1, sect. 3; p. 101.

doxies, the Enlightenment saw the birth of the modern liberal subject.[14] And above all else that bourgeois liberal subject is a bearer of rights. While in the most general sense this way of putting it would seem to carry a truth, it also, unfortunately, begs many questions not least because *the Enlightenment* is itself a contested term. Any cursory glance at the long traditions of the history of political thought would immediately reveal that the Enlightenment has hardly ever been understood as a single movement or as having a singular national identity.[15] Furthermore, the particular qualities of the era called Enlightenment have been characterized in very different ways: Some have wished to see it as "a revolution in ideas" while others have sought to explain its revolutionary character in terms of society and culture, placing the burden of proof on such novelties as the coffee house or the very significant rise in circulation of printed materials.[16] Leaving

14. In some hands, this comes to be seen as the modern invention of "identity." See Dror Wahrman, *The Making of the Modern Self: Identity and Culture in Eighteenth-Century England* (New Haven, Conn.: Yale University Press, 2004). Alasdair MacIntyre understands the "invention" of the "modern individual" as a response to a loss of faith in the theological grounding of morals; this "individual" was a "new social and cultural artefact." See *Whose Justice? Which Rationality?* (South Bend, Ind.: University of Notre Dame Press, 1988), 339.

15. For a good brief overview, see Lester G Crocker, introduction to *The Blackwell Companion to the Enlightenment*, ed. John W. Yolton (Oxford: Blackwell, 1991), 1–10; and for a more philosophical approach see James Schmidt, "Introduction: What Is Enlightenment?," in *What Is Enlightenment: Eighteenth-Century Answers and Twentieth-Century Questions*, ed. James Schmidt (Berkeley: University of California Press, 1996), 1–44. J. G. A. Pocock has been perhaps the most prominent critic of the term *"the" Enlightenment.* See "Post-Puritan England and the Problem of the Enlightenment," in *Culture and Politics from Puritanism to the Enlightenment*, ed. P. Zagorin (Berkeley: University of California Press, 1980), 91–111. More recently, Jonathan I. Israel has completed a gargantuan history of the Enlightenment in three volumes. It would be impossible to characterize in a thumbnail this significant contribution to our understanding of the revolution in ideas that for a century gripped Europe and the colonies, but the essential focus of all three studies is firmly targeted at the "ideas" that circulated within and across national boundaries. See Jonathan I. Israel, *Radical Enlightenment: Philosophy and the Making of Modernity 1650–1750* (Oxford: Oxford University Press, 2001); *Enlightenment Contested: Philosophy, Modernity, and the Emancipation of Man, 1670–1752,* (Oxford: Oxford University Press, 2006); *Democratic Enlightenment: Philosophy, Revolution, and Human Rights 1750–1790* (Oxford: Oxford University Press, 2011).

16. One might want to observe, as Jonathan Israel does, that it was both. See Jonathan I. Israel, *Enlightenment Contested: Philosophy, Modernity, and the Emancipation of Man 1670–1752* (Oxford: Oxford University Press, 2006), v.

aside for the moment these cavils and measured objections, it remains the case that there is a pretty narrow variance in how historians have understood the significance of the French Declaration of the Rights of Man and Citizen (1789) which, building on the American Declaration of Independence (1776), is commonly said to have provided a language for expressing universal human rights.[17] The project of the Enlightenment, at least if one takes an optimistic view of its intervention, certainly included the generation of aspirations for equality on behalf of all citizens.[18] Within this optic, "human rights" are usually taken to be the outgrowth or development of a set of arguments that were made in the early modern politico-legal framework of natural law. "Human rights," according to this view, are the progeny of the long European tradition of thought concerned with natural rights that links in a continuous chain thinkers such as Grotius, Pufendorf, Locke, and Rousseau.[19]

17. Lynn Hunt notes, for example, that "the history of the revolutionary spurts in rights shows that something happened to the conception of rights between 1689 and 1776–1789 to transform them from the rights of a particular people—freeborn English men—into universal natural rights, the French *droits de l'homme* or 'rights of man.' Men—especially men and only later women—began to talk fervently about universal rights in ways that at least implied their equality for all 'men,' remembering that 'men' could mean either males or humankind." See Lynn Hunt, "Paradoxical Origins of Human Rights," in *Human Rights and Revolutions*, ed. Jeffrey N. Wasserstrom, Lynn Hunt, and Marilyn B. Young (Lanham, Md.: Rowman & Littlefield, 2000), 8.

18. For a good conspectus on this, see *Enlightenment, Rights, and Revolution: Essays in Legal and Social Philosophy*, ed. D. N. MacCormick and Z. Bankowski (Aberdeen: Aberdeen University Press, 1989). The pessimistic view has tended to be in the ascendant in more recent times. See, for example, James Schmidt's introduction to his edited volume *What Is Enlightenment?*: "The Enlightenment has been blamed for many things. It has been held responsible for the French Revolution, for totalitarianism, and for the view that nature is simply an object to be dominated, manipulated, and exploited. It has also been implicated in one way or another in European imperialism and the most aggressive aspects of capitalism. While some have insisted that its skepticism about 'absolute values' infects our culture with a 'nihilistic sluggishness,' others have suggested that liberal societies should divest themselves of the Enlightenment's obsession with 'philosophical foundations.'" Schmidt is referring first to the work of Leszeck Kolakowski, "The Ideology of Politics," *Atlantic Community Quarterly* 24 (Fall 1986): 219–30 and then to that of Richard Rorty, *Contingency, Irony, and Solidarity* (Cambridge: Cambridge University Press, 1989), 52–54.

19. A useful and brief account of the importance of the natural rights tradition can be found in Knud Haakonssen, "From Natural Law to the Rights of Man," in *A Culture of Rights: The Bill of Rights in Philosophy, Politics, and Law 1791 and 1991*, ed. Michael J. Lacey and Knud Haakonssen (Cambridge: Cambridge University Press, 1991), 19–61.

In contrast to this smooth linear narrative, recent political theorists and philosophers have begun to develop a different picture.[20] The Oxford moral philosopher James Griffin, for example, has recently asked if the concept of human rights is well formed. Griffin replies in the negative and sets out to provide strenuous arguments on behalf of the idea that the concept is "incomplete."[21] For Griffin and others who take this contrary view, the distinctive contribution of the Enlightenment is the formulation of a *yet to be achieved* "project on human rights." Such views can hardly be detached from a current politics around the establishment and policing of international human rights nor, at the same time, from a set of local and currently more or less energetic arguments about the nature—benign or toxic—of the Enlightenment itself.[22] Although I do not want to completely

---

The most vocal critic of this line of argument is John Philip Reid, who makes a strong case for the irrelevance of natural rights to the colonists. See his *Constitutional History of the American Revolution: The Authority of Rights* (Madison: University of Wisconsin Press, 1986), 95: "The truth is there was little substantive difference between natural rights and positive rights. To dissect a natural right was to find a British right and was natural because the British possessed it." See also his "The Irrelevance of the Declaration," in *Law in the American Revolution and the American Revolution in Law: A Collection of Essays on American Legal History*, ed. Hendrik Hartog (New York: New York University Press, 1981), 46–89.

20. As well they might if one suspects that "ideas" are unlikely to have smooth evolutionary histories: The history of universal rights in the Anglophone tradition is, in fact, very lumpy. Even if a case were made for an eighteenth-century moment of efflorescence (a view that requires considerable qualification in the terms developed below), the almost total absence of interest in the category from the early nineteenth century until 1948 indicates that any continuous narrative of gradual refinement would be faulty. If one were to sketch a long history, it would more likely resemble a fold in time than a continuous arc. On the gulf between 1948 and the era of eighteenth-century revolutions, see the compelling account of nineteenth-century neglect of human rights in Samuel Moyn, *The Last Utopia: Human Rights in History* (Cambridge, Mass.: Belknap Press of Harvard University Press, 2010).

21. See James Griffin, *On Human Rights* (Oxford: Oxford University Press, 2008). Griffin makes the point even more strongly: "The term 'human right' is nearly criterionless. There are unusually few criteria for determining when the term is used correctly and when incorrectly—and not just among politicians, but among philosophers, political theorists, and jurisprudents as well. The language of human rights has, in this way, become debased" (14–15).

22. This is to note that the "postmodern" skepticism with which the emancipatory ideals of the Enlightenment were greeted in the 1970s and '80s has a long tail. See, for example, *Questioning History: The Postmodern Turn to the Eighteenth Century*, ed. Greg Clingham (Lewisburg: Bucknell University Press, 1998); Daniel Carey and Lynn M.

ignore these current political vectors that infuse any contemporary discussion of human rights, the major focus in this chapter concerns whether it is possible to differentiate between different *types* of concept that might fall under the common rubric of "rights" when applied to "man." This is to say, I wish to test the hypothesis, raised in passing by Griffin but more explicitly by Charles Beitz, that the conceptual architecture of natural rights is distinct from (and possibly incommensurate with) the architecture of the concept of human rights.[23]

Natural Rights and Human Rights

Within the discipline of the history of political thought, the history of the concept of rights has been the object of some attention.[24] There are competing accounts—most especially in relation to the importance of Locke's *Two Treatises on Government*—to the development of what Michael P. Zuckert calls the "natural rights republic,"[25] that is, the emergence

Festa, eds., *The Postcolonial Enlightenment: Eighteenth-Century Colonialism and Postcolonial Theory* (Oxford: Oxford University Press, 2009).

23. See Charles R. Beitz, *The Idea of Human Rights* (Oxford: Oxford University Press, 2009). Beitz's solution to the difficulty posed by the demand for a philosophically coherent justification for international human rights is to turn away from parsing the conceptuality of competing notions of such rights toward practical assessments of the efficacy of human rights discourse. Here the difference between his project and mine is very clear: My first aim is to test the coherence of these concepts *historically*, before essaying any observations about how current international human rights discourse may or may not be working with a conceptual architecture that is fit for purpose (howsoever determined). I do, however, fully take the force of his practical turn as a strategy for addressing the difficulties in current conceptualizations. See especially his analysis of what he calls the "conceptual space of natural rights" and its differences from that occupied by international human rights (52ff).

24. See Richard Dagger, "Rights," in *Political Innovation and Conceptual Change*, ed. Terrence Ball, James Farr, and Russell L. Hanson (Cambridge: Cambridge University Press, 1989), 292–308; A. I. Melden, *Rights and Persons* (Berkeley: University of California Press, 1977); John Dunn, *Western Political Theory in the Face of the Future* (Cambridge: Cambridge University Press, 1979); *A Culture of Rights: The Bill of Rights in Philosophy, Politics, and Law, 1791 and 1991*, ed. Michael J. Lacey and Knud Haaksonssen (Cambridge: Cambridge University Press, 1991); Jonathan Gorman, *Rights and Reason: An Introduction to the Philosophy of Rights* (Chesham: Acumen, 2003).

25. See Michael P. Zuckert, *The Natural Rights Republic: Studies in the Foundation of the American Political Tradition* (South Bend, Ind.: University of Notre Dame Press,

of the United States of America, about which I shall have something to say in the following chapter. But this scholarly tradition has a very distinctive outline. Essentially, it is argued, modern conceptions of rights are derived from the long European engagement with classical, especially Roman, models of liberty. This tradition notes that natural rights in a sense recognizable to us were first formulated in the late Middle Ages, but their centrality to how one might understand human society and government did not become apparent until the seventeenth century. Although Aquinas had a very well developed sense of the distinctiveness of humanity, namely its capacity for reason, it was his later epigone, Francisco Suarez, who propelled the natural law tradition toward its embrace of the concept of natural rights.[26] This idea was then developed and extended by the protestant Hugo Grotius writing in the mid-seventeenth century, who is widely held to have been the instigator of the modern secular theory of natural law.[27]

1996). Zuckert aims to combine the republican and liberalism positions, essentially seeing Locke as a contributor to political philosophy, not political science. He notes that "during the Restoration there was a Whig political philosophy—essentially one or another form of modernized natural law philosophy (e.g., Hooker or Grotius)—and a Whig political science. Over the course of the eighteenth century Locke, and to a lesser but still important degree Algernon Sidney, replaced Grotius as the chief authority in political philosophy, but many of the elements of the older Whig political science were carried forward, assimilated to and at least somewhat transformed by their connections to the new Lockean political philosophy" (165). This chapter and the following seek to uncover a fault line in the architecture of the concept of rights that may have been in part created by the distinction between politics as theory and practice, so to this extent I think that Zuckert's combinatory reading is helpful.

26. This suggests that Aquinas would have been unable to derive the modern concept of human rights from his understanding of natural law—a view that some would find contentious. See on this John Finnis, *Aquinas* (Oxford: Oxford University Press, 1998): "Aquinas clearly has the concept [of human rights]. He articulates it when he sums up the 'precepts of justice' by saying that justice centrally concerns . . . what is owed to 'everyone in common' or to 'everyone alike' . . . rather than to determine persons for reasons particular to them" (136). The alternative view, that Aquinas's conceptual toolbox did not allow him to see rights our way, is forcefully argued by Griffin in his *On Human Rights* (Oxford: Oxford University Press, 2008), 9.

27. Commenting on Grotius's contribution to this tradition, Istvan Hont notes: "It was Grotius who first clearly understood that natural jurisprudence could be valid only if it was 'of use for the whole human race.' Positive and arbitrary law must be distinguished carefully from the common or "natural" laws of the whole of mankind. Of these last Grotius provided the first real and complete system." See *Jealousy of Trade: International Competition and the Nation-State in Historical Perspective* (Cambridge, Mass.: Belknap Press of Harvard University Press, 2005), 165; and for an assessment of the

Grotius's interlocutors, among them Samuel Pufendorf and John Selden, helped to shape this tradition, which had a definitive shape and texture by the time Thomas Hobbes and John Locke wrote their significant contributions to modern political thought.[28]

According to the dominant historical narrative, if one were alive in the first half of the eighteenth century in Britain, one could not articulate what was distinctive about the settled constitution under which one enjoyed one's liberties without recourse to those arguments made on behalf of natural rights. Life, liberty, and property, the almost mystic trio of rights intoned mantra-like throughout this tradition, were a birthright at least if one thought of oneself under a particular description of Englishness.[29] Although, as shall become clear, there were competing analyses of the basis for holding those rights—this is where the long running debate between the republican and the liberal interpretations of the American Revolution exposes differences in how eighteenth-century actors understood this long natural law tradition[30]—it nevertheless remained the case that the natural

---

arguments both pro and contra Grotius's founding modern natural law, see Charles Edwards, *Hugo Grotius: The Miracle of Holland* (Chicago: Nelson-Hall, 1981), chs. 2 and 3.

28. The standard work on the emergence of this tradition remains Richard Tuck, *Natural Rights Theories: Their Origin and Development* (Cambridge: Cambridge University Press, 1979). See also Brian Tierney, *The Idea of Natural Rights* (Atlanta, Ga.: Scholars Press, 1997).

29. An early eighteenth-century boast of the wisdom of the ideology of Englishness puts it: "Will you exchange your Birth-right of English Laws and Liberty, for Martial and Club Law, and help to destroy one another, only to be eaten last yourselves?" See Hugh Speke, *The Secret History of the happy Revolution, in 1688. Humbly dedicated to His Most Gracious Majesty King George, by the principal transactor in it* (London, S. Keimer, 1715), 17.

30. The literature around this issue is very extensive. For a good recent overview see Alan Gibson, *Understanding the Founding: The Crucial Questions* (Lawrence: University Press of Kansas, 2007). The three most widely cited texts that set the terms of the revisionary republican thesis are Gordon Wood, *The Creation of the American Republic, 1776–1787* (Chapel Hill: University of North Carolina Press, 1969); J. G. A. Pocock, *The Machiavellian Moment: Florentine Political Thought and the Atlantic Republican Tradition* (Princeton, N.J.: Princeton University Press, 1975); and Bernard Bailyn, *The Ideological Origins of the American Revolution* (Cambridge, Mass.: Belknap Press of Harvard University Press, 1976). The counter position, the thesis based on an account of liberalism, has been put by, among others, Steven Dworetz, *The Unvarnished Doctrine: Locke, Liberalism, and the American Revolution* (Durham, N.C.: Duke University Press, 1990); Joyce Appleby, *Liberalism and Republicanism in the Historical Imagination* (Cambridge, Mass.: Harvard University Press, 1992); Paul Rahe, *Republics Ancient and Modern: Classi-*

rights tradition had so firmly established the concept of "right" that belief in its justness and necessity for a well functioning society was almost
unshakeable.[31]

If one finds this narrative compelling, the movement from "natural
rights" to the "rights of man" can be understood as simply a further refinement or extension of this long tradition of rights discourse. But, as recent
studies have begun to show, the lines of force connecting the heterodox
systems of belief that were woven into the tapestry of eighteenth-century
Anglophone culture were manifold and did not always act in concert with
each other.[32] This is to note that the very local specifics of a particular
set of arguments and beliefs highlight the difficulties of supposing a single, and even less coherent, tradition which allowed a seamless translation
across speech contexts: Although the same words may be have been used
by, say, dissenting colonists and members of the British Parliament, one
should not immediately assume that they operated with a common or even
compatible set of beliefs. What I take this to imply is that, in respect to a
putative concept of rights, one must question whether or not a singular
architecture for such a concept was in circulation. Or, to put that in a way
that will cast significant light on the intervention that Paine's *Rights of Man*
made in the early 1790s in Britain, "rights" (at least in some places and in
some hands) were not only (or could or ought never to be) the plural form
of "right."[33]

---

cal Republicanism and the American Revolution (Chapel Hill: University of North Carolina
Press, 1992).

31. Although British eighteenth-century political discourse found much to contest
in respect to the forms of government that were deemed to be most appropriate, juristic
and legal discourse simply accepted that to be a person one must be a rights holder.
In the conceptual analysis that follows I shall refer to the functionality of this concept of "right" as "load bearing": It enables one to coherently construe the concept of
"person."

32. For a robust exploration of this heterodoxy, see J. C. D. Clark, *The Language of
Liberty 1660–1832: Political Discourse and Social Dynamics in the Anglo-American World*
(Cambridge: Cambridge University Press, 1994).

33. This builds upon an observation made by James H. Hutson in his "Emergence
of the Modern Concept of a Right in America: The Contribution of Michel Villey,"
first published in 1994 and revised in Barry Alan Shain, ed., *The Nature of Rights at
the American Founding and Beyond* (Charlottesville: University of Virginia Press, 2007).
Commenting on the French legal historian Michel Villey's insistence on the distinction
between "right" and "rights": "He [Villey] held that a speaker or author using the singular, right, meant classical objective right, while the use of the plural, rights, indicated
subjective rights" (33).

As noted above, to some extent the outlines of the distinctions I wish to make in respect to the architecture of the concept of rights in the Anglophone eighteenth century can be most clearly seen in the debates of the colonists about their putative separation from the British Empire. One does not need the detail of that argument, however, in order to note that the content, as it were, of the colonists' conceptual lexicon was determining in relation to the justifications they were able to make (or convince themselves were indeed justified arguments) for proposing an end to their sovereign connection to the mother country. And that lexicon did not spring spontaneously from some source. It had deep foundations in their "cultural baggage": their religious beliefs, their education, the codification of their legal system, or, more generally, their social, political, and familial practices, their reading and conversing. This has led to a long-standing disagreement among historians of the colonial period and subsequent revolution: Were the colonists essentially following and adopting the moral strictures laid out by Frances Hutcheson, as Garry Wills has claimed?[34] Or were they deeply immersed in the natural-rights tradition and taking their clues from John Locke?[35]

The most common way of resolving such discrepant accounts is to trace the close histories of texts, readers, and contexts within which those

34. See Garry Wills, *Inventing America: Jefferson's Declaration of Independence* (New York: Vintage Books, 1979).

35. See Michael P. Zuckert, *Natural Rights and the New Republicanism* (Princeton, N.J.: Princeton University Press, 1994), esp. 3–25. T. H. Breen steers a course between the pro- and anti-Lockean account in calling the revolutionary period a "Lockean moment," by which he means to call to mind the fact that although Locke's own works were hardly present to the debates of the colonists they were, nevertheless, happy to use his name as a placeholder. As he writes about the public debates of the era: "Locke became a symbol for a wider, often wonderfully undisciplined exploration of natural and human rights." See T. H. Breen, "An Appeal to Heaven: The Language of Rights in the Eve of American Independence," in *The Future of Liberal Democracy: Thomas Jefferson and the Contemporary World*, ed. Robert Fatton Jr. and R. K. Ramazani (Basingstoke: Palgrave Macmillan, 2004), 68; Yuhtaro Ohmori, "The Artillery of Mr Locke: The Use of Locke's *Second Treatise* in Pre-Revolutionary America, 1764–1776" (PhD diss., Johns Hopkins University, 1988). A slightly different approach is taken by Daniel T. Rodgers, who notes that the language of rights was often incoherent or contested, at the very least far from consistent in its deployment of terms such as "natural rights." Far from their being a "great liberal tradition stretching across the centuries . . . intellectual traditions are the convenient inventions of intellectual historians." See Daniel T Rodgers, *Contested Truths: Keywords in American Politics since Independence* (New York: Basic Books, 1987), 47. I shall have more to say about this in the following chapter.

texts were both produced and read. Since Jefferson, for example, neither owned a copy of Hutcheson's major work nor ever recommended to anyone that they read it, Zuckert makes the point that Wills's attempt to displace Locke as the *eminence grise* behind the Declaration of Independence with Hutcheson is misguided.[36] Or, to take another powerful corrective to the standard account of the basis for revolutionary beliefs in the colonies, J. C. D. Clark's *The Language of Liberty 1660–1832*, unless one reconstructs the precise locales for the utterances of those historical actors and the varying belief systems they upheld—according to Clarke almost entirely determined in and through the varieties of dissent to which these actors subscribed—one runs the risk of completely misunderstanding the meanings of those utterances. Only such careful reconstruction will allow one to respect the varieties of thought present to the period. I take this as axiomatic for the following argument, but I also wish to refract such close contextualizations through the widest possible lens, through the culture at large. This is because the center of my interest is the history of conceptual forms where such forms are taken to be cultural phenomena: I do not see them as the exclusive property of an individual or of a text, even if it is possible to recreate the uses to which a person or a text put specific concepts.

In contrast to a meaning-driven account of conceptuality, the following is based upon the observation that concepts can be understood as given to us or made available by the culture in which we live. They are common unshareable structures for arriving at understanding, the tube or subway maps of my introduction. Consequently, I shall not be concerned to answer the question "What did the rights of man *mean* to historical agents alive in the eighteenth century?" Rather, my aim is to parse the grammar of the concept of rights and to describe its distinctive architecture within the culture of the English language eighteenth century. This entails the discrimination of different functionalities, modalities, and forms for the concept, which in turn reveal a significant difference in conceptual architecture between "right(s)" as it emerges out of the natural-rights tradition and a more complex if also in some ways problematic concept, "rights of man." In the case of the former, a conceptual analysis supports the observation that the ideational concept "right(s)" was most commonly operated for the greater part of the eighteenth century according to a nominal function.[37]

36. See Zuckert, *Natural Rights*, 19.

37. It is useful to recall that all concepts, be they ideational or reificational, have a naming function; the former, however, may also operate in other ways.

A "right" named a title or claim. But that nominal function was not exclusive: The concept "right(s)" could also be operated with either a load bearing or containing function. When, for example, it was claimed that natural law upheld the distinct rights of property and personal safety, the concept "right(s)" functioned as a container for the many distinctive rights that could be claimed. In contrast, when one turns to the phrase the period used most frequently in respect to general rights, *rights of mankind*, it will become clear that a dual function was applied: The "rights of mankind" were both a container for all the specific rights one might claim and also the load-bearing foundation upon which one could construct an account of personhood or understand the political relations between individuals and the state or sovereign. The modality of the concept "right(s)" could also be either schematic, providing the rules or criteria for containing distinct rights within the overall conceptual shell, or axiomatic, enabling one to think the category person or the rather unfamiliar if not new category of national identity: Britishness.[38] It also had the capacity to take on two different forms: It could be both plastic, applied to things that heretofore were not conceived as having rights, and rigid, providing the nonnegotiable basis for grounding a legal conception of person.[39]

This conceptual mobility doubtless provided the opportunity, if not the motor, for "rights discourse" to become so ubiquitous during the period. It was the reason for the fact that, as some recent commentators have noted, rights were so easily and indiscriminately appealed to as to make it almost impossible to extract a common or coherent thread to such ar-

---

38. Recent work on constructions of national identity during the eighteenth century in Britain have placed considerable emphasis on the larger geopolitical environment in which identities are manifest. See Linda Colley, *Britons: Forging the Nation, 1707–1837* (New Haven, Conn.: Yale University Press, 1992); Colin Kidd, *British Identities before Nationalism: Ethnicity and Nationhood in the Atlantic World, 1600–1800* (Cambridge: Cambridge University Press, 1999); Kathleen Wilson, *The Island Race: Englishness, Empire, and Gender in the Eighteenth century* (London: Routledge, 2003); and, for an account that plays into the story legal history in the period told about the centrality of race, see Hugh A. MacDougal, *Racial Myth in English History: Trojans, Teutons, and Anglo-Saxons* (Hanover, N.H.: University Press of New England, 1982). A recent theoretical account of cultural identity asks us to see all such markers of difference in dialectical terms: See Stephen Greenblatt, *Cultural Mobility: A Manifesto* (Cambridge: Cambridge University Press, 2010).

39. For a good account of the particular values applied to and inhering in things during the period, see Wolfram Schmidgen, *Eighteenth-Century Fiction and the Law of Property* (Cambridge: Cambridge University Press, 2002), esp. 104–49.

guments. In this sense, the concept "right(s)" was exceptionally powerful in the political world of the Anglophone eighteenth century because it invoked an ethico-legal doctrine as the basis for a property claim while simultaneously inhabiting a plurality of discursive locales that were at least potentially contestatory. When, as happened on many occasions and in many contexts, the drive to resolve such contestation was ignored or in the descendant, the invocation of "right(s)" usefully left undeclared the precise foundation for holding to a specific moral code: That justification or foundation was left unidentified, residing somewhere in the shadows as the conceptual architecture slid from one configuration to another. And it was also precisely that mobility in conceptual structure that made the connections between "rights," "man," and "universal" seem so enticing for those wishing to bring about the end of the ancien régime. As I shall argue below, it was also the reason why the period was never really confronted with the significant problem of making "human rights" conceptually coherent. All this is to note that the mobility of a conceptual structure may have both enabling and disabling aspects: On the one hand, a "fuzzy" concept allows one to think outside the parameters currently available (this is what Paine will do in the 1790s) while at the same time it prevents the coalescence of a new conceptual form that will generate a truly transformative worldview (this is what happened after the "breakthrough" moment of the separation of the colonies from the mother country in the 1770s).

I recognize that these parsings of the concept of "right(s)" are likely to strike readers as unfamiliar, perhaps even defamiliarizing. They ought to become less so, however, as their frequency increases in the following presentation and interpretation of data. It is not only these parsings, however, that make legible the beginnings of a chronological history of conceptual formation; it is also the connectivity within specific networks that reveals how concepts as cultural entities coalesced over time to form composite clusters for making sense. Thus, a second feature of the conceptual analysis I propose is the reconstruction of the historically contingent conceptual networks within which the concepts "right(s)" and "rights of man" were suspended. This network analysis is intended to augment the parsing of a conceptual grammar and syntax in order to make the larger "architecture" of a conceptual form visible. Here I need to restate that when in the following I refer to the architecture of a concept I take that "architecture" to comprise both the internal structure (what might be seen as self evidently architectural elements) and the external fit or connectivity that enables concepts to operate within networks of related and adjacent conceptual forms and generate the clusters referred to above.

From Natural Rights to Subjective Rights

In order to understand how the data presented in this chapter provide different evidence for a history of ideas, I need to first establish what it is departing from. The following sketch, therefore, intends to provide an albeit highly truncated version of what might be called a standard history-of-ideas approach to rights. As will become clear, the data and their interpretation that follows are intended to test that standard history, with the intention of thickening it where appropriate. Although the scholarly debate has moved on since Richard Tuck published his book *Natural Rights Theories: Their Origin and Development* in 1979, it nevertheless remains the most succinct and persuasive account of the foundations for the tradition of European thought concerned with natural rights.[40] In that book, Tuck traces the evolution of the language of rights by putting it within a specific set of historically inflected political and philosophical arguments. We do not need to follow Tuck's powerful analysis of this tradition in any detail in order to note that within the long history of natural rights discourse there was, as Tuck notes, from "its inception" an "ambiguous character" to it.[41] That ambiguity lies in the operation of the concept of possession: Does property necessarily imply *possessive* individualism and therefore a very particular notion of liberalism? Or, as Tuck argues, is there a different way of articulating the relation of persons to the modern liberal democratic theory of politics that was substantially developed in the context of seventeenth-century England?[42] Much of the following argument seeks to explore in greater detail that ambiguity through the specific lens of what I characterize as the parsing of concepts. Notwithstanding the technicalities of the arguments in political theory, the consensus view firmly holds to the thought that the early modern development of a theory of natural rights was essentially grounded in the notion of *possession*, or property.[43]

40. Attention has moved away from the early modern natural jurists to the inheritance of Roman law in the thinking of the later Christian scholastics. On this, see Annabel S. Brett, *Liberty, Right and Nature: Individual Rights in later Scholastic Thought* (Cambridge: Cambridge University Press, 1997).

41. Richard Tuck, *Natural Rights Theories: Their Origin and Development* (Cambridge: Cambridge University Press, 1979), 3.

42. Tuck is writing against C. B. Macpherson's account in his *The Political Theory of Possessive Individualism* (Oxford: Oxford University Press, 1962).

43. See Tuck: "Already by the fourteenth century it was possible to argue that to have a right was to be the lord or *dominus* of one's relevant moral world, to possess *dominium*, that is to say *property*." *Natural Rights Theories: Their Origin and Development*

Thus, by the time Locke came to write his *Two Treatises on Government*, the discourse of rights was entangled in a set of discriminations and distinctions which sought to hold in tension duty, obligation, property, and rights.[44] The spilling of a great deal of ink occurred throughout the early eighteenth century in the vain hope that this knot of moral and political concepts might be held stable or at least immune from dissolution into a morass of self-interest. Tuck, for example, notes one particularly strenuous attempt by Locke, who argued that "property is explained in terms of a right necessary to the fulfillment of a duty to preserve and benefit mankind as a whole, a duty which men are under naturally as well as civilly."[45] The consensus scholarly view, however, claims that by the end of the eighteenth century in Britain something very different was in the ascendant in respect to the knot around rights referred to above. In place of the delicate balance of rights with obligations, duties and property, rights were now taken to be a person's due *merely on account of being human*. Under this rubric, rights are first and foremost held by and for the person.[46]

Such an account of the legitimacy of rights claims clearly requires the support of another concept: man, person, or the human. If to be human is to have rights—as current international human rights thinks the matter— then the conceptual armature between "rights" and "the human" needs to be understood. Are "rights" the necessary and sufficient condition for

---

(Cambridge: Cambridge University Press, 1979), 3. Note here that Tuck finds the origin of this idea earlier than the then prevailing scholarship was minded to, which suggests that a capacious history of rights might have difficulty with the notion that "human rights" were invented around the time of the French Revolution.

44. Locke did not discriminate very carefully between a number of synonyms for *right—power, title, privilege, claim, liberty*—which makes the legacy claim (eighteenth-century rights discourse is based upon Lockean arguments) more difficult to substantiate than is often assumed. As A. John Simmons points out, "Locke never gives us anything like a definition of right in his works." See *The Lockean Theory of Rights* (Princeton, N.J.: Princeton University Press, 1992), 70; see also n. 11.

45. Richard Tuck, *Natural Rights Theories: Their Origin and Development* (Cambridge: Cambridge University Press, 1979), 171.

46. Care is needed here as to whether "person" is to be taken as a universal category for man. In some versions of the genealogy I sketch out here, this is so, but this needs to be tempered by the observation that such an account is certainly not Lockean. As A. John Simmons reminds us, "natural rights in Locke should not be understood as those rights possessed by all human beings; for there *are* no rights that all human necessarily possess. Rights in Locke are possessed by *persons* (i.e., 'men' in the *moral*, not the biological sense), not by human beings qua humans." See A. John Simmons, *The Lockean Theory of Rights* (Princeton, N.J.: Princeton University Press, 1992), 89n64.

being human, or is it the other way around? The natural-law tradition es-
sayed a number of ways of creating this armature.[47] Henry Home, Lord
Kames, for example, made a very strong case for property as the distinctive concept that enables one to understand the distinctiveness of the human.[48] In doing so, he was taking issue with his Scottish compatriot, David
Hume, who claimed that in a state of nature "there can be no such thing as
property."[49] According to Hume, this is why property must be subsequent
to the concept of justice: In terms of the conceptual architecture that enables this way of thinking, "justice" functions in a load-bearing capacity
with respect to the concept of property. Kames wished to dissent from
this view, noting that "property is founded on a natural sense independent
altogether of agreement or convention"—thereby arguing against Hume's
notion of "justice as convention."[50] This then led Kames to the observation
that even in the rudest state man must have had a sense of property: "What
sort of creature would man be, endued as he is with a hoarding appetite,
but with no sense or notion of property?"[51] Furthermore, the labor that
provides man with the necessities for life is itself a form of property: "A
relation is formed betwixt every man and the fruits of his own labour, the
very thing we call property, which he himself is sensible of, and of which
every other is equally sensible."[52] As far as Kames was concerned, then,
from the very first moment property provided the platform for understanding the human. Arguing against those, like Hume or Hobbes, who
thought that property only gained coherence as a concept once man had
left the state of nature and given up some of his rights in order to enter
into society, Kames saw that very movement into society as predicated
upon the desire to protect and maintain ownership in property. It is for
this reason, according to Kames, that "it is clear, that the sense of property

47. For Locke the point of government was to safeguard rights, renamed by him as
"property," thereby configuring the essence of the human in terms of property. See Michael P. Zuckert, *Natural Rights and the New Republicanism* (Princeton, N.J.: Princeton
University Press, 1994), esp. 216–22.

48. See J. G. A. Pocock, "The Varieties of Whiggism from Exclusion to Reform,"
in *Virtue, Commerce, and History* (Cambridge: Cambridge University Press, 1995), 215–
310 in which he gives an account of how property became the foundation of personality.
See esp. 234–39.

49. Henry Home, Lord Kames, *Essays on the Principles of Morality and Natural Religion*, ed. Mary Catherine Moran (Indianapolis, Ind.: Liberty Fund, 2005), 47.

50. Ibid., 47.

51. Ibid., 48.

52. Ibid.

owes not its existence to society"[53]since, as Kames notes, "every man has a peculiar affection for what he calls his *own*."[54] It therefore follows that our sense of what is right or wrong is tied into this strong attachment to what we perceive to be our own property. Justice, seen from this perspective, is far from being an artificial construct: In fact it is dependent upon the natural relation all human beings have to their fruits of their own labor and to the objects they call their own. To be human is to own things.

Kames's account of the human chimes perfectly with the general tendency towards subjective rights. Over the course of the eighteenth century, the qualifying condition of person or the individual increasingly became independence: No longer understood in a tied relationship to an authority above it (howsoever described: monarch, state, or god), the individual began to be conceived as an independent particular, now cut free from external ties even if through the social contract that independence was tempered by the rules of commercial exchange and the conventions of polite society.[55] According to some historians of ideas, this alteration in the ways in which persons claimed legitimacy for their actions or beliefs is effectively used as the prompt or basis for a story that tells the triumphant emergence and complete hegemony of the liberal subject. The point of rights, in this account, is that they gradually become "refined," well adapted to the singular independent agent who is now understood as a bearer of entitlements, and those very entitlements are precisely the defining characteristics of what it is to be a subject in civil society.[56] Refinement, here, is not a qualitative measure; rather, it is more like a narrowing of focus to a theory of govern-

53. Ibid., 49.

54. Ibid., 50.

55. The difference between holding rights conditionally and absolutely also marks the distinction in conceptual grammar I aim to elucidate. That this difference was visible to the period can be seen from William Roberston's early eighteenth-century account of liberty: "As to *Rights* and *Privileges*, or *Liberties* of the Subject, even *Magna Charta*, the great *Record* of them, tells us, that they are *Grants* and *Concessions* of the King, and not the *Inherent Original Rights* of the People: They are not held *Absolutely*, but upon *Condition* of our firm Allegiance." See *The Liberty, Property, and Religion of the Whigs* (London: John Morphew, 1713), 7. This text was reprinted under a different title four years later. See *The English Realm a Perfect Sovereignty and Empire, and the King a Complete and Imperial Sovereign* (London: n.p., 1717), 6.

56. The origins of this sense of subjective rights have been traced back to the fourteenth-century Franciscan monk William of Ockham. On this, see James H. Hutson, "Emergence of the Modern Concept of a Right in America," in Barry A. Shain, ed., *The Nature of Rights at the American Founding and Beyond* (Charlottesville: University of Virginia Press, 2007), 25–63; esp. 29–33.

ment which enables all persons to have access to the same "buy-in": That is what it means to be enfranchised under certain conditions of political organization. This account of rights has helped to create one version of the liberal state that, in hindsight, has become extremely easy to manipulate as a "trump" on account of its ability to engender a simple identification between person and those rights now said to be each person's due.[57] Rights, in one version of the end of this story, have come to be understood as subjective in the sense that an individual is the sole bearer of rights.[58] That supposed change across the Anglophone eighteenth century, an alteration in the shape or contours of the concept, its internal architecture and external connections, will be subject to considerable scrutiny in this chapter.

Contemporary discussion of rights is not limited to the domain of intellectual history, of course; indeed, the most vigorous and contested area of current debate sits between international law, the politics of liberal democracy, and comparative ethics.[59] For some in this debate, the triumphalist story comes dripping in the ironies and violence of a certain kind of imperialism: Human rights, under this rubric, are what first-world states can afford, or, more pointedly, are counters in an ongoing imperialism which

57. Although the mechanism, insofar as any identification may be said to lack complexity, through which this works is simple enough, the history of its operation is rather more complicated. On this, see John Dunn, *Setting the People Free: The Story of Democracy* (London: Atlantic Books, 2005).

58. The current aggravating interference to this simple truth is provided by those accounts of rights that seek to diminish the hegemony of the human. Most obviously at the current time, I am thinking of those strenuous arguments that put animals back into the picture. Perhaps the most concise exploration of this issue is to be found in Stanley Cavell, Cora Diamond, John McDowell, Ian Hacking, and Cary Wolfe, *Philosophy and Animal Life* (New York: Columbia University Press, 2008).

59. I shall not be concerned to adequately convey the very rich seam in contemporary political philosophy that addresses the issue of rights. My aim is to provide an archaeology for the concept of human rights in terms of its historical conceptual formation with the intention of casting light on some of the tensions that obtain within our contemporary concept of "human rights." This might lead one to conclude, perhaps too hastily, as Sonu Bedi does in a provocative recent book, that we should give up on rights altogether. According to Bedi, since we no longer live (for the most part) in the age of monarchies, we do not need to ensure that our democratically elected governments "protect" our rights but *justify* their actions. See Sonu Bedi, *Rejecting Rights* (Cambridge: Cambridge University Press, 2009). For a good overview of the literature on rights from the standpoint of political theory, see the bibliographical essay in Jeremy Waldron, ed., *Nonsense upon Stilts: Bentham, Burke, and Marx on the Rights of Man* (London: Methuen, 1998), 222–30.

seeks to colonize third-world states through the operation of the trump category "human rights." And for others the operation of "human rights" as a weapon in colonial subjugation often masks the fact that the erstwhile noble values supposedly protected and promoted through universal human rights are ignored by the imperializing powers.[60] Whether or not this is the case, international human rights are most commonly understood to be based in, and justified by, the subjective account outlined above that is said by some to be the outcome of the Enlightenment's discourse of rights. This can be used as the basis for an extreme extension of the doctrine of universal rights that certainly ends up looking like a strong form of moral and political imperialism: The rights I hold as my due by dint of being human must not only be *available* to any and every other human being but must also be *held by them*. Consequently, it is claimed, we are all equal rights holders in contemporary society and where, for local, contingent political or doctrinal reasons, this is not the case we have an obligation and a duty to alter the regimes within which such politics disenfranchise persons from their true personhood. Equality, here, can to some seem like the disguise that is adopted in pursuit of the eradication of difference. If this provides an albeit thumbnail sketch of the current tensions at work within the international community with respect to its common goal of achieved "human rights," the central insight of this chapter can be said to be this: The smooth and continuous evolution of the concept of natural into human rights cannot be upheld on historical grounds. That transformation (the extent of which has yet to be fully sketched out) could not have been realized under the historical rubrics of the concepts involved, which is to say that the architecture of the concept "right(s)" does not allow or enable the smooth transition to a new and differently structured concept, contemporary "human rights."[61] Or, to put that in another and more pointed

60. As Joseph Slaughter argues, "international human rights law appropriated forms and institutions—e.g., the *Bildungsroman*, the public sphere, and human rights themselves—that historically served to legitimate the emergent European nation-state." See *Human Rights, Inc.* (New York: Fordham University Press, 2007), 323.

61. This observation leads to a further important question: Why do contemporary arguments about human rights commonly seek support from historical example? Leaving aside the accuracy of the historical claim, what is the specific value provided by a heritage narrative? If, as I shall argue in the coda to this book, two of the major architectural components of the contemporary concept of human rights that cause problems in their realization, delivery or universal acceptance, are the *tense* and modality of that concept, the repetitive gesture by which the concept is said to have a history—its purported genealogical inheritance—is a symptom of the concept's lack of fit for what we want it

way: Contemporary human rights are supposed legitimated by a mistaken genealogy and built using an inadequate or inappropriate conceptual architecture that can be gleaned from the grammar of the concept. Such human rights are conceived to be "held" by individuals.[62] The failings of this conceptual architecture with respect to universal rights ought to be clearer by the end of this chapter.

Some Enlightenment thinkers would have doubtless found this continuous evolution narrative of human rights and their extension into twenty-first-century geopolitics rebarbative. And some contemporary historians would be unconvinced by any account of a concept's smooth transformation over time. Moreover, the veracity of this specific historical sketch has been challenged by scholars such as Knud Haakonssen, who makes the point that "natural law theory in general was not deeply individualistic and dominated by the idea of subjective rights."[63] For him it is necessary to distinguish between those early modern accounts of rights from within the orbit of politics, between "purely *political* rights discourses" and the tradition of ethical thought commonly referred to as natural law. As Haakonssen notes: "According to most natural lawyers in the seventeenth and eighteenth centuries, moral agency consisted in being subject to natural law and carrying out the duties imposed by such law." This, he indicates, was distinct from rights, which in this tradition were seen as derivative, a "mere means to the fulfillment of duties." For natural lawyers there was a bound reciprocity at the heart of one's being an agent in society: "Each person had a right to the acts he or she was under a duty to do and a right to what others had a duty to render."[64] My purpose, however, is not to settle the score between these

to do. "Rights of man," as I shall go on to develop the architecture of that concept, cannot have a history in the same sense. That is their future strength.

62. The blind spot in most accounts of the conceptual basis for human rights is the emphasis on their legitimation: such rights are legitimated simply by the fact of being, of being human. But it is not only their legitimacy that needs attention; it is also the grammar of the concept itself, which conjugates rights as being "held." They are items or objects capable of possession where to own something provides the conceptual platform for understanding person. Under this regime, the category "universal rights" becomes very difficult to parse.

63. Knud Haakonssen, *Natural Law and Moral Philosophy: From Grotius to the Scottish Enlightenment* (Cambridge: Cambridge University Press, 1996), 5.

64. Ibid., 6. See also his later comment: "Natural rights theory was much less individualistic and anti-authoritarian than it has later been taken to be. Furthermore, the natural law theory of which it was a part was developed by a wide variety of British thinkers so as to accommodate a great deal of traditionalism, including that inherent in

competing accounts of the origins and development of subjective rights but to ask a slightly different question. In terms that may by now have become more familiar, my aim is to open out the concept of rights to a particular form of inspection. Did the Anglophone eighteenth century have access to a singular conceptual form for rights, or operate it with a singular modality? This is to raise the issue that lies at the heart of this book: How do conceptual architectures determine the limits of understanding, or, put in a more pointed way that speaks to our own contemporary situation, how do they render unthinkable precisely what we aspire to understand?[65]

It could be said that these questions (though not put in exactly this way) would be intelligible to both the account of rights given by Tuck and his subsequent interlocutors and to Haakonssen's patient elaboration of the Scottish school's attempt to combine "jurisprudence, civic humanism, and practical ethics in a coherent moral and political outlook."[66] Whether or not this is so, I see the trajectory of the present inquiry as departing slightly from that taken by both Tuck and Haakonssen; I am concerned less about what individuals in the past may have thought, or indeed in what they said or wrote, than about trying to uncover the structures that enabled them to think—that is, in exhuming the deep archaeology of a historically contingent network of culturally dispersed concepts. In order to gain some purchase on that, this chapter will elaborate in some detail the architecture of one those concepts: "right(s)." I shall begin by taking a cue from Haakonssen, who notes that the structure of the concept of rights within the natural law tradition was bipolar. It was articulated like the face and obverse of a coin, on the one side rights and on the other duties. This provides me with my first architectural element: the hinge. Two further elements, the platform and the deposit, will also be encountered in the following section.

English constitutionalism and common law thought. This cluster of doctrines constituted a formidable hindrance to the development of a subjective rights theory proper, that is, a theory according to which rights are the primary and fundamental moral feature of humanity" (311).

65. The point here is that a concept's architecture may prevent one from making sense in precisely the arena thought to be rendered intelligible by the concept. This suggests that if we can identify the conceptual architecture of our contemporary "human rights," we will be better able to see what it helps us think as well as what it renders unthinkable. The source of what for some are frustrations and others incoherence within the contemporary debate over human rights might, then, lay in the concept's architecture. That, at least, is the wager that the current argument wishes to make.

66. Knud Haakonssen, *Natural Law and Moral Philosophy: From Grotius to the Scottish Enlightenment* (Cambridge: Cambridge University Press, 1996), 5.

The Hinge, the Platform, the Deposit

We are used to thinking about rights as having a face and obverse because the long Western tradition of ethical speculation has pretty much
continuously circled around the question over whether a right implies a
corresponding obligation.[67] And perhaps the most robust or influential articulation of this correlation was proposed by the thinker who has cast
a long shadow over modern Western political thought, John Locke.[68]
This, however, covers only *one* tradition of speculation regarding rights,
the ethical or moral philosophical.[69] At least two further traditions, those
of politics and of law, need to be addressed. In the latter case, rights are
most commonly seen as titles or claims, and the work that the concept
is asked to perform is different from its use in the domain of ethics.[70] In
contrast to the ethical blueprint for considerate behavior, which is highly
sensitized to the fact that an individual's actions impinge on others, the
legal concept of rights sets out to adjudicate between competing claims:

67. See the classic essay by H. L. A. Hart, "Are There Any Natural Rights," *Philosophical Review* 64, no. 2 (1955): 175–91; Joel Feinberg, "Duties, Rights, and Claims,"
American Philosophical Quarterly 3, no. 2 (1966); David Lyons, "The Correlativity of
Rights and Duties," *Noûs* 4, no. 1 (February 1970). For the period, the distinction between kinds of natural rights, perfect or imperfect, also needs to be taken into account.
As Hutcheson taught (in this he was not original), "to every imperfect right of individuals there answers a like *obligation* or duty which our conscience plainly enjoins." See
Francis Hutcheson, *Philosophiae Moralis Institutio Compendiaria*, with *A Short Introduction
to Moral Philosophy*, ed. Luigi Turco (Indianapolis, Ind.: Liberty Fund, 2007), 131.

68. And consequently the literature on this topic is voluminous. A good place to
start is W. D. Ross, *The Right and the Good* (Oxford: Oxford University Press, 1930); for
readings of Locke that seek to diminish the strength of this correlation, see John Finnis,
Natural Law and Natural Right (Oxford: Oxford University Press, 1980); and Ian Shapiro,
The Evolution of Rights in Liberal Theory (Cambridge: Cambridge University Press, 1986).

69. And of course that tradition has been put under strain by recent philosophers.
See especially in this regard Ronald Dworkin's refinements to the model in his distinguishing between "right-based," "duty-based," and "goal-based" theories of individual
rights. See Ronald Dworkin, *Taking Rights Seriously*, rev. ed. (London: Duckworth,
1978), 169–73.

70. The tradition of rights discourse in the wake of Bentham's critique of universal
rights insists on the intelligibility of the concept of rights as being derived from positive
law. The most important contemporary outworking of that observation is to be found
in the work of John Rawls. See his classic account in *A Theory of Justice*, rev. ed. (1971;
repr., Cambridge, Mass.: Harvard University Press, 1999) and the later revision to the
thesis in *Justice as Fairness*, ed. Erin Kelly (Cambridge, Mass.: Belknap Press of Harvard
University Press, 2001).

Rights are *to* things or *on behalf of* persons. Within this tradition, it is difficult to imagine a right without the concept of possession, thereby constructing a hinge between two different concepts, rights and possession. In this case the relation between the two is a dependent one: "Possession" functions as load bearing in respect to rights, thereby subordinating the concept of rights to ownership. Politics, in contrast, understood as either a practical craft or as a theoretical enterprise, most commonly thinks of rights as levers for the distribution of scarce goods and ultimately as a set of inflections of power, and it often invokes legal or quasi-legal instruments for securing or protecting those rights.[71] Here the concept of rights functions as a container for specific political rights that can be used for the purposes of obtaining and maintaining power. It is true that these two traditions for thinking about and with the concept of rights, the legal and the political, have plenty of scope for interaction and mutual support. Indeed, by the end of the seventeenth century, as noted above, rights seen from the perspective of politics began to become definitional in respect to person: Hereafter, to be a political or social subject is to have or claim rights. Much the same can be said about contemporary human rights. And, as has also been remarked above, it is said that by the end of the eighteenth century they come to be conceived as inviolable or unalienable from persons, with the concept of "rights" functioning in a load-bearing capacity. One can see the outlines of this way of thinking rights in Blackstone's magisterial system of the common law, which begins by establishing the "rights of persons."[72] One should not, however, assume that such an account of the dependence of the concept "person" on the concept "rights" was intended to legitimate claims for universal rights, since as noted above at least one important, if not dominant, strand of the natural-rights tradition that developed out of Locke thought of personhood as something attainable only in a particular form of political society.[73] Although it would be foolish to

71. One might note—perhaps getting ahead of the argument somewhat—that this is why universal rights prove to be so problematic for liberal democracies.

72. This is not quite accurate since the long introductory material to the *Commentaries on the Laws of England* (4 vols.; Oxford: Clarendon Press, 1765) sets out first to justify the reason for giving lectures on *English* law (this was material he used as a kind of advertisement for the course before the lectures began in earnest), before providing an extremely directed account of the history of England. It is the first book proper, as it were, that begins with the rights of persons, and thereafter this takes up the rest of the first volume.

73. Thus, as A. John Simmons notes: "The natural rights theorist (and certainly Locke) is not committed to asserting that all humans in all places at all times have rights,

imagine that any of these three different ways of conceiving rights could exist entirely independent of the others, there is nevertheless considerable merit in taking them as distinct from each other. In doing so I hope to make good on the claim made above that the cultural conceptual lexicon of the English-language eighteenth century contained two architecturally distinct concepts of rights and that these concepts operated with differences in form, modality, and function.

I am going to begin, however, from a historical point of view that will be insensitive to the distinctions I have just made between legal, political, and ethical senses of rights. The following presents an interpretation of some of the data in table 3 that are intended to provide an initial framework for exploring the overarching architecture of the concept of rights in the English-language eighteenth century. It will be noted that this initial data have been derived by searching across the entire archive, which is to say I have not sorted it by category of text (as defined by Gale), thereby separating legal discussion, say, from ethics. My opening strategy is to sweep the entire database in order to begin developing a picture of the cultural dispersal of a network of related and dependent concepts. These sweeps, therefore, are context insensitive, and the data express the number of texts within which the search terms appear (not the total number of times the terms were used). It should also be noted that these figures include multiple editions or printings of a single text. As this chapter progresses, however, I shall move from this big-picture account to more fine-grained descriptions of some of the conceptual arrays that will be encountered. This will place "rights" within narrower contexts as I begin to develop the distinctions in conceptual architecture that heretofore have been unavailable for inspection.

A perfectly good place to start is the observation made above that rights, at least within one strand of the eighteenth-century tradition, always come bound up with duties.[74] Is this an accurate representation of

---

but only to the claim that all persons naturally acquire certain rights along with their personhood." See *The Lockean Theory of Rights* (Princeton, N.J.: Princeton University Press, 1992), 113.

74. The long-standing European traditions of jurisprudence are deeply committed to the analysis of rights in terms of a correlative obligation or duty. In the early decades of the twentieth century, the philosopher of law Wesley Hohfeld set out to clarify what by then, he thought, had become a very incoherent field in which rights were said to be either active or passive, positive or negative, special or general. His starting point was the observation that rights and the correlative duties were far too broadly conceived. There are, according to Hohfeld, four distinct relations under law: rights and duties, privileges and no-rights, powers and liabilities, and immunities and disabilities. Since

Table 3. Number of eighteenth-century texts in which *rights* appears within five words of *duties*

	1700–1720	1720–1740	1740–1760	1760–1780	1780–1800
rights N5↓ *duties*	140	157	175	349	1,136

Source: Eighteenth Century Collections Online (ECCO), http://galenet.galegroup.com/ servlet/ECCO.

how the period thought with the concept "rights"? Was its primary architectural element the hinge that coupled rights to duties? The first set of data shown in table 3 has been derived from proximity searches, which locate the incidence of two words used within a proximity of a specifiable number of words. Thus, the search operator $xN5y$ will find all those occurrences where the two words x and y appear within a proximity of five words in either order ($xN5y$ and $yN5x$). This first sweep through the archive looks for *rightsN5duties*, that is, all occurrences where *rights* appears within five words of *duties* in either order and it yields data in table 3.

Insofar as these data cast a light on the strength of the hinge *rights/duties*, it indicates that for most of the century it was weak.[75] In order to begin to assess precisely how weak one needs a larger contextualization for the data. Thus, in table 4 a much larger set of terms provides one such context, and

---

Hohfeld proposed this clarification legal scholars have taken up his fourfold characterization and wrestled further with its implications for understanding the concept of rights in a legal framework. For Hohfeld's original contribution to this debate, see *Fundamental Legal Conceptions* (1919; repr. New Haven, Conn.: Yale University Press, 1964), summarized usefully in J. Feinberg, *Social Philosophy* (Englewood Cliffs, N.J.: Prentice Hall, 1973); and for accounts of his analysis, see Jeremy Waldron, ed., *Theories of Rights* (Oxford: Oxford University Press, 1984), esp. 6–8; and Jonathan Gorman, *Rights and Reason: An Introduction to the Philosophy of Rights* (Chesham: Acumen, 2003), esp. chs. 7 and 8. In respect to the eighteenth-century understanding of this reciprocality, see J. J. Burlamaqui: "An inalienable right is a right coupled with a duty; a duty with which no other obligation can interfere," *Principles of Natural Law*, 2nd ed., rev. and corr., 2 vols. (London: J. Nourse, 1763), 1:52.

75. Of course the proximity of five words may not quite take the full measure of that strength. Searches for $N10$ and $N20$ produce very similar data, however: $N10$ returns 166, 195, 210, 435, and 1,287; $N20$ returns 204, 276, 327, 659, and 1,585.

Table 4. Number of eighteenth-century texts in which *rights* appears within five words of search term, by ascending order 1700–1720

	1700–1720	1720–1740	1740–1760	1760–1780	1780–1800
Total texts with *rights*	8,949	8,934	11,395	16,820	26,184
rights N5↓					
imprescriptible	0	1	0	2	255
women	2	15	24	30	231
citizen	5	28	64	144	657
individual	5	3	17	112	553
indefeasible	6	7	13	45	174
inalienable	7	5	5	39	197
woman	7	10	30	66	189
female	9	11	18	54	111
petition	13	44	57	150	277
vote	14	16	24	23	77
happiness	19	18	39	111	482
humanity	22	23	87	580	1,119
universal	24	16	29	60	248
political	24	23	42	218	976
human nature	26	43	78	262	578
injury	34	22	32	53	155
life	37	59	82	209	446
essential	41	46	80	275	433
absolute	41	34	52	132	237
obligations	43	47	72	120	248
unalienable	44	58	79	310	788
elect!!!	52	44	87	217	535
hereditary	54	47	119	183	409
conscience	58	102	221	383	710
equal	58	73	115	314	1,482
truth!	67	60	105	186	349
constitution!!	74	66	169	465	1,070
inherent	82	43	101	255	592
english!!!!	89	62	91	465	631
monarchy	93	79	56	147	201
regal	100	67	65	163	163
human	114	142	232	545	1,183
general	121	155	227	548	1,140

security	126	133	223	396	841
subject	132	121	123	188	293
interests	140	186	299	656	998
duties	140	157	175	349	1,136
original	143	101	130	385	656
majesty	148	162	180	266	265
property	156	143	293	806	2,139
sovereign	164	157	206	335	676
custom!	175	167	189	269	347
immunities	202	220	282	463	595
true	202	136	162	266	614
nature	228	303	438	1,144	2,521
man	231	220	330	736	4,157
royal	243	240	249	329	429
sacred	246	310	488	1,063	2,128
divine	251	199	210	249	446
free!!!!	302	366	611	1,243	2,199
parliament	311	262	323	639	951
god	323	240	274	406	717
person!	336	383	432	777	1,434
mankind	345	475	745	1,619	2,649
natural	377	585	879	1,732	3,185
common	386	498	726	1,438	1,929
legal	399	298	374	612	892
prerogative!	437	419	501	667	947
king	459	457	562	864	1,179
men	518	567	642	1,192	3,114
ancient	578	418	463	870	1,424
people	971	943	1,347	2,482	4,368
law!	999	904	1,187	1,920	3,055
church	1,278	1,008	806	1,073	1,265
civil	1,287	1,047	1,303	1,850	3,139
privileg*	1,604	1,948	2,652	3,766	5,032
libert*	1,971	1,762	2,277	3,102	4,542

Source: Eighteenth Century Collections Online (ECCO), http://galenet.galegroup.com/servlet/ECCO.

it corroborates the point just made, namely that rights and duties were not particularly prone to association for most of the eighteenth century.[76]

These initial searches presented in table 4 help construct a picture of the strength of connection between the concept of rights and those other listed concepts: It enables one to begin assessing what I call the "orbital drag" exercised by one concept upon another. This term captures the proclivity for binding that takes place in a conceptual lexicon: Ideational concepts typically "drag" other concepts in their wake since they often sit in a network that makes fine distinctions between terms. The more focused contexts in which "rights" operates as a way of thinking will be addressed later in this chapter, where it will become apparent that it is not only the strength of orbital drag that needs to be taken into account. Moreover, at the most general level of the global archive, care is needed in respect to the contextual insensitivity referred to above.[77] It is also important to recognize that, although searching across the entire archive provides data for the general dispersal of a conceptual array, it does not provide information as to the frequency with which a hinged concept may have been present to the specific discussion of morals, say, or of legal rights. This qualification notwithstanding, the general sweep of the archive demonstrates that the drag the concept of rights had on duties was not as strenuous as one might have imagined from the standard account in the history of ideas. As a way of testing the common assumption that rights in the eighteenth century were hinged with obligations or duties, it suggests that at the very least the other connections that were considerably more frequent need to be seen alongside. It would be difficult however, given these data, to conclude anything other than that the hinge "rights/duties" was weak in the period 1700–1720: Across the entire published output of works in English that are included in ECCO for this twenty-year span, there are only

76. The immediate common-sense objection, adverted to in the first chapter, that the period may simply have used other words for conveying the concept of "duty" when hinged with "rights" can be answered by the following searches: Over the entire century, *rightsN5dues* appears in 297 texts; *rightsN5respect* in 229; and *rightsN5accountability* in 1.

77. The most careful handling of this is to be found in Knud Haakonssen, *Natural Law and Moral Philosophy: From Grotius to the Scottish Enlightenment* (Cambridge: Cambridge University Press, 1996), esp. 310–22. For a good example of the way in which moral thinkers of the period operated this conceptual hinge, see Thomas Rutherforth, *Institutes of Natural Law*, 2nd ed., 2 vols. (Cambridge: J. Nicholson, 1779), 1:29–30: "obligation and right are correlative terms: where any person has a right, some one or more persons are under an obligation, which corresponds to that right."

140 texts where the two words were used in a proximity of five words.[78] By the twenty-year period 1760–1780, that incidence has risen to 349, but if one compares this with the orbital drag between "rights" and "people" in the same twenty-year segment (*rightsN5people 1760–1780: 2482*), it is still a very low level. The data also pretty consistently suggest that across all search terms frequencies tend to increase most markedly between 1760–1780 and 1780–1800. *RightsN5human* and *rightsN5humanity*, for example, double from the twenty years 1740–1760 to 1760–1780, and then double again over the next twenty-year span. Many search terms show a similar pattern, while *rightsN5man* increases nearly sixfold between 1760–1780 and 1780–1800. Perhaps as noteworthy are the figures at the top of the table: At the opening of the century, rights had no drag at all on "indefeasible," "imprescriptible," or "inalienable."

In these initial extrapolations from the data, one needs to bear in mind that a proximity search for *rightsN5duties* will not identify precisely the same *conceptual* binding as the search for *rightsN5people*. Here one can call to mind the typology set out as a diagram in the previous chapter.

Conceptual Kind	reificational	ideational	noetic
Conceptual Function	nominal	containing	load bearing
Conceptual Structure	rigid	plastic	adaptive
Conceptual Modality	isogetic	schematic	axiomatic
Conceptual Phase	single	dual	continuous

In the first example, *rightsN5duties*, the modality of the concept of rights is most likely to be isogetic with respect to *duties*: The concept of rights operates in a comparative mode, discriminating between rights and duties. When thinking this way, one invokes the fine distinctions that may obtain between rights and other linked ideational concepts—say the differences between rights and dues, rights and obligations, or rights and entitlements. This is perhaps the most common and certainly the simplest functionality for the concept: It names something. In the second case, searching for the proximity *rightsN5people* is more likely to identify those instances where the modality of the concept of rights operates schematically, providing a way of

---

78. Of course the complete picture of the culture at large is not accessible solely through its published print archive (even if that archive were close to 100% complete). We have no record of the speech of historic actors in the period, and the significant quantity of nonprint material has as yet no comprehensive digital form. It would, of course, be extremely interesting if an analysis of this kind revealed very different profiles for printed and nonprinted materials, but one might suspect that this will be unlikely.

thinking about rights when they are applied to something else. Where this occurs, the architectural element in play switches from the hinge to the platform, and the concept of rights provides a support for thinking other concepts, here "people." In this case the structure of "rights" is plastic, applied to a number of categories, say, people, citizen, or mankind. This conceptual heterogeneity, or "fuzziness," caused precisely the problem by which eighteenth-century persons were confronted when attempting to understand rights as universal claims. Could the concept of rights only be applied to those individuals deemed to be legitimate rights holders, or was it plastic enough to be applied to everyone, servants as well as lords, slaves as well as landowners? And if so, on what grounds?

As table 5 shows, rights were also pulled into proximity with concepts designating institutions: Indeed, at the opening of the century, "rights" were more likely to be within the orbit of "church" than anything else. And, although by the last twenty years of the century the concept was attached to "man," until that point it were as likely to be attached to the "king."

Once again, at the very least, the run of these data suggest that we need to attenuate the common assumption that, over the course of the Anglophone eighteenth century, rights were increasingly understood as subjective. Although there is a clear tendency toward the connection between rights and human agency, one should not immediately assume that, where "rights" and "man" are pulled into orbit with each other, the term *man* covers what we think of as individual or individuated agency. And the same can be said for other terms in the list—*men, mankind, people.* In fact what is surprising in these data is that, where there is a clear signal of the subjective, as in, say, "individual" or "citizen," the frequency of uses is paltry up through midcentury and only becomes relatively significant by the last twenty year tranche. As the table indicates there was a long persistence through the century of rights orbiting in the proximity of concepts that could be taken as referring to a general category, say "mankind," "people," "men," or "church," rather than a particularity, say, an individual person. Although I do not take this to be decisive with respect to the standard account of the development of subjective rights over the length of the century, it does nevertheless suggest that this change in architecture occurred during a far narrower window, precisely the last two or three decades of the century.

A third example can be drawn from table 4, where "rights" is held in a dependent relation with a qualifying term. Thus, *rightsN5common* picks up those uses where the concept of rights functions as a container: "Rights" provides a repository for different kinds of right. This is the third architec-

Table 5. *Rights as platform.* Number of eighteenth-century texts in which *rights* appears within five words of search term, by ascending order 1700–1720

	1700–1720	1720–1740	1740–1760	1760–1780	1780–1800
total texts with *rights*	8,949	8,934	11,395	16,820	26,184
rights N5↓					
women	2	15	24	30	231
woman	7	10	30	66	189
citizen	5	28	64	144	657
individual	5	3	17	112	553
monarchy	93	79	56	147	201
majesty	148	162	180	266	265
property	156	143	293	806	2,139
sovereign	164	157	206	335	676
man	231	220	330	736	4157
parliament	311	262	323	639	951
god	323	240	274	406	717
person!	336	383	432	777	1,434
mankind	345	475	745	1,619	2,649
king	459	457	562	864	1,179
men	518	567	642	1,192	3,114
people	971	943	1,347	2,482	4,368
church	1,278	1,008	806	1,073	1,265

Source: Eighteenth Century Collections Online (ECCO), http://galenet.galegroup.com/servlet/ECCO.

tural element, the deposit. If one compares this search with, say, another containing example in same time segment, *rightsN5inherent 1700–1720*, the relative orbital drag can be seen to favor common: *rightsN5common:386* compared to *rightsN5inherent:82*. Table 6 lists these.

A preliminary observation suggests that the deposit "rights/common" was around five times more likely to be operated in the English-language cultural conceptual lexicon during the years 1700–1720 than was the deposit "rights/equal." By the end of the century, as table 6 shows, this ratio was slowly but surely increasing in favor of "rights/equal."[79]

79. *Equal*: 0.6% of texts containing rights in 1700–1720; 5.6% in 1780–1800. *Common*: 4.3% in 1700–1720; 7.3% in 1780–1800.

Table 6. *Rights as deposit*. Number of eighteenth-century texts in which *rights* appears within five words of search term, by ascending order 1700–1720

	1700–1720	1720–1740	1740–1760	1760–1780	1780–1800
total texts with *rights*	8,949	8,934	11,395	16,820	26,184
rights N5↓					
imprescriptible	0	1	0	2	255
individual	5	3	17	112	553
indefeasible	6	7	13	45	174
inalienable	7	5	5	39	197
universal	24	16	29	60	248
political	24	23	42	218	976
essential	41	46	80	275	433
absolute	41	34	52	132	237
unalienable	44	58	79	310	788
hereditary	54	47	119	183	409
equal	58	73	115	314	1,482
inherent	82	43	101	255	592
english!!!!	89	62	91	465	631
regal	100	67	65	163	163
human	114	142	232	545	1,183
general	121	155	227	548	1,140
original	143	101	130	385	656
true	202	136	162	266	614
royal	243	240	249	329	429
sacred	246	310	488	1,063	2,128
divine	251	199	210	249	446
natural	377	585	879	1,732	3,185
common	386	498	726	1,438	1,929
legal	399	298	374	612	892
ancient	578	418	463	870	1,424
civil	1,287	1,047	1,303	1,850	3,139

Source: Eighteenth Century Collections Online (ECCO), http://galenet.galegroup.com/servlet/ECCO.

These initial analyses are intended to be provisional: They begin the task of recovering the networks within which the concept of rights was suspended across the English-language eighteenth century from data generated out of ECCO. Now, by looking at more specific examples, these first impressions can be tested and adjusted. So far I have claimed that rights were in general, across the entire archive, far from frequently connected in a hinge with duties, but does this picture change once one investigates the more specific terrain upon which the discussion of rights as a political, legal, and moral concept was played out? Returning to the first example of *rightsN5duties*, one can break the incidence of 349 for the segment 1760–1780 into component discursive contexts by using the tags operated in ECCO. When one does this, one finds that the most frequent incidence of *rightsN5duties 1760–80* appears in texts classified by ECCO as law (118—or 2.8% of texts classified as law), closely followed by social sciences (94—that is, 1.1% of texts classified as social sciences).[80] This is much as one might expect since the legal tradition operates cumulatively, building on precepts as jurisprudence adapts to case law. Its modes of argumentation and presentation are repetitive and agglutinative, citing precedent and refining past arguments in a process of augmentation. Moreover, the pressure on the legal operation of the concept of rights was very likely to drag duties into its orbit as rights in the sense of *iura* were distinguished from rights as duties.

Even so, in taking this more detailed snapshot into account, if one is to assess the penetration of this hinged concept "rights/duties" into the culture at large, these figures need to be placed in the context of the initial data presented above. Thus it remains the case that 349 occurrences of *rightsN5duties* throughout the entire text base in the years 1760–1780 is not a particularly high number (2.42% of texts containing the word *rights* in the twenty-year period). By the last twenty years of the period, however, the sweep of the entire archive indicates an increase by a factor of over two: The incidence in the years 1780–1800 is 1,136 (5.17% of texts containing rights in the twenty-year period).[81] One can also note from my sweep of

80. It is important to bear in mind that the criteria for classification according to type of text in ECCO are not transparent.

81. Care is needed when moving from the raw numbers that count texts in which these proximity searches appear. Expressing them as percentages of all those texts in which single terms appear (in this case, *rights*) needs to be contextualized in relation to the overall number of texts printed. All of the runs of data across the century in twenty-year slices that are used in this study indicate increasing frequencies (with some very few exceptions which are commented upon below) that are consistent with a rising produc-

rightsN5x (table 4) that *rightsN5duties* moved from the thirtieth most common in 1700–1720 to the twenty-first most common in 1780–1800.[82] Although the data clearly indicate that there was an increasing propensity for rights and duties to orbit more closely over the course of century, it is nevertheless worth remarking that the greatest orbital drag between ideational concepts (*rightsN5liberties*) shows up in 20.6 percent of all texts containing rights in the last twenty years of the century. This is to say, it is four times more common to find rights coupled to liberties than to duties.

If one takes another example of the drag between the concept of rights and a related ideational concept, to "rights/obligations," one finds an even smaller incidence: Between 1700 and 1720 *rightsN5obligations* appears in 43 texts (0.5% of texts containing rights); by 1780–1800 that has risen to only 248 (1.1% of texts containing rights). It seems uncontentious to conclude from these data that the incidence of rights being within a close orbit of either duties or obligations in the print culture at large over the course of the century was low. Even if it might be argued that the literature of moral improvement or guidance gave great weight to the balance between rights and duties or obligations, this hinge had a very low presence in the conceptual lexicon of the culture in general. I need to insert a caveat here

---

tion of print across the century. But as far as I can see, there is no real evidence to support the view that, after the 1774 ruling in *Donaldson v. Becket* in which perpetual copyright could no longer be lawfully held, the number of printed books rapidly increased by approximately twofold. The number of records in ECCO for 1775 is 5,687 (records are not the same thing as numbers of books printed, and they may also hide cases where texts were issued with title pages different from in the initial print run); in 1777 the number of records falls to 4,796, by 1783 it has risen to 5,380, and, by 1789, to 7,941. It is true that by the end of the century the number of records has reached 9,329, a rise of two-thirds. The most forceful account of the effect of *Donaldson v. Becket* claiming the twofold increase in production is to be found in William St. Clair, *The Reading Nation in the Romantic Period* (Cambridge: Cambridge University Press, 2004), esp. ch. 7. Others have contested this view: See Richard B. Sher, *Enlightenment and the Book: Scottish Authors and their Publishers in Eighteenth-Century Britain, Ireland, and America* (Chicago: University of Chicago Press, 2006); James Raven, *The Business of Books: Booksellers and the English Book Trade, 1450–1850* (New Haven, Conn.: Yale University Press, 2007). I also wonder if St. Clair's claim that the rush to produce "classics" from 1780 onward meant that the market became flooded with a very narrow range of titles (see p. 131) is tenable.

82. The selection of the lexical items is based upon my own observation of proximate terms. Unfortunately my request that Gale provide a complete list of proximate terms was not met, which means that the rankings here are merely intended to give an impression of relative movements.

and to make clear what these data are beginning to get in focus. It would, I think, be reasonable to raise a common-sense objection to the observation I have just made, and point out that *rights*, *obligations*, and *duties* are concepts that are most likely to be found in proximity to each other where matters of a moral or legal character are under discussion.[83] Since the culture at large produced fewer texts about or, in a broad sense, engaged with the law or morality than those engaged with, say, travel, it is bound to be the case that the incidence of *rightsN5duties* across the entire text base is going to be relatively small. While this is true, it also misses the point of the methodology here employed, tracking incidence through proximity, which is intended to provide a snapshot of the networks within which concepts were suspended in the culture at large. It is useful to remember that the concept of rights was not exclusively operational within the domain of ethics or law, and its architecture as a cultural conceptual entity cannot be identified by only examining its uses in those discursive environments.[84] Thus in tables 7 and 8 (*rightsN10*, *rightsN20*) I present some data that bear upon the larger networks within which the concepts of rights gained coherence through binding at greater orbital distances.

These tables indicate that the network connection "rights/man" and "rights/human" consistently increased in usage across the century and at all orbital distances. This should not, however, be taken to imply that the concept of universal human rights was available to the late eighteenth century. Here I wish to insist on the specifics generated by the kind of conceptual analysis I have been developing: Were the eighteenth-century rights of man, for example, structured through the element of the deposit? That is to say, was the period hampered in thinking rights as universal by the conceptual architecture that determined rights as a set of distinct claims or entitlements whose distinctiveness lay in the difference of person? Contrariwise, does our own contemporary deployment of the concept of human rights as a platform lead us to confound the universality of rights with the differences of person, thereby eradicating those differences in a common "humanity"? For the moment these questions will be left hanging, but they will become increasingly germane as this study progresses.

I want to underline the fact that these proximity searches are merely one way of beginning to identify the architectural elements of the concept of

83. For the classic textbook account, see Blackstone, *Commentaries on the Laws of England*, 1:2.

84. Note that this begs the question as to whether or not "rights" comprises a singular conceptual form. This will be discussed below.

Table 7. Number of eighteenth-century texts in which *rights* appears within ten words of search term, by ascending order 1700–1720

	1700–1720	1720–1740	1740–1760	1760–1780	1780–1800
total texts with *rights*	8,949	8,934	11,395	16,820	26,184
rights N10↓					
inalienable	6	10	6	40	169
citizen	7	36	83	186	765
individual	16	6	41	190	793
human nature	29	56	79	255	578
unalienable	40	60	82	289	724
obligations	69	71	118	193	361
inherent	92	61	107	254	566
regal	119	83	86	183	220
conscience	121	138	247	412	761
english!!!!	123	90	140	620	951
equal	124	122	196	494	1,666
truth!	125	130	184	425	689
human	142	184	294	617	1,378
monarchy	157	105	117	203	345
life	162	192	284	516	1,112
duties	166	193	210	435	1,287
subject	167	156	170	281	420
original	177	145	169	480	830
property	217	211	385	1,019	2,550
sovereign	236	206	314	560	930
security	238	235	328	572	1,117
majesty	261	301	362	480	518
divine	298	248	281	393	635
scared	349	367	578	1,194	2,345
mankind	393	540	808	1,640	2,620
royal	398	340	377	601	768
nature	402	498	627	1,467	3,013
man	496	509	683	1,360	4,459
human right*	532	872	1345	2,231	3,617
prerogative	565	537	666	929	1,345
god	584	466	489	692	1,129
person!	590	661	743	1,346	2,149
free!!!!	598	720	1,041	1,950	3,292
king	871	809	1,047	1,576	2,155
civil	1,239	1,047	1,250	1,916	3,064
people	1,252	1,172	1,550	2,771	4,814
libert*	1,511	1,750	1,993	3,133	4,211
privileg*	1,525	1,840	2,437	3,582	4,820

Source: Eighteenth Century Collections Online (ECCO), http://galenet.galegroup.com/servlet/ECCO.

Table 8. Number of eighteenth-century texts in which *rights* appears within twenty words of search term, by ascending order 1780–1800

	1700–1720	1720–1740	1740–1760	1760–1780	1780–1800
total texts with *rights*	8,949	8,934	11,395	16,820	26,184
rights N20↓					
inalienable	9	10	6	42	178
regal	177	126	128	283	375
obligations	111	134	185	315	486
monarchy	234	175	200	323	571
inherent	106	75	141	307	651
subject	221	209	248	396	658
human nature	46	73	102	315	702
unalienable	46	63	95	311	756
majesty	509	478	637	851	984
conscience	262	227	356	567	991
divine	456	381	439	662	993
citizen	19	51	117	268	1,029
original	254	216	257	689	1,187
individual	37	24	71	316	1,198
royal	595	542	618	981	1,278
english!!!	187	129	216	879	1,458
sovereign	382	337	522	925	1,465
truth!	268	319	461	864	1,500
duties	204	276	327	659	1,585
security	419	340	496	828	1,612
prerogative!	722	640	819	1,257	1,789
human	203	282	457	912	2,048
god	1,151	893	1,003	1,308	2,148
equal	217	216	357	790	2,197
life	382	446	658	1,218	2,335
sacred	500	483	708	1,457	2,787
mankind	473	617	882	1,831	2,971
person!	1,042	1,079	1,273	2,162	3,401
property	348	368	568	1,456	3,413
civil	1,403	1,206	1,471	2,279	3,688
king	1,470	1,335	1,764	2,684	3,764
nature	704	791	1,014	2,156	4,102
free!!!	962	1,061	1,541	2,741	4,766
privileg*	1,618	1,963	2,598	3,920	5,411
man	923	976	1,220	2,388	5,913
human right*	925	1,607	2,428	3,858	6,098
people	1,613	1,559	2,011	3,450	6,146
libert*	2,321	2,733	3,211	4,809	6,562

Source: Eighteenth Century Collections Online (ECCO), http://galenet.galegroup.com/servlet/ECCO.

Table 9. Number of eighteenth-century texts containing the phrase *rights and liberties*

	1700–1720	1720–1740	1740–1760	1760–1780	1780–1800
total texts with *rights*	8,949	8,934	11,395	16,820	26,184
rights and liberties	1,458	1,270	1,649	2,123	2,643

Source: Eighteenth Century Collections Online (ECCO), http://galenet.galegroup.com/servlet/ECCO.

Table 10. Number of eighteenth-century texts containing the phrase *rights and duties*

	1700–1720	1720–1740	1740–1760	1760–1780	1780–1800
total texts with *rights*	8,949	8,934	11,395	16,820	26,184
rights and duties	82	99	95	218	568

Source: Eighteenth Century Collections Online (ECCO), http://galenet.galegroup.com/servlet/ECCO.

rights as it appeared in the English-language eighteenth century. A refinement is provided by searching for the exact phrase *rights AND x*. Running this type of search through the database provides the results in table 9, and this can be compared with the contents of table 10.

These figures can also be expressed in terms of their relative frequencies: *rights and liberties* appears in 18.9 percent of texts containing *rights* in the first twenty years of the period compared with 1.6 percent for *rights and duties*.[85] These more specific searches confirm what has already been noted from the proximity searches above: Across the century, rights were

85. The most comprehensive search, picking up both *rights and liberty* as well as *rights and liberties* gives a drag coefficient of: *rightsN5libert**: 1,971, 1,762, 2,277, 3,102, and 4,542; this can be compared with *rightsN5privilege**: 1,604, 1,948, 2,652, 3,766, 5,032. See table 4.

most likely to be hinged with liberties. Furthermore, the orbital drag for *rightsN5libert** across the century tied the two concepts together in the compound phrase *rights and liberties*: *rightsN5libert* 1700–1720*, for example, throws up an incidence of 1,971, and in 1,458 of those cases the exact phrase *rights and liberties* was used. The data provide a similar pattern across the century.

Conceptual Grammar

Conceptual forms have their own distinctive grammars that provide the rules for "ways of thinking something." The typology of concepts I have proposed is intended to make that grammar more evident. I now want to enhance the picture of the concept of rights in the English language eighteenth century that is emerging by parsing its grammar. By this I do not only mean to observe uses of terms in relation to standard English grammar, although that is a good place to start. One can note, for example, that standard English makes no preference in respect to the order of the terms *rights* and *liberties* when combined. This is to say, one can perfectly grammatically say "liberties and rights" as well as "rights and liberties." The ECCO database allows us to ascertain the relative frequency of use for each of these sequences, thus for *liberties and rights* we find the results presented in table 11. And the search results for *rights and liberties* appear in table 12. We find precisely the same grammar in the second most prevalent hinge, *rights and privileges* (table 13)—compared with *privileges and rights* in table 14.

Table 11. Number of eighteenth-century texts containing the phrase *liberties and rights*

	1700–1720	1720–1740	1740–1760	1760–1780	1780–1800
total texts containing *rights*	8,949	8,934	11,395	16,820	26,184
liberties and rights	159	175	218	322	359

Source: Eighteenth Century Collections Online (ECCO), http://galenet.galegroup.com/servlet/ECCO.

Table 12. Number of eighteenth-century texts containing *rights and liberties*

	1700–1720	1720–1740	1740–1760	1760–1780	1780–1800
total texts with *rights*	8,949	8,934	11,395	16,820	26,184
rights and liberties	1,458	1,270	1,644	2,123	2,643

Source: Eighteenth Century Collections Online (ECCO), http://galenet.galegroup.com/
servlet/ECCO.

Table 13. Number of eighteenth-century texts containing *rights and privileges*

	1700–1720	1720–1740	1740–1760	1760–1780	1780–1800
total texts with *rights*	8,949	8,934	11,395	16,820	26,184
rights and privileges	1,393	1,737	2,312	3,270	4,188

Source: Eighteenth Century Collections Online (ECCO), http://galenet.galegroup.com/
servlet/ECCO.

Table 14. Number of eighteenth-century texts containing *privileges and rights*

	1700–1720	1720–1740	1740–1760	1760–1780	1780–1800
total texts containing *rights*	8,949	8,934	11,395	16,820	26,184
privileges and rights	128	140	217	284	376

Source: Eighteenth Century Collections Online (ECCO), http://galenet.galegroup.com/
servlet/ECCO.

In both of these cases, the preference for putting rights first is grammatical in the sense that the concept of rights operates according to a rule or set of rules wired into the conceptual form. Those rules are in effect a grammar. This "correct" sequence (correct only in the sense that it is preferred—this is to say the reverse, *liberties/privileges/rights*, can also be found during the period since it was a perfectly acceptable instance of English usage) was preferred because the concept of rights functioned as load bearing. Rights provided the support for understanding the concept of liberty. Although one might have expected this relation to be reversed (liberty providing the support for rights), the data confirm the former: In the first twenty years of the century, one finds *libertiesW5rights* in 235 texts; in the last twenty-year segment, in 538. This can be compared with *rights W5liberties*, mentioned 1,659 (1700–1720) and 3,049 (1780–1800) times. Expressing this as a percentage of occurrences in all those texts containing *liberties*, the results are: 3.1 percent for *liberties-rights*, 21.7 percent for *rights-liberties* in the first twenty-year segment; 3.1 percent and 17.9 percent in the last segment. The same statistic for all those texts containing *rights* in the twenty-year period 1700–1720 is 2.6 percent for *liberties-rights* and 18.3 percent for *rights-liberties*. For the last twenty-year segment, those figures are 1.9 percent and 11.2 percent, respectively. As can be seen by all these measures, wherever *rights* and *liberties* appear in proximity to each other, *rights* is the preferred first term. I take this grammar to indicate that rights come before liberties in a conceptual sense: Where rights and liberties are both invoked, the former provides a platform for the latter. Although it was possible to think with the concept of liberty without joining it to rights, the orbital drag was strong enough to mean that in 21.7 percent of texts in which liberties occurred during 1700–1720, this hinge was present.

The foregoing conceptual analysis leads to the conclusion that rights functioned in a load-bearing capacity with respect to liberties and privileges across the English-language eighteenth century. Now my earlier caveat about the more precise contexts for the use of conceptual forms needs to be borne in mind. We shall need to address whether, for example, this observation holds true when "rights" was operating in a legal as opposed to a political context. For the moment, however, I want to continue with this larger picture. One can, for example, parse the grammar of the concept "rights" across the Anglophone eighteenth century by searching for more elaborate strings of words. Table 15 presents the data for the string *rights-liberties-privileges* in all possible word-order sequences.

The data here confirm the observation made above with respect to the placement of the first term: *Rights* on the whole comes before either *liberties* or *privileges*, and it is least likely to come last in the sequence. This leads one to ask: Why does the sequence *privileges, liberties and rights* appear to seem so awkward to the period (and perhaps to us as well)? If not awkward or inelegant, why is it so clearly disfavored for over half a century and only

Table 15. Number of eighteenth-century texts containing permutations of *rights*, *privileges*, and *liberties* within five words of each other

	1700–1720	1720–1740	1740–1760	1760–1780	1780–1800
total texts with *rights*	8,949	8,934	11,395	16,820	26,184
privilege! W5 libert!! W5 right!	12	8	8	33	46
libert!!! W5 privilege! W5 right!	24	26	25	46	43
libert!!! W5 right! W5 privilege!	28	62	61	99	74
privilege! W5 right! W5 libert!!!	32	43	52	36	41
right! W5 libert!!! W5 privilege!	84	105	154	257	231
right! W5 privilege! W5 libert!!!	90	73	110	145	106

Source: Eighteenth Century Collections Online (ECCO), http://galenet.galegroup.com/servlet/ECCO.

gains extremely moderate exposure from 1760 onward? The answer lies in the grammar of the concept of rights: Rights uphold or safeguard privileges and liberties. It should be pointed out here that I am not attending to the meanings, or shades in meaning, that might be generated by these differences in sequence. It is, of course, the case that emphasis can be created by position within a sequence, and it is likely, if not certain, that on some of the occasions where these different sequences occur the reason for variance is determined by the precise sense *in this case*. However, the purpose of sweeping the full archive is to diminish the weighting of specific uses in order to first construct the larger picture of a particular concept's architecture. Once that has been established, it will be tested against more specific cases below.

One more point can also be made here: The period encountered difficulty in thinking with the concept "rights" when applied universally because of the strong drag on both "liberties" and "privileges." And this difficulty increased as the century lengthened and rights became ever more attached to person. Although one can think "liberty" in a universal mode, the period constructed its understanding of the political—and certainly the geopolitical—across a divide that separated the free from the enslaved. Liberties, for the most part and for the majority of those who thought about the matter consecutively, certainly were not universally available or perhaps even universally attainable. This can be seen so clearly in the ideology of the "freeborn Englishman" who considered his position to be unique and perhaps incapable of replication. Precisely the same can be said with respect to privileges. Although it was possible to construct an antithetical relation between rights—universal and held equally—and privileges—special entitlements for the few—the period constructed their relation as dependent. Rights guaranteed both liberties and privileges, and eighteenth-century thinking, guided by the concept of "right(s)" saw no problem in claiming legitimacy for rights on the basis of their being held in common by mankind while at the same time using rights claims to uphold privileges. Although some people crashed hard into this hindrance for thinking rights as universal, it was the conceptual architecture that stood in their way. As I shall argue in the concluding chapter, the same observation is applicable to our contemporary situation with respect to "human rights."

Another way of bringing into view some of the differences in grammar for each of the concepts "privileges," "rights," and "liberties" is provided by table 16.[86] This table presents data in respect to how the period "declined" the concepts of rights, liberties and privileges. As can be seen, it understood both privileges and liberties as things to be "enjoyed" more frequently than it did for rights; moreover, the declension of rights through the verb *enjoy* decreased in frequency over the century.[87] Why did this alteration in grammar occur? The answer, I believe, is to be found in the emergence of a new architecture for the concept of rights that began to become visible from the 1770s onward. Evidence for that new architecture is also provided by other aspects of the data. As can be seen from the table, the verb *declare* was very infrequently applied to rights, privileges, or liberties. I take this to indicate something about the grammars of these concepts: All three were prone to avoid both the active and passive senses of being declared. Rights, however, as can be seen from the table, were increasingly declined through the act of making a declaration.[88] When compared with the other two concepts, one can note that a declaration of privileges was very uncommon and only marginally more likely to occur with liberties.

86. The *W* search operator finds the terms in the exact order.

87. *EnjoyW5liberties* in the last twenty-year period occurs in 6.2% of texts containing *libert!!!*; *enjoyW5privilege!* in 10%; *enjoyW5rights* in 3.8%. In the first twenty-year period, *enjoyW5rights* occurs in 7.8% of texts containing rights.

88. A fivefold increase, from 1% of texts containing *rights* in 1700–1720 to 5% in 1780–1800. *Declaration/libert!!!* declines over the century from 1% in 1700–1720 to 0.7% in the last twenty years. In the case of *privileges*, it remains pretty stable: 0.16% increasing to 0.2%.

Table 16. Number of eighteenth–century texts containing *privileges*, *rights*, and *liberties* within five words of search term

privilege/ rights/ liberties	W5 privilege!					W5 rights					W5 libert!!!				
	1700–1720	1720–1740	1740–1760	1760–1780	1780–1800	1700–1720	1720–1740	1740–1760	1760–1780	1780–1800	1700–1720	1720–1740	1740–1760	1760–1780	1780–1800
all texts	8,260	10,797	14,007	20,221	29,664	8,949	8,934	11,395	16,820	16,184	17,955	19,077	24,494	32,997	47,833
rescind	1	1	0	1	0	0	0	0	4	2	1	1	0	1	2
guarrantee	4	1	0	8	19	2	8	6	14	136	4	7	5	8	79
subvert	8	10	12	37	21	43	33	44	78	54	81	88	121	156	219
usurpation	3	6	18	12	22	53	53	56	110	238	25	33	35	42	40
declare	21	29	30	42	46	27	33	19	55	94	78	95	90	107	137
protect	2	5	8	18	42	26	21	50	107	224	25	42	86	85	159
vindication	35	25	30	48	79	124	99	123	168	399	94	86	75	116	123
usurp	10	23	25	56	79	28	48	42	97	131	32	30	28	49	28
declaration	14	33	24	48	84	94	66	132	307	1,325	210	209	184	245	378
invade	42	72	90	71	87	293	253	327	494	726	179	196	233	227	239
violate	43	68	67	97	113	78	61	140	198	503	41	36	41	74	136

vindicate	45	30	33	75	113	130	102	200	416	836	118	106	160	238	306
invasion	24	30	46	89	116	177	135	182	359	589	133	114	121	212	235
restore	26	52	65	93	114	73	65	126	168	358	242	358	459	595	883
preservation	46	60	73	150	153	190	214	221	367	531	438	426	620	777	952
assert	35	67	80	137	183	178	169	256	622	1,089	205	212	305	330	396
protection	29	36	40	137	188	13	19	16	58	144	23	41	63	146	339
possess	16	21	36	82	237	13	15	21	60	164	11	28	42	94	209
secure	81	70	93	165	238	198	134	176	297	674	430	408	546	640	1,105
defend	119	131	145	212	255	492	418	500	830	1219	489	453	649	900	1,076
defence	84	124	140	222	310	354	293	432	783	1153	713	892	1314	1657	1,949
preserve	146	170	224	355	367	339	305	423	487	735	624	635	898	1001	1,317
enjoyment	104	142	286	431	638	172	212	307	446	948	261	258	459	799	1,368
breach	280	311	356	755	958	36	21	27	97	91	85	80	66	123	73
enjoy	869	1,177	1,398	2,164	2,995	307	286	374	658	1,003	1,075	1,304	1,649	2,120	2,981
have	1,585	2,059	2,442	3,452	4,987	703	644	817	1,468	2,883	4,595	5,532	6,306	8,168	10,649

Source: Eighteenth Century Collections Online (ECCO), http://galenet.galegroup.com/servlet/ECCO.

The point I wish to extract from this is that the grammar of the concept of rights determined the modalities of sense making available to eighteenth-century actors. To say "I declare my rights" is conceptually incoherent if the primary architectural element of the concept of rights was not what I call the deposit, which is to say eighteenth-century persons were unlikely to have made much sense of a speech act that intended to declare what we call subjective rights. If one were to make sense in this case, one must hold fast to the idea that persons may have close attachments, even express those attachments as rights claims, rights that one claims as one's own, one's own to declare.

In fact, the period became increasingly familiar with a different conceptual form whose primary architectural element was the platform. This concept marked the distinction between a "right" and "rights" and operated with an axiomatic modality.[89] Under this rubric, the grammatical accidence of making a declaration of rights feels much more correct. This is because a public announcement, making a declaration, is intended to derive legitimation from the act itself: Making a declaration of rights is akin to what the philosopher of language J. L. Austin considered to be an illocutionary act. Speaking or acting this way, making a declaration of rights feels much more like an assertion on behalf of a collective, the many, rather than a claim made by a singular, subjective actor. Unlike a "right," a title or a claim for which one might seek redress through the law, a "declaration of rights" takes rights to be self-evidently legitimate and inseparable from the collective on whose behalf the declaration is being made.[90] This difference in grammar has consequences: It determines the distinct networks within which the concept of rights was inserted over the course of the century.

The table also shows that, although both rights and liberties might have been said to be defended, the frequency of defending privileges was considerably smaller. In addition, liberties were deemed to be preserved almost twice as often as rights, and around three times more frequently than privileges. Once again it is useful to remember that the differences revealed in this kind of analysis are only marginally caused by the vagaries of the natural language English. It is, for example, perfectly intelligible within the language to speak of the "preservation" of one's privileges, yet,

89. Compare *declarationW5right*: 115, 95, 127, 221, 557 to *declarationW5rights*: 94, 66, 132, 307, 1,325.

90. I take this to indicate why universal rights do not connect very easily with subjective rights: The basis for the claim in each case is conceptually distinctive enough to make them incompatible. I shall have more to say about this in my concluding chapter.

as the table shows, the period did so markedly less often than it spoke of
the preservation of one's rights, and even less so than the preservation of
one's liberties. A common-sense retort to this observation would be that
in terms of the politics of action it is easier to understand how one might
go about preserving liberties—say through legislation—than preserving
privileges, although to put it that way instantly arouses suspicion with respect to a specific sense of politics and a freighting of privileges in terms
of elitism. It is hardly surprising that arguments on behalf of preserving
the privileges of the few were thin on the ground in a political context that
was increasingly sensitive to the qualifications for enfranchisement. But
that is my point: The concepts of liberty, privilege, and rights have distinctive grammars that are themselves determined by their specific conceptual
architectures. Now it becomes possible, I think, to begin to see how the
concept of rights was itself internally segmented, or, to put that in terms
of the specific type of conceptual analysis I am promoting, functioned in
different ways. There were two architectures. I shall mark this distinction from now on by using "*right(s)*" to refer to the concept developed up
through the early modern tradition of natural rights. The concept from
which it will be distinguished will be referred to as "*rights of man.*"

Ideational concepts create and retain coherence through being held in
tension with other concepts. Unlike reificational concepts, which simply
require demarcation from all other concepts, ideational concepts are more
commonly counterbalanced by neighboring conceptual forms: They are
held in suspension in varyingly complex networks. These networks comprise connections of varying strengths and topologies. An ideational conceptual network, therefore, has complex geometries that can be recovered
by searching the database with more fine-grained operators. As I have already had occasion to remark, my initial searches have flattened out the
distinctions between discrete discursive environments since I have been
seeking to provide only a preliminary account of the architecture of the
concept of rights in general. Consequently, my glosses on the data have
been insensitive to the differentiations between, say, civil and political
rights, or between rights in the juristic sense and rights as a moral category. Some of these differentiations can now be recovered in returning to
the raw numbers presented above.

The numerical values in table 17 present in broad brush strokes the
relative incidence of using the term *rights* within the close orbit of other
terms. That long focus can be shortened by turning to the specific-use
contexts within which rights operated. I shall start by assuming that the
combinatorial term in each case in this table helps one identify (even if

Table 17. Number of eighteenth-century texts containing *rights* within five words of search term, ascending order 1700–1720

	1700–1720	1720–1740	1740–1760	1760–1780	1780–1800
total texts with *rights*	8,949	8,934	11,395	16,820	26,184
rights N5↓					
people	971	943	1,347	2,482	4,368
law!	999	904	1,187	1,920	3,055
church	1,278	1,008	806	1,073	1,265
civil	1,287	1,047	1,303	1,850	3,139
*privileg**	1,604	1,948	2,652	3,766	5,032
*libert**	1,971	1,762	2,277	3,102	4,542

Source: Eighteenth Century Collections Online (ECCO), http://galenet.galegroup.com/servlet/ECCO.

very weakly) an area of discursive activity.[91] The following hypothesis gains support from the data: At the beginning of the century, rights were as commonly inserted into environments in which the church figured as into those in which civil matters might be addressed.[92] By the end of the century, however, the incidence of use of rights in an ecclesiastical context runs at around the same figure as at its start. This represents a significant decline since the total number of texts printed in the last twenty-year seg-

91. I offer the following merely as a suggestion for fine-tuning the kind of analysis I have been presenting. A far more extensive and complex method for distinguishing between discursive environments would require the rights holder of ECCO to open up its database and allow researchers to write specifically targeted algorithms that would identify more precisely a text's discursive milieu.

92. In a culture that increasingly had to reconcile orthodox and dissenting traditions of religious observance, the issue of an individual right to conscience was keenly debated. This religious context generated the most common network for rights being seen as untouchable: Robert Craghead speaks for many when he complains about Papists "in these and other matters of religion, they will not allow men such a liberty to judge for themselves, nor to act according to that judgment. But to me nothing can be more evident, than that this liberty is one of the most essential unalienable rights of human nature, which no man, nor body of men have authority to deprive us of; nor are we our selves at liberty to make a surrender of it." Robert Craghead, *The True Terms of Christian and Ministerial Communion founded on Scripture alone* (Dublin: J. Smith, 1739), 11.

ment was substantially larger than that of the first segment. In the case of legal contexts, for the moment taken to be indicated by the presence of the word *law*, the hypothesis suggests that there was a marked increase.[93] Over the course of the century the largest increase in the table above is *rights N5people*. Although at this stage we are dealing only with raw numbers, it is nevertheless possible to perceive an outline to the changes that occur across the century, that is, to begin to develop a history of conceptual change based on data. Extrapolating from these data values that help determine the architectural elements of a concept, it becomes possible to identify variations in the shape or form of the concept "rights" over the century. This can be done by taking all those texts in which *rightsN5liberties* appears and then profiling *rights Nx* where *x* is *law*, *church*, and so on within that subset. The same kind of profiling for all those texts that contain *rightsN5church* can then be compared by running the same searches as before (*rightsN5*, *-people*, etc.).[94] Such profiles of the frequencies of connections between concepts provide a window onto the specific networks within which different conceptual forms were active. In this case, the picture that emerges suggests that political rights were structured through the network rights → liberties → people (where → indicates a dependent conceptual relation). Since each of these independent concepts was also networked in distinct ways, it would require a sophisticated multiform diagram to represent the complex geometries of the interlocking networks within which they individually and collectively circulated.[95]

93. I mean for these more local analyses to be merely suggestive. Of course texts where the word *law* is found in proximity to *rights* are unlikely to be exclusively what we might identify with any precision to be *legal texts*. The point here is to suggest ways in which the database, as currently constructed and searchable, runs out of road while at the same time opening onto vistas that might, in the future, yield more precise information. Insofar as these suggestive narrowing of discursive environments contribute to the argument I am pursuing, they support the view that the concept of rights over the course of the century changed its network connections in ways that are consistent with the earlier interpretation of data.

94. For the twenty-year segment 1760–1780, the following profiles appear: *rights-N5libert** → *N5people* (34%) → *N5 mankind* (20%). *RightsN5law* → *N5people* (29%) → *N5 libert** (26%). These two can be clearly distinguished from *rightsN5civil* → *N5 libert** (41%) → *N5people* (32%) and *rightsN5church* → *N5libert** (29%) → *N5people* (20%).

95. I have experimented with various computational diagrammatic expressions— word clouds, cluster diagrams, and so forth—that are now very easily created using open-source software. But I am yet to be convinced that such diagrams enhance my understanding of the relations between conceptual forms and networks. They certainly make for attractive presentation, but I continue to find the raw numbers more helpful.

The Architecture of Rights of Mankind

The general picture that has thus far emerged can be refined by turning to some specific examples. I shall begin with a striking fact: As noted above, the phrase *rights of man* was essentially absent from the Anglophone print culture of the first half of the eighteenth century, but by its close it was everywhere.[96] The phrase *rights of mankind*, on the other hand, was in quite wide circulation and continued to be used up through the end of the century. This leads to the question: Why did the phrase *rights of man* come to such prominence in the 1790s, and more importantly, did the phrase name a concept whose architecture was distinct from that of the concept "rights of mankind"? The point here is to test if these two concepts were structured through different architectural elements or networked in strikingly different configurations. Thus one might ask if the concept "rights of man" was built as a platform while "rights of mankind" operated as a deposit. At first glance it might appear that the answer to the first of these questions is relatively easy to grasp since Thomas Paine's *Rights of Man*, for reasons detailed in Chapter 4, put the *phrase* into extremely widespread use. This does not necessarily mean, however, that the *concept* "rights of man" was ubiquitously employed. The answer to the second question can be gleaned by paying particular attention to the distinction between "right" and "rights" as it was deployed across the century.

The first occurrence in the eighteenth century I have found for the phrase *rights of mankind* appears in a text of 1703 where the context is a discussion of Protestantism and the sovereign's role in the defense of "injur'd liberty" and "for the recovery of the just rights of mankind."[97] The main concern of this pamphlet is the congeries of arguments that post-1688 sought to justify the "manners" of the time being circumscribed through the profession of Protestantism. Here it is useful to call to mind that the so-called bill of rights that emerged from the glorious revolution was intended to secure the rights of Parliament and not the rights of individuals, even if its subsequent reception and altering uses (especially in

---

A word cloud, for example, only seems capable of giving an impression of relative values (by using size or color, shape and so forth). The big picture is made more legible, but the devil, as always, is in the detail.

96. The Burney collection of newspapers indicates thirteen uses up to 1760 and eighty-four in the twenty-year period 1760–1780. In the last twenty years of the century, that had risen to 2,980.

97. *Some Expedients without Which England Cannot Be Happy. Humbly Offer'd to the Consideration of Both Houses of Parliament* (London: J. How, 1703), 14.

the colonies) did turn its provisions in the direction of persons generally and away from parliamentarians exclusively.[98] For most of the century the effect of the Declaration of Rights passed in 1689 was, as Alan Ryan argues forcefully, "to secure that Britain remained a protestant country"[99] and continued to discriminate against dissenters, Catholics, and Jews within the polity. "Mankind" in this particular discursive and ideological context was never intended to embrace the universal. With this firmly in mind, one might wonder how or in what senses the rights of mankind were understood to be "just." In the text of 1703, it is clear that the author deems it important to "recover" these rights; given this, what kind of thing does he suppose rights to be? Are rights conceptually of a kind that might be lost or given away, as he seems to imply? Or was he working with a more aggressive formulation: Rights were understood to have been taken away and now needed to be recovered? One might attempt to answer these questions by placing the discussion within the context of a debate about a "mixed" religious polity, but attention to such a close context does not close down the conceptual issue around rights I have just raised. Would a right that had been rescinded, for example, be the same right on its return? Or be legitimated in the same way, or granted from the same authority? In the back of this there lays another, more telling issue that will increasingly surface: Are "just rights," those that need to be recovered, any old rights that had simply been rescinded or lost over time, their justness derived simply from the fact that they were applied to mankind howsoever understood? Or, alternatively, were they just because they were to be *derived* from a universal, from man in general? What is at stake here is this: Are rights of mankind to be understood as a set of specific rights that construct and maintain the balance of power between state and individual, or sovereign and subject whose legitimacy is derived from the social and political compact, or, rather, are they to be taken as a general set of unspecifiable rights (or at least without need of specification) that are a given by dint of being human?

There are two further points I wish to take from this. First, does this way of thinking with the concept of rights recognize a difference in kind: Some rights are just while others are unjust? Second, does the qualifier *just*

98. For most of the period, political rights were instruments used for the limitation of government rather than the liberation of individuals.

99. Alan Ryan, "The British, the Americans, and Rights," in *A Culture of Rights: The Bill of Rights in Philosophy, Politics, and Law 1791 and 1991*, ed. Michael J. Lacey and Knud Haakonssen (Cambridge: Cambridge University Press, 1991), 366–439; 385.

primarily indicate that such rights of mankind are justifiable or held with justification?[100] In both cases, rights of mankind may be understood either as a composite nonspecifiable category or as a set of specific rights that might also be bundled up in that composite. In this particular instance, the text does not go on to examine or even make reference to specific rights which might fall under the umbrella heading *rights of mankind*, so here one must conclude that the latter sense, if it is at all activated, sits quietly in the background.[101]

It was quite common to qualify the rights of mankind in this way: During the first twenty years of the century, rights are said to be just in 18.5 percent of texts where the phrase *rights of mankind* appears. This can be compared with the most frequent qualifier for the phrase *rights of mankind*, which is *natural*, occurring in 30 percent of those texts where the phrase *rights of mankind* appears. A typical example can be found in Richard Steele's *The Englishman*, where writes of being "obliged to support common Sense, and the Natural rights of Mankind."[102] It may be the case that the phrase *rights of mankind* is operating as a substitute for *rights of man* or, to put that more pointedly, the concept "rights of man" (where *man* gives the sense of individuation) may be operating alongside or simultaneously with the concept "rights of mankind" (where *mankind* gives the sense of generality). This is because the commonplace invocation of natural rights always implies that they are held by an individual, by a man, even if they may also held by everyone, by mankind.

100. The sense of emphasis falling on the "justness" of these rights is perhaps even stronger in Samuel Johnson, *The Works of the Late Reverend Mr Samuel Johnson, Sometime Chaplain to the Right Honourable William Lord Russel* (London: Andrew Bell et al., 1710): "when men fight for a Country and Constitution . . . and Death it self is the least damage of the two, they are ready to sacrifice themselves for it: Especially when what they defend are the just Rights of Mankind" (32). The difference in conceptual shape between a right that might be "recovered" and one that might be "defended" is what I am trying to ascertain.

101. It is important to note what this analysis is intended to reveal: Although attention is being paid to the sense or meaning of the phrase *just rights*, it is not its semantic value that I mean to highlight. The discrimination in senses between *just* as a qualifier implying differences in kind (just rights, unjust rights, etc.) and *just* implying a difference in quality (rights held justifiably) is being used to reveal the extent to which the concept of rights functions either as containing (it includes a number of distinct rights that can be named) or as load bearing (rights of mankind is an undifferentiated knot of claims). It is not, then, a difference in semantic value that I am concerned with but the architectural support—deposit or platform—which stabilizes the concept that interests me.

102. Sir Richard Steele, *The Englishman*, 2 vols. (London: J. Roberts, 1716), 2:212.

This does not, however, address the issue of the qualifier *natural*. As outlined above, the Lockean argument makes no claim for universality even if the general sense of his account of rights suggests a distinction between contractual or consensual rights and those that could have been possessed independently of civil society.[103] "Natural rights," therefore, are most easily understood as those obtaining in an unencumbered "state of nature."[104] But this still leaves hanging the question over universality: Are those rights held in a state of nature common to all humanity? Is it this commonality that makes them natural? Or, is it actually the other way around: The fact that they are held in a state of nature, are natural in that regard, has the consequence of their being held in common? Furthermore, if one alters where the emphasis falls in Steele's expression (of course Steele is merely exemplary for the purposes of this argument) one can begin to perceive the distinctions that are going to become more telling as my argument progresses. The natural rights of *mankind*, for example, could imply that other agents or beings might also have natural rights—say, animals—but it could also be taken to indicate that only the universal category "mankind" is entitled to natural rights (i.e., it distinguishes between natural rights of mankind and other kinds of rights claims that may be made by individual men, say, a right to property). Mankind in general has a claim to rights based in nature, whereas man in society has other rights claims—say, civil or political. This distinction shall be marked by the difference between rights of *man* and the rights of *men*. Since the state of nature is a fiction, real men, as it were, only ever operate in society, and there they have civil or political rights. These are the rights of *men*. The nub of the argument now becomes clearer: Are the rights of man simply transferable to the rights of men? Or are these rights that are held by individuals different in kind from those held on behalf of all mankind, humanity?

In an early text of 1718, one can see how retailing elements of the account of man's entry into society that sit at the heart of the natural law tradition sets in motion the different architectures I am attempting to un-

103. For a good account of Locke's lack of clarity with respect to "natural right," see A. John Simmons, *The Lockean Theory of Rights* (Princeton, N.J.: Princeton University Press, 1992), 89–94.

104. This is the distinction upheld by many eighteenth-century commentators between positive, legally protected rights and those that derive their authority from nature alone. In the case of the second, natural rights, "they are *the only foundation* of all just Authority; and, *the sole Reason* for all Laws: Whatever are the Rights of Men *in this Age*, were their Rights *in every Age*; for, Rights are independent of *Power*." *Daily Gazetteer* 6 (July 5, 1735).

cover. John Jackson, the rector of Rossington in Yorkshire, described the distinctions between civil and ecclesiastical laws by placing the former in relation to the rights of mankind: "The *Nature* of the *Civil* Laws of all Nations is founded . . . in the Principles of Natural Reason" and it has, he says, "a necessary Relation to the Natural Rights of Mankind."[105] As the conventional set up has it, men are said to give up part of their liberty in a state of nature by entering society and, once within the polis, they are beholden to the laws each of us subscribe to as a consequence of making that move. Civil laws, then, are not protective of natural rights since they apply in the state of society and not in the state of nature, but, as Jackson notes, they have a "relation" to the natural rights of mankind. Are those rights to be understood as a compound, an unarticulated bundle of natural rights that come attached to mankind, the rights of man, or are they to be taken as containing a set of distinct rights, the rights of men? Is the concept "right(s)" functioning as load bearing, providing the platform for understanding what it is to be a person, or as containing, supplying the deposit for gathering under one rubric a set of distinct rights, the rights of men? Once again, it is difficult to be certain in this matter, since there is an evident circularity to Jackson's argument about the removal from the state of nature where natural reason holds sway: The purpose of man entering society, he notes, is "the preservation and security of which Rights." Such compounded reasoning—natural rights are protected by civil rights, civil rights are distinct from natural rights and required on account of the removal from the state of nature—often appears in the natural-rights tradition where a defense of the move into society is required. It is not the reasoning itself that I want to highlight but the potential within the conceptual network for operating two distinct architectures. "Natural rights of mankind" conceptualizes rights as specifiable and at the same time unspecifiable. The geometry of the network within which the concept "right(s)" was suspended allowed for both, thereby enabling different ways of making sense of rights: It was a fuzzy concept. Jackson, then, in common with the standard account of the removal from the state of nature, sees the purpose of society as to protect the "rights of mankind" (a bundle), perhaps as an aspiration or an ideal, and at the same time to secure specific rights (say the right to personal security). He makes this clear in the comment that comes in its wake: "Men enter into Society, and consent to the making of

105. John Jackson, *The Grounds of Civil and Ecclesiastical Government Briefly Consider'd, by John Jackson, Rector of Rossington in Yorkshire. To Which Is Added a Defence of the Bishop of Bangor, against the Objections of Mr Law*, 2nd ed. (London: James Knapton, 1718), 8.

Laws; the Design of which, is to secure to every particular Member his own private Rights."[106]

It should be noted again that there is nothing original to this view, which was commonly offered as a support for the adoption and promulgation of positive rights. There is, however, an opening in the fabric of this thinking that throws light on the precise architecture supporting this particular concept of "right(s)": Its form is plastic, allowing rights to be claimed by any single person as their own, "his own private rights," while its modality is axiomatic, applied without need of justification to every particular member of society. In this case, the concept functions nominally, making clear which rights any particular person claims as his own. The legitimacy for these rights is derived from the axiomatic modality thereby precluding the need for consensually agreed rights, rights held by all for all. Such a consensus is natural in the sense not of a preordained legitimacy but of a contractual one. This is how liberty and rights are joined together in civil society. As Jackson notes, "no Man can *naturally* have a Right to govern any Society, without Their *Consent* who are to be governed."[107]

Again I need to make it clear that there is nothing particularly original in this claim, and it will be seen in the following chapter how the colonists in America during the constitutional crisis made a great deal of noise about precisely this characterization of the nature of liberty; what I do want to call attention to, however, is the character of the conceptual architecture, its instability. For the most part, in the chronological history of the conceptual formation of "right(s)" the concept was mobile. One can see this from the preceding discussion in which the "natural rights of mankind" could have been taken to refer either to a set of distinct claims that were respected in a state of nature or to a state in which an unarticulated bundle of rights operated. The architecture of the concept conformed to the shape or form I call the deposit, in the first case, and the platform in the second. In the example above, John Jackson takes advantage of the fact that the two forms can effectively be fused: Rights are entities that might be contained within a deposit, but at the same time those rights are not generalizable or universal; they remain private or personal. Here a dual phase cognitive process is set in motion: First, "right(s)" provides a platform for understanding the condition of man in society, and, second, those rights are distinguishable as a group of distinct private rights held by a person. Even though in a state of nature one does not consent to the making of laws, and

106. Ibid.
107. Ibid.

therefore the right to govern cannot be called a natural right, by making the step into society, one makes the right to require consent for government into a natural right. As far as Jackson is concerned, the requirement for consent is nonnegotiable. What can one now understand from the initial context of his remarks in which Jackson points out that civil laws and natural reason are not rights, and, as such, they merely have a *relation* to the natural rights of mankind? In order to answer that question, the network of relations within which the concept of "right(s)" was suspended in the early decades of the eighteenth century needs to be investigated.

As the following sets out to demonstrate, the geometry of the network within which the concept of "right(s)" sat was comprised of a set of reflections or equivalences: Rights are to mankind as nature is to equality, and equality is to rights as mankind is to nature. Taking Jackson's invocation of the principle of equality as an index to this geometry, what has just been identified as the requirement for consent in being governed is legitimated through the network that connected natural rights to the equality of any and every man. As Jackson notes, "all Men are *equal* in nature, and have *equal* Natural Rights."[108] Because this is the case, "one Man cannot *naturally* have any more Power over another, than another over him."[109] This, I think, begins to reveal a set of connections within a conceptual array: "Man" and "rights" connect through the other two concepts, "nature" and "equal." Now the following thought might gain some coherence: Men are equal, and men in a state of nature have natural rights; therefore, natural rights are equal. In this example, the protocols for connectivity between "man," "right," "nature," and "equality" are mutually intelligible. Or, to put that in a more visualizable fashion, the complex geometry of network connections is made possible because the outlines or shapes for each concept present edges that fit. The period established a similar compatibility for connecting the rights of mankind to what is said to be common.[110] Thus, in precisely the same way that rights are held to be natural, so they are said to be common: That commonality derives from the fact that man or mankind holds rights. If one were attending to the mode of argument,

108. Ibid.
109. Ibid.
110. Matthias Earbery, for example, in his *The History of the Clemency of Our English Monarchs* (London: printed by author, 1717) writes "in defence of the common rights of mankind" (2). The incidence of *common W5 rights* in the first twenty years of the century in those texts where *rights of mankind* appears is 57, or 25.7% of those texts. It is slightly less in the last twenty-year period—21%.

one would note that this is syllogistic reasoning, but I wish to direct attention to the substrate of this way of thinking, to the architecture of its conceptual support.

I do not want to lose sight of the overarching thought that initiated these parsings: Are the rights of mankind to be understood as a set of distinctive rights, or, rather, are they an undifferentiated group that gives coherence to what it might be to be human? I have argued that this question cannot be easily decided, a point that is reinforced when one considers a close verbal cousin, the "common rights of mankind." Precisely the same can be said with respect to this phrase as it occurs in Jackson's text: The concept of "right(s)" operates in both a load-bearing capacity, its architectural element being the platform, and in a containing capacity, its element being the deposit.[111] However, when one turns to a slightly different discursive context, to those texts that sought to establish a more legalistic understanding of the rights of mankind, this picture begins to alter.

It is hardly surprising, given the legal framework within which rights were conventionally considered, that alongside the general account of rights examined above we also find in the first decade of the eighteenth century a disaggregation of "rights" into specific right(*s*), the rights of men: Here the longstanding early modern conceptualization of a right hinged with justice is much in evidence. One can find it in a text of 1705: "*People* have a *Right* to the *Protection* of their *Governors*. And a *Property* in their *Possessions*."[112] These rights are the exfoliation of what the author in the preceding paragraph calls the "Rights of *Mankind*." Thus rights are explicitly specified: a right *of* protection, *of* property, and so forth because the concept functions first as a container for all those claims that are justified under the rubric of a "right" to ensure, protect, or deliver justice. In the switch that follows, it functions as load bearing, precisely providing the platform upon which such claims can be made sense of as right(*s*). Over the course of two centuries, the juristic tradition slowly evolved all manner of claims that were based in the same switching between functionalities of the concept of "right(s)." To a great extent this was the conceptual motor

---

111. Of the twenty-three pages on which *rights* appears in Jackson's text, almost half of the uses fall into the element I call the deposit—as in "natural rights" (8), "private civil rights" (20), and half the platform, as in "rights of mankind" (8); "common rights of mankind" (11).

112. [Charles Leslie] *Cassandra (but I Hope Not). Telling What Will Come of It. Num 1 in Answer to the Occasional letter* (London: printed and sold by the Booksellers of London and Westminster, 1705), 4.

driving the legal and political discussions seeking to promote, justify, or criticize liberalism. Without it, the ways in which the early modern period conceptualized both the relations between state and individual and intrapersonal relations would be unintelligible. But if its functionality switched from load bearing to containing and the cognitive processing occurred in a dual phase, its modality was strictly uniform.

In part this can be explained as a habit of thinking long engrained in Western accounts of complex systems. It has the heft of history supporting its modus operandi, which doubtless enhances its feeling of being "natural" or self-evident. The European natural-rights tradition developed in dialogue with Roman law through the early modern period and was fed into the British tradition through the teaching of Hutcheson and Turnbull in Glasgow in the first half of the century. Although, as Knud Haakonssen points out, the seventeenth-century natural-law tradition was not a single coherent body of work, it nevertheless used a singular modality in its operation of the concept of "right(s)": schematic.[113] Within this tradition, rights are said to be "perfect" or "imperfect": Life and liberty were deemed to be "perfect" rights on account of their certainty in respect to claims made on behalf of their infringement. They were also deemed to be either innate or natural or, conversely, adventitious, or acquired. Rights that were acquired or said to be adventitious, such as kindness or benevolence, were usually designated as imperfect since they were too vague to be enforceable through a legal code and were distinguished from those *iura* said to be "perfect."[114] Rights also applied either to persons or to larger groupings of individuals, to societies, and rights were also seen to be either alienable or inalienable. This schematic modality is evident in thinkers as far apart in ideological, social, and geographical terms as Blackstone and Reid: It was the standard accepted way of thinking rights from within a legal and moral framework.[115]

113. See Knud Haakonssen, *Natural Law and Moral Philosophy* (Cambridge: Cambridge University Press, 1996), ch. 1.

114. The conception of imperfect rights allowed leeway in thinking about distributive justice because such rights were not considered to entail a strict reciprocal obligation. See Istvan Hont, *Jealousy of Trade: International Competition and the Nation-State in Historical Perspective* (Cambridge, Mass.: Belknap Press of Harvard University Press, 2005), 423–43.

115. The tradition was not without dispute and is, therefore, more various than I am conveying in this broad sketch. Thomas Reid, for example, took issue with the strict distinction between perfect and imperfect rights. On this see Knud Haakonssen, *Natural Law and Moral Philosophy* (Cambridge: Cambridge University Press, 1996), 201–5, and

From Rights of Mankind to Rights of Man?

So far I have highlighted some specific contexts within which the concept of rights in general and the rights of mankind in particular appeared during the first two decades of the eighteenth century. My examples have been taken from religious, political, and legal discourse, and I have been at pains to examine how the concept of "right(s)" made available a distinctive way of thinking through "right." My larger aim in doing this should not be lost sight of: These forensic analyses are intended to test whether or not *rights of mankind* was the term used in the eighteenth century for our own contemporary "human rights." There are a number of issues compacted in this. First, is the term *rights of mankind* a verbal formulation for the *concept* human rights? Or are both terms dedicated to the specific concepts they name, which supposes that the two concepts are distinct and, if so, built upon different structures? This implies that they do not share a common foundation in "right."

I am going to address these complexities by moving further into the century since another term, *rights of man*, began to feature more prominently as the century lengthened. The first thing to note is that the phrase *the rights of man*, whatever it may have been taken to name, was hardly available to persons in the first thirty or so years of the eighteenth century. Notwithstanding this fact and the relatively low incidence of the phrase *rights of mankind* when in the orbit of rights,[116] can a case be made that the later and far more prevalent use of the phrase *the rights of man* referred to what our own period calls human rights?[117] Once again, the specific kind

---

his exemplary introduction to Reid's lectures, *Practical Ethics* (Princeton, N.J.: Princeton University Press, 1990), esp. 103, where Haakonssen presents a diagram representing the schematic way in which Reid thought about philosophy. For Blackstone's thinking through this modality, see William Blackstone, *Commentaries on the Laws of England*, 4 vols. (Chicago: University of Chicago Press, 1979), esp. 1:118.

116. *Rights of mankind* appears in 2.8% of texts where *rights* appears, 1700–1720, and 4.5% in 1720–1740.

117. This leaves to one side the question as to whether the period understood the same thing by *rights of mankind* and *the rights of man*. The evidence would suggest that this was not the case. See, for example, George Lyttleton, *Letters from a Persian in England, to His Friend at Ispahan*, 3rd ed. (London: J. Millan, 1735), 180; *The London Magazine* (London: T. Astley, 1736–1746), 197; *The Old Whig: or, the Consistent Protestant. In Two Volumes* (London: W. Wilkins et al., 1739), 1:268; M. L'Abbe Duguet, *The Institution of a Prince*, 2 vols. (London: R. Dodsley, 1740), 1:vi; Charles Dodd, *The Church History of England, from the Year 1500, to the Year 1688*, 3 vols. (London: n.p., 1737–1742), 2:3.

of forensic conceptual analysis I have been promoting will provide us with some answers.

Although the following will be presented as a chronology in outline, it would be a mistake to suppose that the archive provides good quality evidence for a singular narrative sequence that might be thought of supporting the hypothesis that a "transformation" in conceptual architecture occurred between, say, 1730 and 1790. Care is needed here because the instances I shall pull out of the archive are precisely that—instances. They are essentially spikes in an otherwise continuous ground bass that conceived of general rights as merely the plural form of a right. This, however, leaves hanging how much weight or value should be given to such spikes in an historical explanatory framework: Does the instance speak only for its eccentricity from the norm, or is it the expression of a more deep-rooted and widespread current that runs through it? In terms of the immediate argument, do these instances provide evidence for a divergent conceptual form that was immanent to the architecture of "right(s)"? This will be taken up in more detail in the third chapter; first, one must examine the instances.

In 1733 there is what I believe to be the first evidence for the period beginning to generate an account of rights that understood them as *conceptually varied*, or, to put that more precisely, evidence that suggests the grounds for conceiving rights differed in respect to the kind or type of concept in play. In the course of outlining the "pretensions" of the dissenters John Perceval, earl of Egmont, asks, "What are the *natural Privileges* of Mankind?"—by which is to be understood mankind in general. He cautions, however, that "we must take care not to be confus'd in our *Ideas* of them" since they are not of a single piece. They are often, he remarks, understood sometimes as *"one Thing*, and then *another*; they are often us'd to signify *Two things indifferently*." These ideas are, he notes, used to signify "both *the Rights of Man* in a *State of Nature*, and his *Rights* in a *Society*."[118] What is important here is not the standard distinction between rights in the state of nature and those in society—as noted above, this discrimination of natural from civil rights is to be found everywhere in the natural-law tradition—but the observation that the "ideas" grounding the difference in rights are themselves different. In the terms I have been developing, I take Perceval to be noting that there are two distinct architectures supporting two different concepts of rights. Although Perceval's contribution to the

118. John Perceval, Earl of Egmont, *A Full and Fair Discussion of the Pretensions of the Dissenters, to the Repeal of the Sacramental Test* (London: J. Roberts, 1733), 14.

debate over dissenters' rights was far from groundbreaking, and although his forensics in respect to the confusion that seemed to him to characterize discussion of rights had little impact, there is nevertheless a feature of his intervention that needs remarking. Concepts, Perceval seems to be saying, are tied to the signification of terms: If we are unclear in how we use words, we are also unclear in our conceptualizations. It is this confusion, he notes, that enables dissenters to "draw a great advantage" in their arguments for repealing the Test Acts. Fuzzy concepts have their uses.

Between 1740 and 1760, the frequency of the phrase *rights of mankind* is ten times greater than *rights of man*; even so, there begins to develop a nascent sense that the latter phrase may do some of the same work.[119] An initial hypothesis, then, is that the second phrase merely replaces the first: *Rights of man* simply designated the same concept as "rights of mankind." One can get the measure of this from a text published in Dublin in 1748: "What is Power," James Digges La Touche asks, "according to the Rights of Man, but so much of the natural Liberty of each Member of Society, vested in one or more, in order to be the more strongly exerted, when occasion requires, for the good of the community?"[120] In this case there is a distinct sense that "the Rights of Man" might refer to a body of pre-scribed rights, a set of specific claims or ethical desiderata comprising, as it were, a code for conduct and even potentially a legal doctrine with force. Where earlier in the century this containing functionality of the concept of "right(s)" almost exclusively operated under the rubric of the "rights of mankind," by midcentury there is clear evidence that the same functionality began to appear with regard to the "rights of man." The same sense of the rights of man being an identifiable set that might be "asserted" is found in Thomas Cooke's *Pythagoras an Ode*.[121]

One of the senses of the "rights of mankind" that has already been re-marked is those rights that are held exclusively by the general category. Although this sense is not particularly active in the natural-rights tradi-tion, it was available to it. The reason for this is that natural law could not

119. *Rights of mankind* appears in 560 texts in the twenty-year segment; *rights of man*, in 53.

120. James Digges La Touche, *A Freeholder's Fourth Address, to the Merchants, Trad-ers, and Others, the Freemen and Citizens of the City of Dublin* (Dublin: Peter Wilson, 1749), 11–12.

121. Thomas Cooke, *Pythagoras an Ode. To Which Are Prefixed Observations on Taste, and on Education* (London: R. Francklin, 1752), 7: "In *Sidney's* more extended plan / He shall assert the Rights of Man." The point here is that an assertion of an undifferentiated collocation is weaker than of a set of distinct and identifiable rights.

operate with respect to the generality of mankind; it could only arbitrate or legislate in the case of claims made by men, by individuals. "Mankind" had no agency in such a legislative context even if supra-individuals, so-called corporations, effectively did so. But this other conceptual configuration whereby one might impute to the general class properties that were not held in common by its particularities—that is, rights held by mankind but not by men—could be said to provide an instance within the historical formation of the concept of universal human rights. Although that hypothesis awaits further clarification with respect to the architecture of "universal human rights," it has a more certain purchase with respect to the period's development of the concept "rights of man."

In one of the most important treatises penned by a Scottish enlightenment thinker, Francis Hutcheson's *A System of Moral Philosophy*, this tension between the universal and the particular, between *man* as a placeholder for mankind and, at the same time, a marker for a singular subject, is explored with reference to the idea that "mankind" might operate systematically.[122] In the terms I am using Hutcheson operated the concept "mankind" schematically. He notes that one might consider "the rights and obligations peculiarly respecting certain individuals" but also observes that "each individual is a part of this system," by which he means the "system of mankind."[123] It is clear from how he uses this phrase *system of mankind* that he considers the general category "mankind" to have a kind of agency. It could, therefore, be a rights holder on its own behalf. As Hutcheson comments about the obligations of parents to their children in respect to their becoming "proper members of society," "so mankind as a system, and every society, have a right to compell them to discharge these offices."[124] Furthermore, "mankind as a system have a like right to prevent any perversions of the natural instinct from its wise purposes, or any defeating of its end."[125] The difference that is being marked, between "mankind" and "mankind as a system," is used to disarticulate kinds of rights. Thus

122. For a useful account of system in Hutcheson's thinking, see J. Moore, "The Two Systems of Francis Hutcheson: On the Origins of the Scottish Enlightenment," in M. A. Stewart, ed., *Studies in the Philosophy of the Scottish Enlightenment* (Oxford: Oxford University Press, 1990), 37–59; Knud Haakonssen, *Natural Law and Moral Philosophy: From Grotius to the Scottish Enlightenment* (Cambridge: Cambridge University Press, 1996), esp. 77–85.

123. Francis Hutcheson, *A System of Moral Philosophy, in Three Books*, 3 vols. (Glasgow: R. and A. Foulis, 1755), 2:104, 105.

124. Ibid., 2:107.

125. Ibid., 2:207.

the rights of mankind are distinct from the specific rights individuals might claim, but the basis upon which mankind stakes a rights claim is similar: Agency has been transferred from the individual to the collective. Hutcheson was able to conceive it this way because he differentiated rights according to types of agency: In the text that he probably wrote before the *System*, he stated that the "rights of men" are "divided into *private, publick*, and *common to all*," thereby maintaining the distinction between rights of *men* and rights of man.[126] Here, then, I think there is clear evidence for a difference in conceptual architecture that was operated in an important text of the midcentury. But that difference, between "rights of mankind" and "rights of men," had yet to bite with respect to political and aspirational uses to which the concept "rights of man" might be put. Although, as will be seen in the following chapter, this potential would be exploited by the colonists in their justification for separation from the mother country, it would not be until the 1790s that it had any real exposure in Britain. And even then the clarity of the distinction was far from universally appreciated, or, where perceived was fudged in the cut and thrust of the debate over constitutional reform. The reasons for that and how it came to pass will be dealt with in the fourth chapter.

If there begins to be an admittedly low incidence of "rights of man" conceptualized as a container for specific and identifiable rights, as "*the* rights of man," there is also the first glimmer of a different conceptual architecture, the basis for the noetic concept I call "rights of man." In Thomas Pownall's *Principles of Polity*, for example, a discussion of the limited powers of government is inflected through an insistence on the "Right" of "Individuality," a right which nevertheless has its limitations "as it is circumscribed by the Obligations of the universal Communion of Nature in general, so is its Extent limited by the Rights of Man."[127] In this case the concept "rights of man" enables one to understand the comparative weighting of and balance between individual persons and the general polity. That balance is not predicated upon a specific right or set of rights; rather, the concept of rights, put in play, operates like a mini-theory providing the means for understanding something other than rights. Its modality is axiomatic, and it functions nominally, designating a general principle or belief rather than a set of entitlements or grounds for making claims against other persons.

126. Francis Hutcheson, *Philosophiae Moralis Institutio Compendiaria*, ed. Luigi Turco (Indianapolis, Ind.: Liberty Fund, 2007), 128.

127. Thomas Pownall, *Principles of Polity, Being the Grounds and Reasons of Civil Empire* (London: Edward Owen, 1752), 61.

In Pownall's text the concept "rights of Man," for example, is used in order to make sense of the nature of the individual: rights → person. In the
examples above, where the concept of "right(s)" was found to function as
load bearing in respect to person—that is, where the category "person"
gave coherence through its hinge with the concept of possession or entitlement thereby underpinning the concept of "right-as-claim"—it was the
other way around. The hinge provided stability for thinking through person: person → right. This marks the difference between noting that to be a
person one must have rights and to have rights one must be a person. Our
contemporary efforts at operating the concept of universal human rights
consistently trips over precisely this distinction.

Here one needs to return to the issue of the weighting that might be
given to these spikes in the continuous history of formation of a conceptual
architecture. If, as I have argued, a different way of conceiving rights began
to emerge, why did this have so little take up? In part this can be explained
by what I have been calling the mobility of the concept of "right(s)." The
uses to which the period could put a fuzzy concept were not only politically expedient; they were also conceptually satisfying—one can do more
and different things with concepts that operate in a dual phase and have
a plastic structure. Thus, to continue the chronological sketch across the
century, it is evident that the natural-rights tradition was deeply grounded
in the cultural landscape, and within that body of ethico-legal doctrine
the rights of mankind were constructed upon the ideational concept of
"right(s)" functioning in a dual phase. A good example of how the concept
operated under this rubric is provided by John Currie's defense of the right
to elect one's own pastor. Such a right, described as an "inviolable right of
human Nature," explains how a man has "as much Liberty to chuse a Pastor for his Soul, as a Physician for his Body, or a Lawyer for his Estate."[128]
The concept of "right(s)" here allows one to understand its application in
each of these cases, operating a dual phase schematic modality with both a
load-bearing and a containing function.

The power and persistence of the natural-rights argument was not
achieved without some attention to the varied ways in which it was used
and abused. As with all conceptual forms understood as cultural entities,
use necessarily entails a set of negotiations. From time to time, then, cor-
rections or alterations in emphasis or direction were bound to occur. In a
course of lectures given in Cambridge in the 1750s by the then–professor

128. John Currie, *A Full Vindication of the People's Right to Elect Their Own Pastors*
(Edinburgh: David Oliphant et al., 1733), 106.

of divinity Thomas Rutherforth, one can track precisely such a negotiation.[129] These lectures were intended to clarify the prevailing—loose— talk about rights by outlining the theories of Grotius in some detail. The term *natural rights*, Rutherforth noted, was frequently used in a confusing way, to refer, for example, not only to the rights that belong to mankind "by the gift of nature" but also to those adventitious rights "as either did subsist, or might have subsisted, in a state of nature."[130] He counsels that the term be used in a more strict sense in which the rights of mankind can be said to be "natural," this distinction being derived from the fact that they fall under the protections of the "law of nature," and this "law forbids the violation of them."[131] As an illustration of the point he adds "The legislative power of a civil society, or the legislative body of such a society, is a right of this sort."[132] The observation I want to take from this is that "the rights of mankind" were taken by Rutherforth to be simply the plural form of "right": "natural rights" comprised, therefore, merely one kind of right. As Rutherforth makes clear, the concept of rights simply refers to multiple instances of a right. Although this might be an understandable reaction to the possible confusion created by a fuzzy concept, it was unlikely to succeed because the architecture of the concept was far from stable. Or, seen from a different perspective, it was protean, plastic, malleable: open to structural reconfiguration.

In all of the specific texts that have been examined so far the phrase *rights of mankind* appears far more frequently than *rights of man*. It is only in the period 1760–1780 that one begins to find an incidence of the use of this alternative phrase that could—with some effort and special pleading—be said to be gaining a foothold in the culture at large.[133] And it is noteworthy that such rights of man begin to be described as either *sacred* or *inalienable* (and sometimes both). In the case of the first, the *sacred rights of man*, the

129. Rutherforth was deeply attached to Cambridge latitudinarianism, which held that the actions of men could be weighed in the balance of moral goodness. For a good account of this intellectual and religious milieu, see John Gascoigne, *Cambridge in the Age of Enlightenment: Science, Religion, and Politics from the Restoration to the French Revolution* (Cambridge: Cambridge University Press, 1985), esp. ch. 5.

130. Thomas Rutherforth, *Institutes of Natural Law Being the Substance of a Course of Lectures on Grotius de Jure Belli ac Pacis Read in St Johns College Cambridge*, 2 vols. (Cambridge: J. Bentham, 1754), 2:222.

131. Ibid.

132. Ibid.

133. The incidence is 198, or 4.7% of texts, containing *rights* in the segment 1760–1780.

qualifier suggests that such rights are out of human reach and, therefore, do not fall within the purview of the law. These rights, it is implied, are given by God (a point that will return in the following chapter). If they are untouchable they can be neither added to nor diminished, and when seen this way the sacred rights of man tend to be conceptualized as a unit, an undifferentiated whole. In the case of the second qualifier, rights that are said to be *inalienable*, a similar sense operates: These rights are untouchable. Whether said to be inalienable or sacred, the justification or legitimacy for such rights is derived from the same conceptual configuration, which I characterize as a hinge. Rights that are inalienable are set up upon the hinge "rights-man," where the second term is networked strongly with the concept of "the human." This is why rights could come to be understood as being legitimated by or derived from the fact of being human. But the period also worked a distinction between these kinds of inalienable rights and those that were in the opposite camp, those that are said to be alienable. John Gray, for example, in a critique of Richard Price's tract on civil liberty, made the argument that Price had confused the two.[134] What one begins to see emerging in these arguments is a distinctive architecture for a concept of rights that was split across the division between the man made and the God given, or between the legal and civil and the ethical or moral. Sacred and unalienable rights are not up for grabs; they are not subject to the whim of human intervention and lie outside the machinations of human jurisprudence. Alienable rights, on the other hand, are subject to human desires or the politics of social practice. Although this division is marked within the natural-law tradition (indeed this is its source), the emerging conceptual form has features that differ from the concept of "right(s)" found there. Drawing in part on the natural-rights tradition and in part on the ecclesiastical account of God's sacred rights (often expressed as our duty to God to act in particular ways) this emerging concept of "rights of man" will turn out to be inapplicable to *men*—hence, the architectural distinction between right(*s*) of *men* and "rights of man."

I do not want to exaggerate the presence of this emergent conceptual form. For most of the century, rights were not often thought of as either inalienable or unalienable, whether or not those rights were inflected by the human, as in "rights of man(kind)."[135] And up until the 1760s the com-

---

134. See John Gray, *Doctor Price's Notions of the Nature of Civil Liberty, Shewn to Be Contradictory to Reason and Scripture* (London: T. Becket, 1777), 74.

135. The period used both *unalienable* and *inalienable* to refer to a property that could not be transferred, but the term *inalienable rights* appears in only eleven texts

pound phrase *sacred and unalienable rights* hardly has any dissemination, only becoming noticeable by the last twenty years of the century, where it can be found used in 542 texts. Notwithstanding these data, Gray's text pushes the notion of inalienable rights more forcefully than does any previous tract.[136]

"Rights of Man" as an Emergent Concept

So far I have been arguing that the preferred phrase over most of the century for referring to general rights, *rights of mankind*, could not have been understood by eighteenth-century persons as designating universal human rights. Nor, in the evidence so far, is there a good reason to suppose that the alternative phrase *rights of man* was used to mark a distinction in conceptual architecture between it and the more common phrase *rights of mankind*. But by the 1760s there is a feature of the increasing use of the phrase *rights of man* that does suggest an alteration. Although not very strenuously marked—I think of it more as a kind of play, in the sense of a machine's variability in the function of its moving parts, than a transformation in conceptual form—it could be argued that this opened up the possibility for a new conceptual architecture to become established. Put in the terms for conceptual analysis I have been developing, what I shall push hard at in the following are these three possibilities for parsing the concept of rights: The ideational concept "right(s)" functioned in two phases, both containing and load bearing, as had been the case within the natural-law tradition (the above "fuzzy concept"); it functioned nominally with an isogetic modality as had been developed in the political discourse of the period; or, finally, a new architecture began to be developed that points to an emerging noetic concept, "rights of man," which understood rights as indivisible and uncountable. Thus, what I shall try to answer is this: Is it possible to identify the prototype for the concept that I shall argue in Chapter 4 threatened to be unleashed within the popular political culture of reform in early 1790s Britain?

To begin with, it is easy enough to identify those uses where "right(s)" is conceived in terms of a bundle of specifiable items: John Gray, for ex-

---

between 1700 and 1760, rising to 151 in the last twenty years of the century. *Unalienable rights* is hardly more common, appearing in 131 texts up to 1760 and reaching 642 during the period 1780–1800.

136. The phrase occurs seven times.

ample, in the text referred to above, writes of some rights as "not among
the inalienable rights of man,"[137] where it is made clear that, whatever inalienable rights might be, it is possible to distinguish among them. They
are, therefore, specifiable. Another example is provided by the Irish writer
Charles Francis Sheridan when he speaks of the "three primary rights of
mankind."[138] But more ambiguous uses sit alongside these: The qualification of rights by "common" or "sacred" has already been encountered, and
in these cases right(*s*) may have been taken as countable or as uncountable,
as individual civil or political rights (say, the right to elect governments)
or as the sacred and common "rights of man." In this case not much help
is provided by the data in respect to the specific grammar of the concept
of "right(s)" since the assertion of rights, for example, might be either an
assertion of specific rights or of the bundle "rights of man."[139] It is possible,
however, to identify movements within table 18 that begin to provide a
profile for the difference in conceptual structure for "right" as opposed to
"rights."[140]

A good place to start is the significant difference in incidence between
claimW5right and *claimW5rights*.[141] Further noteworthy comparisons in the
table can be made between *maintain right/rights* and *knowing right/rights*.[142]
These declensions of the concepts of "right" and "rights" are intended to
open out the specific grammar of uses in each case in order to begin identifying the structural difference between the ideational concept of "rights(s)"
and the noetic concept "rights of man." In the case of the concept of right

137. John Gray, *Doctor Price's Notions of the Nature of Civil Liberty, Shewn to Be Contradictory to Reason and Scripture* (London: T. Becket, 1777), 51.

138. Charles Francis Sheridan, *Observations on the Doctrine Laid Down by Sir William
Blackstone, respecting the Extent of the Power of the British Parliament* (Cork: Robert Dob-
byn, 1779), 37.

139. *AssertW5rights* appears in the following numbers of texts: 178, 169, 256, 622,
and 1,089.

140. It needs to be borne in mind that there is some noise in these data: Running
a search with the operator *right* in ECCO will not disarticulate the three senses of the
word (right as a claim, right as correct, and right as opposed to left). This noise, however, should not be substantial since the qualifiers are not commonly attached to right in
the last two senses. Notwithstanding this observation, the comparative data below needs
to be tempered by this limitation in the ECCO search protocols.

141. *ClaimW5right*, 1700–1760, appears in 7.9% of texts in which *right* appears;
claim W5 rights, in 1.3% of texts where *rights* appears. In the period 1760–1800, the differential is maintained: 8.8% for *claimW5right*, 2.4% for *claimW5rights*.

142. *MaintainW5rights*: 5.2% in 1700–1760, 4.5% in 1760–1800; *maintainW5right*:
2.4% and 2.2%, respectively. *KnowW5rights*: 0.7%, 1.17%. *KnowW5right*: 5.5%, 6.2%.

Table 18. Number of eighteenth-century texts containing *right* and *rights* within five words of search term, ascending order *rights* 1760–1800

	1700–1760	1760–1800		1700–1760	1760–1800
right	65,965	83,439	*rights*	28,342	42,210
W5 right↓			*W5 rights↓*		
protect	38	91	declare	76	149
preservation	160	196	lose	146	196
usurpation	162	263	grant	136	241
violate	136	274	use	163	291
invasion	306	416	protect	95	327
restore	431	471	usurpation	159	343
enjoyment	207	512	know	199	496
vindicate	447	531	restore	260	518
secure	446	579	violate	272	683
charter	227	606	charter	166	700
declare	554	695	preservation	612	879
lose	554	695	invasion	484	923
declaration	357	850	secure	499	962
preserve	857	947	claim	373	1,042
defence	921	1,220	preserve	1,043	1,204
grant	715	1,255	vindicate	419	1,226
defend	1,211	1,285	exercise	240	1,249
enjoy	889	1,403	enjoyment	666	1,378
maintain	1,636	1,891	declaration	290	1,607
assert	1,260	1,980	enjoy	938	1,634
use	2,088	2,437	assert	586	1,680
exercise	730	2,716	defence	1,043	1,904
know	3,688	5,205	maintain	1,502	1,924
claim	5,238	7,415	defend	1,368	2,015
have	23,869	34,047	have	2,098	4,274

Source: Eighteenth Century Collections Online (ECCO), http://galenet.galegroup.com/servlet/ECCO.

as it comes out of the natural-law tradition, there is a clear tendency for its grammar to include "claim," "know," "use" and "maintain." This provides information about how a right was conceptually mobilized; it gives one an outline for an architecture. In contrast, when "right" moved into the plural "rights" the grammar slightly altered so that one finds the most frequent ways of declining rights were "maintain," "defend," "defence," and "preserve." Perhaps even more noteworthy is the tendency to use "preservation" in respect to rights but not in respect to "right," since in constructing the architecture for the new concept "rights of man" these distinctions will be important: One might know one's rights if they are conceived in terms of specific claims, but, as shall become clear, rights of man are in a fundamental way unknowable. Most importantly, as has already been noted, one needs to keep firmly in mind the subtle distinction between a declaration of right and of right(*s*), the topic for further investigation in the following chapter.

There is also a marked distinction between right and rights with respect to the agency making the claim. As the following table suggests, it was less common to think of plural rights as the property of a single individual than a specific right. Moreover, rights in general were not imagined as general property, as it were, in the ownership of the collective. The singular "right," however, was declined through ownership ("have"), even if a specific right need not be called to mind. And this held for the collective as well: As can be seen from table 19, corporations were more likely to lay claim to ownership of a right than rights.

It is worth noting that the incidence of use for the phrase *rights of man* in legal texts throughout the century is very low when compared with other textual genres. This provides evidence for the tight grammar that determined the use of the concept of "right(s)" in the legal context, where the orbital drag of rights upon "claims" was strong. Within the jurisprudential tradition, rights were understood as attached to persons: It would have been conceptually coherent, therefore, to speak of the "rights of men" as merely indicating the general case for the basis of any rights claim. But since *man* has a potential universal sense, the legal conception of right as a claim, as a positive right, becomes incoherent if one speaks of rights as applying to an unassignable person, to man in general. This is why Bentham, famously, called the rights of man "nonsense on stilts."

I do not want to imply that what I have above called the play that existed in the phrase *rights of man* was unique to it: The phrase that predominated throughout the century, *rights of mankind*, could also set in motion a similar play. Thus, in the 1770s some examples where both phrases seem to

Table 19. Number of eighteenth-century texts in which *right* and *rights* appear two words after *has* and *have*

	1700–1720	1720–1740	1740–1760	1760–1780	1780–1800
total texts with *right*	8,949	8,934	11,395	16,820	26,184
has W2 right	1,784	2,399	3,483	5,692	8,259
have W2 right	3,214	3,605	4,835	7,384	10,371

	1700–1720	1720–1740	1740–1760	1760–1780	1780–1800
total texts with *rights*	8,949	8,934	11,395	16,820	26,184
has W2 rights	39	22	42	74	194
have W2 rights	122	98	139	243	422

Source: Eighteenth Century Collections Online (ECCO), http://galenet.galegroup.com/servlet/ECCO.

open the possibility of a new architecture include: "our kingdom is more friendly to the rights of man than Holland"; "but if you are determined that your Ministers shall wantonly sport with the rights of mankind"; "it is the opinion of the best friends to the rights of mankind"; "and propagating universally the laws of nature and the inherent rights of man."[143] The most clear-cut case, however, appears in Thomas Percival's *A Father's Instructions to His Children* where he writes of supporting "the cause of liberty and the rights of man." Here "cause" may govern both the concept "liberty" and the compound concept "rights of man" so that it may be read as referring to a "cause" labeled "the rights of man."[144] These, however, are once again incidents in a long history of conceptual formation and deployment that was effectively immune to such alterations in architecture. This is to note that, up through the 1770s, there is no real presence of an alternative conceptual form that I am calling rights of man.

But from the early 1780s things begin to change. At this point it does become possible to identify more securely uses of the phrase *rights of man* that were grounded in a different conceptual form whose modality was axiomatic. We can begin to identify, for example, instances in which rights of man were increasingly seen as referring to an undifferentiated and undifferentiable knot of rights whose legitimacy was found neither in the legal concept of title or claim nor in the political concept of enfranchised political agent. It was to be derived from the fact that to be human was to be one in the many. "Person," under this rubric, began to give way to the collective as the primary legitimating basis for government. As the following chapter outlines in detail, this move was far more advanced in the colonies than in Britain, and, as the new republic refined its understanding of political character, the collective *we* became the foundation for a newly conceptualized polis. At the same time, back in Britain this move was never likely to gain widespread support or even comprehension as the deeply en-

143. Percival Stockdale, *Six Discourses* (London: N. Conant, 1777), 104; *Extracts from the Votes and Proceedings of the American Continental Congress, Held at Philadelphia on the 5th September, 1774* (Annapolis: printed by Anne Catherine Green, 1774), 23; Thomas Bradley Chandler, *A Friendly Address to All Reasonable Americans, on the Subject of Our Political Confusions: In Which the Necessary Consequences of Violently Opposing the King's Troops, and of a General Non-importation Are Fairly Stated* (New York: printed for the purchasers, 1774), 20; *Civil Liberty Asserted, and the Rights of the Subject Defended, against the Anarchical Principles of the Reverend Dr Price* (London: J. Wilkie, 1776), 71.

144. Thomas Percival, *A Father's Instructions to His Children; Consisting of Tales, Fables, and Reflections; Designed to Promote the Love of Virtue, a Taste for Knowledge, and an Early Acquaintance with the Works of Nature* (London: J. Johnson, 1776), 105.

trenched differences of rank, class, gender, and race proved to be far more resilient than the reform movement imagined. Its lack of success, however, should not divert attention away from the fact that the architecture of the concept of rights *did* alter. The network within which it was suspended *did* change shape. As table 20 shows, the conceptual geometry altered over the course of the century, and the crisis points in that change are consistent: between 1740 and 1760, between 1760 and 1780, and again in the last twenty-year segment.

The most clear-cut change over the sweep of the entire century is hardly surprising: Rights were less and less frequently in contact with any terms that referred to the sovereign. Thus the only orbital drag that has an absolute downward trajectory by the end of the century is *rightsN5majesty*: 266 occurrences in 1760–1780 falling to 265 in the last twenty-year segment. And all the other terms that are associated with the sovereign move substantial distances in the list if we compare the opening twenty years with the last.[145] If one is to assume an overall continuous increase in printed materials over the course of the century, these decreases are even more significant than the raw numbers might at first indicate.[146]

Increasing frequencies are also perhaps unsurprising: *rightsN5man* shows the largest jump into the last twenty years of the century (from 736 in 1760–1780 to 4,157 in 1780–1800). Moreover, the movement of *rightsN5man* across the century, from twenty-second on the list in the first twenty years to fourth in the last twenty years, provides ample evidence that the conceptual network with which "rights" was suspended had a very strong orbital drag on "man." One should not hurry to conclude from this that the alteration in architecture I have been at pains to identify supplanted the previous configuration, that "right(s)" were transfigured into "rights of man." A salutary corrective to that view is provided by the fact that, as has already been observed, the phrase *rights of man* was in fact very seldom used. My point is more exploratory: I wish to claim merely that this new conceptual form was available as a resource for thinking rights in a different and more open way (where "open" refers to Weitz's notion of an open concept). That resource had the potential to enable one to understand the full implications and difficulty of thinking rights through the

145. *RightsN5regal* moves from 35th to 58th place; *rightsN5majesty*, 28th to 49th; *rights N5 monarchy*, 36th to 54th; *rightsN5royal*, 21st to 45th; *rightsN5king*, 9th to 20th.

146. *RightsN5majesty*: 148, 162, 180, 266, 265; *rightsN5regal*: 100, 67, 65, 163, 163; *rightsN5monarchy*: 93, 79, 56, 147, 201; *rightsN5royal*: 243, 240, 249, 329, 429; *rightsN5king*: 459, 457, 562, 864, 1179.

Table 20. Number of eighteenth-century texts containing *rights* within five words of search term, comparing ascending order 1700–1720 and 1780–1800.

rights N5↓	1700–1720	1720–1740	1740–1760	1760–1780	1780–1800
imprescriptible	0	1	0	2	255
women	2	15	24	30	231
citizen	5	28	64	144	657
individual	5	3	17	112	553
indefeasible	6	7	13	45	174
inalienable	7	5	5	39	197
woman	7	10	30	66	189
female	9	11	18	54	111
petition	13	44	57	150	277
vote	14	16	24	23	77
happiness	19	18	39	111	482
humanity	22	23	87	580	1,119
universal	24	16	29	60	248
political	24	23	42	218	976
human nature	26	43	78	262	578
injury	34	22	32	53	155
life	37	59	82	209	446
essential	41	46	80	275	433
absolute	41	34	52	132	237
obligations	43	47	72	120	248

rights N5↓	1700–1720	1720–1740	1740–1760	1760–1780	1780–1800
vote	14	16	24	23	77
female	9	11	18	54	111
injury	34	22	32	53	155
regal	100	67	65	163	163
indefeasible	6	7	13	45	174
woman	7	10	30	66	189
inalienable	7	5	5	39	197
monarchy	93	79	56	147	201
women	2	15	24	30	231
absolute	41	34	52	132	237
universal	24	16	29	60	248
obligations	43	47	72	120	248
imprescriptible	0	1	0	2	255
majesty	148	162	180	266	265
petition	13	44	57	150	277
subject	132	121	123	188	293
custom!	175	167	189	269	347
truth!	67	60	105	186	349
hereditary	54	47	119	183	409
royal	243	240	249	329	429

unalienable	44	58	79	310	788
elect!!!	52	44	87	217	535
hereditary	54	47	119	183	409
conscience	58	102	221	383	710
equal	58	73	115	314	1,482
truth!	67	60	105	186	349
constitution!!	74	66	169	465	1,070
inherent	82	43	101	255	592
english!!!!	89	62	91	465	631
monarchy	93	79	56	147	201
regal	100	67	65	163	163
human	114	142	232	545	1,183
general	121	155	227	548	1,140
security	126	133	223	396	841
subject	132	121	123	188	293
interests	140	186	299	656	998
duties	140	157	175	349	1,136
original	143	101	130	385	656
majesty	148	162	180	266	265
property	156	143	293	806	2,139
sovereign	164	157	206	335	676
custom!	175	167	189	269	347
immunities	202	220	282	463	595
true	202	136	162	266	614
nature	228	303	438	1,144	2,521
nature	231	220	330	736	4,157
man	231	220	330	736	4,157

essential	41	46	80	275	433
life	37	59	82	209	446
divine	251	199	210	249	446
happiness	19	18	39	111	482
elect!!!	52	44	87	217	535
individual	5	3	17	112	553
human nature	26	43	78	262	578
inherent	82	43	101	255	592
immunities	202	220	282	463	595
true	202	136	162	266	614
english!!!!	89	62	91	465	631
original	143	101	130	385	656
citizen	5	28	64	144	657
sovereign	164	157	206	335	676
conscience	58	102	221	383	710
god	323	240	274	406	717
unalienable	44	58	79	310	788
security	126	133	223	396	841
legal	399	298	374	612	892
prerogative!	437	419	501	667	947
parliament	311	262	323	639	951
political	24	23	42	218	976
interests	140	186	299	656	998
constitution!!	74	66	169	465	1,070
humanity	22	23	87	580	1,119
duties	140	157	175	349	1,136
general	121	155	227	548	1,140

(continued)

Table 20. (continued)

rights $N_5\downarrow$	1700–1720	1720–1740	1740–1760	1760–1780	1780–1800
sacred	246	310	488	1,063	2,128
divine	251	199	210	249	446
free!!!!	302	366	611	1,243	2,199
parliament	311	262	323	639	951
god	323	240	274	406	717
person!	336	383	432	777	1,434
mankind	345	475	745	1,619	2,649
natural	377	585	879	1,732	3,185
common	386	498	726	1,438	1,929
legal	399	298	374	612	892
prerogative!	437	419	501	667	947
king	459	457	562	864	1,179
men	518	567	642	1,192	3,114
ancient	578	418	463	870	1,424
people	971	943	1,347	2,482	4,368
law!	999	904	1,187	1,920	3,055
church	1,278	1,008	806	1,073	1,265
civil	1,287	1,047	1,303	1,850	3,139
privileg*	1,604	1,948	2,652	3,766	5,032
libert*	1,971	1,762	2,277	3,102	4,542

rights $N_5\downarrow$	1700–1720	1720–1740	1740–1760	1760–1780	1780–1800
human	114	142	232	545	1,183
church	1,278	1,008	806	1,073	1,265
ancient	578	418	463	870	1,424
person!	336	383	432	777	1,434
equal	58	73	115	314	1,482
common	386	498	726	1,438	1,929
sacred	246	310	488	1,063	2,128
property	156	143	293	806	2,139
free!!!!	302	366	611	1,243	2,199
nature	228	303	438	1,144	2,521
mankind	345	475	745	1,619	2,649
law!	999	904	1,187	1,920	3,055
men	518	567	642	1,192	3,114
civil	1,287	1,047	1,303	1,850	3,139
natural	377	585	879	1,732	3,185
nature	231	220	330	736	4,157
man	231	220	330	736	4,157
people	971	943	1,347	2,482	4,368
libert*	1,971	1,762	2,277	3,102	4,542
privileg*	1,604	1,948	2,652	3,766	5,032

Source: Eighteenth Century Collections Online (ECCO), http://galenet.galegroup.com/servlet/ECCO.

concept of the human where the "human" was thought under the rubric of the singular universal. This shows up as a historical potentiality most clearly in the colonies during the imperial crisis, the topic for the next chapter.

One can get a sense of how that conceptual innovation began to infect the culture from a moment in Tobias Smollett's encomium to George the first, who, Smollett noted, was "well disposed to assert the rights of mankind in general,"[147] or from William Woodfall's *An Impartial Sketch of the Debate in the House of Commons of Ireland, on a Motion Made on Friday, August 12, 1785*, when he writes of the "natural rights *of man*." Here the italicization marks that the concept "man" operates in both its collective and individual sense, thereby opening the door to "rights of man."[148] It is, however, in a tract that is firmly opposed to constitutional reform that the difference in architecture of the concept of "rights of man" is for the first time made explicit: "Though all true friends to the cause of liberty and the *natural rights* of mankind would wish that *every man* should vote for his representative in the national council, without any other description of *right*, or qualification, than that of *being a man*." Rights, here, are held simply by dint of being. This, Granville Sharp notes, is not "*adviseable*, at least at present."[149] Perhaps Sharp's damning observation on the dangers of the human being a truly universal category carries more weight today than many might suspect. Sharp's comment, however, indicates that present to his culture was a resource, a conceptual form that would allow those who grasped it to think rights differently. Paine certainly took advantage of that as he tried to turn rights away from entitlements, in the possession of individuals, so that they could become aspirations, yet-to-be-realized potentialities held by the totality of human being on behalf of all persons.

This chapter has demonstrated that for most of the eighteenth century the rights of mankind were built upon the concept of "right(s)." This concept was used to make the hinge "person → right" even if an emergent possibility, the hinge "rights of man → person", also began to be explored. This made experimentation with the noetic concept "rights of man" intelligible, as shall be seen in the following chapter. It is important to under-

147. Tobias George Smollett, *The History of England, from the Revolution to the Death of George the Second*, 5 vols. (London: T. Cadell, 1785), 3:284.

148. William Woodfall, *An Impartial Sketch of the Debate in the House of Commons of Ireland, on a Motion Made on Friday, August 12, 1785* (Dublin: Luke White, 1785), 25.

149. Granville Sharp, *An Account of the Ancient Division of the English Nation into Hundreds and Tithings* (London: Galabin & Baker, 1784), 244.

stand why this innovation had so little impact or take-up: Something is lost by embracing the noetic concept, precisely the clarity of those specific rights that may be argued as essential protections for liberty. It is also the case that the gain in thinking through the noetic concept—aspirational universal rights and humanity grounded in the singular universal—entailed risk. Too much would be given away in consigning specific rights to the politics of self-interest, and the politics of aspiration remained too vague and without clear indications for specific action. This left rights where they were at the century's start: As claims that could be used in the propagation of both justice and injustice. But in 1776 the delegates to the Second Continental Congress convinced themselves and the greater part of their colonial constituencies that the risk was worth taking. How that came about is the subject of the next chapter.

CHAPTER 3

"There Are, Thank God, Natural, Inherent and Inseparable Rights as Men . . .": The Architecture of American Rights

The previous chapter has tracked the alterations in the conceptual architecture of rights across the eighteenth century in English: In the early
decades of the century, rights understood in the most general sense were
conjugated through an early modern juristic conception of "right," where
that concept was hinged to a claim and tied to an ethico-theological description of society. The purpose of a right (and of rights, therefore) was to
uphold and protect both civic and religious institutions within which the
subject appeared as a coherent and cohesive social entity. Although such
entities could only, also, be political, it was not the purpose of a right to
provide one of the major defining characteristics of person or underscore
the internal coherence of the notion of the individual or subject; rather, its
aim was firmly at the level of the polis and state. Rights, coming out of the
political settlement of 1688, were a matter for the collective and collectivities and calibrated the ratios of power that held the estates general in tension. By the end of the century, "right(s)" were more frequently taken to
protect and give definition to individual commonwealths, political goods
desired by individuals whose primary objective was to maintain a tensile
relationship between rights, liberties and privileges such that the space

for action and well-being within civic society provided opportunities for
the expression of personhood now understood as an independent particular. Both of these accounts were plausibly constructed upon a conceptual
framework that utilized the same core building blocks, the networked connections that comprised part of the architecture of the concept "right(s)."
But, as I have argued, another conceptual entity also began to gain coherence and consistency: "rights of man," which was networked in different
ways and whose grammar and syntax contributed to the establishment of a
new conceptual architecture.[1]

This emergent alternative architecture can be seen most clearly for the
first time in the imperial crisis, whose resolution created the first modern
republic, the United States of America.[2] If one were to narrow the moment
at which this occurred to its tightest (and doubtless absurd) range, the best
candidate, perhaps, would be July 2, 1776, when the committee instructed
with the task of bringing a document to the Second Continental Congress
proposing independence presented its arguments. Jefferson has tradition-
ally been given the role of author for this document, but as he himself
noted later in life, when he penned his era-defining lines—"We hold these
truths to be self evident, that all men are created equal, that they are endowed by their Creator with certain unalienable Rights, that among these
are Life, Liberty and the pursuit of Happiness"—he was merely giving his

1. This opens up a very intriguing and complex set of negotiations in the history of
conceptualizations of the human subject. The current argument is certainly intended
to bring a part of that history to light, but the larger picture which must for reasons of
coherence remain only in the background should be called to mind here. In the century
preceding that taken for detailed analysis throughout this book, political theorists—not
exclusively writing in the English language—refined and recomposed some of the concepts that from the early modern period onward had become central for thinking in and
about the social and political. Hobbes's notion of "person," for example, has a peculiar
structure that both individuates and collectivizes. "Persons" are both agents sui generis
and multiple constituents of the state. Rousseau, perhaps riffing on Hobbes's account,
constructed a robust account of the *volonte generale* that mapped easily onto the concept
"man" as universal. At the same time individuated notions of man, such as Kant's deployment of the "citizen" were placed in tension with "person" or "subject," the latter
of course a major conceptual hub in the ancien régime's configuration of state, society,
and polis. I am grateful to Jonathan Lamb for pressing me with these comparative and
extending observations.

2. The campaign around Wilkes in the early 1760s was focused on liberty, not
rights. Although the two are hinged the specific inflection given to rights, that is, political rights, Wilkes and his supporters meant that the concept "right(s)" was more than
adequate for making sense of the crisis.

version of what was common to the American mind.[3] The purpose of this chapter is to recover the concept of rights understood as a cultural entity within the colonial context leading up to the revolution, and to map the architecture of that concept. It sets out to provide in considerable detail the process by which a new concept is "cultured," that is, given common currency within a closed community. My aim, therefore, might be described as an attempt to draw the outlines of the American mind alongside a finer, more detailed picture of a specific concept held within it. This is to note that I shall not be concerned with an adjacent issue, the political meanings and origins of the concept of rights as used by the colonists, because in a general sense they are both easily inspected and have been subjected to substantial scholarly scrutiny. If one were to redact that body of work to its essential outlines, those meanings and origins would be unintelligible outside the orbit of what has become known as "Whiggism,"[4] even if that Whiggism took on particular inflections within the more rarefied locale of the colonies, where Whig ideology was grafted both happily and unhappily upon varieties of dissent.[5] The traces of that political and intellectual lin-

---

3. Writing to Henry Lee on May 8, 1825, Jefferson retracted from any sense that the Declaration of Independence was in a strong sense original: The object of the declaration was not, he wrote, "to find out new principles, or new arguments, never before thought of, not merely to say things which had never been said before; but to place before mankind the common sense of the subject, in terms so plain and firm as to command their assent, and to justify ourselves in the independent stand we are compelled to take." And, in the words that have since become renowned, he continued: "Neither aiming at originality or principle or sentiment, it was intended to be an expression of the American mind, and to give to that expression the proper tone and spirit called for by the occasion." *Life and Selected Writings of Thomas Jefferson*, ed. Adrienne Koch and William Peden (New York: Random House, 1944), 656. In the terms of the current argument, Jefferson's characterization of his purpose looks very much like an attempt to convey a culturally embedded concept. I have written about Jefferson's role in drafting the Declaration in my *The Fourth of July and the Founding of America* (London: Profile Books, 2007), esp. 10–30.

4. Albeit a "sentimental Whiggism"; see Kenneth Silverman, *A Cultural History of the American Revolution* (New York: Thomas Y. Crowell, 1978).

5. Throughout this chapter, when I refer to "the colonies" and to the "colonists," I mean to gather together those colonies that could be accurately termed "British" and those settlers who either themselves came from Britain or who were descended from British stock. This is to note that the more recent history of the transatlantic world in this period has, quite properly, begun to address the Anglocentric focus of much that speaks under the rubric of the history of the colonies in prerevolutionary America. I make no apology for this Anglocentric approach since the current work is entirely

eage are still legible today, even if the ideology informing Whig principles of independence and improvement were subject to mutation when transplanted onto colonial soil, becoming transformed as the powerful motor of the nascent republic's drive toward imperial supremacy began to fashion a new and different characterization of the American mind that today finds its home in free-market individualism. That home, insofar as it represents the terminus of the colonists' speculations outlined in this chapter, would most likely have surprised some, if not all, of the founding fathers. For whatever claims might be made today on behalf of a certain conception of citizenship, of the human subject as a bearer of rights, the conceptual universe that provided the context for the founding of the new republic was entirely innocent of what we have learned to call subjective identity rights. Free-market individualism, as has been noted by others, presents particular difficulties when one tries to think rights as universal, and even if the founding fathers subscribed to Jefferson's "all men are equal" thesis, it would be a mistake to conflate how the mid-eighteenth century thought through the concept of rights (in either of its guises) with how our own period thinks through the concept of identity. Whatever the connections may be between our own senses of "rights" and those circulating in the Enlightenment, contemporary defenses of subjective identity rights that are based on claims of historical precedent are spurious.

While it should be pointed out that the historiography of the period contests the extent to which the colonists adopted Whig ideology wholesale, it would nonetheless be perhaps accurate to state that across the various colonies a meld of then recent and not-so-recent liberal British interpretations of the nature of government and society came to predominate.[6] The colonists were certainly inward with the classic account of liberty, which insisted on the defense of certain inalienable rights as it also, simultaneously, recognized that, in the movement from a state of nature to society, certain alienable rights must be given up. But they were also pragmatists faced with what they slowly came to perceive as a unique and

---

directed at the formation of concepts within the English language. For the sake of elegance, wherever I use the term *colonist(s)* I do not mark it with the qualifier *British*, but this is what is meant.

6. The most extensive account of the roots of colonial political ideas is to be found in Craig Yirush, *Settlers, Liberty, and Empire: The Roots of Early American Political Theory, 1675–1775* (Cambridge: Cambridge University Press, 2011), commented upon below. See also Garry Wills, *Inventing America: Jefferson's Declaration of Independence* (Garden City, N.Y.: Doubleday, 1978); James H. Kettner, *The Development of American Citizenship, 1608–1870* (Chapel Hill: University of North Carolina Press, 1978).

singular situation: the necessity for founding a state on newly minted republican principles.

For over forty years, arguments within the history of the colonial period and the revolution that brought it to an end have circled around the so-called theses of "republicanism" and "liberalism," essentially arguing pro or contra the importance of various writers and texts for the colonists (wherever they stood on the issue of separation from the mother country) as they struggled to formulate a coherent account of the legitimacy (or not) of their actions.[7] The arguments have drawn upon a variety of sources: the voluminous correspondence of some of the most high-profile founding fathers (Jefferson and Adams prime among them) as evidence for reconstructing the intellectual formation of various actors during the revolutionary period,[8] evidence (scant though it is) for the holdings of various colonial libraries,[9] and an increasingly sophisticated and detailed book history that has begun to map the transatlantic travel of printed materials over the course of the eighteenth century.[10] My own approach in

7. This long-standing debate has proposed a number of key texts. Among them are Locke's *Two Treatises*, various works of Hutcheson, Grotius, Pufendorf and Sidney, Burgh's *Political Disquisitions*, and Trenchard and Gordon's *Cato's Letters*. The following argument does not seek to join this debate as the emphasis I shall place on conceptual forms intends to demonstrate the emergence of something newly minted within the culture of the 1770s. For a concise account of the historiographical debate, see Alan Gibson, *Understanding the Founding: The Crucial Questions* (Lawrence: University Press of Kansas, 2007), ch. 4; and for the reception of republican ideas in the context of late eighteenth-century America see Daniel T. Rodgers, "Republicanism: The Career of a Concept," *Journal of American History* 79, no. 1 (1992): 11–38.

8. Did Jefferson read Hutcheson? Was he ignorant of Locke's *Two Treatises on Government*? These two linked questions have taken on particular emphasis in the work of Garry Wills and both his defenders and detractors. See Garry Wills, *Inventing America: Jefferson's Declaration of Independence* (Garden City, N.Y.: Doubleday, 1978); and, for a contrary view, Kenneth Lynn, "Falsifying Jefferson," *Commentary*, 66 (Oct. 1978), 66–71; Ronald Hamowy, "Jefferson and the Scottish Enlightenment," *William and Mary Quarterly*, 3rd ser., 31 (1979): 502–23; Steven Dworetz, *The Unvarnished Doctrine: Locke, Liberalism, and the American Revolution* (Durham, N.C.: Duke University Press, 1990). According to Donald Lutz, Hutcheson did not figure among the thirty-five most cited thinkers during the founding era. See Donald Lutz, *The Origins of American Constitutionalism* (Baton Rouge: Louisiana State University Press, 1988), 142.

9. See David Lundberg and Henry F. May, "The Enlightened Reader in America," *American Quarterly* 28 (1976): 262–71; H. Trevor Colbourn, *The Lamp of Experience* (Chapel Hill: University of North Carolina Press, 1965), esp. 200–32.

10. See James Raven, "The Importation of Books in the Eighteenth Century" in *A History of the Book in America*, ed. Hugh Amory and David D. Hall (Chapel Hill: Uni-

this chapter, however, will not attempt to adjudicate between various con-
tenders for the status of founding texts that are supposed to have formed
the intellectual substrate that helped colonists make sense of their lives and
political filiations.[11] I shall not be concerned to characterize the "American
mind" by reconstructing its library. In contrast, I intend to trace the ways
in which the architecture of the concept of rights began to mutate as the
colonists came under pressure to articulate clearly how they understood
their legal and political relations to Britain.[12] That attempt at understand-

---

versity of North Carolina Press, 2007), 1:183–98; David D. Hall, "Learned Culture
in the Eighteenth Century," in *A History of the Book in America*, ed. Hugh Amory and
David D. Hall (Chapel Hill: University of North Carolina Press, 2007), 1:411–33. For
an account of the commerce in ideas between the mother country and the colonies, see
Colin Bonwick, *English Radicals and the American Revolution* (Chapel Hill: University
of North Carolina Press, 1977), esp. Ch. 2; for the reception of Locke, see Eric Slau-
ter, "Reading and Radicalization: Print, Politics and the American Revolution," *Early
American Studies* 8 (2010): 5–40; and, for the role of one bookseller in the dissemination
of ideas throughout the colonial world. see Eric Stockdale, *'Tis Treason, My Good Man!:
Four Revolutionary Presidents and a Piccadilly Bookshop* (London: British Library, 2005).

11. For a good window onto the educated world of the colonists, see D. W. Rob-
son, *Educating Republicans. The College in the Era of the American Revolution, 1750–1800*
(Westport, Conn.: Greenwood, 1985).

12. The debate over the importance and significance of Locke's *Two Treatises on
Government* was first prompted by John Dunn in his seminal essay of 1969, "The Politics
of Locke in England and America in the Eighteenth Century." In this magisterial essay,
Dunn argues strenuously for the irrelevance of Locke's text to the colonists in the prerevolutionary era, noting that for the first half of the eighteenth century it was "almost
unknown as a work of his [Locke's]." And in the colonies there is, he writes, "no reason
to suppose that many people had read it [*Two Treatises*] with care . . . by 1750." See John
Dunn, *Political Obligation in Its Historical Context* (Cambridge: Cambridge University
Press, 1980), 76. Since its first publication, there has been a vigorous discussion with
many voices entering the fray either pro or contra Dunn's position; see above, ch. 2
note 23. Although, as Michael P. Zuckert notes, some evidence about the presence of
Locke's text in the colonies has come to light since Dunn wrote his essay, there nevertheless remains a very large question as to whether, when referring to "Locke on government," colonial writers were explicitly referring to his text, or indeed that they had
anything other than a scant awareness that such a text existed. It remains the case that
Dunn's characterization of the principles and political concepts mobilized by the colonists as far from specifically or uniquely Lockean must be correct. See *Natural Rights and
the New Republicanism* (Princeton, N.J.: Princeton University Press, 1994), esp. 20–25.
As the following seeks to demonstrate, the cultural embedding of a concept like rights
is both complex and mobile and cannot be derived from a single source or authority.
This is so even if, as critics of Garry Wills have taken pains to establish, certain phrases
in the Declaration have antecedents in Locke's *Two Treatises* since the presence of these

ing the political, legal, and cultural maelstrom they found themselves in set in motion a process through which diverse views and opinions (far from uniquely articulated around the issue of pro or contra the then-current colonial structures) came to be focused on a set of common aspirations and objectives that would eventually give definition to a new nation. In doing so, it also began the game-changing process of forming a new culture that was not only going to require heretofore separate colonial societies (understood here in the round, as distinctive legal, religious, linguistic, and political entities) to connect in ways that had yet to be figured out but also going to create common tokens—call them concepts—that would allow something like efficient communication between them.[13] This, it should be pointed out, was not simply a matter of agreeing upon a means of communication—say, a standard linguistic praxis or medium of telecommunication—still less, a legislative or constitutional code that could be commonly applied across what was to emerge as a federal state. It was also something far more difficult to achieve, a matter of constructing a new conceptual lexicon that could be adopted by and within the polis as whole.[14] The argument of this chapter is that the crucible for generating that new conceptual lexicon was the imperial crisis in general, but I shall take a far narrower perspective since the rubric under which the first Continental Congress

---

echoes, exactly as Jefferson noted, can indicate the *cultural dispersion* of these ideas as easily as they can be said to prove a conscious borrowing from Locke's text. This of course begs the question as to the difference between a *cultural dispersal* of ideas and borrowing the meanings of someone else's words. On the parallels between the Declaration and the *Two Treatises*, see Zuckert, *Natural Rights and the New Republicanism* (Princeton, N.J.: Princeton University Press, 1994), 323n47. It is perhaps worth noting that Locke's name hardly appears in the database of Eighteenth Century American Newspapers until the last twenty years of the century. The data for *Locke* are: 1, 13, 97, 523, 3,512.

13. The institution of Committees of Correspondence across the colonies was a technological innovation that had significant effects on the outcome of the imperial crisis. See William Warner, "Transmitting Liberty: The Boston Committee of Correspondence's Revolutionary Experiments in Enlightenment Mediation," in *This Is Enlightenment*, ed. Clifford Siskin and William Warner (Chicago: University of Chicago Press, 2010), 102–19.

14. That such a transformation took place was the opinion of one of its key players, John Adams, who commented in a now-famous remark: "But what do we mean by the American Revolution? Do we mean the American War? The Revolution was effected before the War commenced. The Revolution was in the minds and hearts of the people; a change in their religious sentiments. Of their duties and obligations . . . *This radical change in the principles, opinions, sentiments, and affections of the people was the real American Revolution.*" John Adams to Hezekiah Niles, *Niles Weekly Register*, March 7, 1818.

met provided a very specific locale for the "culturing" of a new conceptual architecture for rights.

One can see in snapshot how Jefferson's formulation captures the sense of tension that I have described in the preceding chapter. Jefferson, like his compatriots, inherited a notion of rights that understood them as prescriptible, both specifiable and countable, and therefore built upon the architectural element of the deposit. That architecture began to mutate under the pressure of providing a legitimating scaffolding for the colonists' moves toward separation and eventual independence.[15] In contrast to the concept of rights configured as a deposit containing specifiable and countable rights claims, another architecture began to become discernible— one that provided a different kind of support. This platform for thinking with the concept of "rights" allowed rights to remain comfortably vague, in no need of being specified or precisely enumerated. In its most developed state, this different architecture can best be understood as providing support for a different concept of rights altogether. One can get a glimpse of that difference by noting that embedded in Jefferson's formulation— "among these" rights are liberty, and so forth—is the potential sense that the full range of rights need not be supplied and perhaps could never be listed. I do not doubt that this reading of his famous words can be placed next to a more conventional gloss that assumes the full range of rights to be countable—those are the "certain" rights that Jefferson refers to—but on this occasion Jefferson chose to select only three.[16] One can, however, make a case for a different analysis of the conceptual universe present to Jef-

15. For a good account of the complexities of Declaration's use of rights, see Barry A. Shain, "Rights Natural and Civil in the Declaration of Independence," in Barry A. Shain, ed., *The Nature of Rights at the American Founding and Beyond* (Charlottesville: University of Virginia Press, 2007), 116–62.

16. There are further potentialities of meaning in these famous words. When Jefferson writes that men are endowed with "certain inalienable rights," does he mean to indicate that those rights are "certain" in the sense that they are given and beyond dispute? This reading is somewhat attenuated by the following "among them," which seems to pull the sense away from certitude toward the sense of "some as yet to be fully determined." It is this second sense that I shall explore in the larger context of the constitutional crisis in the 1770s. It should also be noted that Jefferson's first draft read "inherent and inalienable rights." This suggests that in the discussion that followed the submission of his draft (either to the drafting committee or to the full committee of Congress, or indeed to both) there was dissent about the content of "rights." It suggests that some wished to preserve a distinction between alienable and inalienable based on the claim to such rights being inherent. The substitution of *certain* then, in the sense of a lack of specificity, suggests that a compromise was brokered. On this see Pauline

ferson's formulation. In outline I shall argue that the concept of "right(s)" was under pressure (for reasons explored below) that led to the growth—almost like a viral infection within the concept of "right(s)"—of a different concept with a distinctively different architecture. That concept I have called "rights of man," rights understood as prospectively realizable in the collective on behalf of all persons.[17] The distinction between this conceptual architecture and that which supports contemporary human rights will become clearer as this chapter progresses: Its outline can be seen in the difference between rights understood as aspirations voiced in the collective and rights understood as a property held by the individual. It will also become evident that it is incautious to assume that the architecture of the concept of the "human" is chrono-invariant, essentially identical over the stretch of time from the eighteenth century to today, or indeed that it had a singular shape within the confines of the eighteenth century.

One can get the measure of this observation by looking at the ways in which ideas about "human nature" circulated in colonial America. There in that context it was, for example, used as one of the ways in which the sexes were distinguished.[18] Humanity came associated with sentiment and affect; it demarcated an area of sensitivity that persons might experience when considering others. Given this, it had the potential to weaken one's resolution with respect to rights. As John Adams noted, "we all know that human nature itself, from indolence, modesty, humanity or fear, has always too much reluctance to a manly assertion of its rights."[19] This suggests that Adams, and by extension the cultural environment in which he lived and thought, would have found it awkward to combine "rights" and "humanity." For them, the sentiments associated with respect for others were not

---

Maier, *American Scripture: How America Declared Its Independence from Britain* (London: Pimlico, 1999), esp. 134–50.

17. I offer this in full knowledge of the fact that, as Michael Zuckert points out, the exact phrase *rights of man* had hardly any circulation during the 1770s in America. See Michael Zuckert, "Natural Rights in the American Revolution: The American Amalgam," in *Human Rights and Revolutions*, ed. Jeffrey N. Wasserstrom, Lynn Hunt, and Marilyn B. Young (Lanham, Md.: Rowman & Littlefield, 2000), 59. See also table 22 below.

18. As G. J. Barker-Benfield points out, Adam Smith associated humanity—that is, the feeling for fellow humans—with unmanliness. Humanity, he maintained, was a virtue of women; men were more prone to generosity. See G. J. Barker-Benfield, *Abigail and John Adams: The Americanization of Sensibility* (Chicago: University of Chicago Press, 2010).

19. John Adams, *Dissertation on the Feudal and Canon Law* (1765).

Table 21. Number of times *human rights* appears in eighteenth-century American newspapers

	1700–1720	1720–1740	1740–1760	1760–1780	1780–1800
human rights	0	0	0	4	102

Source: Early American Newspapers, http://www.readex.com/content/early-american
-newspapers-series-1-9-1690-1922.

conducive to the "manly" task of defending rights.[20] This observation at the very least asks us to consider the extent to which the concept of the "human" across the English-language eighteenth century shared an outline or architecture with our contemporary form. A good argument can be made, for example, that for Adams and his peers the category of the "human" had only a weak connection to "mankind." The very sparse incidence of use for the term *human rights* in American newspapers bears this out, as table 21 shows. Those data can be compared with the use of the phrase "rights of man" (table 22).

For Jefferson and his peers at the time of the Declaration, the claim that all men are created equal entailed at the very least scrutiny of the potential consequences for the claim to universality. Indeed, for many colonists the discrepancies between what they professed and what they actually did caused considerable anguish.[21] As it turned out, however, following the revolution the resources of this second conceptual architecture were in little demand. The colonists quickly discovered that both the federal and state constitutions adopted over the 1780s, and the eventual Bill of Rights, could

20. See G. J. Barker-Benfield, *Abigail and John Adams: The Americanization of Sensibility* (Chicago: University of Chicago Press, 2010), esp. 115–26.
21. The literature on the question of slavery and the founding of America, a topic that has received considerable attention, puts this in its proper light. See, among others, David B. Davis, *Was Thomas Jefferson an Authentic Enemy of Slavery?* (Oxford: Oxford University Press, 1970); Robert McColley, *Slavery and Jeffersonian Virginia* (Urbana: University of Illinois Press, 1973); David B. Davis, *The Problem of Slavery in the Age of Revolution, 1770–1823* (Ithaca, N.Y.: Cornell University Press, 1975); John Diggins, "Slavery, Race, and Equality: Jefferson and the Pathos of Enlightenment," *American Quarterly* 28 (1976): 2016–28; John C. Miller, *The Wolf by the Ears: Thomas Jefferson and Slavery* (New York: Macmillan, 1977).

Table 22. Number of times *rights*, *rights of man*, *rights and liberties*, *rights and privileges*, and *sacred rights* appear in eighteenth-century American and British newspapers

American newspapers

	1700–1720	1720–1740	1740–1760	1760–1780	1780–1800
rights	578	3,523	9,070	41,488	198,585
rights of man	0	1	0	45	3,532
rights and liberties	2	23	56	797	724
rights and privileges	0	31	78	735	721
sacred rights	0	2	7	95	415

British newspapers

	1700–1720	1720–1740	1740–1760	1760–1780	1780–1800
rights	3,728	8,508	7,849	28,430	53,248
rights of man	3	8	2	84	2,980
rights and liberties	241	775	619	2,061	1,286
rights and privileges	266	1,015	739	2,513	2,899
sacred rights	6	19	3	4	134

Sources: Early American Newspapers, http://www.readex.com/content/early-american-newspapers-series-1-9-1690-1922, and the Burney Collection, http://www.jisc.ac.uk/news/stories/2009/01/burney.aspx.

all function adequately under the rubric of positive law and find legitimacy in the authority of the much-longer-standing concept of "right(s)." To a considerable extent, it can be argued that this sealed the fate of "human rights" for the following two centuries. Perhaps to our continuing cost, the colonists discovered that there was no immediate crisis, no compellingly immediate reason to embrace the differently structured concept of "rights of man." They also saw very clearly that any attempt to make this other concept over into a generally applied cognitive tool was bound to require significant political will and strenuous (perhaps inhuman) efforts at persuasion. As history was to later indicate, the political difficulties of turning an aspiration for universal rights into an achieved legislative and social program all too easily ended up in devastating violence, civil war. Such difficulties have proven to be extraordinarily persistent, all the more so as their shape, form, and expression continuously alter under the pressure of capitalism's inexhaustible capacity for reinvention. The civil rights movement of the late twentieth century certainly did its best to disrupt the repetitive return to self-centered rights, but capital has the knack of infecting every pore of the skin that protects polity. Perhaps one should not be surprised, therefore, when our own attempts to think universal rights continually stumble over the hinge that connects the concept of rights to property. Seen in this light, one might remark that, far from inheriting the Enlightenment's thinking vis-à-vis rights, we have ignored what I consider to be its major and significant discovery, that "rights of man" could never be held by men. It is almost as if the period's work in conceptual analysis never existed, its careful delineation of the conceptual architecture of "right(s)" good for nothing.

The American Mind before the Revolution, ca. 1760–1774

Within the longstanding historiographical tradition of the American revolution, significant contributions to our understanding of the intellectual milieu of the colonists have focused upon the natural-rights tradition as it developed through the seventeenth century in England in particular and in Europe more generally.[22] As I have pointed out above, this account has been challenged or attenuated by others who seek to replace a monolithic

---

22. The European influence on colonial cultures is tracked through two important essays: David Lundberg and Henry F. May, "The Enlightened Reader in America," *American Quarterly* 28, no. 2 (1976): 262–93; and Donald S. Lutz, "The Relative Influ-

natural-law tradition with more nuanced intellectual, social, cultural, and religious histories of the period. To some degree, debate continues to ebb and flow over the extent to which a civic-humanist tradition exhumed by J. G. A. Pocock among others featured in the colonists' mental landscape, in contrast to the moral and political thought taught within the Scottish university system.[23] Did Scotland (and Ireland) provide the most congenial environment for developing the political, legal, and moral ideas that were to provide example and sustenance for the colonists, or was the formation of the American mind an outworking of early modern Florentine political philosophy?[24] This question requires a more detailed formulation since, as

ence of European Writers on Late Eighteenth-Century American Thought," *American Political Science Review* 78, no. 1 (1984): 189–97.

23. This literature is by now vast, but I mean to call to mind, among other significant contributions, Caroline Robbins, *The Eighteenth-Century Commonwealthman* (Cambridge, Mass.: Harvard University Press, 1959); Garry Wills, *Inventing America: Jefferson's Declaration of Independence* (Garden City, N.Y.: Doubleday, 1978); J. G. A. Pocock, *Virtue, Commerce, and History* (Cambridge: Cambridge University Press, 1985); Steven Dworetz, *The Unvarnished Doctrine: Locke, Liberalism, and the American Revolution* (Durham, N.C.: Duke University Press, 1990); Isaac Kramnick, *Republicanism and Bourgeois Radicalism: Political Ideology in Late Eighteenth-Century England and America* (Ithaca, N.Y.: Cornell University Press, 1990); Gordon S. Wood, *The Radicalism of the American Revolution: How a Revolution Transformed a Monarchical Society into a Democratic One Unlike Any That had Ever Existed* (New York: Vintage Books, 1991); Bernard Bailyn, *The Ideological Origins of the American Revolution*, enl. ed., (Cambridge, Mass.: Harvard University Press, 1992); Joyce Appelby, *Liberalism and Republicanism in the Historical Imagination* (Cambridge, Mass.: Harvard University Press, 1992); J. C. D. Clark, *The Language of Liberty 1660–1832: Political Discourse and Social Dynamics in the Anglo-American World* (Cambridge: Cambridge University Press, 1994).

24. A recent characterization of the debate puts it thus: "Dominated in the last generation by the 'classical republican' challenge to an older 'liberal' interpretation of the founding, [scholarship on early American political thought] has reached an impasse, with the republican contention that a classical politics of virtue dominated early American political theory proving unsustainable in the face of the strong counter-evidence that liberal ideas of rights, property, and consent, often associated with John Locke, were an important part of the ideology of the revolution." See Craig Yirush, *Settlers, Liberty, and Empire: The Roots of Early American Political Theory, 1675–1775* (Cambridge: Cambridge University Press, 2011), 5. The links between Scotland and the colonies have been the subject of long-standing and substantial research. See, among others, D. Sloan, *The Scottish Enlightenment and the American College Idea* (New York: Teachers College Press, 1971); R. Hamowy, "Jefferson and the Scottish Enlightenment," *William and Mary Quarterly* 36 (1979): 503–23; D. Walker Howe, "Why the Scottish Enlightenment Was Useful to the Framers of the American Constitution," *Comparative Studies in*

has rightly become necessary, differences in the variety of dissent present to prerevolutionary America need to be taken into account.[25] Those differences bit hard in respect to the *sensus communis* that shaped distinct colonial territories. Although the pressure of the imperial crisis would change things for good, for the first half of the eighteenth century communication between far-flung colonies was intermittent and often deeply instrumental (regarding trade, for example). Even within colonies, different communities with distinctive cultural, religious, social, and political practices often had only scant need to remark such differences: The colonies were a loose collection of independent particulars. Not only did the specific varieties of dissent determine the character of local cultural traditions, the legal and political structures that operated in each locale had little need for conformity: Each colony worked with and under its particular charter or contract.[26] Given this heterogeneity, the effects of allegiance to one or another variety of dissent were perhaps not decisive but certainly significant, and they drew upon a range of intellectual goods whose compatibility rarely surfaced as an issue.

This tradition of scholarship, moreover, has become very sensitive to the detailed conditions—social, political, legal, religious, and intellectual—that prevailed in colonial America.[27] It would, therefore, be foolish

Society and History 31, no. 3 (1989): 572–87; R. B. Sher and J. R. Smitten, eds., *Scotland and America in the Age of the Enlightenment* (Princeton, N.J.: Princeton University Press, 1990). The Lockean legacy is treated in John Dunn, "The Politics of Locke in England and America in the Eighteenth Century," in *John Locke: Problems and Perspectives*, ed. J. W. Yolton (Cambridge: Cambridge University Press, 1969), 45–80; T. L. Pangle, *The Spirit of Modern Republicanism: The Moral Vision of the American Founders and the Philosophy of Locke* (Chicago: University of Chicago Press, 1988); and, for a different perspective that seeks to place the founding of America in relation to the ancient world, see Carl J. Richard, *The Founders and the Classics: Greece, Rome, and the American Enlightenment* (Cambridge, Mass.: Harvard University Press, 1994).

25. An outstanding recent account of the complex social and political map of the colonies can be found in Richard R. Beeman, *The Varieties of Political Experience in Eighteenth-Century America* (Philadelphia: University of Pennsylvania Press, 2004).

26. As Richard R. Beeman, remarks, "on the eve of the revolution . . . it becomes impossible to talk about a single *American* political culture; rather, the essential fact of political life in the American colonies in the eighteenth century is that there existed numerous, diverse political cultures, diffuse and fragmented, often speaking altogether different political languages." See Richard R. Beeman, *The Varieties of Political Experience in Eighteenth-Century America* (Philadelphia: University of Pennsylvania Press, 2004), 2.

27. On the legal complexities, see Max Radin, "The Rivalry of Common-Law and Civil Law Ideas in the American Colonies," in *Law: A Century of Progress 1835–1935*,

to characterize this extremely extensive tradition as comprising a singular approach to the description and archaeological exhumation of that intellectual milieu that Jefferson called "the American mind."[28] Notwithstanding this caveat, for the most part this scholarly tradition does, nevertheless, rely upon well-established models of intellectual history (howsoever contested) which seek to track the lineage of ideas. This is why there is such debate over the importance of, say, Hutcheson or Locke in the formation of the colonists' political discourse.[29] It is why Burgh's *Political Disquisitions* or Trenchard and Gordon's *Cato's Letters* have attracted particular attention. It can be quite fairly said that a history of thought is necessarily a history of the people who held such thoughts and of the texts within which they gave expression to their ideas.[30] In the first part of this chapter, my own approach will be somewhat different, however, since I shall begin by

---

ed. Alison Reppy (New York: New York University Press, 1937), 2:404–31; George Athan Billias, ed., *Law and Authority in Colonial America* (Barre, Mass.: Barre, 1965); William E. Nelson, *Americanization of the Common Law: The Impact of Legal Change in Massachusetts Society, 1760–1830* (Cambridge, Mass.: Harvard University Press, 1975); Morton J. Horwitz, *The Transformation of American Law, 1780–1860* (Cambridge, Mass.: Harvard University Press, 1977); A. G. Roeber, *Faithful Magistrates and Republican Lawyers: Creators of Virginia Legal Culture, 1680–1810* (Chapel Hill: University of North Carolina Press, 1981); Peter S. Onuf, *The Origins of the Federal Republic: Jurisdictional Controversies in the United States, 1775–1787* (Philadelphia: University of Pennsylvania Press, 1983). For the religious complexities, see J. C. D. Clark, *The Language of Liberty 1660–1832: Political Discourse and Social Dynamics in the Anglo-American World* (Cambridge: Cambridge University Press, 1994), esp. 141–217. For the social complexities, see Jack Greene, *Pursuits of Happiness: The Social Development of Early Modern British Colonies and the Formation of American Culture* (Chapel Hill: University of North Carolina Press, 1988). For cultural diversities, see *Strangers within the Realm: Cultural Margins of the First British Empire*, ed. Bernard Bailyn and Philip D. Morgan (Chapel Hill: University of North Carolina Press, 1991).

28. The best account in terms of a rigorous philosophical examination of ideas— committed to the influence of Locke on the colonists—remains Morton White, *The Philosophy of the American Revolution* (New York: Oxford University Press, 1978).

29. A recent contribution to this debate proposes a new line of inquiry, essentially proposing that Locke established a radical theory of natural liberty that took issue with Filmer and disengaged from the tradition that stretched from Grotius to Hobbes. See Lee Ward, *The Politics of Liberty in England and Revolutionary America* (Cambridge: Cambridge University Press, 2004), esp. 209–40.

30. This approach is exemplified in some of the finest accounts of the "American mind" during the colonial period. See in particular Carl Becker, *The Declaration of Independence: A Study in the History of Political Ideas* (New York: Alfred A. Knopf, 1942); Daniel J. Boorstin, *The Lost World of Thomas Jefferson* (Chicago: University of Chicago

asking a very specific question: What is the shape or modality of the concept of rights as it appears in particular locales within the colonial situation during the prelude to revolution? Hence, I shall arbitrarily take a slice through a continuous history as I attempt to take the pulse of the beating heart of colonial dissent at a particular moment—effectively the ten or so years before the Declaration of Independence—thereby setting a marker or establishing a context for what transpired in the hothouse of the First Continental Congress in Philadelphia between September 5 and October 26, 1774, which is the topic for second part of the chapter. It should be pointed out that my characterization of the prerevolutionary context is not intended to imply that the ideas and conceptual structures I identify were only present to this decade or so, nor is it meant to occlude the fact that many of the opinions and arguments I present had long-standing and deep roots in the colonial experience stretching back into the previous century. I wish to focus on this tight historical window because it provides me with a very unusual opportunity for testing the general hypothesis presented by this book: that concepts are cultural entities, and, as such, they may be "cultured" in a set of social practices. Thus, the conditions in which the delegates to the First Continental Congress met—essentially in a "black-box" environment, cut off from external communication—created a kind of experimental laboratory for generating conceptual forms. Most especially, it provided a delimited and constrained environment—a loco-specific culture—within which the stresses in the architecture of the concept of "right(s)" could be discovered and attempts initiated for the "culturing" of a new concept of universal rights that enabled the colonists to understand the basis for claiming their rights as "American"—and, as will become very clear with consequences under which we continue to operate, for claiming the universality of rights to lie precisely in their being American.

I also need to signal at the outset that I do not mean to sideline the extremely useful work that provides the modern scholar with the resources for reconstructing in some detail the larger intellectual milieu of the founding fathers, even if the scholarship in this matter has often been contested. It seems to me that J. C. D. Clark is correct in insisting on the discrimination between versions of dissent that permeated the colonial experience in the first half of the eighteenth century, just as I would also agree with J. G. A. Pocock in his distinguishing between radically different ways of conceiving the relations of the citizen to the state that found

---

Press, 1948); Bernard Bailyn, *The Ideological Origins of the American Revolution*, enl. ed., (Cambridge, Mass.: Belknap Press of Harvard University Press, 1992).

favor during the colonial period and note with respect to these differences that a common or harmonious mélange was as likely as George III inviting the founding fathers to an evening at Vauxhall Gardens.[31] In essence those differences came down to the investment in a juristic or legal account of the state, on the one hand, or, on the other, a political or ideological account conveyed by the term *liberalism*. This might look like a feeble reluctance to adjudicate in a debate that at times has appeared to will the destruction of opposing points of view, but my purpose is to demonstrate that the optic I shall bring to bear on the formation of the American mind—my insistence on the historical exploration of concepts as cultural entities—sheds light on the many sides and issues in this debate.[32] Even if I shall take care to remind myself that any broad brushstroke account of the "mental universe" within which the colonists operated immediately falls prey to qualification and counterqualification, I shall nevertheless propose that characterizations at the most general level of distinctive conceptual networks within a culture are both possible and revealing.[33] Thus, with due consideration to the preceding caveat, I want to enter a very general

31. Good accounts of the dissenting tradition during the period can be found in H. McLachlan, *English Education under the Test Acts, Being the History of the Non-Conformist Academies, 1662–1820* (Manchester: Manchester University Press, 1931); Anthony Lincoln, *Some Political and Social Ideas of English Dissent, 1763–1800* (New York: Octagon, 1971); J. Seed, "Gentlemen Dissenters: The Social and Political Meanings of Rational Dissent in the 1770s and 1780s," *Historical Journal* 28, no. 2 (1985): 299–325.

32. The following observation seen from the perspective of conceptual form helps one get behind, as it were, the thought that words are not concepts. This is Pocock's useful way of putting it: The early modern English-speaking world contained among others the following strains of political discourse: "common law, republican civic humanism, Protestant apocalyptic and eschatology, natural jurisprudence, political economy, and the Enlightenment assault of the concept of Christ's divinity." See his "The Language of Political Discourse and the British Rejection of the French Revolution," in E. Pii, ed., *I Linguaggi Politici delle Rivoluzioni in Europa XVII–XIX Secolo* (Firenze: L. S. Olschki, 1992), 20.

33. For those qualifications and counterqualifications, see among others John Shy, *A People Numerous and Armed: Reflections on the Military Struggle for American Independence*, rev ed., (Ann Arbor: University of Michigan Press, 1990); Bernard Bailyn, "Religion and Revolution: Three Biographical Studies," *Perspectives in American History* 4 (1970): 85–169; J. G. A. Pocock, "Virtues, Rights, and Manners: A Model for Historians of Political Thought," in *Virtue, Commerce, and History* (Cambridge: Cambridge University Press, 1985): 9–33; J. C. D. Clark, *The Language of Liberty 1660–1832: Political Discourse and Social Dynamics in the Anglo-American World* (Cambridge: Cambridge University Press, 1994).

observation that ought to attract wide assent: Whatever their specific allegiances, interests, or competencies in the byways of political and legal history, the colonists began from the position that in terms of their rights they understood themselves to be British.[34] Their legal charters asserted that in the words of Stephen Hopkins, governor of Rhode Island in 1764, emigrants to the colonies "were to remain subject to the King and dependent on the kingdom of Great Britain." This, he noted, had a reciprocal component: "In return they were to receive protection and enjoy all the rights and privileges of freeborn Englishmen."[35] And why would they not

34. As the second codicil of the Stamp Act Congress Declaration had it: "his Majesty's Liege Subjects in these Colonies, are entitled to all the inherent Rights and Liberties of his Natural born Subject, within the Kingdom of *Great-Britain*." See "Declarations of the Stamp Act Congress," in *The American Republic: Primary Sources*, ed. Bruce Frohnen (Indianapolis: Liberty Fund, 2001), 118. This, of course, cannot be simply taken to indicate that what it meant to be British was a single and agreed-upon thing. Nor does it mean to suggest that they felt themselves to be *first* British and then, say, Virginian. It leaves open, for example, whether or not the primary identification for many colonists was that of belonging to a particular tradition and inflection of dissent and, as it were, only British by accident of birth or descent. This is to open up the very significant chasm that separated vast numbers of emigrants to the colonies from Britain, people who had left the mother country precisely on account of perceived or actual persecution for their religious convictions. And many, if not the greater part of those emigrants came, of course, from Scotland and Ireland. In spite of this, as John Phillip Reid points out, the colonists throughout the constitutional crisis "never sought Scottish rights and the last thing they wanted were Irish rights." See John Phillip Reid, *Constitutional History of the American Revolution* (Madison: University of Wisconsin Press, 1968), 2:10, hereafter referred to as *The Authority of Rights*. For a slightly different emphasis in an account of the persistence of Scottish and Irish identities in the early republic, see Michael Durey, *Transatlantic Radicals and the Early American Republic* (Lawrence: University Press of Kansas, 1997).

35. Hopkins was, of course, merely intoning what had become the orthodoxy within the colonies upheld by those of British descent by the first half of the eighteenth century. Richard West, legal council to the Privy Council, had formulated this doctrine in 1720: "The Common law of England is the Common law of the Plantations, and all statutes in affirmance of the Common Law passed in England, antecedent to the settlement of a colony, are in force in that, unless there is some private Act to the contrary; though no statutes made since those settlements, are there in force, unless the colonies are particularly mentioned. Let an Englishman go where he will, he carries as much of law and liberty with him, as the nature of things will bear." Cited in George Chalmers, *Opinions of Eminent Lawyers on Various Points of English Jurisprudence* (Burlington: C. Goodrich, 1858), 207. See also Stephen Hopkins, *The Rights of Colonies Examined* (Providence: n.p., 1764), 5. Cf. the petition sent by the New York assembly to the British House of Lords: "*My Lords* we are *Englishmen*, and as such, presume ourselves intitled to the Rights and

claim allegiance to what the pamphlet *British Liberties* claimed was "the most perfect" government in Europe?[36] Why would they not want to be a part of what the great British jurist Sir William Blackstone maintained was "the only nation in the world, where political or civil liberty is the direct end of its constitution"?[37] Such an identification raises the specter of the peculiarly fraught allegiances embedded in the distinction between Britishness and Englishness, allegiances which cut deep into the cultures of dissent that came to settle in colonial America.[38] At the most general level, however, one can begin to see how the architecture of the concept of rights provided the colonists with a common cause—call it common sense—

Liberties, which have rendered the Subjects of *England* the Envy of all Nations," Petition of the New York Assembly to the House of Lords (December 31, 1768), *Boston Post-Boy*, May 1, 1769; and similar petitions sent by New Jersey and North Carolina legislators: "The subjects thus emigrating, brought with them, as inherent in their persons, all the rights and liberty of natural-born subjects within the parent-state," New Jersey Petition to the King, May 7, 1768, *Scots Magazine* 30 (1768): 522; North Carolina Petition, November10, 1768, *Boston Chronicle*, March 20, 1769. Thomas Pownall, former governor of Massachusetts, indicated to a British readership in 1764 that the colonists were aiming to establish "their rights and privileges as *Englishmen*," *Gentleman's Magazine* 34 (1764): 105, and this was indeed the case. See Daniel Dulany, *Considerations of the Propriety of Imposing Taxes in the British Colonies for the Purpose of Raising a Revenue by Act of Parliament* (New York: n.p., 1765): "The right of exemption from all taxes *without their consent*, the colonies claim as British subjects. They derive this right from the common law, which their charters have declared and confirmed . . ." in *Tracts of the American Revolution*, ed. Merrill Jensen (Indianapolis, Ind.: Hackett, 1966), 104.

36. Additionally, "it is the indispensable interest and duty of every true *Briton* to maintain those privileges . . . upon which all our temporal (and in great measure our eternal) happiness, safety, and well being depends." See *British Liberties* (London: Edward and Charles Dilley, 1766), 161–62.

37. Sir William Blackstone, *Commentaries on the Laws of England* (Chicago: University of Chicago Press, 1979), 1:141. Blackstone's *Commentaries* were deeply entangled in the colonial development of the practice of law. Although there are differences between the new England colonies and those in the south, especially Virginia in respect to the training of lawyers (the southerners almost required trainee lawyers to spend a sojourn in London and be exposed to the legal profession's arcane conventions and modes of jurisprudence inculcated through the inns of court, whereas the New England colonies tended to look more toward the Scottish system and to maintain close links between the pulpit and the law). For a good account of these differences, see Anton-Hermann Chroust, *The Rise of the Legal Profession in America*, 2 vols. (Norman: University of Oklahoma Press, 1965).

38. The most extensive treatment of this topic in the period is Francis Plowden, *Jura Anglorum: The Rights of Englishmen* (London: K & R Brooke, 1792).

even if its differently networked connections inevitably caused from time to time the need for negotiation. It was precisely the weighting of these connections that generated pressure on the concept of rights in the context of the unfolding politics of the prerevolutionary decades. In making the claim to English rights and privileges, a pretty constant ground bass to the colonists' self-presentation throughout the first half of the century that had its roots in the long-standing conceptualization of the legal and political arrangements of the polis developed in England up through the seventeenth century,[39] a number of important subclaims were implied.[40]

39. The most detailed account of this prehistory to the revolutionary moment is to be found in Craig Yirush, *Settlers, Liberty, and Empire: The Roots of Early American Political Theory, 1675–1775* (Cambridge: Cambridge University Press, 2011). Seventeenth-century colonial assemblies seemed to think of their rights as directly derived from the Bill of Rights or Magna Carta and to claim authority for those rights and privileges from what were loosely held to be "natural-law" principles operating unproblematically within a common-law framework. On this, see Charles F. Mullett, *Fundamental Law and the American Revolution* (New York: Columbia University Press, 1933).

40. See, among many such claims to the rights of Englishmen, Patrick Henry's renowned resolves passed in the house of Burgesses in Virginia, May 1765: Tthe Virginians, it was stated, were entitled to "all the Liberties and Privileges, Franchises and Immunities, that have at any Time been held, enjoyed, and possessed by the people of *Great Britain*," adding for clarification that "for all intents and purposes" this was "as if they had been abiding and born within the realm of *England*," Edmund S. Morgan, *Prologue to the Revolution: Sources and Documents on the Stamp Act Crisis, 1764–1766* (Chapel Hill: University of North Carolina Press, 1959), 47–48. Two things are noteworthy in this formulation of the colonists' rights: The first is the seeming ease with which *British* flows into or out of *English*. The second, about which I will have more to say below, is the temporal accidence of the claim: The colonists assert that they are entitled to all the liberties, etc., that had been held "at any time." This alerts us to the fact that, within the common law interpretation of rights, specific rights might become more relevant or require stating at particular moments, but the identification of rights with Englishness implied that the total basket of rights was timeless. They were coincident with the forging of the English nation, "time out of mind," as Blackstone characterizes the origin of common law. Note also Delaware's House of Assembly vote that the colonists had "been in possession of, and now are entitled to, all the inherent Rights and Liberties of His Majesty's Subjects in Great-Britain, or elsewhere," Delaware resolves, June 3, 1766, *Votes and Proceedings of the House of Representatives of the Government of the Counties of New Castle, Kent and Sussex, upon Delaware. At Sessions held at New Castle in the Years 1765–1770* (Dover, Del.: n.p., 1931), 54; Boston town meeting: "British privileges we hold in common with our fellow subjects who are natives of Britain," Instructions of Boston, May 28, 1764, in *The Massachusetts Gazette and Boston News-Letter* (1764); the suggestion that freeholders in Carolina elect representatives "who will use their best endeavours to *preserve, support and defend the enjoyment of every* CONSTITUTIONAL

Perhaps most significant for the story I shall tell is the inference that to be British was to enjoy those liberties that had been hard won during the glorious revolution; rights that were, of course, inherent and unalienable as noted by Stephen Hopkins: "British subjects in America have equal rights with those in Britain," but they did not hold them "as a privilege granted them" or, indeed, "enjoy them as a grace and favour bestowed." They held them as an "inherent, indefeasible right, as they and their ancestors were freeborn subjects," which entailed that they were "naturally entitled to all the rights and advantages of the British constitution."[41] Although within the parochial context of British politics this sense of liberty came attached to a specific political ideology, to Whiggism, I am less concerned here as to whether or not or to what extent that specific inflection carried into the colonial context.[42] More significant for the argument I am going to

LIBERTY, RIGHT *and* PRIVILEGE *that has been handed down to us by our* FOREFATHERS, *and which we* CLAIM *as* BRITISH SUBJECTS," *South-Carolina Gazette*, October 5, 1765; "We have the highest respect and reverence for the British parliament, which we believe to be the most august and respectable body of men on earth. . . . We consider ourselves as one people with them, and glory in the relation with them," *The Constitutional Courant*, Burlington, N.J., Sept 21, 1765.

41. Stephen Hopkins, *The Rights of Colonies Examined* (Providence, R.I.: 1764), 9. In a similar vein, the Virginia House of Burgesses petitioned George III on June 22, 1770, "to secure to us the free and uninterrupted Enjoyment of all those Rights and Privileges, which from the Laws of nature, of Community in general, and in a most especial Manner, from the Principles of the *British* Constitution, particularly recognized and confirm'd to this Colony by repeated and express Stipulations, we presume not to claim, but in common with all the rest of your Majesty's Subjects, under the same or like Circumstances." *Journals of the House of Burgesses of Virginia*, ed. John Pendelton Kennedy (Richmond, Va.: n.p., 1905–1907), 12:102. Gordon S. Wood points out that by the time of the imperial crisis "it was natural for colonists like Arthur Lee of Virginia to call in 1768 for 'a bill of rights' that would 'merit the title of the Magna Carta Americana.'" Wood is quoting Lee from Bernard Bailyn, *Ideological Origins of the American Revolution* (Cambridge, Mass.: Harvard University Press, 1992), 189. See Gordon S. Wood, "The History of Rights in Early America," in *The Nature of Rights at the American Founding and Beyond*, ed. Barry Alan Shain (Charlottesville: University of Virginia Press, 2007), 237; and for good accounts of the glorious revolution and its relation to the Declaration of Independence, see Elizabeth Read Foster, "Petitions and the Petition of Right," *Journal of British Studies* 14 (1974): 21–45; Lois G. Schwoerer, *The Declaration of Rights, 1689* (Baltimore, Md.: Johns Hopkins University Press, 1981).

42. Hopkins was not making an original claim since this view had long been in circulation throughout many colonies. William Penn's *The Excellent Privilege of Liberty and Property Being the Birth-Right of the Free-Born Subjects of England* was printed in Philadelphia in 1687, a pamphlet that abridged the radical Whig Henry Care's *English*

pursue is the friction caused by invoking British rights at the same time as holding on to the distinction and distinctiveness of the American context.[43] John Dickinson was perhaps the most dogged lawyer of the revolutionary period who consistently worked away at the interface of these two (potentially) conflicting identifications. He maintained that "If then the colonies are equally intitled [*sic*] to Happiness with the Inhabitants of Great Britain," and if also "Freedom is essential to Happiness" then the colonists were "equally intitled [*sic*] to Freedom."[44] This led him to conclude that "the inhabitants of these colonies are entitled to the same rights

---

Liberties: Or, the Free-Born Subject's Inheritance of 1682, wherein these views are robustly expressed. There is a complicated publishing history of these texts and their overlapping content. On this, see Winthrop S. Hudson, "William Penn's *English Liberties*: Tract for Several Times," *William and Mary Quarterly* 26, no. 4 (1969): 578–85. Care's text was republished seven times between 1688 and 1766 in Britain, and there was a Boston edition in 1719 and one in Providence, R.I., in 1774. Another digest, entitled *British Liberties* (London: Edward and Charles Dilly, 1766) was also published in 1766 and intended for export to the colonies. On this, see Lois Schwoerer, *The Ingenious Mr. Care, Restoration Publicist* (Baltimore: Johns Hopkins University Press, 2001). For the complexity of Whig doctrine over government and its exposure in the colonies, see Michael Zuckert, *Natural Rights and the New Republicanism* (Princeton, N.J.: Princeton University Press, 1994), esp. chs. 4 and 5.

43. One way of doing that and causing minimal friction was to make the case that at the time of the first settlements the original charters provided the basis for the colonists' claims to English rights; thereafter, however, they developed their own legal codes. See, for example, Christopher Gadsden in a letter sent to both William Samuel Johnson and Charles Garth on December 2, 1765: "For my own part I have ever been of opinion that we should all endeavour to stand upon the broad common ground of those natural and inherent rights that we all feel, and know, as men, and as descendants of Englishmen we have a right to, and have always this bottom amply sufficient for our present, important purpose. . . . A *confirmation* of our essent'l Common rights as Englishmen, may be pleaded from Charters safely enough, but any further dependence on them may be fatal." See *The Writings of Christopher Gadsden*, ed. Richard Walsh (Columbia: University of South Carolina Press, 1966), 66–67. Gadsden was one of the staunchest defenders of American liberties, an early and unwavering advocate of independence and served as a delegate for South Carolina in both the First and Second Continental Congresses.

44. John Dickinson, "Address to Friends and Countrymen," in *The Writings of John Dickinson: Political Writings 1764–1774*, ed. Paul Leicester Ford (Philadelphia: Historical Society of Pennsylvania, 1895), 202. See also William F. Dana, "Political Principles of the Declaration," in *A Casebook of the Declaration of Independence*, ed. Robert Ginsberg (New York, 1967), 117: "The Colonists spoke for, and in the name of, themselves, as British subjects, the equals, in all respects of those native-born within the kingdom. The instances of this character are so numerous as almost to defy recapitulation."

and liberties WITHIN these colonies, that the subjects born in *England* are entitled to WITHIN that realm."[45] What I referred to as the interface above is illuminated by the following consideration: Did equality provide the legitimation for Americans claiming their distinctive rights, or, rather, were they claiming a right to equality that had no specific distinction as a peculiarly *American* right? To put that schematically, was equality a source for the rights that came in its wake, did the concept provide a platform for thinking American rights, or was it merely a constitutional or civil right, hinged with the concept "citizen" and derived from the entry into society? The same friction arises in the claim made by Dickinson that Americans had equal rights to freedom and happiness, since in its wake the question of kind and of the source for legitimation immediately follows: Were those rights precisely the same as British rights?[46]

Seen from one perspective, they could not be since if, as some loud voices in Britain including many (though not all) in Parliament believed

45. John Dickinson, *A New Essay [By the Pennsylvania Farmer] on the Constitutional Power of Great Britain over the Colonies in America; with the Resolves of the Committee for the Province of Pennsylvania, and Their Instructions to their Representatives in Assembly* (London: J. Almon, 1774), 4.

46. One can get the measure of the problem when it is put like this: If one emigrated to, say, Philadelphia from Nottingham (as Joseph Priestley did), the rights one held as an Englishman would apparently move as well. But how long would one have to be resident in Philadelphia before those rights lapsed and, in some mysterious way, transformed into American rights? Or, to put the same case in a more telling light for many residents of the colonies at the time of the Stamp Act, if one's father or grandfather held onto British rights, were these inherited by his progeny? It is clear, for example, that some argued for the inalienable rights of Englishmen without perceiving a distance between themselves as colonists and the inhabitants of the mother country, while for others the difficulty of a view like the following, expressed by James Duane, one of the delegates to the First Continental Congress, lay precisely in the identification with Englishness: "The priviledges of Englishmen were inherent. They were their Birth right and of which they could only be deprived by their free Consent. Every Institution legislative and Juridical, essential to the Exercise & enjoyment of these Rights and priviledges in constitutional Security, were equally their Birth right and inalienable Inheritance." *Letters of Delegates to Congress: 1774–1789*, ed. Paul H. Smith (Washington, D.C., 1976–1981), 1:53. What should be noted here is the use of the past tense: By casting this in the past, it suggests that the settlers—for whatever reason—could no longer claim the same authority for rights. For a contrary view, see Daniel Dulany, *Considerations of the Propriety of Imposing Taxes in the British Colonies for the Purpose of Raising a Revenue by Act of Parliament* (New York, 1765): ". . . their [the colonists'] privileges as English subjects, should be effectively secured to themselves, and transmitted to their posterity." *Tracts of the American Revolution*, ed. Merrill Jensen (Indianapolis, Ind.: Hackett, 1966), 106.

it was fully within the rights of the British to tax their colonial brethren on whatever they pleased, and those rights were, it was also believed, precisely the qualifying identification of being English—this is what it meant to have hard won the liberties and privileges of Englishmen—then how could the colonists claim legitimacy for their rights as *the same* as British rights?[47] Was it not the case that hostilities were entered into precisely over the issue of an infringement of American rights?[48] Rights immediately appear here as a contested ground upon which a claim to person is made: If colonists were in fact subjects of the crown, how could they also have distinct rights—in their own right, as it were—*as colonists*? How could the action of the British government on behalf of the King, the passing of legislation that taxed pretty much every use of paper in the widely detested Stamp Act, essentially break apart a concept of rights that heretofore had been held in common by both residents of the mother country and those in her colonies? Did this not imply that Americans held their rights as Americans?[49] As John Wesley, an opponent of the patriot colonial claims, was harshly reminded by a pro-American, the British Parliament had "no

47. An alternative view is expressed in a pamphlet published in New York during the Stamp Act crisis in which it is argued that Americans were faced with only one course of action, to "claim *an alienable Right* to all the Privileges of Englishmen.—As Freemen, Subjects of the same Prince, They consider themselves upon an *equal Footing* with the Freemen of Great-Britain." See *Considerations upon the Rights of the Colonists to the Privileges of British Subjects, Introduc'd by a Brief Review of the Rise and Progress of English Liberty, and Concluded with Some Remarks upon our Present Alarming Situation* (New York: John Holt, 1766), 17. Note here the play of terms indicating national identification: *British, English.*

48. See the North Carolinans' urging of the Continental Congress "to take such measures as they may deem prudent to effect the purpose of describing with certainty the rights of *Americans*; repairing the breaches made in those rights; and for guarding them for the future." *South Carolina Gazette*, June 16, 1766. See also Edmund Pembleton, the Virginian delegate to the First Continental Congress, writing to Joseph Chew on June 20, 1774: "Our Assembly was sitting last Month, when we received [an] Authentic copy of the Act of Parliament for stopping the trade and harbour of Boston [which] we could not avoid considering as a common Attack upon American Rights." *The Letters and Papers of Edmund Pembleton, 1734–1803*, collected and edited by David John Mays (Charlottesville: Virginia Historical Society, University Press of Virginia, 1967), 1:93.

49. Roger Sherman, one of the Connecticut delegates at the First Continental Congress, after having read James Otis, *The Rights of the British Colonies Asserted and Proved* (Boston: Edes and Gill, 1764), thought that "the Rights of America" had been conceded away. See John Adams, *Diary and Autobiography of John Adams*, ed. L. H. Butterfield (Cambridge, Mass.: Belknap Press of Harvard University Press, 1961), 2:100.

right to *grant* privileges to a people, who *have* as much themselves, an *inherent indefeasible* right to those privileges."[50] The consequence of this way of thinking meant that from then on the colonists would have to find an alternative source of legitimation for what they claimed as their rights. One way of doing that would be the generation and adoption of a legally binding document that set into stone the rights of Americans, as Benjamin Franklin noted in 1774.[51] As can be seen from the many instructions issued by the different bodies in each colony (assemblies, House of Burgesses, etc.) who sent delegates to the First Continental Congress the need to "ascertain" American rights had become urgent.[52] In putting it this way, I mean to draw attention to the strains and pressures within the architecture of the concept of rights putatively held in common between the colonists and the British that began to surface as the patriots tried to find justification for what many felt to be increasingly unavoidable: separation from the mother country.[53] In the terms I am going to develop, they were then

50. *A Second Answer to Mr John Wesley. Being a Supplement to the Letter of Americanus, in Which the Idea of a Supreme Power, and the Nature of Royal Charters, Are Briefly Considered* (London: Wallis and Stonehouse, 1775), 13.

51. See Benjamin Franklin, letter from London to Joseph Galloway: "I wish most sincerely with you that a Constitution was form'd and settled for America, that we might know what we are & what we have, what our Rights and what our Duties in the Judgment of this Country as well as in our own." *The Writings of Benjamin Franklin*, ed. Albert Henry Smyth (New York: n.p., 1906), 6:196.

52. See Pennsylvania assembly instructions: "There is an absolute necessity that a Congress of deputies . . . form and adopt a plan for the purposes of obtaining redress of American grievances, ascertaining American rights upon the most solid and constitutional principles . . ." July 22, 1774; North Carolina sent instructions: "to effect the purposes of describing with certainty the rights of Americans," September 14, 1774; Massachusetts sent delegates authorized to enact measures "for the recovery and establishment of their just rights and liberties," June 17, 1774; New Hampshire sent its delegates to "secure and perpetuate their rights," July 21, 1774. All in *American Archives, Fourth Series* (Washington, D.C.: n.p., 1837), 1:893–94.

53. This was a conceptual problem common to all in the colonies, not just those who either strenuously or reluctantly advocated rebellion. It is important to recall, however, that far from all colonists agreed with the Second Continental Congress and its declaration of independence issued in 1776. Furthermore, within the complexities of colonial social and political life, the identification with Britishness was to become inflected in rather strange ways once hostilities commenced since, as we now know in rather greater detail that heretofore, a number of slaves joined forces with His Majesty's troops in opposition to Washington's army. The differences between the colonial and British contexts within which the concept of rights was networked can be gleaned from data developed out of the Burney collection of English newspapers and the database

forced to explore other ways of legitimating their claims, and this in turn opened up the possibility of discovering or inventing a different architecture for the concept of rights.[54]

The opening of this new account for the legitimacy of rights claims can be detected in one of the most substantial documents on the topic penned in 1764 by James Otis and published in Boston on July 23 of that year. Although Otis retracted many of the opinions expressed in this pamphlet the following year, his formulation of the distinctiveness of different kinds of rights played into the problem that was going to emerge in the years leading up to independence. Furthermore, his sensitivity to the differences in how the rights-bearing person was described (which is to say under which rubric one claimed a right) focused—perhaps unwittingly—upon the issue of a singular architecture for rights in a very eye-catching manner. Thus, in asking his reader to imagine a parliament that might "give a decisive blow to every charter in America, and declare them all void," he says such a thing would be impossible: "What could follow from all this," he asks, "that would shake one of the essential, natural, civil or religious rights

---

Early American Newspapers. Over the course of the century, for example, to *secure rights* appears 285 times in American newspapers and 20 times in English; to *preserve* appears 248 times in American and 26 times in English newspapers. This powerfully indicates how the colonists thought differently about rights in comparison to their compatriots in England.

54. Part of the conceptual issue here concerns the nature of emigration. If, as many colonists believed, when they left the mother country they brought with them their British rights (as a petition to George III from New Jersey pointed out, "the subjects thus emigrating, brought with them, as inherent in their persons, all the rights and liberty of natural-born subjects within the parent state"; *The Scots Magazine* 30 (1768), 522), did this imply that now, when on colonial soil, those rights remained "British"? Or were they also required at the same time to acknowledge "subjection to the mother state" as another writer put it in the same journal? See letter of June 3, 1774, *The Scots Magazine* 36 (1774), 282. This matter is, of course, complicated by the fact that many emigrants were fleeing a restrictive, if not repressive, regime with regard to the freedom of conscience. As the Massachusetts House of Representatives noted, the "great Design of our Ancestors, in leaving the Kingdom of England, was to be freed from a Subjection to its spiritual Laws and Courts, and to worship God according to the Dictates of their Consciences." The point was to remove themselves from the jurisdiction of Parliament, which "might make what ecclesiastical Laws they pleased, expressly to refer to them [the colonists], and place them in the same Circumstances with respect to religious Matters, to be relieved from which was the Design of their Removal." See John Phillip Reid, ed., *The Briefs of the American Revolution* (New York: New York University Press, 1981), 70–72.

of the Colonists?" Immediately he supplies the answer: " Nothing."[55] What needs to be noted here is the list of qualifiers attached to rights. Although he does not say it—and indeed one way of reading this list is to simply take it as a set of overlapping terms that leave no remainder—the list implies a set of differences and qualifications among kinds of rights. And those differences are amplified by the description of rights holders that follows in the next sentence: "They would be men, citizens and British subjects after all."[56] Once again, although it is possible to read this as a list of overlapping terms, that to be a man is identical to being a citizen and a British subject, it is also the case that it can be read as indicating the differences between them. That difference would be marked even more strongly if the list were to read "they would be men, citizens and American subjects." It could be said that some of the patriot colonists' most intransigent opponents would have been more comfortable with the order of these terms reversed, moving from the general to the specific: Rights holders were first British subjects, second citizens, and only lastly in any qualifying sense "men" because it was only in Britain that rights were truly protective of civil liberty.

Otis takes pains to douse his readers' fears that their rights might be traduced by the British Parliament in his assertion that "there are, thank God, natural, inherent and inseparable rights as men, and as citizens, that would remain after the so much wished for catastrophe"[57]—once more strengthening the reading proposed above in which the distinctions and differences between holding rights as a man and as a citizen are respected. Furthermore, as Otis makes clear, although the rights that are "inherent and inseparable" may include the aforementioned civil or religious rights, there is also a possibility that they do not. Here, then, is the opening of the thought that these inherent rights are different in kind. And the most important difference is that such rights may not be susceptible of full enumeration. Thus, in a phrase that is going to have extraordinary weight twelve years later in Jefferson's characterization of the colonists' rights, Otis intones the common argument about the Britishness of the rights he is claiming: "Every British subject born on the continent of America," he notes, "is by the law of God and nature, by the common law, and by act of parliament (exclusive of all charters from the Crown) entitled to all the natural, essential, inherent and inseparable rights of our fellow subjects

55. James Otis, *The Rights of the British Colonies Asserted and Proved* (Boston: Edes and Gill, 1764), 33.

56. Ibid.

57. Ibid., 34.

in Great Britain."[58] So far, so good: The argument of commonality stated once again. And then the phrase appears: "Among those rights are the following . . ."[59] It is, I believe, a significant moment in which the thought that such rights could never be fully articulated enters the culture.[60] Although the impact this thought had was negligible in 1764, twelve years later it set a fire whose effects were the establishment of the first modern republic grounded upon a concept of rights that to this very day builds aspirations for a form of equality that would be truly liberating.

Two years later Richard Bland, a Virginian who served in the Virginia House of Burgesses from 1742 until 1775 and was a delegate to the First Continental Congress, published a pamphlet that provides further evidence for this emergent new architecture for the concept of rights. Bland was considered to be one of the most reliable authorities on colonial legal history, and his *An Inquiry into the Rights of the British Colonies* was first published on March 7, 1766, reprinted in the *Virginia Gazette* on March 30, 1766, and subsequently published in London in 1769. As will become clear, the contractarian account of civic rights was to some extent common currency across the colonies, upheld by both those who came at the question of rights from a predominantly religious perspective as well as those whose entry point was the law. Bland, in noting that "Men in a State of Nature are absolutely free and independent of one another as to sovereign jurisdiction," is merely echoing what by then, in 1766, was certainly in the common mind of America: that all men are created equal.[61] He continues: "But when they enter into a Society, and by their own consent

58. Ibid., 35.

59. Ibid.

60. The phrase was adopted by the freeholders of Boston in 1772 in a document that was possibly written by Samuel Adams: "All Persons born in the British American Colonies are by the laws of God and nature . . . entitled to all the natural essential, inherent and inseparable Rights Liberties and Privileges of Subjects born in Great Britain, or within the Realm. Among those Rights are the following . . ." See [Samuel Adams?], "A State of the Rights of the Colonists," in *Tracts of the American Revolution*, ed. Merrill Jensen (Indianapolis, Ind.: Hackett, 1966), 239.

61. Richard Bland, *An Inquiry into the Rights of the British Colonies* (Williamsburg, Va.: Alexander Purdie & Co, 1766), 9. See also Abraham Williams, *An Election Sermon* (Boston: n.p., 1762): "All Men being naturally equal, as descended from a common parent"; John Tucker's *Election Sermon* delivered in Boston in 1771: "All men are naturally in a state of freedom, and have an equal claim to liberty" (13). And being created equal it followed that they were *equal in rights* to their British forebears and current masters. In some hands this view meant that equality functioned as load bearing in respect to the concept of rights. On this, see John Phillip Reid, *Constitutional History of the Ameri-*

become members of it, they must submit to the Laws of Society according to which they agree to be governed."[62] This submission to law, however, does not dissolve an individual's inherent rights since, "though they must submit to the laws, so long as they remain members of the Society, yet they retain so much of their natural freedom as to have a Right to retire from the Society, to renounce the Benefits of it, to enter into another Society, and to settle in another Country."[63] Such a right, Bland notes, is built upon a singular original right to happiness: "This natural Right," Bland continues, "remains with every Man, and he cannot justly be deprived of it by any civil Authority."[64] If there is an essence to being a man, then, a quality that is both nonnegotiable and, at the same time, constructive, that which determines its specific character, it is the right to happiness. In terms of the distinctive form of conceptual analysis I have been developing, the right to happiness operates with an axiomatic modality, and its function is load bearing. "Man" becomes intelligible when thought through the concept of "rights." Of course this still leaves hanging the precise utilities of "happiness."

I do not want to suggest that Bland is either original or distinctive in his characterization of a natural right as something retained by a citizen in society, nor am I particularly concerned with the precise details of the transmission of these ideas.[65] Rather, I wish to highlight the problem that

can Revolution: The Authority of Rights (Madison: University of Wisconsin Press, 1968), ch. 10.

62. Richard Bland, *An Inquiry into the Rights of the British Colonies* (Williamsburg, Va.: Alexander Purdie & Co, 1766), 9–10. As John Phillip Reid points out, the crucial issue for the colonists was "consent": If the colonists' consent was to be defined by the British Parliament, it removed the link between ownership and consent that made the latter incoherent. See John Phillip Reid, *Constitutional History of the American Revolution: The Authority of Rights* (Madison: University of Wisconsin Press, 1968), 41–44.

63. Richard Bland, *An Inquiry into the Rights of the British Colonies* (Williamsburg, Va.: Alexander Purdie & Co, 1766), 10.

64. Ibid.

65. For debates about the presence (determining or not) of the natural law tradition in the formation of the colonists' political ideology, see J. C. D. Clark, *The Language of Liberty 1660–1832: Political Discourse and Social Dynamics in the Anglo-American World* (Cambridge: Cambridge University Press, 1994), esp. 93–110; Michael Zuckert, *The Natural Rights Republic: Studies in the Foundation of the American Political Tradition* (Notre Dame, Ind.: University of Notre Dame Press, 1996); and, for a reliable and detailed account of the natural law tradition in its wider context, see Knud Haakonssen, *Natural Law and Moral Philosophy: From Grotius to the Scottish Enlightenment* (Cambridge: Cambridge University Press, 1996).

became increasingly evident as the colonists attempted to conceptualize their rights under the aegis of a government that many saw as acting ultra vires.[66] Bland's way of thinking is initially directed by the architectural element of the deposit; for him, as for Jefferson, the natural rights tradition provided the concept of "right(s)" operating with a containing function, thereby identifying a specific set of rights that could be marshaled together under one rubric, a coherent and politically effective bulwark against the encroachments of a potentially repressive (and self-interested) government. Thus Bland states that "members of the society have a Right to retire from the Society, to renounce the benefits of it" along with a right to "enter into another society, and to settle in another country," all, of course, associated

66. There is a subtle distinction that needs to be made here between the authority Parliament may have claimed and the authority of the King. If one subscribed to the tripartite allocation of power after 1688, that is, to the classical Whig account of mixed government, the proper jurisdiction of the colonies was to be seen in a very distinct light. As Thomas Pownall put it, the colonies "were dominions of the King of England; although, according to the language of those times [pre-Restoration], not yet annexed to the crown." In those days, he noted, "parliament itself" did not think it "proper to pass bills concerning America." But, at the Restoration "the constitution of the colonies received their great alteration: the King participated the sovereignty of the colonies with the parliament." It was the tripartite nature of the sovereign that upheld the distinctively British form of liberty. See Thomas Pownall, *The Administration of the Colonies. Wherein Their Rights and Constitution Are Discussed and Stated*, 4th ed. (London: J. Walter, 1768), 48–49. Benjamin Franklin was less easily persuaded that this account of sovereignty was coherent, writing to Lord Kames on February 25, 1767: "The Sovereignty of the King is . . . easily understood. But nothing is more common here than to talk of the *Sovereignty of Parliament*, and the *Sovereignty of this Nation* over the Colonies; a kind of Sovereignty the Idea of which is not so clear, nor does it clearly appear on what Foundation it is established." See Benjamin Franklin, *The Papers of Benjamin Franklin*, ed. Leonard W. Laborce (New Haven: Yale University Press, 1960), 14:68–69. It was precisely the issue of sovereignty, or the basis for political and legislative authority, that would exercise the Second Continental Congress. How could one found a political institution on the quicksand of the mercurial demands of individuals? If one could not turn to divine right, or to God, then who or what provided the source for legitimacy? The answer they came up with, of course, was "the people," but it took a considerable effort to convince enough of the delegates that this would be robust enough to withstand the ebb and flow of political challenge. As John Dickinson, a skeptic to the end and the only person in the room on July 4, 1776, to dissent from the majority view, noted: "A sovereignty composed of several bodies of men not subject to established constitutions, and not combined together by confirmed articles of union, is such a sovereignty that has never appeared." Quoted in W. P. Breed, *Presbyterians and the Revolution* (Philadelphia: Presbyterian Board of Publication, 1876), 159–60.

with and intended to provide legitimacy for the action undertaken by most of his audience (or if not themselves certainly their immediate forebears), namely their emigration from Britain. According to this account, "rights" are simply the plural of *right*; they come in a singular common form and structure and can be collated as a set of entitlements with identical claims to legitimacy.[67] The general shape or form of each of these rights is held in common or, if not, is easily connected to or overlaid upon another: While the right to retire from society has a corresponding positive balance in the right to enter another society, both share a conceptual shape or form. One might think of them as having the same outline. In contrast, however, Bland also recognizes that the right to settle in another country is not simply the obverse of the right to enter another society: Here the shapes of the concepts overlap in some respects (doing one may entail doing the other) but maintain an area of noncoincidence. If one were to overlay one upon the other, there would be a remainder. This right, an entitlement for leaving behind the mother country, moreover, is followed in Bland's argument by something that has a very different shape or structure, a right that "remains with every man." If it is true that Bland began by operating the concept of "right(s)" through a containing function, his desire to see rights in some fundamental sense as natural led him to reach for a second conceptual functionality. Thus, when he introduces the notion of universality, the gears begin to grind: The "right that remains with every man" is not to be taken as the property of a privileged few. It is, as he remarks, "natural." This, however, can be taken in two ways. First, since Bland has already referred to the situation men find themselves "in a State of Nature," this right is natural in the sense that it belongs to that state of nature.[68] But it

67. It is noteworthy that procolonial British opinion tended to see this in a slightly different light, as the extension of *constitutional* rights to their colonial brethren. See Allan Ramsay: "Nothing will contribute so much to the peace, harmony, and order of our distant provinces, as a thorough conviction, in their own minds, that they are perfectly secure in the enjoyment of all their constitutional rights," *London Gazetteer*, April 7, 1775, quoted in *American Archives*, 4th ser. (Washington, D.C.: St. Clair Clarke and Peter Force, 1837), 1:242. Of course the issue over the constitutionality of those rights played differently in the colonies since they were in the business of evolving their own state constitutions as primary and determining legal instruments.

68. A contrary view seeks to explode this myth of origin, putting in its place the rational account of positive law: Natural rights, according to Anthony Bacon, an MP at Westminster who had formerly lived in Maryland, "have no meaning: for men are born members of society, and consequently can have no rights, but such as are given by the laws of the society to which they belong." See [Anthony Bacon], *A Short Address to*

also may be taken to be natural in a stronger sense, as "original," a reading strengthened by his observation that "every person therefore who is denied his share of the legislature of the state to which he had an original right . . . must be subject to the Laws . . . he . . . consents to."[69] Although he does not say it, the drift of the argument is that this "original right" must in some sense trump all those others that come in its wake. It certainly looks, then, as if the functionality of this concept of a right that "remains with every man" is load bearing and its modality schematic: It may be used to construct a set of subsidiary rights that rest upon this one original.

One way of describing this move in Bland's text would be to characterize his reaching for a "trump" natural right as the turn toward the language and discourse of natural law, something that was well established in the mother country. This, however, presents a problem on account of Bland's opening gambit, which is to question the legitimacy of the British government's right to tax the colonies. He goes even further, in fact, since after a lengthy description of the British constitution and its laws, he states that the "laws of the Kingdom" (by which is meant Britain) were not in fact applicable to the colonies. In other words, his turn toward the "law of nature" is explicitly meant as an alternative source of legitimation for *American* rights.[70] Something of the same problem can be seen in the background of a comment made in 1774 by James Wilson from Pennsylvania when he asks, "can the Americans," who are, he is careful to point out, "descended from British ancestors" and who "inherit all their rights," be blamed "*by their bretheren in Britain* for claiming still to enjoy those rights" if they are at the same time "bound by the acts of a British parliament?"[71] Since the most recent acts of that Parliament were manifestly antilibertarian, they reduced Americans to the state of slavery.[72] In both these cases I want to

---

the *Government, the Merchants, Manufacturers, and the Colonists in America, and the Sugar Islands, on the Present State of Affairs* (London: G. Robinson, 1775), 5.

69. Richard Bland, *An Inquiry into the Rights of the British Colonies* (Williamsburg, Va.: Alexander Purdie & Co, 1766), 10.

70. Ibid.,14.

71. James Wilson, *Considerations on the Nature and Extent of the Legislative Authority of the British Parliament* (1774), in *The Works of James Wilson* (Cambridge, Mass.: Harvard University Press, 1967), 2:731. Wilson became a justice of the Supreme Court and professor of law at the College of Philadelphia. He was a staunch advocate of the doctrine that, as he put it, "the *vital* principle" of the new American republic was that "the supreme or sovereign power of the society resides in the citizens at large" (1:169).

72. Throughout the long gestation of American unhappiness with the attitude of their British compatriots, the colonists increasingly thought of themselves as slaves.

highlight where the stress falls or the pressure point occurs: It requires Bland or Wilson (and others of the same view) to either reach toward a slightly different culturally available concept of rights (if such existed and could be identified) or to begin the task of building a new concept. Put another way, the shape and modality of the concept "right(s)" as it operated within the natural-law tradition would not quite do the work the colonists needed it to do. They needed the concept of "rights of man." It is instructive to follow why that is the case.

As has been outlined above, within the natural-rights tradition the concept of "right(s)" most commonly functions as containing with a schematic modality. If this conceptual architecture were to be applied in this case, all Bland (who for the purposes of the present argument is merely a stake holder for the aggrieved colonists) would need to do is propose (or discover) a new right that would apply to the colonists' situation. "American rights" would then be defined by their exceptionalism from all other rights: As British rights were to natural rights, so American rights are to universal rights.[73] He does not do this because he feels that there is another primordial conceptual architecture that is being traduced, the original right each and every citizen has to a share in the legislature. From the position of the colonists attempting to justify their insurgence this ur-right might be dif-

---

See "Containing Matters Interesting to Liberty, and No Wise Repugnant to Loyalty," a piece appearing in the *Courant*, a New Jersey newspaper, on September 21, 1765: "the true lovers of liberty and their country, who detest and abhor the Stamp Act from principle, and a certain knowledge of their rights, violated by that act, are far from countenancing, or being pleased with these violences [in the eastern colonies]; on the contrary, they hear of them with concern and sorrow, not only as they must necessarily involve many innocent persons in distress, who had no share in the guilt that excited the public resentment; but also as they injure a good cause, and check the spirit of opposition to an ant illegally obtruded upon us, to deprive us of our most sacred rights, and change our freedom to slavery, by a legislature who have no authority over us." See *Tracts of the American Revolution*, ed. Merrill Jensen (Indianapolis, Ind.: Hackett, 1966), 87; On July 31, 1770, the Massachusetts House of Representatives took Lieutenant Governor Thomas Hutchinson to task over the same issue. Hutchinson in reply said, "Your quotation from Mr Locke, detached as it is from the rest of the treatise, cannot be applied to your case. I know of no attempt to enslave or destroy you. . . ." Thomas Hutchinson, *The History of the Colony and Province of Massachusetts-Bay* (Cambridge, Mass.: Harvard University Press, 1936), 3:395.

73. Of course this parallelism has continued to be vexatious for Americans who buy into the notion of universal rights. At the heart of rights-speak, American style, there is an identification issue that needs to be negotiated: How to revalue the exceptionalism of the American founding?

ferent in kind; it could not simply be the original form that contained each subsequent identification of a claim or entitlement; that is, its function could not be containing, and its modality could not be schematic, applied to every case in which a claim might be made. Moreover, it was difficult to understand if its lineage could (or should) be traced back to the traditions of political theorizing that were so well established in the mother country. There, back home, within the natural-law tradition the fiction of the presocietal state of mankind was openly declared: No one was supposed to think that man was ever in a state of pure nature.[74] It was, in effect, a legal fiction.[75] Bland, however, is trying to find a basis for legitimating a course of action that did not depend upon a concept of rights built upon the fragile foundations of a fiction. He therefore holds to a literal interpretation of the founding story: In the beginning, man was in a pure state of nature. As far as he was concerned there *was* a time before society. And the only way we can connect back to it is through our invocation of natural law: "As then we can receive no Light from the Laws of the Kingdom, or from ancient History, to direct us in our Inquiry, we must have recourse to the Law of Nature, and those Rights of Mankind which flow from it."[76]

74. Pufendorf is commonly attributed with the most forthright articulation of this position. For him the only historical fact that could be defended in respect to the "state of nature" proposition was that early mankind had been in a "state of *Natural Liberty*." See Samuel Pufendorf, *The Whole Duty of Man, According to the Law of Nature*, ed. Ian Hunter and David Saunders (Indianapolis: Liberty Fund, 2003), 169.

75. It would be fair to say that some attempted to claim that the original contract was a historical fact; most, however, agreed that although a fiction it was nevertheless treated within the common law as a reality. On this, see William Paley, *The Principles of Moral and Political Philosophy* (London: R. Faulder, 1785), esp. 417–18. It is important to note that when the term *contract* was used by eighteenth-century commentators on rights, a certain ambiguity surrounded it: On the one hand, they may have been referring to the "social contract" and, on the other, to what was called "the original contract." Blackstone, for example, denied that there was a social contract, putting great stress on the original contract as a source of legitimation for constitutional power. Locke, however, is said to have confused the two, or to have seen the original contract as kind of exchange of reciprocal promises. On this see John Phillip Reid, *Constitutional History of the American Revolution: The Authority of Rights* (Madison: University of Wisconsin Press, 1968), 132–38; "Introduction" in John Locke, *Two Treatises of Government*, ed. Peter Laslett, 2nd ed. (Cambridge: Cambridge University Press, 1967), 113.

76. Richard Bland, *An Inquiry into the Rights of the British Colonies* (Williamsburg, Va.: Alexander Purdie & Co, 1766), 14.Within the context of escalating hostility from the British government, Nathaniel Niles delivered a sermon on June 5, 1774, in which he noted that "we are now called on . . . to struggle for the preservation of those rights of

On first reading this might look like an appeal to the natural-law tradition coupled to the contractarian account of the move from the state of nature to society. It looks as if natural rights are to be somehow converted into positive constitutional rights. But Bland resists that move, arguing instead that, since neither do the laws of Britain provide guidance in the current situation in the colonies nor can any other historical precedent of any use be found, another source for the legitimation of the rights the colonists were claiming must be ascertained.[77] One must look back to the moment before man entered society, where "man" is understood not only as a generality embedded in deep history but also as a specific case now in the present, as precisely the colonists themselves. Bland is effectively stating that the colonists have in some strange way returned to the state of nature, thereby occupying both the present and the moment of human origin simultaneously.[78] And there in that strangely foreshortened historical temporality they have access to a different concept of rights, one which draws its legitimacy from its being coeval with being itself. This temporality—I shall call it the historic continuous present—is one of the signatures of a different architecture for a concept of rights that has the potential for enabling one to think the social and political differently. It is important to note here that the issue of priority is only marginal in relation to this

---

mankind which are inexpressibly dear." *Two Discourses on Liberty* (Newburyport, Mass.: I. Thomas and H. W. Tingers, 1774), 32.

77. The same issue over the source of legitimation for American rights was raised with respect to the authority of textual precedent in Silas Downer's *A Discourse at the Dedication of the Tree of Liberty*, given in 1768. Downer notes that "it is of the very essence of the *British* constitution, that the people shall not be governed by laws, in the making of which they had no hand." This is enshrined in the "great charter of liberties, commonly called *Magna Charta*." But is not this document that gives "the privileges therein mentioned" legitimacy, nor do the charters under which the independent colonies operated provide the authority for colonial rights. These documents, Downer notes, are merely "declaratory of our rights." As shall become evident, the force of this observation and what it meant to "declare" rights took on especial significance for the colonists as they found their way to independence. See *The American Republic: Primary Sources*, ed. Bruce Frohnen (Indianapolis, Ind.: Liberty Fund, 2001), 141.

78. During the debate on whether the Second Continental Congress could legitimately "institute" government held between the thirteenth and fifteenth of May 1776, James Wilson, one of the Pennsylvania delegates, argued that if the colonists effectively destroyed the proprietary governments they worked under (essentially acting according to the principles established by their various charters), "the people will be instantly in a State of Nature." See John Adams, *Diary and Autobiography of John Adams*, ed. L. H. Butterfield (Cambridge, Mass.: Belknap Press of Harvard University Press, 1961), 2:240.

difference in architecture. In claiming that one has "recourse to the Law of Nature," understood as the *first* law, one is merely insisting on there being a trump. The real difference in shape or form for the concept is determined by the fact that its tense allows one to think an origin without a future. Thinking this way prevents the stacking of one right upon another as the ur-concept bears that load, as it also prevents the corralling of rights within a single frame or container. Both of these conceptual functions, the load bearing and containing, are prone to produce sequential and chronological thinking. In this case a linear narrative would adequately explain the situation of the colonists in terms of their rights: First, man is in a state of nature, then he enters society, then positive law is formulated in order to maintain and promote its well-being. In contrast, the distinctive feature of the historic continuous present is that everything happens, always, at once. It blocks or suspends thinking in hierarchies and confounds the construction of linear temporal narratives. Although Bland does not go so far as to say this, his notion of the "law of Nature" is completely "un-natural" if by *natural* one means subject to the rhythms of the natural world, the cyclical patterns of growth and decay. What he really means to get at is the essence of rights that flow from an unchanging nature. Rights, he seems to be saying, at their origin and in perpetuity—that is, rights considered in their "natural state"—can only ever be general and indeclinable, "rights of mankind."[79]

According to this view, the rights of mankind are not a set of distinct or specific rights corralled into a group; "right(s)" is not functioning as a container for a number of different items, say property or civil rights, nor does it provide the supporting structure for the establishment of these (or other) kinds of rights, which is to say it is not functioning as load bearing. In order to see clearly the functionality of the concept in this case, one needs to attend to its most significant feature: its grammar in respect to temporality, to its tense. What Bland is trying to think with is a concept that allows him to understand how—and then make the claim that—in the beginning and for all time, as it were, Men have rights *as Men.* This is precisely the architecture that Paine will use in his proclamation of "Rights of Man." My purpose here is to carefully open out the difference between a trump concept (rights in the original state of nature) functioning as load bearing, the trump here being that which provides a structure for a set of subsidiary rights, say the right to quit society, and a different kind of con-

79. As will become clear in the following chapter, the disagreement between Burke and Paine over the nature of rights crucially identified the issue of tense.

cept that I call noetic, which operates as a trump providing the pathways within which rights in general, unassigned and without labels, may come to be understood as intelligible. And what that effectively means is that the concept "rights of man" enables one to think the human as an origin without a future. One could think of it, at the descriptive linguistic level, as the difference between natural rights taken to be a set of interlinked claims (an ideational concept whose modality is schematic) and "natural rights" understood as a singular indeclinable concept (a noetic concept whose modality is axiomatic). I think one can begin to pick up on this subtle distinction in Bland's observation "that when Subjects are deprived of their civil Rights, or are dissatisfied with the Place they hold in the Community, they have a natural Right to quit the Society of which they are Members, and to retire into another Country."[80] When they do this, they "exercise this Right, and withdraw themselves from their Country," thereby recovering "their natural Freedom and Independence."[81] Here Bland seems to be claiming that the original state of nature *is* recoverable, men are able to regain what they agreed to give up in part on entering society, their "Freedom and Independence."[82] In effect they turn the clock

80. Richard Bland, *An Inquiry into the Rights of the British Colonies* (Williamsburg, Va.: Alexander Purdie & Co, 1766), 14.

81. Ibid.

82. Throughout the constitutional crisis, colonial opponents to the British government encouraged each other in the task of "regaining" their rights. There is, however, an ambiguity over what this may have meant—and indeed it could easily have meant either and both of the following at different times and in different contexts. On the one hand, it might refer to a specific right or set of rights, say the right to decline paying taxes without representation on the body (the British government) issuing such legislation. On the other, it might refer to the return to the first state of society when, as it were, men were in the purest state of freedom. Precisely this ambiguity can be seen in a letter of June 22, 1769, sent by Christopher Gadsden to the planters, mechanics, and freeholders of the province of South Carolina. The second sense is uppermost in his comment "tis the general opinion of most thinking men in this province, supported by that of all America . . . that Such a Conduct [the repeal of the offending acts], *firmly*, *faithfully*, and *generally*, adhered to, must inevitably answer our expectations, regain our rights; and restore us again to the *honourable rank* of Freemen." The first sense, however, is implied three pages later in the following: "Though, I am persuaded, many of you must think, *every thing ought to be risked*, rather than lose the *two main rights* we are contending for, the distinguishing characteristicks of Englishmen. . . ." The two rights he has in mind are "trial by jury and the law of the land." See *The Writings of Christopher Gadsden*, ed. Richard Walsh (Columbia: University of South Carolina Press, 1966), 78, 82, 86.

back and start again from scratch: "The Jurisdiction and Sovereignty of the State they have quitted ceases; and if they unite, and by common Consent take Possession of a new Country, and form themselves into a political Society, they become a sovereign State, independent of the State from which they separated."[83] Furthermore the "compact" that they make is precisely identical in structure and form to that which was made in the country they have left behind: "The terms of the compact must be obligatory and binding upon the parties" and these terms "must be the Magna Charta, the fundamental principles of government, to this new society."[84]

When one begins to see the architecture of the concept in this way his invocation of the "Rights of Mankind" seems to be intended to do rather different work from the concept of natural rights as it was articulated in the long European juristic tradition and associated with thinkers such as Grotius and Pufendorf. Although Bland calls this a "natural right," the right to relinquish one's country, and he takes it to be in some sense an "original" and therefore unalienable right, he is not invoking the legal definition of perfect natural rights, which were understood to be protected by the natural-law tradition.[85] Those rights are conceptually structured through both containing and load-bearing functionalities: Innate perfect rights such as the right to life and liberty fall into the latter, while imperfect acquired rights like kindness, benevolence, or gratitude fall into the former.[86] Bland, however, as noted above, reaches to a different conceptual architecture structured through a temporality that melds the long distant past (mythically construed or not) with the present: the historic continuous present.

83. Richard Bland, *An Inquiry into the Rights of the British Colonies* (Williamsburg, Va.: Alexander Purdie & Co, 1766), 14.

84. Ibid., 14. A Boston town meeting in 1772 went even further: "All Men have a Right to remain in a State of Nature as long as they please. . . ." See *The Votes and Proceedings of the Freeholders and Other Inhabitants of the Town of Boston, in Town Meeting Assembled, according to Law* (Boston: n.p., 1772), 2.

85. Care is needed here since the colonists were far from one mind with respect to what that natural-law tradition legitimated. It has been suggested, for example, that over one hundred and twenty different constructions of the term *natural law* can be shown to have been available. On this, see Paul Foriers and Chaïm Perelman, "Natural Law and Natural Rights," in *Dictionary of the History of Ideas: Studies of Selected Pivotal Ideas*, ed. PhilipWiener (New York: Scribner, 1973), 3:13–27.

86. For a good account of these distinctions and of the natural-law tradition in general, see Knud Haakonssen, *Natural Law and Moral Philosophy: From Grotius to the Scottish Enlightenment* (Cambridge: Cambridge University Press, 1996), esp. 117–20.

Perhaps the most explicit example of how this different architecture enabled the colonists to understand their grievances with the British government is to be found in a pamphlet written by a British sympathizer, Mathew Robinson-Morris, the second baron Rokeby. Robinson-Morris was an independent Whig, fellow of Trinity Hall, Cambridge, and former member of Parliament for Canterbury. He was moved to write a condemnation of the government's handling of the colonial crisis after the North ministry had proposed its Massachusetts Government Act of May 20, 1774. This act essentially nullified the colony's charter. *Considerations on the Measures Carrying on with Respect to the British Colonies in North America* was published in London in 1774, with seven American editions quickly following. The first pages of the tract set out how Robinson-Morris saw the "back story" to the conflict. Although the inhabitants of the colonies were not "themselves the original people of the country," they had in general been born and bred there; they "divided themselves into several different governments" and had undertaken considerable tasks in making the land habitable: "They have felled the forests; they have cleared and tilled the land, they have planted it, they have sown it, they have stocked it with cattle."[87] He goes on to characterize their legal and commercial activities and then begins an enumeration of what can be taken to be their minimum rights: "They are by nature entitled to welfare and happiness,"[88] he says, and have also "a right to freedom in their governments and security in their persons and properties."[89] No one, he states, could be warranted to deprive them of these things. And the reason why this is so is because the inhabitants of the colonies are entitled to the "essential, inherent rights of human nature."[90]

87. [Baron Rokeby] *Considerations on the Measures Carrying On with Respect to the British Colonies in North America*, 2nd ed. (London: R. Baldwin et al., 1774), 6.

88. Ibid.

89. Ibid., 7.

90. Ibid. My earlier suspension of the distinction between British and English rights has purchase here. An important strand in the period's understanding of rights in a colonial context sought to clarify the distinct legal provision for settlers against those settled. The issue here rested on whether the colonists had acquired the land they occupied or, rather, whether those lands were the fruit of conquest. Given the earlier colonial context within which Ireland was placed, the qualifier "English" as against "British" had a certain valency. This distinction was used in both the American arguments vis-à-vis the jurisdiction of the crown and/or Parliament and British accounts of the reach of British law. While earlier legal doctrines placed great emphasis on conquest, and therefore found no reason to suppose that those conquered had their own claims to make under

All of this is pretty standard stuff, taken out of the liberal tradition that Robinson-Morris explicitly attaches himself to.[91] But then the grammar of the concept of universal rights, the historic continuous present, makes its entry: The rights he has enumerated "were conferred upon them [the colonists] by the great Author of their being when he was pleased to endow them with the faculties of men."[92] These faculties enabled them to tell good from evil and provided them with the means for self-preservation and self-defense. And, he notes, "they are common to all mankind." Not only

---

their own legal systems, the seventeenth-century interpretation of the law of conquest tended to stress that the indigenous peoples in colonial America had no settled law or government and therefore no property rights. On this, see Hans S. Pawlisch, *Sir John Davies and the Conquest of Ireland: A Study in Legal Imperialism* (Cambridge: Cambridge University Press, 1985); Martin Flaherty, "The Empire Strikes Back: *Annesley v. Sherlock* and the Triumph of Imperial Parliamentary Supremacy," *Columbia Law Review* 87, no. 3 (1987): 593–622; Daniel J. Hulsebosch, "Edward Coke and the Expanding Empire: Sir Edward Coke's British Jurisprudence," *Law and History Review* 12 (2003), 439–82; Craig Yirush, *Settlers, Liberty, and Empire: The Roots of Early American Political Theory, 1675–1775* (Cambridge: Cambridge University Press, 2011), esp. 34–50.

91. He associates his position with "Whigs before the revolution" and explicitly refers to "the principles which such men as Mr Locke, Lord Molesworth and Mr Trenchard maintained with their pens, Mr Hampden and Lord John Russell with their blood and Mr Algernon Sydney with both; names, which must surely by all Englishmen ever be revered, as those of some of the first among men." [Baron Rokeby] *Considerations on the Measures Carrying On with Respect to the British Colonies in North America*, 2nd ed. (London: R. Baldwin et al., 1774), 10. This position contrasts with the standard Tory reading of the legal basis for Parliament having jurisdiction over the colonies. That case is put most succinctly by Blackstone, who contrasts, on the one hand, "an uninhabited country . . . discovered and planted by English subjects" in which "all the English laws are immediately there in force" and, on the other, "conquered or ceded countries, that have already laws of their own." In this second case, "the king may indeed alter and change those laws." According to Blackstone, "our American plantations are principally of this latter sort, being obtained in the last century either by right of conquest and driving out the natives (with what natural justice I shall not at present enquire) or by treaties." And it is for this reason that "the common law of England, as such, has no allowance or authority there." The colonies were, then, "subject . . . to the control of the parliament; though (like Ireland, Man, and the rest) not bound by any acts of parliament, unless particularly named." See Sir William Blackstone, *Commentaries on the Laws of England*, facsimile of 1st ed., 1765–1769 (Chicago: University of Chicago Press, 1979), 1:104–5.

92. [Baron Rokeby] *Considerations on the Measures Carrying On with Respect to the British Colonies in North America*, 2nd ed. (London: R. Baldwin et al., 1774), 8.

this, however; they also "subsist at all times, in all regions and all climates," adding for emphasis and clarification "in Turkey, in Spain, in France, in Old England and New, in Europe and America."[93] Although he quickly qualifies this last comment—"I don't mean that they are in all these places always, or at this time possessed and enjoyed as they ought to be"—the tense of the concept of rights he is using is clear enough: They subsist at all times. It is perhaps not surprising that this different conceptual form found fertile ground in a culture deeply versed in those stories in the Bible that could be used for making the colonists' situation intelligible.[94] For some, the good book provided a literal description and history of man before he entered society, but even if that literalism was in the descendant, the historic continuous present became a powerful tool in thinking the legitimacy of the claims the colonists were increasingly making with one voice.

This observation leads to a distinction that needs to be respected if one is to gain a substantial purchase on the intellectual milieu of the colonists. While on the one hand colonial America developed its legal traditions within the shadow of both the English common law and the Scottish account of natural law and morals, both of which helped to define and police what it meant to be a citizen or subject, on the other it was deeply immersed in another version of the legitimacy of the state and the relations of individuals to it and each other derived from strenuous articulations of religious conviction (howsoever differently inflected).[95] In this second optic, the grounding or legitimation of rights could eventually be traced back to the gift of the Almighty.[96] Although not all denominations had identical attachments to this line of argument, there was a large constitu-

---

93. Ibid.

94. One aspect of their situation that has only recently received the attention it requires was the necessity of addressing the rights of the colonized, that is the indigenous peoples the settlers divested of their property. For the most part, the colonists understood themselves as rightful owners of their new land either through purchase or the right of conquest. For a good introduction to these issues, see Daniel Richter, *Facing East from Indian Country: A Native History of Early America* (Cambridge, Mass.: Harvard University Press, 2001).

95. For a good account of the complexities of those convictions, see A. Gregg Roeber, "The Limited Horizons of Whig Religious Rights," in *The Nature of Rights at the American Founding and Beyond*, ed. Barry Alan Shain (Charlottesville: University of Virginia Press, 2007), 198–229.

96. This is not to say that the same commitments to a broadly Christian account were lacking in Britain.

ency that bought into the outlines, if not the detail, of an account such as Daniel Shute's.[97] In a sermon delivered in Boston in 1768 he noted that "Life, liberty, and property, are the gifts of the creator, on the unmolested enjoyment of which their happiness chiefly depends."[98] Or as John Dickinson, a lawyer not a minister, argued, rights were not given by kings or government; rather "we claim them from a higher source—from the King of Kings, and Lord of all the earth."[99]

Shute accepted that the pursuit of happiness was, as he put it, the "end of creation" and that "the whole plan of things is so adjusted as to promote the benevolent purpose."[100] This belief, completely at ease with a corresponding espousal of the rationality of man, entailed the observance of a "moral obligation" to "promote their own, and the happiness of others."[101] This way of thinking was characteristic of the Scottish school of moral theory

97. For an account of these overlapping denominational investments, see John Frederick Woolverton, *Colonial Anglicanism in North America* (Detroit: Wayne State University Press, 1984); Jay Fliegelman, *Prodigals and Pilgrims: The American Revolution against Patriarchal Authority, 1750–1800* (Cambridge: Cambridge University Press, 1982); Timothy L. Smith, "Congregation, State, and Denomination: The Forming of the American Religious Structure," *William and Mary Quarterly*, 25, no. 2 (1968): 155–76; A. M. C. Waterman, "The Nexus between Theology and Political Doctrine in Church and Dissent," in *Enlightenment and Religion: Rational Dissent in Eighteenth-Century Britain*, ed. Knud Haakonssen (Cambridge: Cambridge University Press, 1996).

98. Daniel Shute, *An Election Sermon* (Boston, 1768), 9. Shute was a graduate of Harvard and a Congregationalist minister in the town of Hingham in Massachusetts. The concepts of liberty and property were often joined as a hinge; see *Boston Gazette*, February 22, 1768: "*Liberty* and Property are not only join'd in common discourse, but are in their own natures so nearly ally'd, that we cannot be said to possess the one without the enjoyment of the other."

99. John Dickinson, *An Address to the Committee of Correspondence in Barbados* (1776), in *The Writings of John Dickinson*, ed. Paul Leicester Ford (Philadelphia: 1895), 1:262. Dickinson began by arguing for the rights of the colonists as being founded in natural law, but such arguments seems to have found little support. His draft of resolutions for the Stamp Act Congress moved the ground to religious doctrine, noting that the right of no taxation without consent was a "Sacred Right." See John Dickinson, "An Address to the "Friends and Countrymen" on the Stamp Act. . . . November, 1765" (broadside), in *The Writings of John Dickinson*, ed. Paul Leicester Ford (Philadelphia: Historical Society of Pennsylvania, 1895), 1:197. And on this point, see J. C. D. Clark, *The Language of Liberty 1660–1832: Political Discourse and Social Dynamics in the Anglo-American World* (Cambridge: Cambridge University Press, 1994), 96–97.

100. Daniel Shute, *An Election Sermon* (Boston, 1768), 6.

101. Ibid., 8.

that melded the natural-law tradition with Presbyterian accounts of duties and responsibilities. A right, according to this tradition, is the obverse of an obligation, and both were deemed to be "naturally" a part of the "order and harmony of the moral system, and so the general good."[102] Within this type of religious discourse, rights are "natural" in the sense that they are granted by God to man at his first appearance in the world.[103]

The move into society is also seen as a natural consequence of human nature since, as Shute states, "society will afford vastly more happiness" to man than solitary existence. Consequently, as "each individual living in a separate state would be preventive of the happiness for which men were evidently formed" and as "this happiness can only obtained in a social state," it follows that the formation of society "must be not only in their interest" but also "their duty."[104] Once within society it becomes necessary, according to Shute, to create some rules or codes for behavior, but these are once again subordinate to the first command, as it were, the pursuit of happiness: "The design of mankind in forming a civil constitution" is "to secure their natural rights and privileges, and to promote their happiness."[105] This, of course, was to become one of the supporting structures of the ideology of the new republic: As Jefferson will claim in 1776, governments are instituted among men in order to uphold those rights.

It has already been observed that this formulation of the move from a state of nature to society is commonly understood to have been derived from the European traditions of political thought. Within the English-language stream of that tradition, Locke's *Two Treatises on Government* have most frequently been said to play a significant role in the colonists' evolu-

102. Ibid., 7.

103. As Shute puts it, "Though in the constitution of things it does not belong to man to live alone, or without government in society; yet he is invested with certain rights and privileges, by the bounty of the creator, so adapted to his nature that the enjoyment of them is the source of his happiness in the world, and without which existence here would not be desirable." Furthermore, "mankind have no right voluntarily to give up to others those natural privileges, essential to their happiness, with which they are invested by the Lord of all," which leads him to note, contra Hobbes, that civil government is not a "resignation of their natural privileges" but in fact a "method of securing them Given that mankind is," as already stated, "morally obliged" to secure happiness this, the trump right, determines that "in the constitution of things" men can "naturally have no rights incompatible with this, and therefore none to resign" Ibid., 20–21.

104. Ibid., 9.

105. Ibid., 25.

tion of arguments for the legitimacy of self-government.[106] While it would be a mistake to pay no attention at all to this tradition of political theory, one also needs to recover the religious contexts of the prerevolutionary decades if a balanced view is to emerge. For many colonists, the local minister needed to look no further than the Bible for sources of legitimation with respect to rights.[107] And in some respects it is here, in the biblical account of providentialism, that the fault line opens up most spectacularly: Are the rights the colonists brought with them from the mother country, their birthright as British citizens, the same kind of rights bestowed on man by his creator?[108]

106. This was certainly one of the accusations made by British opponents. See, for example, Allan Ramsay, *Letters on the Present Disturbances in Great Britain and Her American Provinces* (London: n.p., 1777), 24: "[The] People of England will be able to see through all the sophistry of the American Pamphleteers, who, having no sense of their own, borrow some from Locke." But note that in his record of the debate held in Congress on September 28, 1774, John Adams indicates that Joseph Galloway's contribution to the discussion of his *Plan of a Proposed Union between Great Britain and the Colonies* included a passage in which he referred to "Burlamaqui, Grotius, Pufendorf, Hooker." No mention is made of Locke. See John Adams, *Diary and Autobiography of John Adams*, ed. L. H. Butterfield (Cambridge, Mass.: Belknap Press of Harvard University Press, 1961), 2:142. Also note that Locke's name only really began to circulate in American public arenas—at least insofar as newspapers provide a window onto them—in the last twenty years of the century. A search through the database of Early American Newspapers gives the following data for *Locke*: 1, 13, 97, 523, 3,512.

107. This should not be taken to imply that only ministers used the authority of religious texts. As A. Gregg Roeber points out in the case of James Otis, a lawyer, "Otis did not have to be explicit in acknowledging his indebtedness to a specifically Christina definition of 'doing justice,' for he knew his audience would understand the biblical basis for his argument. Otis, as a Protestant Lawyer, argued from the local traditions of New England society when he insisted that rights were tied to duties and were quite different from privileges and immunities." A. Gregg Roeber, "The Limited Horizons of Whig Religious Rights," in *The Nature of Rights at the American Founding and Beyond*, ed. Barry Alan Shain (Charlottesville: University of Virginia Press, 2007), 216.

108. There is a very substantial tradition of scholarship that seeks to unveil the role of evangelical religious doctrine and the development of the social, familial, and political ideologies that coalesced into what has become known as American exceptionalism and individualism. That story has not been exclusively focused on the issue of rights, but the current argument should certainly be taken as complementing it. See among others A. Heimert, *Religion and the American Mind: From the Great Awakening to the Revolution* (Cambridge, Mass.: Harvard University Press, 1966); R. H. Bloch, *Visionary Republic: Millennial Themes in American Thought, 1756–1800* (Cambridge: Cambridge University

In 1771 John Tucker, pastor of the First Church in Newbury, reminded his congregation in an election sermon that "the great and wise Author of our being, has so formed us, that the love of liberty is natural."[109] He was undoubtedly drawing upon a common understanding of the basis for holding this view and its implications with respect to rights. Rights, his congregants supposed, were only considered necessary in order to protect liberties, a view derived equally from the juristic and political theory of rights as well as from the Christian account that Tucker goes on to flesh out. But for him and his congregation, the "natural" love of liberty was first and foremost a gift from our maker; it would, therefore, be an error to conflate the rights that follow on from that observation with those rights that are protected and upheld by civil society. As he writes, "Civil and ecclesiastical societies are, in some essential points, different," and this means that "our rights, as men, and our rights as Christians, are not, in all respects, the same."[110] Here very explicitly, then, is a description of rights as differential: The rights one may claim by dint of being human are *not* identical to those one may lay claim to as a Christian.[111] But does that imply they are supported by different conceptual architectures? Tucker's initial inclination is to claim that there is no friction between civil and religious rights because our maker has arranged things thus: "As this divine polity, with its sacred maxims, proceeded from the wise and benevolent Author of our being," it must follow that "none of its injunctions can be inconsistent with that love of liberty he himself has implanted in us," nor can they "interfere with the laws and government of human societies, whose constitution is consistent with the rights of men."[112] Albeit formed out of different rough-hewn matter, civil rights were no different from religious with respect to the source for their legitimation. Thus, Tucker notes on the one hand that the legitimacy of civil government "from whence all authority in the state must take its rise" is "said to be from man." On the

Press, 1985); H. S. Stout, *The New England Soul: Preaching and Religious Culture in Colonial New England* (New York: Oxford University Press, 1986).

109. John Tucker, *An Election Sermon* (Boston, 1771), 5.

110. Ibid., 6.

111. The Boston Whigs in their public statement of rights in 1772 seem to have considered their rights to come in three different inflections. As the *Votes and Proceedings* note, they needed to state their rights "as men, as Christians, and as Subjects." See *The Votes and Proceedings of the Freeholders and Other Inhabitants of the Town of Boston* (Boston: Edes and Gill, 1772), iii.

112. Ibid., 7.

other, however, he cautions against this being taken to imply "that civil government is not from God."[113] Furthermore, one should not mistakenly attribute to any man an "indefeasible right to rule over others."[114] At the end of the day, then, Tucker relegates his rights as a man to his faith, to his rights as a Christian, which define his sense of duty to God.[115] Although he seems to want it both ways—rights derive their legitimacy from God and from our acceding to civil society—he cannot quite find a conceptual architecture that will allow them to sit together comfortably.

So, to conclude this section with a summation of the argument thus far, within the natural-law tradition, the functionality of the concept "right(s)" is twofold. On the one hand the concept functions as load bearing, allowing one to understand how innate, perfect rights (to life or liberty) are fundamental and effectively fixed in number even if a set of subsidiary rights may be built upon them. On the other hand, it functions as containing, allowing one to understand how imperfect acquired rights have the capacity to increase in their number. Within the biblical account, the primary architectural element of the concept of rights is what I call a hinge: The concept of "right(s)" is held in tension with dues or obligations that have been given to us by the maker. In bringing both the natural-law and biblical accounts to bear on the colonists' predicament, Tucker, like most of his compatriots, was unable to reconcile the load-bearing and containing function of "right(s)" without subordinating it to another concept, liberty. Christian obedience and submission to government are held in tension by "a sense of our duty to God" *and* to "civil authority": Both, Tucker notes, are "animated by a sense of liberty." As long as one continues to strive for the welfare and "happiness of all," there will be no danger of carrying

113. Ibid., 11.
114. Ibid.,12.
115. This articulation of rights and duties is a common feature of colonial religious justifications for action. See, for example, Samuel West, *On the Right to Rebel against Governors* (Boston: n.p., 1776), an election-day sermon reprinted in Charles S. Hyneman and Donald. S. Lutz, *American Political Writing during the Founding Era 1760–1805*, 2 vols. (Indianapolis, Ind.: Liberty Fund, 1983), 1:419: ". . . when a people find themselves cruelly oppressed by the parent state, they have an undoubted right to throw off the yoke, and to assert their liberty, if they find good reason to judge that they have sufficient power and strength to maintain their ground in defending their just rights against their oppressors; for, in this case, by the law of self-preservation, which is the first law of nature, they have not only an undoubted right, but it is their indispensable duty, if they cannot be redressed any other way, to renounce all submission to the government that has oppressed them."

"liberty beyond its just bounds."[116] Throughout the eighteenth century across the British Empire, the specter of an unlicensed authority legislating beyond its legitimate boundaries appeared in the background of much political discussion. Within the Whig tradition, rights, under this cloud, were first and foremost guarantors of freedom from oppressive government. Rights stood between the citizen and slavery. Small wonder, then, that the colonists increasingly invoked the pitiful lot of the slave in their attempts to formulate the grievances they held against their masters in His Majesty's government.[117]

The preceding discussion has opened up the various ways in which the concept of "right(s)" was mobilized in the heterodox cultures of the colonies in the immediate lead-in to revolution. I have argued that the two predominant traditions the colonists drew upon, the natural-law tradition and the biblical (howsoever interpreted in distinct denominational contexts), failed to provide either singly or conjointly an architecture for a concept of rights that would enable the discernment and proclamation of *American* rights. Such rights, by necessity within the politico-legal framework assumed by the colonists to define their situation, needed to be seen to be based on an unimpeachable authority.[118] The solution to this problem was to be found elsewhere, in the invention of a new conceptual architecture.

116. Ibid., 39.

117. The ubiquity of the charge of being "enslaved" by the British underlines the complexity of the colonists conceptual map for understanding their position since the concept of slavery is networked to biblical ideas of free will, political ideas of justice and socioethnic conceptions of national identity. Britons, it was commonly stated, could never be slaves. For a good account of this, see Joyce Appelby, "Liberalism and the American Revolution," in *Liberalism and Republicanism in the Historical Imagination* (Cambridge, Mass.: Harvard University Press, 1996), 140–60, esp. 155–58.

118. For a parallel account of the ways in which the colonists combined natural-law theory and Protestant moral law see Knud Haakonssen's comment: "The problem concerning the inalienability of rights was central to Americans' understanding and justification of their dispute with Britain. . . . If certain basic rights were to be the moral touchstone by means of which the conduct of all instituted authority was to be checked, such rights must exist on a basis that made them transcend all institutions of authority. They must somehow be inherent to the human species and thus continue to be justifiably held by persons in society as well as out of it." See "From Natural Law to the Rights of Man," in *A Culture of Rights: The Bill of Rights in Philosophy, Politics, and Law 1791 and 1991*, ed. Michael J. Lacey and Knud Haakonssen (Cambridge: Cambridge University Press, 1991), 47. For a contrary view of the authority of nature, see John Phillip Reid, *Constitutional History of the American Revolution: The Authority of Rights* (Madison: University of Wisconsin Press, 1968), 91: "At every important occasion when the American

The Culturing of Rights in the First Continental Congress

In 1774 the colonies delegated representatives to a congress for the purpose of coordinating their individual efforts at resistance to the increasing interference in their affairs by His Majesty's government in Westminster.[119] The background to this attempt at operating politically across the colonies at a manifestly cooperative level was the increasing frustration and anger many colonists felt at the British government following the Stamp Act of 1765.[120] In many ways that act, which had attempted to levy a tax on virtually every kind and use of paper in the colonies, provided dissidents with the first clear focus for collective action and over the next decade the pros and cons of various forms of resistance were debated throughout the colonies. It is important to remember a variety of viewpoints were expressed from within those constituencies minded to stand up to His Majesty's government, and these stood alongside opposing positions expressed by those who continued to support the British. This is to note that the decade or so from 1765 was characterized by vigorous debate within the colonies in which various fault lines were exposed: between different religious convictions, different social and political affiliations within and across settled communities in distinct colonies.[121] These differences were grounded in a

---

Whig leadership gathered to claim rights and state grievances, nature was rejected as the sole authority of rights." As will be seen below, the delegates to the First Continental Congress took no chances: They claimed legitimacy for their rights from as many sources as they could.

119. For a good overview, see Jack N. Rakove, *The Beginnings of National Politics: An Interpretive History of the Continental Congress* (New York: Alfred A. Knopf, 1979); also see Merrill Jensen, *The Founding of a Nation: A History of the American Revolution, 1763–1776* (New York: Oxford University Press, 1968); Pauline Maier, *From Resistance to Revolution: Colonial Radicals and the Development of American Opposition to Britain, 1765–1776* (London: Routledge & Keegan Paul, 1973).

120. The colonists had first sent delegates to a collective meeting in October 1764, following the Stamp Act. On that occasion, rights had also been at the forefront of their deliberations, as the document issued attests: They declared it their "indispensable Duty, to make the following Declarations of our humble Opinion, respecting the most Essential Rights and Liberties of the Colonists. . . ." *The American Republic: Primary Sources*, ed. Bruce Frohnen (Indianapolis, Ind.: Liberty Fund, 2001), 117. On this, see Edmund S. Helen and M. Morgan, *The Stamp Act Crisis: Prologue to Revolution* (Chapel Hill: University of North Carolina Press, 1953).

121. For a good account of the emergence of a common resistance movement, see David Ammerman, *In the Common Cause: American Response to the Coercive Acts of 1774* (Charlottesville: University Press of Virginia, 1974).

range of investments in the real or perceived ancestral links to the mother country (and those were also split between regions within Britain).[122] Only slowly and occasionally painfully did a consensus begin to emerge across the colonies for creating a singular political and legislative entity intended to replace the diffuse and multiple associations that had characterized colonial interactions since settlement.[123] I want to begin, then, by signaling the complex and often conflictual nature of the political discourse that animated the period between the Stamp Act and the Declaration of Independence in 1776. We need to keep in mind that many differences in opinion could be found at town meetings, in chapel or church, and across colonial settlements. If one were carefully reconstructing the meanings of discrete contributions to this political discourse, it would be necessary to attend to who was speaking, the context within which they spoke (in all senses of context, including the occasion for the speech, and the religious, professional, geographical and social filiations of the speaker) and the purposes of their speech. Such a reconstruction would very quickly reveal that not all the actors in this very varied terrain would have understood precisely the same things from the use of similar or identical words. The present study, however, takes a different focus: My aim is to expose how differences in understanding were determined by or encouraged within a culturally dispersed conceptual network. Furthermore, it is my contention that this network connected a set of distinct concepts that were themselves structured or built in very precise ways. By attending to that structuration I intend to recover the architecture of some of those concepts and demonstrate how a difference in structure necessarily determined specific ways of understanding that were held in common. My strong thesis is that concepts, considered as cultural entities, are the commonly held building blocks of

122. A good example of the need for collective thinking is provided by John Dickinson's attempts to bring the seriousness of the situation to the attention of the colonists. Writing after New York's legislature had been suspended by an act of the British Parliament, Dickinson noted that "if the parliament may lawfully deprive *New-York* of any of *her* rights, it may deprive any, or all the other colonies of *their* rights." See *Letters from a Farmer in Pennsylvania, to the Inhabitants of the British Colonies* (Philadelphia: printed by David Hall and William Sellers, 1768), 5.

123. The real crisis over what such a single entity might mean in terms of the future development of heretofore fiercely proud individual colonial jurisdictions was to be delayed until the immediate threat from His Majesty's troops had been diminished. Much ink would be spilled before delegates once again came together to broker a deal over the eventual shape and form of the union that would emerge from the Constitutional Congress that closed on September 17, 1787.

a sense-making community. This section seeks to demonstrate how a very tightly restricted community, the delegates to the First Continental Congress, who kept shut the doors and windows to the room they met in and who were pledged to maintain secrecy in relation to their deliberations until such time as they agreed to publish communiqués, built or came to share a conceptual network.[124] It is intended, then, as a very focused case study for the exploration of the "culturing" of conceptual forms.

I began by noting that the delegates to the First Continental Congress came from many backgrounds and from all over the settled regions of the continent—the opinions they brought, either their own or those they were delegated to represent, were unsurprisingly varied in their rhetorical clothing and divergent in respect to the aims or objectives they sought to achieve. Some, for example, sought to protect regional or colonial autonomy, while others saw great benefit to the evolution of institutions and practices that would lead to closer association between distant communities. On the one hand, this diverse group of delegates could be said to represent the range of difference across the culture at large of colonial America in the 1770s. On the other hand, their diversity ought to be attenuated by the fact that they were, in effect, a self-selecting group who shared a very small number of characteristics: They had been sent by their respective communities because they were deemed to be men in good, even high, standing, nearly half of them were lawyers, a good few counted themselves among the wealthiest inhabitants in the colonies, most had some (considerable) experience in local politics and administration, and all of them had agreed to represent their communities at a collective congress which aimed (or perhaps fantasized, in the first instance) to filter out the noise of difference

---

124. James Duane's notes of the debates for Tuesday September 6, 1774, indicate that it was "resolved that the doors of Congress be kept shut during the debates and that every Member be obligd under the strongest obligation of Honor to keep secret the proceedings of the Congress until they shall be ordered to be published by the Congress." See Paul H. Smith, ed., *Letters of Delegates to Congress, 1774–1789* (Washington, D.C.: Library of Congress, 1976) 1:31. They met in secrecy, of course, because they were mindful of the fact that under British law they could be accused of treason. That such a view prevailed can be seen from the various minutes of Congress's deliberations, which sought to uphold the distinction between the sovereign and Parliament. See, for example: "To support our laws, and our liberties established by our laws, we have prepared, ordered, and levied war: But is this traitorously, or against the King? We view him as the Constitution represents him: That tells us he can do no wrong. The cruel and illegal attacks, which we oppose, have no foundation in the royal authority." Minutes of December 6, 1775.

in the hope of determining a common set of objectives.[125] If they arrived with a great variety of opinions it was possible if not quite likely that they would part speaking in one voice. To a significant extent this did indeed transpire, and the reasons for that are in part to be found in the precise historical conditions within which their deliberations took place, the events outside Philadelphia that gave a shape and focus to their meetings. Thus, although only the northern colonies and especially the port of Boston were directly in the firing line of the forceful imposition of British rule in the later months of 1774, most delegates in Philadelphia were keenly aware that the same force was likely to be used elsewhere in the colonies. Much of the discussion, therefore, concerned the practicalities of raising an armed force that might resist such strong-armed tactics. This is to note the part that *real politik* played in the construction of a common conceptual lexicon: The pressure to find a coherent plan, not to say resources, for collective defense was a powerful force in driving the delegates toward unity.[126] I am not, however, so concerned as to the reasons why they came to share a view about a future course of action (to be formalized in the Declaration of Independence two years later at a second congress whose participants were not identical) or the precise causes (events, political maneuvering, military needs and requirements, economic and financial realities) that made argu-

125. John Adams, one of the Massachusetts delegates to the First Continental Congress, writing to his wife Abigail on September 8, 1774, from Philadelphia noted that "There is in this Congress a Collection of the greatest Men upon this Continent, in Point of Abilities, Virtues and Fortunes." See *My Dearest Friend: Letters of Abigail and John Adams*, ed. Margaret A Hogan and C James Taylor (Cambridge, Mass.: Belknap Press of Harvard University Press, 2007), 42. See also John Adams's diary entry for August 29, 1774: "By a computation made this Evening by Mr McKean, there will be at the Congress about 56 Members, twenty two of them lawyers." See John Adams, *Diary and Autobiography of John Adams*, ed. L. H. Butterfield (Cambridge, Mass.: Belknap Press of Harvard University Press, 1961) 2:115.

126. By the time they came to meet at the Second Continental Congress in May 1775 the battles at Lexington and Concord had occurred (on April 19) and the siege of Boston was underway. In such circumstances, armed resistance came to be seen as a justified response and much of the time spent in deliberation at the Second Congress took place against a background of bulletins from the continental army. In such circumstances, the push toward compromise and coherence in debate is all too readily explained by the fact that the colonies were now engaged in a civil war within the British Empire. The extent to which American independence was secured as the result of a civil war has only relatively recently been appreciated; see J. C. D. Clark, *The Language of Liberty 1660–1832: Political Discourse and Social Dynamics in the Anglo-American World* (Cambridge: Cambridge University Press, 1994), esp. 296–303.

ments tack this way or that. My aim, rather, is to trace the close detailed history of the construction of a common conceptual lexicon, which became an increasingly valuable resource for the delegates as they attempted to think through the tangled aims, objectives, loyalties, and antagonisms that surfaced repeatedly in their deliberations.

In the preceding pages I have sketched out how the shape of the concept of rights appeared in a few texts published in Boston and Virginia. The geographical specificity is not unimportant, but in turning to the debate and discussion that animated the First Continental Congress one can see the differences and distances of origin, Christian denomination, profession, rank, and class softening as the delegates slowly found a common tongue that was able to speak on behalf of colonial grievances. In turning to the *Journals of the Continental Congress*, then, I want to suggest that, no matter how sparse and sketchy these records are, they nevertheless provide (howsoever imperfectly) a window onto the conceptual universe of colonial America. Of course in respect to that universe in its most general guise—the "American mind"—they provide almost no information since the records for the most part simply note the barest outlines of discussions and record the resolutions taken. And most of this bears witness to the practicalities that were in urgent need of attention. But hidden in these rather sparsely written journals, like traces upon a misted window pane, are the outlines of the convictions held by the delegates that were tested and refined, altered and challenged as they began to construct a common conceptual framework for understanding their predicament. And that process of debate, argument, persuasion, and collective publication—which, as will become clear, had the very significant form of the declaration—effectively created a kind of petri dish within which the concept or concepts of rights were now going to be (newly) cultured. This, at least, is the hypothesis I wish to test.

When the delegates first met on Monday, September 5, 1774, they took as their initial point of business the selection of a president, unanimously electing Peyton Randolph from Virginia. They then appointed as secretary Charles Thomson before turning to the so-called credentials supplied by each colony as the bona fides endorsing their chosen delegates. These documents also outlined the briefs given to each colony's representatives. In the cases of New Hampshire, Massachusetts, Rhode Island, and Pennsylvania, these "credentials" share a remarkably similar language; they find the same justifications for making common cause against the injustices of the British government and, most importantly for the present argument, they closely echo a very restricted formulation in their assertions of colonial rights. Although these four colonies were not in the majority, we shall see how the language of their credentials set in motion the construction of a common conceptual network for rights that I now want to explore in detail.[127]

In the words of the New Hampshire instructions, its delegates were to "attend and assist in the General Congress of delegates," to "devise, consult, and adopt measures" that would have the most likely "tendency to extricate the Colonies from their present difficulties." And, further to that, they were to "secure and perpetuate their rights, liberties, and privileges."[128] The House of Representatives of Massachusetts instructed its delegates to "deliberate and determine upon wise and proper measures" for the "establishment of their just rights & liberties."[129] Rhode Island put it similarly to its delegates who were to consult "upon proper measures to establish the rights and liberties of the Colonies," adding that these were to be "upon a just and solid foundation."[130] The language of the Pennsylvania instructions is not quite so close, but it does indicate that the task of the congress ought to be "ascertaining American rights upon the most solid and constitutional principles."[131]

To some extent the correlation in these documents is far from surprising: As the constitutional crisis gained momentum in the colonies, a fair amount of correspondence was communicated between the various bodies (houses of representatives, burgesses, etc.) that oversaw their respective administrative activities.[132] They were already talking to each other and therefore beginning to share a language for expressing common concerns.

127. The colonies whose "credentials" do not conform to this description were Connecticut; New York; New Jersey; the three counties Newcastle, Kent, and Sussex on Delaware; Maryland; Virginia; and South Carolina.

128 *Journals of the Continental Congress*, ed. Chauncey Ford (Washington, D.C.: Library of Congress, 1904), 1:15.

129. Ibid., 1:16.

130. Ibid., 1:17.

131. Ibid., 1:20. The deputies from North Carolina did not present their bona fides until Wednesday, September 14, but their instructions were very close to the previous: They were to "effect the purpose of describing with certainty the rights of Americans, repairing the breaches made in those rights, and for guarding them for the future from any such violations done under the sanction of public Authority." Ibid., 1.30.

132. Committees of correspondence had mushroomed during the constitutional crisis, and these provided channels of communication that not only kept distant communities across the colonies abreast of ongoing events; they also began to develop a common language and conceptual lexicon for stating and understanding their predicament.

Moreover, the Boston Whigs' foundation of a Committee of Correspondence on November 2, 1772, had a decisive role in linking many towns and communities into a correspondence network that developed the beginnings of a common language for resistance.[133] The procedures adopted by similar committees throughout the colonies and the protocols they followed in their deliberations formed an extraordinarily solid base upon which rebellion could stand. The first real sign of a concerted effort at pooling resources came in 1773, when a group of legislative bodies from four colonies wrote to Pennsylvania suggesting a system for intercolonial communication.[134] The "talking shop" of the continental congress, then, consolidated what had been developing over the two previous years. I shall argue below that the decision to send delegates to this talking shop was instrumental in changing the conceptual network within which "rights" was suspended; indeed it established a new conceptual architecture that enabled the colonists to understand their situation and provide them with "credentials" for the revolutionary move of separation from the mother country.

It is noteworthy that, when the delegates met the next day for the business of drawing up the rules of conduct for their discussions and the determination of the topics or questions, they were to deliberate only one of the resolutions passed has anything at all to say about the content of future discussion. That fifth resolution, passed unanimously, was to appoint a committee "to State the rights of the Colonies in general, the several instances in which these rights are violated or infringed, and the means most

133. John Adams noted in 1815 that there is "another large tract of inquiry to be travelled in the correspondence committees of the town of Boston with the other towns and States, commonly called the committees of correspondence." This inquiry, he maintained, would be crucial since without it "the history of the United States never can be written." John Adams to Jedidiah Morse, Dec 22, 1815, in John Adams, *The Works of John Adams, Second President of the United States*, ed. Charles Francis (Boston: Little, Brown and Company, 1850–1856), 10:196–97. See Richard D. Brown, *Revolutionary Politics in Massachusetts: The Boston Committee of Correspondence and the Towns, 1772–1774* (Cambridge, Mass.: Harvard University Press, 1970); and for an account of how the protocols of the Boston committee was instrumental in creating the revolution, see William B. Warner, *Protocols of Liberty: Communication Innovation and the American Revolution* (Chicago: University of Chicago Press, 2013).

134. The four colonies were Virginia, Massachusetts, Rhode Island, and Connecticut. For an account of how this played out in Pennsylvania, see Richard Alan Ryerson, *The Revolution is Now Begun: The Radical Committees of Philadelphia, 1765–1776* (Philadelphia: University of Pennsylvania Press, 1978), esp. 22–23.

proper to be pursued for obtaining a restoration of them."[135] This made good sense, given the background of the previous two years worth of "correspondence" around the colonies: They were doing as a collective group with representatives from twelve of the colonies what had been happening in towns and communities all over. The format had essentially been laid down by the Boston Committee of Correspondence in its *Votes and Proceedings* of 1772. In that document, the first item was "to state the Rights of the Colonists and of this Province in particular."[136] But of course the fact that communities of American Whigs around the colonies had been formulating their own version of these statements did not necessarily mean that they conceptualized their predicament, still less the basis upon which they found legitimacy for their rights claims, in identical ways. It would be fair to say, then, that at its commencement the most pressing concern was to state what the delegates *could agree* were the rights of the colonies and, having done so, to list those that had been violated. Thus, within the formulation "to state the rights of the Colonies in general," and certainly within the Pennsylvania credentials, there lurks a less confident or settled account of colonial rights. Are we to take this as the rights that apply to all the colonies, the "colonies in general," or as the "general rights" that apply? This is to note that the "statement of rights" was not a simple matter, nor could it be assumed that all would agree immediately to the content of such a statement. It may have been the case that each of the colonies had a well-developed understanding—local, traditional, inherited, or recently articulated—of their rights, but were all these accounts severally and individually coherent? Were there any "general rights" of the colonies in the sense that all would have agreed not only what they were but what such a generality could be? Furthermore, as the Pennsylvania credentials put it, surely the purpose of the Congress must also be to "ascertain American rights upon the most solid and constitutional principles."[137] Thus, in the terms I have been developing, their purpose was to make explicit both the conceptual network that sustained the concept of rights and, perhaps more urgently, provide an account of the sources or forms of legitimation for the rights claims they were going to

135. *Journals of the Continental Congress*, ed. Chauncey Ford (Washington, D.C.: Library of Congress, 1904), 26.

136. See *The Votes and Proceedings of the Freeholders and Other Inhabitants of the Town of Boston* (Boston: Edes and Gill, 1772), 2.

137. In the credentials for the delegates from North Carolina presented on September 14, this sense is also very clear: Their brief was to "effect the purpose of describing with certainty the rights of Americans." See *Journals of the Continental Congress*, ed. Chauncey Ford (Washington, D.C.: Library of Congress, 1904), 1:30.

make.[138] It was inevitable that in the course of doing that work the delegates rubbed up against each other and discovered that they did not hold identical views or beliefs, but of course part of the purpose of the congress was to iron out such differences. That process effectively placed the concept of rights under great pressure, and, where it was found wanting, considerable effort was required in order to explore ways in which what I call the architecture of the concept might be altered. I want to see their deliberations, then, as a kind of "culture" in the biological sense, which had the capacity to grow a new concept or set of networked concepts.

On September 7, twenty-two delegates, two from each colony, were appointed to the committee to "state the rights etc." It would seem that this large committee met the next day and the day following and came to the conclusion that it was too large to be effective. The first meeting, for example, lasted all day on September 8 and produced vigorous discussion. According to John Adams, "a most ingenious and entertaining debate" was had.[139] It is possible to reconstruct some of the debate from Adams' diary entry for that day, although it is necessary to bear in mind that his account must be taken as partial. Colonel Lee, Adams noted, argued that the colonists' rights were based on "a fourfold foundation," that is, on "Nature, the British Constitution, on Charters," and on "immemorial usage."[140] John Jay, the lawyer from New York, insisted that "it is necessary to recur to the Law of Nature, and the British Constitution" in order to "ascertain our Rights." But, he went on, the British Constitution "will not apply to some of the Charter Rights."[141] Lee argued against the view that charter rights were foundational, claiming that the "Crown had no Right to grant such Charters." Another voice, that of William Livingston from New Jersey, noted that "it will not do for America to rest wholly on the Laws of England," which elicited from Roger Sherman, from Connecticut, the thought that common law had been adopted by the colonies as the "highest reason," not because it was the law of England.[142]

138. It might be stretching things too far to claim that they were explicitly setting out to ascertain the architecture of the concept(s) of rights, but that in effect is what they did.

139. *Journals of the Continental Congress*, ed. Chauncey Ford (Washington, D.C.: Library of Congress, 1904), 28n1.

140. See John Adams, *Diary and Autobiography of John Adams*, ed. L. H. Butterfield (Cambridge, Mass.: Belknap Press of Harvard University Press, 1961), 1:128.

141. Ibid., 2:128.

142. Ibid., 2:129. Adams himself was strongly in favor of adhering to natural-law principles, noting in his diary: "Whether we should recur to the law of nature, as well

When they met again on the following day, a consensus seems to have emerged, and again according to John Adams they "agreed to found our rights upon the laws of Nature, the principles of the English Constitution, and charters and compacts."[143] Although various voices had been raised against basing their rights on the law of Nature (Joseph Galloway, one of the delegates from Pennsylvania who was on the committee, was perhaps the fiercest opponent of this argument) the full range of possible sources for the legitimacy of American rights was agreed upon.[144] It appears that the discussion in a committee of twenty-two was too fragmented or cumbersome (too much grandstanding for John Adams) to make much headway since a subcommittee was appointed to carry the brief forward.[145] This met from the tenth to the fourteenth, when it reported back to the larger, twenty-two man committee. That day it was also decided to appoint another subcommittee to "state the infringement of our rights." On September 22, a report was presented to the full congress and read aloud. Even though there seems to have been little discussion of the text that day, it was nevertheless agreed to order a copy be made for each colony. Two days later, on Saturday, September 24, the full congress had its first chance to debate the document at length, but once again there would seem to have been an unfocused discussion that was unable or unlikely to find a resolution since the committee of the whole decided to restrict discussion "to the consideration of such rights

---

as to the British constitution, and our American charters and grants. Mr Galloway and Mr Duane were for excluding the law of nature. I was very strenuous for retaining and insisting on it, as a resource to which we might be driven by Parliament much sooner than we are aware." See John Adams, diary, Sept 8, 1774, in ibid., 2:370–74.

143. *Journals of the Continental Congress*, ed. Chauncey Ford (Washington, D.C.: Library of Congress, 1904), 1:28n1.

144. Ibid. Galloway was extremely conservative in his views about possible action to be taken in response to the imperial crisis. For an extensive account of the local Philadelphia politics during the 1770s, see Richard Alan Ryerson, *The Revolution Is Now Begun: The Radical Committees of Philadelphia, 1765–1776* (Philadelphia: University of Pennsylvania Press, 1978).

Journals of the Continental Congress, ed. Chauncey Ford (Washington, D.C.: Library of Congress, 1904), 1:26.

145. John Adams refers to the long, drawn-out debates in Congress more than once in terms that suggest he began to lose patience: "The Deliberations of the Congress are spun out to an immeasurable Length. There is so much Wit, Sense, Learning, Acuteness, Subtilty, Eloquence, & among fifty Gentlemen, each of whom has been habituated to lead and guide in his own Province, that an immensity of Time, is spent unnecessarily." John Adams, *Diary and Autobiography of John Adams*, ed. L. H. Butterfield (Cambridge, Mass.: Belknap Press of Harvard University Press, 1961), 2:150.

only as have been infringed by acts of the British parliament since the year 1763."[146] This did not preclude their taking the larger brief of the committee at a later time, as can be seen from the resolution passed that day: "Further consideration of the general state of American rights" would have to be postponed to a "future day."[147] At the very start of this extremely intricate and difficult process, then, an explicit distinction was made between those rights which they agreed had been infringed by British acts of Parliament, that is, precisely legally protected civil rights and those that were "general" and said to be either exclusively or not "American."[148]

But the concern over the specific nature of "American Rights" would not simply lie down and fade into a sedate future postponement. Even the more skeptical and less war-mongering faction of the congress understood what hung on that specification. Four days later, for example, Joseph Galloway, the most vocal advocate of reconciliation with the British government, proposed a motion to adopt a plan for "political union" between the colonies and the mother state. While recognizing that the colonists could not be represented in the British Parliament, Galloway nevertheless wished to preserve the political bonds between the mother country and her colonies. In his words, the "Colonies hold in abhorrence the idea of being considered independent communities of the British government."[149] But even Galloway, whose *Plan of Union* set out at length what he considered to be the error of going further down the path of independence, maintained that the colonists had rights that were specifically theirs, that they needed to secure the "Rights and Liberties of America."[150] As the congress had

146. John Adams, *Diary and Autobiography of John Adams*, ed. L. H. Butterfield (Cambridge, Mass.: Belknap Press of Harvard University Press, 1961), 1:42. John Adams noted that specific mention of natural rights was discussed by the congress and rejected: "Two days afterwards [September 22] it was determined, against the views of Mr Adams, that nothing should be said, at that time, of natural rights. This is said to have been caused by the influence of the conservative Virginia members, still anxious to avoid stumbling-blocks in the way of a possible return of good feeling between sovereign and people." See John Adams, *Diary and Autobiography of John Adams*, ed. L. H. Butterfield (Cambridge, Mass.: Belknap Press of Harvard University Press, 1961), 1:160.

147. Ibid., 1:42.

148. It is unclear as to whether the delay in this discussion hinged upon the general quality of such rights or on their more specific identity as *American* rights.

149. *Journals of the Continental Congress*, ed. Chauncey Ford (Washington, D.C.: Library of Congress, 1904), 1:49.

150. Galloway admitted that his report met with "very considerable opposition" and caused the committee to debate it for nearly three weeks. Confusion, he states, was the result: "They did not come to a single resolution for better than a fortnight, nei-

noted the day before, on September 27, their immediate business was to consider "the means most proper to be used for a restoration of American rights."[151] There is no getting around the fact that, by the time of the First Continental Congress, public discourse within the colonies had moved behind the idea that even if Americans brought English rights, as it were, with them when they settled and even if the legitimation for any rights they might claim could only be found in the juristic or moral traditions developed within Britain, there were nevertheless infringements of rights that pertained only to the American case.[152] Although loyalists continued to express solidarity right up through the civil war with their compatriots back in the mother country (and sometimes explicitly wished simply to claim the same rights as Englishmen), it nevertheless became common currency across political factions to speak of "American rights" even if a detailed account of those rights, either in general and as a conspectus or in relation to their specific American character, was lacking.[153]

The First Continental Congress set out to address this very issue, but, as has been seen above, the delegates kicked into the long grass the more

---

ther in stating their rights or their grievances." *Journals of the Continental Congress*, ed. Chauncey Ford (Washington, D.C.: Library of Congress, 1904), 1:63.

151. *Journals of the Continental Congress*, ed. Chauncey Ford (Washington, D.C.: Library of Congress, 1904), 1:43.

152. James Duane made the point in the following way: "It has hitherto been a receivd Maxim that we brought over as our Birth right the Common Law of England, and such Statutes, applicable to our locale Circumstances, as existed at the Time of our colonization; and that these, with our Charter Rights, and provincial Codes, form our Colony Constitutions." See Paul H. Smith, ed., *Letters of Delegates to Congress, 1774–1789* (Washington, D.C.: Library of Congress, 1976) 1:38–39.

153. It needs to be remembered here that opinion in the colonies was divided over the extent and cause of the grievance they suffered. There were, we need to recall, two sides to the debate, one of which continued to support the actions of His Majesty's government and troops even after the first shots had been fired. Given this, the congress was continually faced with the problem of finding a language that would unite the disparate views of its delegates whose task it was to represent their particular colonial assemblies. New York, for example, right up to the month before British troops broke out hostilities in Concord, petitioned the King making it clear that they wished "only to enjoy the rights of *Englishmen*, and to have that share of liberty. And those privileges secured to us, which we are entitled to upon the principles of our *free and happy constitution*." March 25, 1775, in *American Archives, Fourth Series* (Washington, D.C.: M. St. Clair Clarke and Peter Force, 1837), 1:1314. And it was New York, of course, that held out right to the very end before agreeing to become signatories to the document that would finally give a form of words to another kind of right, the Declaration of Independence.

difficult discussion concerning "general" rights; inevitably, then, when speaking of rights they were most likely to be thinking of the specific infringements of rights for which they were seeking redress. But the bigger picture would not simply go away. This is partly because in these early meetings there is a pretty continuous ambivalence in how they conceived of rights.[154] Rights were understood to be both claims the colonists could make under the law they shared with the mother country and at the same time principles for conduct outlined in works of ethics or, more pointedly as we have seen above, in the Bible. "American rights," then, referred simultaneously to specific rights the colonists felt they had "lost," that had been violated or infringed, to which they had a legal claim under the prevailing jurisdiction, and to the more nebulous or at least unspecified-as-yet rights they held as distinctively *American* citizens. The minutes of Thursday, October 6, 1774, for example, indicate that the Congress resumed "consideration of the means proper to be used for a restoration of American rights."[155] Four days later, on Monday, October 10, a unanimous resolution ostracized their colonist opponents for continuing to support the British Parliament, which in turn was characterized as "preparing to destroy those rights, which God, nature, and compact, have given to America."[156] Such statements create tension between these two senses of American rights: They find their conceptual substructure in a shaky conflation of the deposit and the platform. On the one hand the colonists were stating a legitimate claim to the same positive rights held by citizens in the mother country, claims that were upheld by the regimes of natural and common law, while on the other they keenly felt their difference and the need to uphold—to declare, as we shall see—those unique rights Americans held *as Americans*. Quite aside from the basis upon which these American rights were to find legitimacy and justification, there was another glaring obstacle in their path. How could such rights be common to America when the colo-

---

154. John Adams dined on September 7, 1774, with Miers Fisher, a Quaker, and a large number of lawyers the evening before the committee to ascertain rights first met. He reports in his diary that Andrew Allen, the attorney general, asked him, "From whence do you derive your laws? How do you intitle yourselves to English Priviledges?" See Paul H. Smith, ed., *Letters of Delegates to Congress, 1774–1789* (Washington, D.C.: Library of Congress, 1976), 1:33–4.

155. *Journals of the Continental Congress*, ed. Chauncey Ford (Washington, D.C.: Library of Congress, 1904), 1:55.

156. Ibid., 1:60.

nies were distinct legal and political entities that operated under different codes, practices, and traditions of legislation?[157]

Whether or not this incompatibility across colonial institutions of government was felt to be negotiable, it is clear that the delegates were most exercised about the legitimacy of their rights claims. They needed to arrive at a common understanding of the basis upon which they held rights. This is why the "Propositions" that James Duane's submitted to the committee on rights placed such emphasis on the derivation of the rights of the colonists. He claimed that they were first legitimated "From the Common Law of England and such antient Statutes applicable to our local Circumstances, as existed at the time of our Colonization," adding that these rights "are fundamentals in our Constitution." Second these rights were derived from "our respective Charters confirming those rights" and lastly from "our several Codes of provincial Laws."[158] But the to and fro of debate over these first hectic weeks failed to settle the issue. On October 10, a resolution was passed that, in common with the language used by some of the colonial assemblies, took no chances: The legitimation of their rights was to be derived from the three most powerful sources—God, natural, and common law.[159] In this case the delegates were almost certainly echoing the resolutions made in the county of Suffolk, Massachusetts, on Tuesday, September 6, which had been forwarded to the congress and laid before the meeting on September 17. The third of those resolves (which in their entirety issued as a broadside became known as the "Suffolk Resolves")

157. A point endorsed by James Duane's notes on the debates of early September 1774. He states that "much debate" was entered into concerning "the different Rights of the several Charter Governments & their Infringements which must be best known to their respective Representatives were insurmountable Objections. . . ." See Paul H. Smith, ed., *Letters of Delegates to Congress, 1774–1789* (Washington, D.C.: Library of Congress, 1976), 1:36. It is worth bearing in mind that Philadelphia's ruling Quaker elite throughout the Stamp Act crisis and up to September 1768 held on to possibility that they might alter the terms of their legislative constitution and become a royal colony. See James H. Hutson, *Pennsylvania Politics, 1746–1770: The Movement for Royal Government and Its Consequences* (Princeton, N.J.: Princeton University Press, 1972).

158. In Paul H. Smith, ed., *Letters of Delegates to Congress, 1774–1789* (Washington, D.C.: Library of Congress, 1976), 1:40.

159. John Adams notes Colonel Lee proposed four derivations: "The Rights are built on a fourfold foundation—on Nature, on the British Constitution, on Charters, and on immemorial usage." See Paul H. Smith, ed., *Letters of Delegates to Congress, 1774–1789* (Washington, D.C.: Library of Congress, 1976), 1:46.

states that infractions to those rights "to which we are justly entitled by the laws of nature, the British constitution, and the charter of the province" had occurred.[160] And in the fourteenth it was indicated that the inhabitants of Suffolk voted to cease trading with Great Britain—an action they recommended to others—until such time as "our rights are fully restored to us."[161]

The second subcommittee charged with the brief of preparing a report stating the infringement of the colonists' rights had been appointed on September 7. Its eleven members took over a month to prepare their draft, which came before the full congress on October 14.[162] The *Journals* present this draft alongside the annotated document, which records the resolutions as agreed and taken.[163] A comparison of these two documents allows one to inspect the result of six weeks' discussion, debate, argument, and persuasion. The final form of words agreed by the congress not only provided a language for describing the colonists' "rights and grievances" but also the building blocks of a new conceptual storehouse, the armory they needed in order to think "rights" in a more efficacious way. Those long, drawn-out debates were the process by which they collectively participated in the task of conceptual refinement, batting back and forth ideas and arguments that resulted in the culturing of a new conceptual architecture that would enable them to make sense of their predicament. Between "Sullivan's draft" and the agreed text there lies a hinterland of talk that cannot be recovered. Talk over refreshments and food in the City Tavern. Talk in the heated confines of Carpenter's Hall with its "excellent library."[164] Talk at private

160. *Journals of the Continental Congress*, ed. Chauncey Ford (Washington, D.C.: Library of Congress, 1904), 1:33.

161. Ibid., 1:35.

162. Contemporary scholarship has failed to identify the author of the first draft of this document, but by convention it is said to be John Sullivan. The source for that attribution is the draft of an unknown state of the document that appears in the Adams papers, but the most recent scholarship suggests that it is the handwriting of John Dickinson. See John Adams, *The Works of John Adams, Second President of the United States*, ed. Charles Francis (Boston: Little, Brown and Company, 1850–1856), 2:535–42; and Paul H. Smith, ed., *Letters of Delegates to Congress, 1774–1789* (Washington, D.C.: Library of Congress, 1976) 1:193–94.

163. The *Journals* print on the left-hand side of the page the first (Sullivan) draft and on the right the resolutions as passed by Congress.

164. *Journals of the Continental Congress*, ed. Chauncey Ford (Washington, D.C.: Library of Congress, 1904), 1:13.

dinners in the houses two or three blocks away.[165] Talk on the way to the chapel, meeting house or church. Talk in the late Autumnal light, talk late into the night.[166] But the results of that conversation are easily inspected in the common conceptual architecture for American rights that would now provide legitimacy for the course of action they were to embark upon. Just under two years later, the die was cast and the first steps toward the new republic founded upon an aspiration for universal rights were taken. Here then, in the interstices of these texts, one can find the clear outline of a new conceptual architecture being constructed.

It is, perhaps, extraordinary given the preceding discussion of the context in which this first draft was penned that it is to all intents and purposes silent with respect to those specific rights the colonists believed to have been traduced by the British government. It is true that it begins with a long list of grievances formulated in the language of the petition of right: "whereas" the King has "claimed a power of right," "whereas . . . orders have been issued by the King," and so forth. And eventually it rounds upon a "declaration" whose purpose is to vindicate and assert their "rights and liberties." But these are not formulated as a set of specific rights claims. Instead, the draft "declares" the basis upon which their rights and liberties find legitimacy. Thus the "power of making laws for ordering or regulating the internal polity of these colonies" is said to be "within the limits of each Colony" and "respectively and exclusively vested in the Provincial Legislature of such Colony."[167] Consequently any interference from without—by which they have in mind a statute passed by the British Parliament—is said to be "illegal and void." The drift of this is easy enough to discern: The aim

---

165. John Adams's diary entries present a record of his dining companions, noting, for example, that on October 11 he "dined with Mr McKean in Market Street, with Mr Reed, Rodney, Chace, Johnson, Paca, Dr Morgan, Mr R. Penn, &." *Letters of Delegates to Congress, 1774–1789*, ed. Paul H. Smith (Washington, D.C.: Library of Congress, 1976), 1:173.

166. The delegates worked hard—harder perhaps than they had anticipated. Silas Deane sketched out a typical day in the following manner: "We meet at Nine, & set until half past Three, then adjourn until the Next Morning, this brings Us to Dinner at Four or afterwards, which being generally in parties, on invitation out, or at Our Lodgings concludes the Day. We have sat, now, Six Weeks, We have not had One day's respite." Paul H. Smith, ed., *Letters of Delegates to Congress, 1774–1789* (Washington, D.C.: Library of Congress, 1976), 1:202.

167. *Journals of the Continental Congress*, ed. Chauncey Ford (Washington, D.C.: Library of Congress, 1904), 1:67.

is to state *why* they felt aggrieved. What is lacking is anything that might pass muster as "rights talk." It is as if the draft were answering the brief of the other subcommittee.

The text continues with further examples of statutes passed without the colonies, for taxing "the people of said colonies," extending the jurisdiction of Courts of Admiralty for the collection of "rates and duties," the raising or keeping of a standing army within the colonies, and the dissolution or prorogation of colonial assemblies; all are said to be "illegal and void." But once again they are not said to be infringements of rights. It is only in the eighth point under the advertised "declaration" that the word *right* appears, and here it is used to claim "the right of the subjects to petition the King." Another three numbered paragraphs pass by before a general statement about rights appears: "They [the colonists] do claim, demand, and insist, on all and singular the rights and liberties before mentioned as indubitably belonging to them."[168] Although it is clear that everything in the preceding has been intended as a list of "rights and liberties"—the "before mentioned"—the draft fails to make explicit that their grievances are infringements of rights. Indeed its caution in respect to the language of rights is everywhere in evidence. Perhaps it could be argued that the committee charged with the responsibility of drafting a document setting out the specific infringements of their rights was uncomfortable going further. Perhaps they assumed that as British subjects, if that indeed was the consensus in how they saw themselves, they had little room for maneuver. Their best bet was to look to precedent, to the previous petitions of right that had been presented to the monarch.[169] Or perhaps it was simply that a more forceful declaration of rights failed to gain consensus within the committee. The record is silent, but the tracks in the sand left behind by the revisions to the document speak with great eloquence, for the resolutions that were passed have an entirely different character. They are, precisely, couched in terms of specific rights claims.

Although the congress preserved the opening statements of grievances—"whereas . . ."—albeit in truncated form (ten paragraphs in the Sullivan draft as opposed to eight in the adopted resolutions), it was far less shy about openly claiming that rights had been violated. The fifth paragraph ends: "All which statutes are impolitic, unjust and cruel, as well as unconstitutional," adding that there were also "most dangerous and

---

168. Ibid., 1:71.

169. See Pauline Maier, *American Scripture: How America Declared Its Independence from Britain* (London: Pimlico, 1999), 50–59.

destructive of American rights."[170] Then following the same language in Sullivan's draft about the "means of attaining the ends foresaid" for "asserting and vindicating" (word order reversed from Sullivan's "vindicating and asserting") their rights and liberties they proceed to declare "that the inhabitants of the English Colonies in North America . . . have the following Rights." A set of numbered resolutions were then passed, each one specifying a distinct right. And for the most part these rights are explicitly grounded as a set of entitlements.

Thus the first set of rights are said to be "life, liberty & property" to which the colonists claim they are entitled. The second are "rights, liberties, and immunities of free and natural born subjects, within the realm of England."[171] Again the colonists claim that they have an entitlement to these rights. The same term is used in the third (emigration does not surrender previously held rights), fifth (the colonists were entitled to the common law of England), sixth (entitled to those English statutes that existed at the time of colonization), and seventh (entitled to immunities and privileges granted to them by royal charters). Each of the ten numbered resolutions is intended to describe and specify the "many infringements and violations" of what, in the tenth resolve, are referred to as the "foregoing rights." Between the first draft and the adopted resolutions, a sea change has occurred: In the first document rights are almost invisible; in the final approved version of it one could not mistake the fact that the delegates were stating rights claims. And those rights were explicitly designated as *American*.

Almost all of those specific rights would have been recognized by someone versed in the natural law tradition who was also familiar with Blackstone's account of civil rights. There is little here of a specific nature that could be said to disturb a very well established set of principles that had long been the bedrock of liberty as conceived within the Whig tradition. But there are two moments when one can glimpse something slightly different. In stating that colonial assemblies had been dissolved by the British, the delegates claimed that such action was "contrary to the rights of the people."[172] Although this language is not exceptional, it does open the door to a different architecture for the concept of rights; that difference lays in the way in which one might begin to conceptualize universal human rights.

170. *Journals of the Continental Congress*, ed. Chauncey Ford (Washington, D.C.: Library of Congress, 1904), 1:66.

171. Ibid., 1:68.

172. Ibid., 1:66.

The second moment contains a locution that pushes even further in the same direction. It occurs in the fourth resolution, which begins by noting that the "foundation of English liberty, and of all free government" is a "right in the people to participate in their legislative council." This rights claim is unexceptional enough: Of all the grievances outlined by the colonists, the "right to representation" played the loudest tune across the Atlantic, recognized in Britain by both supporters and detractors from the colonists' cause as an issue to be settled.[173] What is worth remark, however, is the formulation that a right *inheres* within the people. This is only a small step away from a very different conceptual architecture, a way of thinking rights that understands the collective to hold them on behalf of the individual. A way of thinking that utilized a noetic concept with an axiomatic modality and adaptive form.

The pressure continued throughout October; a further document was discussed on Wednesday, October 19, referred to as the "address to the people of Great Britain," which set out the colonists' case for a trade embargo.[174] Amendments were agreed and the final draft brought to the committee of the whole on Friday, October 21st. The language around rights in this document is even more revealing in respect to the ongoing "culture" of a common conceptual network. The second paragraph, for example, speaks of the "glorious ancestors" of the inhabitants of Great Britain as having "transmitted the rights of men" to their "posterity."[175] This is the first time the phrase *rights of men* appears in the *Journals*; toward the close of this document we also find the phrase *rights of Mankind*.[176] Now the ar-

173. Detractors never failed to point out that many inhabitants of regions of Britain were in the same situation, both taxed and without any sitting members of Parliament. The notion that two wrongs do not make a right was not, however, frequently inserted into the debate.

174. The draft of this document was prepared by John Jay, one of the delegates from New York. See *The Correspondence and Public Papers of John Jay*, ed. Henry Johnston (New York: Burt Franklin, 1890), 1:17n1.

175. *Journals of the Continental Congress*, ed. Chauncey Ford (Washington, D.C.: Library of Congress, 1904), 1:82.

176. Ibid., 1:89. I do not mean to imply that this form of words had never been used before this occasion. As table 22 shows there is a small but almost negligible incidence of the phrase in American newspapers up until 1774. Perhaps a more useful indication of the phrase having a general presence in the discussion of the Congress is provided by a letter sent from the Virginia delegates to the representatives of the Freeholders of Augusta County in March 1775. In that document, the signatories—Peyton Randolph, Patrick Henry, Richard Lee Henry, Richard Bland, George Washington, Benjamin Harrison, and Edmund Pembleton—wrote that they were pleased to find

chitecture of the predominant inherited concept of "right(s)" can be seen to be undergoing considerable stress, or, to put that another way, a different architecture is beginning to emerge. The same language appears in the second long document approved that day, the memorial to the people of British America, in which the inhabitants of England are described as "the defenders of true religion, and the assertors of the rights of mankind."[177]

It must have been around this time—early October—when talk of rights insistently turned toward the general or universal and the architecture of a new concept, "rights of man," began to become more stable. Evidence for this is provided in a letter Silas Deane wrote to Thomas Mumford on October 16. Of course the change in structural shape I am pointing to cannot be located precisely—it did not suddenly occur—and we cannot know how many of the delegates were involved in discussions outside the formal meetings where this new conceptual form began to emerge. But it is clear that, by October 16 at least, Deane was beginning to work with a concept of rights whose shape was undergoing alteration. He tells his correspondent that the task the congress set itself was easily determined: "Three capital, & general Objects were in View from the First—A Bill of American rights,—A List of American Grievances,—And Measures for redress."[178] He comments that the first of these, what he calls the "bill of American rights," was properly considered the most important and that the delegates all recognized the need to "fix" them "rightly, with precision, yet sufficiently explicit." Above all, these rights required a "durable basis, such as the Reason & Nature of things, the Natural Rights of Mankind, The Rights of British Subjects, in general, and the particular, & local privileges, rights, & immunities of British American Subjects."[179] Deane was following the majority view that had emerged in debate that took as wide or inclusive a reach as was possible in respect to the derivation of rights. As has been outlined above, the delegates thought it wise to use as much firepower as they could muster, claiming the authority of British common law,

---

that their efforts met with approbation, and that the assurances of the people of Augusta in support of the measures adopted by Congress "give us the highest satisfaction, and must afford pleasure to every friend of the just rights of mankind." See *The Letters and Papers of Edmund Pembleton, 1734–1803*, ed. David John Mays (Charlottesville: Virginia Historical Society, University Press of Virginia, 1966), 1:101.

177. *Journals of the Continental Congress*, ed. Chauncey Ford (Washington, D.C.: Library of Congress, 1904), 1:100.

178. Paul H. Smith, ed., *Letters of Delegates to Congress, 1774–1789* (Washington, D.C.: Library of Congress, 1976), 1:201.

179. Ibid., 1:201.

the original charters as well as natural law. Notwithstanding the niceties of the bases for holding to all of these legitimating principles simultaneously, for the most part at the commencement of their discussions they had traded argumentative points around the issue of whether rights were to be understood as specifically American. Here, however, by October 16, one can begin to see a more universal application of rights in Deane's disarticulation of the "natural rights of Mankind" from other local and particular rights, held by both British subjects and what he refers to as "British American subjects." Like the "Address to the People of Great Britain" that was signed off on October 21, the "rights of men" are now understood through the noetic concept "rights of man" operating an axiomatic modality. The forty-five delegates to the congress had adopted a common unshareable conceptual architecture. They had persuaded themselves and each other that American rights were not simply an extension or type of natural right; they were not just British rights planted on colonial soil. American rights were now universal: the rights of all men, wherever they may be, whatever their nationality or allegiance. American rights were coincident with the rights of man. Small wonder, perhaps, that this foundation for American rights would, under the auspices of the Universal Declaration of Human Rights, come back to bite us in the face.

On Wednesday, October 26, the last in this series of long documents was approved. This one was intended to conscript the inhabitants of Canada to the colonists' cause and was referred to as the *Letter to the Inhabitants of the Province of Quebec*. The document begins by noting that the inhabitants of Quebec had also been abused by His Majesty's ministers, who had withheld from them "the fruition of the irrevocable rights to which you were justly entitled."[180] It then continues by outlining what are referred to as the "grand," or "great," rights. The first is "that of the people having a share in their own government," a right also insisted upon by Bland above, which grants to the legislature power to make laws only insofar as they are approved by the people. This, the document notes, "is a bulwark surrounding and defending their property,"[181] thereby linking together one of the principle rights within the jurisprudential tradition, the right to property, with the political right to representation. And the influence of this "first grand right" is said to "extend" still further. There are two things I wish to note about this. First, the concept of "right(s)" is here

180. *Journals of the Continental Congress*, ed. Chauncey Ford (Washington, D.C.: Library of Congress, 1904), 1:105–13.

181. Ibid., 1:107.

functioning in a load-bearing capacity, but its architectural element is the order of the deposit rather than the platform. It is a hybrid or mixed form. Second, the authority and legitimacy of what is taken to be an innate natural right, the right to property, is being carried over into the political right to representation. I do not mean to suggest that there is anything novel in this observation since the banner headline under which the colonists were to come together, "no taxation without representation," was so well entrenched in the colonists' perception of their grievances with the mother country. But what is worth remarking is the transferred legitimacy that is effected by basing the specific right to political representation on the prior inherent right (the first grand right) of having a share in government. I am suggesting here that the authority of the rights claim to political representation in Westminster is founded in a move that essentially embraces a different structural form for the concept of "right(s)," a transition from a plastic or rigid structure to an adaptive one. What one can see happening is the construction of an alternative conceptual architecture as the elements of the deposit and the platform intertwine.

The delegates to the convention clearly conceived of the "irrevocable rights" as specifiable and countable since the document goes on to describe the "the next great right" as that of trial by jury, "another right" relates to the liberty of person, a fourth right is that holding lands by the tenure of easy rents, and the fifth is the freedom of the press. All these named rights are intelligible under the conceptual framework of "right(s)" as it is formulated in the European juristic tradition. These are the rights that government is supposed to protect: positive constitutional rights. They are specific rights "without which a people cannot be free," rights that citizens are "entitled to."[182] Most importantly such rights are held or claimed by persons: They reside, as it were, within the singularity of each individual. But at the same time, hovering in the background, another form of rights began to emerge within the conceptual network that became common property for the delegates to the Congress. And the architecture of this form is slightly different: It embraces the nonspecification of rights, for "rights of man," and for the grammar of these rights to be declined in the form and tense of a declaratory act that speaks in the present-future. Its most transparent appearance can be found in the extraordinary resolution passed by the congress on Wednesday, October 26, 1774: "That we should consider the violation of your rights," that is the rights of the citizens of Canada, "by the act for altering the government of your province, as a

182. Ibid., 1:108.

violation of our own."[183] Two things are noteworthy in this formulation. First, the injury is not to a specific individual or group of individuals; it is to "Man" in general. Second, and perhaps more importantly, it implies a futurity: that we "should consider," not that we "do consider" or "have considered." We should now, in the historic continuous present, in the future-present.[184]

It has been argued by John Phillip Reid that natural law was irrelevant to the colonists in their claims for the authority of rights. By this he means that nature was never cited as the *sole* authority for rights: "Just as claims to natural law are stated in the alternative to claims to constitutional and charter law, so claims to natural rights stated alternative authority."[185] Furthermore, the actual rights that the colonists claimed in their resolutions and declarations were in every case either a "constitutional right or a right derived from the authority of custom, the original contract, the migration purchase, or the second original contract," and where nature was adverted to it was merely to reinforce "the authority for positive or what can be called non-natural rights."[186] This, Reid asserts, was the norm for colonial Whig claims to rights. The point here is that according to Reid the colonists in their official documents never made a claim on any right that was not "already extant in British constitutional theory or English common

183. Ibid., 1:112–13.

184. This sense is strengthened by the closer context: The paragraph begins, "In this present Congress, beginning on the fifth of last month, and continued to this day, it has been, with universal pleasure and an unanimous vote, resolved, That we should consider the violation of your rights. . . ." Ibid., 1:112.

185. John Phillip Reid, *Constitutional History of the American Revolution: The Authority of Rights* (Madison: University of Wisconsin Press, 1968), 91. He does qualify this blanket claim by also noting that one can find claims to rights on the authority of nature alone in various anonymous newspaper and pamphlet accounts. For Reid the fact that the qualified claim—that nature was only one source for rights—is to be found in every "official" petition, resolution, or declaration carries more weight in respect to the colonists' conceptualization of the legitimacy of their rights claims. He does note in passing that this qualified claim is *not* made in either the Boston declaration of 1765 or the preamble to the Declaration of Independence, where nature is said to be the sole source for legitimation. The current argument is derived from an analysis of the cultural dispersion of a conceptual architecture for rights, and, in terms of that analysis, the significant point I wish to make is that each of these ways of claiming authority for rights is founded on a distinctive conceptual architecture.

186. Ibid., 92.

law."[187] In a way this is hardly surprising since the official documents he has in mind—resolutions, petitions, and declarations—were themselves written in the language and according to the conventions of the law, the inherited English common law tradition that underpinned colonial legal institutions. One of the most telling and problematic aspects of the constitutional crisis within the colonies—what made it so singular and troubling—was the fact that once the authority of the institutions of government in the mother country had been rejected (an act that would change everything, from external relations with regard to trade and international relations to the legitimation of courts internally), there was an open field. Eventually, as we know, the solution was to ground the institutions of the state in the consent of the people to be governed, but during the decade or so in which the colonists had to work hard at understanding the legitimacy of their rights claims in the light of a potential separation from the mother country, it is hardly surprising, indeed it was inevitable, that they held on to the current legal code and its conventions. In their official documents they had to couch their claims in terms that would be recognized *in law* by the mother country. That is why, as has often been pointed out since Carl Becker's exhaustive commentary on the document, the major part of the Declaration of Independence took the form of a set of grievances couched in the legal terminology of the English Declaration of Rights that terminated the reign of James I.[188]

In terms of the larger argument I want to make, Reid's assessment of the difference between official and nonofficial accounts of rights claims in the colonies provides further evidence for what I have been tracking: the stress or fault line in the architecture of the concept of "right(s)." It was this that prevented the colonists from fully understanding the basis upon which their action of separation could be justified. The concept of rights they inherited, in both its containing and load-bearing functions, would not do that work. This is why a distinct and new conceptual architecture needed to be cultured, a noetic form that would allow them to make a claim for rights as universal whose modality was axiomatic and form adaptive. It was

187. Ibid.
188. See Carl Becker, *The Declaration of Independence: A Study in the History of Political Ideas* (New York: Alfred A. Knopf, 1956), and for an outstanding account of the legal and political context within which the text was inserted, see Pauline Maier, *American Scripture: How America Declared Its Independence from Britain* (London: Pimlico, 1997), esp. 126–27.

this concept that would provide them with a blueprint or theory for understanding their new republic: Among these rights are . . .

The foregoing account of the early days of the First Continental Congress has been focused on the gradual emergence of a common language for describing the colonists' predicament. That language, I have argued, provides evidence for their increasing frustration with the concept "right(s)," which simply would not allow them to think the exceptionalism of "American rights" with confidence in their legitimacy. On the one hand they were comfortable operating the concept of "right(s)" as a containing form, corralling the separate claims that could be legitimately made within their inherited version of civil society. On the other hand, they recognized that their predicament required the support of a different conceptual architecture for rights that allowed them to find legitimation in a presocietal state that was both recoverable and at the same time an aspirational futurity. They needed a platform that would support the weight of a claim to universality made by the collective on behalf of the individual. The formulation that Jefferson was to come up with two years later, his raid on the conceptual storehouse of the "American Mind," perfectly combines these two: Legitimation for American independence is derived from a set of "truths" said to be "self-evident." Men are equal, and their being is coincident with the possession of rights. Some of those rights are nameable, the civil rights of life and liberty, but others remain unnamed and potentially unnameable. The concept of "right(s)" could now be bolstered by a trump claim that trumped all others, a claim to "rights of man," where "man" is the singular universal in a common unshareable culture.

Coda: The American Mind Post-Declaration

If the foregoing has accurately identified the different conceptual architectures available to or fabricated by the delegates to the First Continental Congress, what transpired following the historic "Declaration" of independence nearly two years later? This is to ask, what happened between 1776 and 1791 when the Bill of Rights was enacted as a set of amendments to the Constitution? How did the aspirational force put into circulation by thinking through the noetic concept of "rights of man" fail to set its mark on the documents that enshrine to this day Americans' sense of belief in their rights? How did the ideational concept of "right(s)" that had been found wanting during the imperial crisis return to center stage and provide the cognitive structure that, down to the present day, determines the way of thinking rights? Although a single answer to this question would be unlikely to carry conviction—the debates and compromises that sealed the fate of the Constitution are extremely complex—there is a contender: The noetic concept "rights of man" required a form of politics and structure of civic polity that the new republic could not realize. Perhaps both are, in an important sense, unrealizable. If that is so, it may have deep consequences with respect to the afterlives of the Enlightenment revolutions that created the ground plan for contemporary Western democracies and their attempts to embrace fully and deliver adequately universal human rights. I shall have more to say about this in my concluding chapter; here in conclusion to the present one I want to add a grace note to the preceding argument.

In the context of the war and its immediate aftermath, Americans no longer needed to justify their decision to separate from the mother country, that was now a fait accompli. But as the various states began to work out what it meant to stand alone, no longer indentured, as it were, by fiat of a charter or similar legal document to the Parliament in Westminster, they consistently gestured toward the contractarian account of government. It turned out they were, in fact, happiest with the account of liberties and rights that for so long had held in tension government and the citizen. And in that account the distinction between two types of ownership of rights, the alienable and the inalienable, were consistently remarked. The new citizens of the first modern republic discovered that this was all they needed. How this was applied can be seen in a document that makes the case for closing the courts in Berkshire County, Massachusetts, as a reaction to the removal of the legitimating instruments of colonial rule.[189] There it is noted that "the people at large are endowed with alienable and unalienable rights."[190] In his commentary upon that document, William Whiting spells out the theory of government that entails men resigning their "alienable natural rights into the hands of the community," thereby submitting

189. Following the Declaration of Independence, residents in western Massachusetts argued that the courts should be closed since the courts derived their legitimacy from the fact they were yoked via British common law to the sovereign and his Parliament in London and now, post-separation, that legitimacy no longer applied. For about four years following the Declaration this situation persisted. In the fall of 1778 the Massachusetts legislature sent a delegation to Pittsfield, in Berkshire Country, to hear complaints about this state of affairs. The document quoted argues the case for the suspension of the courts. William Whiting, a member of the investigating committee, wrote a response to that document, portions of which are quoted below.

190. Charles S. Hyneman and Donald S. Lutz, eds., *American Political Writing during the Founding Era, 1760–1805* (Indianapolis, Ind.: Liberty Fund, 1983), 1:456.

"to be governed by such laws and rules as may be prescribed by the free representatives of the people."[191] Explaining further what this amounts to, he states that while "all mankind are born equally free, and that, by nature, no one is above another" it is nevertheless the case that on entering civil society "they give up, into the hands of the society, many of their natural rights and liberties." But they also possess "other natural rights which they cannot divest themselves of." These, he says, "are called the *unalienable rights of mankind.*"[192] Unlike those documents that were written before the Declaration of Independence that worry so insistently about the source of legitimation for specific colonial rights, and therefore about the purported commonality between the rights held by freeborn Englishmen and their colonial progeny, those accounts after the declaration no longer need concern themselves with the past, or with the grounds for legitimating a difference in rights. Just like the eternally estranged mother country, the citizens of the new republic found all they needed was a concept of "right(s)" functioning as both containing and load bearing. The ideational concept of "right(s)" will do the work required: It provides the rubrics under which specific positive rights can be applied, defined, and defended as it operates with the element of the deposit. And, at the same time, it provides a platform for upholding the legitimacy of rights claims in the originating moment that constructs the polity: The move from the state of dependence to independence.

By the time the new republic came to adopt a constitution that was to bind the states into a federal entity, this way of working with and through the concept of "right(s)" was deeply embedded in the intellectual culture of Americans. It was there before the imperial crisis produced the conceptual problem I have described, sitting at the heart of the natural-law tradition. In fact, it never completely went away. Its essential moves, the sequence of thought it promotes can be discerned in a document published in Exeter, New Hampshire, in the context of increasing dissent over the future form and shape of American government. "The important end of government,"

191. Ibid., 1:464–65.

192. Ibid., 1:474. On August 14, 1776, Congress resolved that "it has been the wise policy of these states to extend the protection of their laws to all those who should settles among them of whatever nation or religion they might be . . ." This gesture was to be made in the context of a "Britannic majesty" who had set out to "destroy our freedom and happiness" and who would seek to return those British supporters of the colonial cause to the "despotism of their prince to be by him again sold to do the drudgery of some other enemy to the rights of mankind." By this time the concept of a universal right, noetic in conceptual structure, had firmly taken root.

it states, "is the good of the whole."[193] Governments cannot be established, it goes on to opine, unless "individuals . . . give up, by a civil compact, some of their natural rights, for securing to themselves others which they would retain."[194] Liberty is assured as long as the government acts in accordance with this compact. Freedom, under this description, could never be absolute or unconstrained: It is precisely the point that some freedom is given up in the initial compact. In the words of this document, "it is directly incompatible with the end of government" as of "every civil constitution" for subjects "to claim the exercise of those natural rights which they have given up by their civil compact."[195] For if they did make such a claim, "all ideas of civil government would be exploded," the net result of which would be that they had returned "in the most strict sense" to a *state of nature.*" And, with great emphasis, this situation is said to be incoherent: "A state of nature, and a state of civil government, are in the nature of things repugnant the one to the other."[196] John Locke would have smiled.

193. *Address to the Public, Containing Some Remarks on the Present Political State of the American Republicks, etc* (Exeter, N.H.: Lamson and Ranle, 1786), 4. See also Benjamin Trumbull: "Is it not that the original great design of civil Government is the good of the community? The maintaining and securing the rights, liberties, privileges and immunities of mankind? The impartial and faithful administration of justice? Must not whatsoever, therefore, tendeth to deprive mankind of these important rights, and to prevent the impartial administration of justice, be contrary to the great design of government, and subversive of its noble institution?" Benjamin Trumbull, *Discourse, Delivered at the Anniversary Meeting of the Freemen of the Town of New-Haven, April 12, 1773* (New Haven, Conn.: Thomas and Samuel Green, 1773), 31.

194. *Address to the Public, containing some remarks on the present political state of the American Republicks, etc* (Exeter, N.H.: n.p., 1786), 4.

195. Ibid.

196. Ibid., 5.

CHAPTER 4

"The Rights of Man Were but Imperfectly Understood at the Revolution": The Architecture of *Rights of Man*

Any historical account of the concept of human rights in the eighteenth century must negotiate the reputation of Thomas Paine's *Rights of Man*, for, whatever else may be said or believed about this book, it is incontrovertible that Paine's counterblast to Edmund Burke's *Reflections on the Revolution in France* has had a very energetic afterlife. Claims on its behalf—as to its notoriety, the number of readers it attracted, and the corresponding number of copies either sold or printed—have been extravagant: It is not uncommon to see figures in the millions as indices to its readership.[1] Although at the time of its publication it can accurately be said that it was a succès de

---

1. Samuel Edwards, in his biography of Paine, claims: "The first printing (Jordan) of 10,000 copies sold out overnight, and thereafter Jordan kept his press running twenty four hours each day in an attempt to meet the demand. Within the next year many hundreds of thousands of copies were sold in Great Britain and the United States, and still more, in a translated edition, in France. No records were kept, but it has been estimated that as least 2 million copies of the work were sold in the three countries." *Rebel! A Biography of Thomas Paine* (London: New English Library, 1974), 142–43. A less exaggerated estimation is provided by W. E. Woodward, *Tom Paine: America's Grandfather* (London: Secker and Warburg, 1946), 22: ". . . the *Rights of Man* was having a large sale.

scandale since both the author and publishers were prosecuted under the law for seditious libel, we still cannot say with any great confidence how many copies of this book were in circulation.[2] For reasons that will become clear, this uncertainty about the size of circulation is far from insignificant in relation to the arguments put forward on behalf of the book by Paine and his supporters as well as his antagonists.[3] It is important, in this regard, to note that it was certainly *said*, and perhaps by some if not many also *believed*, to have an unprecedented circulation. This feature of the event that was the publication and reception of Paine's most famous text has undoubtedly contributed to our current conceptions of the history of "human rights," which are conventionally said to find their origin in the late eighteenth century. If the claim to universality is taken to be the particular signature of the concept, then the ubiquity of Paine's text as the means for its dissemination generated a parallel claim to the universal. Although I do not mean this observation to imply that a supposedly very large scale circulation of Paine's text (certainly not universal, but nevertheless said to be larger than any other text of the period) is identical to a claim for its presenting or encapsulating ideas that were taken to be universal, or that could be said to speak for (and to) humanity at large, it is nevertheless my intention to remark the easily made elision between the very wide circulation of specific ideas within a culture and a claim to universality. When the

---

It was the leading best seller in England during that period. By the end of 1793 more than two hundred thousand copies had been bought by the public."

2. A far more convincing case is made by William St. Clair in his *The Reading Nation in the Romantic Period* (Cambridge: Cambridge University Press, 2004), 623: "Although the number of copies produced was unusually large, and the circulation unusually wide, some of the claims and estimates made and repeated, such as the 'many hundreds of thousands' of copies of *The Rights of Man* said to have been 'rapidly sold' after 1792, the '200,000 copies sold in the first year,' mentioned in a contemporary pamphlet, and the 'hundreds of thousands of copies' [which made Paine's writings known] 'in every village on the globe where the English language is spoken' defy credibility when compared with what is recoverable from archival sources." It should also be pointed out that hard evidence for the size of print runs and therefore accurate estimates of circulation are very difficult to establish for the period since the records that would provide the requisite information have either been lost or were not kept.

3. The claim about the size of circulation could work in many ways. The Rev. George Neale, for example, in his *A Short but Complete Analisis* [sic] *and Refutation, of "Paine's Rights of Man." In a Letter Addressed to the Candour and Good Sense of the People* (London: Andrews and Son, 1791), pointedly dismisses the claim to substantial readership and makes a pitch for his own substantial sales by providing a digest of Paine's arguments in seven pages.

idea in question is itself one that is founded on its absolute generality—a human right is said to be the most general there can be since it is coeval with being—particular care needs to be exercised in order to ensure that distinct applications of the notion of universality are not confused. Consequently, no matter what Paine himself may have thought or believed, it is not wise to uncritically assume that "the rights of man" were either intended to describe the most general or common attribution of rights to the species, or even prospectively desired to become universal, if one is to understand that claim to universality as having its basis in the essence of the human. In other words, one should be constantly on the lookout for the easy enfolding of our contemporary senses of "human rights" in the eighteenth-century's "rights of man." Moreover, given the preceding argument, I shall try to make the careful distinction between the architecture of the concepts "right(s)" and "rights of man" bite throughout this penultimate chapter. From the outset, then, I shall take care to resist the slippage that occurs when one makes the lazy assumption that "rights of man" are identical to the period's sense of the rights of mankind. Indeed, as this chapter sets out to demonstrate, the circulation of the concept "rights of man" as I have characterized it was in fact negligible. To that extent, Paine's intervention was a spectacular failure even if the discourse about "rights" for a heated few years was everywhere in the culture. In order to understand why, we need a far more accurate account of the publication and dissemination of Paine's text than is commonly available. The first part of this chapter provides that.

A second preliminary observation will help in the appreciation of the overall shape of this chapter. The preceding has set out a way of considering concepts as cultural entities as opposed to subjective mental entities. This distinction clearly implies a minimal threshold with respect the differences between a culture (taken as a large unit of sociality) and a coterie or subset of the cultural domain. It suggests that conceptual forms, insofar as they are cultural entities, must circulate above a certain threshold within a cultural environment.[4] Whether or not Thomas Paine and both his sup-

---

4. This of course leaves hanging what that threshold might be; furthermore, that issue is clearly contaminated by the specifics of the cultural environment: One might want to lower the threshold significantly if one is investigating a coterie, or insist on its being elevated if one is working with national politics. The following examination of the details surrounding the publication of *Rights of Man* seeks to establish a solid ground for assessing the extent to which the concept "rights of man" circulated in the *print* political culture of the 1790s in Britain.

porters and detractors recognized this fact, it was nevertheless the case that they collectively put into very wide circulation a phrase, *the rights of man*. The aim of this chapter is to investigate the extent to which that phrase was grounded in or connected to a conceptual form, "rights of man," thereby subjecting to detailed scrutiny the commonly held assumption that contemporary human rights find their conceptual origin in the 1790s.

It must be said, however, that for both Paine and his adversaries there were more pressing political motives in regard to the claimed level of circulation of *Rights of Man*. While Paine and the advocates of constitutional reform were keen to have their movement perceived as attracting widespread support, the government was happy to endorse such a perception (real or imagined) since it played into the strategy they adopted for whipping up fear of violent rebellion. Consequently, the estimation of the size of readership or the extent of circulation of Paine's ideas were crucial elements in the wider political struggle around the text. My primary focus, however, will be not on the political, economic and social struggle for constitutional reform in the 1790s but on the *conceptual* environment in which that struggle occurred. The following sets out, then, to ascertain the extent to which Paine's text contributed to the cultural construction and dissemination of a noetic concept "rights of man." In trying to deliver on that aim, I shall use the form of conceptual analysis developed in this study in order to explore the ways in which the modality of the concept "rights of man" operated axiomatically and schematically during the 1790s.

Estimation of the size of the readership for Paine's text, and correspondingly the number of the copies in circulation was not only important to the 1790s: In the afterlife of the text's publication, down through the nineteenth century and up to the present day, claims on behalf of the text's circulation and readership are key supports for assessments of the book's significance.[5] Such claims do not necessarily make an elision between the

---

5. A recent example is the following: "*Rights of Man* inspired similar raptures and anathemas. As with Burke, many of the eighty or so pamphlets written in reply were hostile but the estimated quarter of a million copies of *Rights of Man* sold by 1793 (with possibly twice that number by the end of the decade) reveal the scale of the positive response." David Duff, "Burke and Paine: Contrasts," in *The Cambridge Companion to British Literature of the French Revolution in the 1790s*, ed. Pamela Clemit (Cambridge: Cambridge University Press, 2011), 49. Gregory Claeys estimates that around six hundred titles were "generated in the ensuing debate," but he does not indicate the criteria for inclusion in this list. He may have been following the list compiled by Gayle Trusdel Pendleton, who claims about three hundred fifty titles constitute the fall out of the publication of *Rights of Man*. See Gregory Claeys, *Thomas Paine: Social and Political*

text's significance in terms of its (assumed) unprecedented circulation and its significance in terms of the ideas said to be contained within it, but for the most part precisely that elision is either silently allowed to stand or, more problematically, it is used as an argument for the historical origin of the widespread promotion of "human rights." Having said this, it is also the case that while most accounts of Paine in the last forty or so years have wished it to be the case that *Rights of Man* was the single most read book of its era, there have also been others which seek to correct estimates of its uniquely swollen circulation figures.[6]

We do not know, and perhaps will never be able to know with any certainty, how many readers *Rights of Man* attracted at the time of its complicated publication.[7] But it is possible to gauge how successful the publication event was in putting the phrase *rights of man* into circulation.[8] And in noting this, one also needs to observe that right up close, on the heels of its publication, the misreading of the title also occurred. Paine's text, even

---

Thought (Boston: Unwin Hyman, 1989), 112; Gayel Trusdel Pendleton, "Towards a Bibliography of the Reflections and Rights of Man Controversy," *Bulletin of Research in the Humanities* 85 (1982): 63–103. Claeys seems to have modified this estimate by 1995 in the introduction to his invaluable four-volume collection of *Political Writings of the 1790s* (London: William Pickering, 1995), 1:xxxiii. In note 1 on that page, he states that there were "probably about eighty works which concentrated exclusively on Paine's book." By my reckoning the number of pamphlets or books directly commenting on or taking issue with Paine's text between 1791 and 1793 is about forty. (The approximation is necessary because some pamphlets only raise Paine in passing which leads to a judgment call: What percentage of the publication needs to be about Paine's text for it to qualify?) It is noteworthy that, from 1794 onward, activity around "rights of man" began to significantly decrease; this is commented upon in more detail in the last section of this chapter. As to Duff's estimation of the size of circulation of *Rights of Man*, this claim must be wrong. On this, see below, p. 213ff.

6. See especially William St. Clair, note 2 above.

7. Anecdotal evidence as to the notoriety of the text is easy enough to come by, but this should be seen in the light of the politics outlined above. See J. T. Mathias, *Pursuits of Literature*, 2nd ed. rev. (London: T. Becket, 1797), 4:ii: "Our peasantry now read the *Rights of Man* on mountains, and moors, and by the wayside"; *Cursory Remarks on Paine's Rights of Man* (London: Parsons, 1792), 8: "I have frequently been in company when the question has been put to me, "Have you read Mr PAINE'S Book? Is it not an astonishing performance?" The author of this critical text goes on to argue that "Mr PAINE'S principles" do not survive close scrutiny. See below, p. 233ff, for a discussion of what is compacted in the term *principle*.

8. See table 27.

in the 1790s, was referred to as *The Rights of Man*,[9] and, when one looks in detail at the text one finds that even Paine himself did not consistently mark the distinction I shall be at pains to identify between the concept of "right(s)" as it had been articulated through the length of the eighteenth century and "rights of man." When Paine's contemporaries referred to *the* rights of man, they were operating with a concept of "right(s)" that explained such rights as claims or titles. That is, they were activating a conceptual network that had a very long-standing tradition within the politico-ethical project of natural law and thinking through the conceptual functionality of rights as a container with a schematic modality. But an alternative conceptual form was also embedded in Paine's text that operated according to a different grammar and syntax and with an axiomatic modality. Like the colonists in the 1770s, the pro-reform movement of the 1790s in Britain opened up the possibility of an alternative future for universal human rights. The purpose of this chapter is to assess how widespread that alternative architectural element, the platform, became in constructing and supporting the concept "rights of man."

I begin from the assumption that what I understand to be exaggerated claims on behalf of the circulation of *Rights of Man* can best be seen as symptomatic of the history of reception of the text. Indeed, that reception is largely determined by readings and, more commonly, misreadings of *merely* the title of the book.[10] Thus, a good deal hangs on the difference between "*the* rights of man" and "rights of man," the latter of course being

9. The 1795 London edition published by Eaton, for example, is titled *The Rights of Man*, as is the 1797 Philadelphia edition. John Parsons, a bookseller who had premises in Paternoster Row, brought printings of both Part I and Part II of Paine's work to the market in 1792 with the title *Rights of Men*. In 1792 Paine's text was reprinted by a Sheffield printer with the title *An Illustration of the Rights of Man: Being an Answer to Mr Burke's Attack on the French Revolution* (Sheffield: J. Crome, 1792). There are also references to a book entitled "*Rights of Men*." See note 63 below.

10. A critical pamphlet published in 1791 begins: "I have read the Rights of Men, and sit down to impugn the system, of Mr Paine, and to search the important subject which his book brings before me; a subject far more full of intricacies than he seems aware of." *Rights of Citizens; Being an Inquiry in Some of the Consequences of Social Union, and an Examination of Mr Paine's Principles Touching Government* (London: J. Debrett, 1791), 2. There is a Dublin edition of the same text, slightly altered, which indicates it was written "by a barrister." See *Rights of Citizens, Being an Examination of Mr Paine's Principles, Touching Government* (Dublin: Henry Watts, 1791). The significance of the term *principles* is discussed below, p. 237.

the title Paine gave to his book.[11] These are not equivalent, still less identical, titles. Second, whatever the actual circulation of his text may have been
at the time of publication, by far the most important effect of its appearance was the very significant increase in use of the phrase *rights of man*,
disseminated through reviews of Paine's book, arguments in pamphlets and
books both pro and contra his ideas, digests of his prose in the form of
"maxims" and so forth, songs, and, perhaps most ubiquitously, commentary of a mainly political kind in newspapers, journals, and broadsheets
on the efforts of Paine and his allies to bring about constitutional reform.
Although Paine himself may well have only been dimly aware of some of
the intricacies I am going to outline, it nevertheless remains the case that
the actual title Paine gave his text, *Rights of Man*, allied to the extraordinary level of circulation of the phrase in the culture at large disrupted the
conceptual network within which the concept of "right(s)" theretofore had
most conspicuously circulated. This chapter sets out to assess the degree
to which that disruption altered the architectonics of two putative conceptual formations bearing on rights: Was it merely a short-lived affair that
had insignificant ramifications in regard to how late eighteenth-century
persons understood citizenship, or did it open up a new way of conceiving the relations between citizens, their connection to the state or polis,
and, perhaps most importantly, what it meant to be human? The burden
of this alteration in conceptual structure falls on whether the distinction
between rights as specifiable and countable, rights as the plural of *right*,
and rights as unspecifiable and uncountable holds steady in the emergence
of a new conceptual network that supported the noetic concept "rights of
man." Whether or not that was case—that a clearly differently networked
conceptual form can be shown to have operated—there is nevertheless
very strong evidence to suggest that this distinction between a "right" and
"rights," howsoever parsed, was clearly visible to Paine and his contemporaries. This was so not only for those who proposed reform but also for
those, like Burke, who opposed it. It is surely the case, then, that whatever
else Paine's *Rights of Man* may have prompted, whatever the force of his
arguments or the scale of uptake of his ideas may have been, the significant cultural *dispersal* of the phrase generated activity within the nexus of
concepts that supported or connected to rights. The conceptual networks

---

11. Christopher Hitchens, in his book on Paine, consistently refers to *The Rights
of Man*, a point made by John Barrell in his review "The Positions He Takes," *London
Review of Books* 28, no. 23 (2006): 14–15.

within which concepts such as "rights" (howsoever understood), "man," the "human," "person," "citizen," and "liberty" were suspended certainly came under sever pressure. Even so, it is important to note that this increase in use of the phrase *the rights of man* does not provide evidence for a generally accepted or understood concept of universal or "human rights" in any significant sense.[12] In fact, as the first section of this chapter demonstrates, the penetration of Paine's *ideas*, certainly the widespread use of a different architecture for the concept "rights of man," was far less significant than has been supposed. In order to understand why, one needs to disentangle a number of things: the myths about the event that was the publication of *Rights of Man*, the likely extent to which the substance of the text was absorbed within the political debates of the time, and its immediate reception history.

The Publication of Rights of Man

There are elements of the following story that have become firmly embedded in the reception of Paine's book and to some extent are now taken to be the currency that comprises any account of the language of politics in the 1790s, and that discourse is commonly seen to be at least in part determined by not only *Rights of Man* but also the entry of theretofore disenfranchised persons into the cultural and political sphere. In this, at least, Paine the man was a kind of placeholder or emblem for a changing landscape of social and political engagement. It is worth remarking, moreover, that the story of Paine himself—what we have come to know and believe about him, his ideas and his life—has become intricately bound up with a set of claims, most of them unsubstantiated and unsubstantiatable, about the publication and circulation of *Rights of Man*.[13]

12. I mean to keep the distinction between what might be understood by "human rights" derived from "right(s)" and "rights of man" very clear. The second, as my last chapter argues, means that such rights only find coherence or intelligibility in the mood of an aspiration. If, as I have been arguing, we derive "human rights" from the first, we shall constantly come up against their indeclension as universal.

13. This is a feature of the telling of Paine's life from the very first biographies. J. T. Sherwin, for example, in his biography of 1819 noted that "with respect to the merits of the work [*Rights of Man*] as a composition, its immense circulation and immediate effect in exciting an inquiry into the abuses of the English government, will answer for

It is sometimes forgotten that Edmund Burke and Thomas Paine were friends during the late 1780s. Paine returned to England from the United States in 1787 knowing that Burke had been one of the colonists' strongest supporters in Parliament. Sometime during the second half of that year, the two men met and then, the following summer after Paine had been in France for seven months, they spent a week together at Burke's home in Beaconsfield.[14] In January 1789, Paine reported to Thomas Jefferson, at that time the American minister in France, that he was "in some intimacy with Mr Burke," and throughout the early months of that year Paine supplied information to Burke about events in France which he, Paine, learned about through his correspondence with Jefferson.[15] In late 1789, Paine returned to France to witness events there on his own account, and through 1790 he corresponded with Burke, noting in one letter that "almost every thing related in the English papers as happening in Paris is either untrue or misrepresented."[16] Burke, as is also well known, quickly revised his view about the revolution in France, and this change of heart can be tracked in the correspondence with Paine through January and February of 1790. Where Paine urged Burke to "introduce Revolution in England, by its established name of Reform!,"[17] Burke for his part was horrified at the thought that what he considered to be the epitome of enlightened government, the English constitution, might be undone. He is reported to have said to Paine, "Do you mean to propose that I, who have all my life fought for the constitution, should devote the wretched remains of my days to conspire to its destruction? Do you not know that I have always opposed the things called reform; to be sure, because I did not think them

this part of the subject." See *Memoirs of the Life of Thomas Paine* (London: R. Carlile, 1819), 104.

14. Burke wrote to Dr. French Laurence on August 18, 1788, saying, "I am going to dine with the D[uke] of Portland in company with the great American Paine, whom I take with me." Edmund Burke, *The Correspondence of Edmund Burke*, ed. Thomas W. Copeland (Cambridge: Cambridge University Press, 1958–1978), 5:412.

15. Cited in Thomas W. Copeland, *Our Eminent Friend: Edmund Burke* (New Haven, Conn.: Yale University Press, 1949), 160. The letter from Paine to Jefferson is dated January 15, 1789.

16. Paine to Burke, January 17, 1790, in Edmund Burke, *The Correspondence of Edmund Burke*, ed. Thomas W. Copeland (Cambridge: Cambridge University Press, 1958–1978), 6:69.

17. Cited in George Croly, *Life of Edmund Burke* (Edinburgh: W. Blackwood & Sons, 1840), 1:298.

reform."[18] Following this exchange, Burke is said to have broken off "all intercourse with Payne."[19]

Burke's unease—perhaps this needs to be more strongly expressed—his consternation at the events unfolding in France, which predated the excesses of the Terror, prompted him to denounce the Revolution in the House of Commons on February 9, 1790. According to Alfred Owen Aldridge, Paine was surprised by Burke's change of heart, most especially by the force, even violence of his criticism, and on learning that Burke intended to pen a longer attack on the revolution he began to write a pamphlet in support of it.[20] It was Paine's intention that this pamphlet would answer Burke's. This caused some inconvenience to Paine since Burke took longer than might have been expected to complete his text; in fact, Paine had to wait almost nine months before his—now—adversary's text appeared in print. While awaiting the publication of Burke's text, Paine thought it would be sensible to refrain from meeting him once he had returned to London. We know, however, that they did in fact meet even if the condition of their doing so included the gentlemanly agreement that no mention of France would be made.[21] Burke's *Reflections on the Revolution in France and on the Proceedings in Certain Societies in London Relative to That Event in a Letter Intended to Have Been Sent to a Gentleman in Paris* appeared on November 1, 1790.

My purpose in providing this preamble is to establish a very significant fact: Burke and Paine shared a discursive environment founded first on friendship and the (at the very least) mutual assumption that they were of common enough mind if not to "speak the same language" then at least to translate effectively between their own idioms. This is to say that they were individually and collectively bound in a relation of conversation. That this friendship was to be broken on the rocks of their different hopes and aspirations for constitutional reform in Britain does not change the fact that their conceptual lexicons were bound to have overlapped to a significant extent. According to the model of concepts as cultural entities that I am

18. Cited in Robert Bisset, *Life of Edmund Burke*, 2nd ed. (London: George Cawthorn, 1800), 2:285–86.

19. The source of this remark is Countess Bentinck, cited in Aubrey Le Blond, *Charlotte Sophie, Countess Bentinck* (London: Hutchinson & Co., 1912), 1:163.

20. Alfred Owen Aldridge, *Man of Reason: The Life of Thomas Paine* (Philadelphia: J. B. Lippincott Co., 1959), 126–27.

21. Paine mentions this in his *Letter Addressed to the Addressers on a Late Proclamation* (London: printed for the booksellers, 1792), 38. Printings of this text were also brought to market by Symonds and Rickman as well as Eaton.

employing, both Burke and Paine can be said to have access to and, even more significantly, were directed in their thinking and understanding by a common set of concepts, though it would be pushing the point too far, indeed counterintuitive, to suggest that they had identical conceptual sets. Individuals are, of course, variously inserted into the cultures within which they live. If one wanted to begin constructing an instrumental account of how those concepts were both formed and then disseminated, the exchange both in print and in conversation between these two men would be a good place to start. But it would be inaccurate to suggest that Paine was the author of the distinctly structured concept of "rights of man," or, if not that, was consciously invoking this distinct concept in his proposals for and justifications of republican government. It would equally be misleading to claim that it was Burke, assuredly the more structured and informed intelligence, who put this new conceptual form into play. He was, of course, deeply committed to arguing *against* a particular investment in rights that he saw as vacuous. As the previous two chapters have attempted to demonstrate, the concept of "right(s)" contained a noetic latency identifiable from early in the eighteenth century. By midcentury that latency was sufficiently accessible to the colonists as to enable them to begin exploring the ways in which a different architecture to the concept of rights might help justify the basis for armed rebellion. This chapter is not, then, or certainly not only, a story of two men and their verbal exchanges. I do mean, however, to elaborate a close account of the ways in which the noetic latency within the concept of "right(s)" surfaced in the division and disagreement between Burke and Paine, and to argue, therefore, that a differently structured concept of rights can be said to have been available to the political culture of the 1790s in Britain. I begin, therefore, with a reading of the two signal texts published in the first years of the decade, one deeply critical of the revolution in France, the other open in promoting its principles.

When, in late 1790, Paine began writing his reply to Burke in earnest, the political situation in Britain was febrile. Pitt and his government were locked in a battle with both the Whig pro-reformers in Parliament and those outside Parliament, to a large degree but not exclusively members of the laboring class, who had begun to create associations for the promotion of "constitutional information." The Revolution Society had been established some time before 1788, when it became revivified around the centenary of the glorious revolution of 1688.[22] Its main objectives were the repeal of the

22. For an account of the society, see Rémy Duthile's entry in the online *Oxford Dictionary of National Biography.*

Test and Corporation Acts and to agitate more generally for parliamentary reform.[23] Following the revolution in France, its membership and activities increased although there seems to have been considerable overlap with another association, the Society for Constitutional Information, which had been founded in 1780, itself also recently reinvigorated by the events across the channel in 1789. Both of these organizations were identified by the government as fomenting dissent and radical proposals for constitutional change.[24] Matters became even more fraught after Richard Price's sermon espousing the cause of reform to the London Revolution Society in November 1789. It was this speech, of course, that was the immediate prompt for Burke's own *Reflections* published the following year. The Pitt government almost immediately began to suppress the reform movement wherever and howsoever it could. In 1790, for example, it initiated legislation that required printing presses to possess state licenses. Government spies were dispatched under instruction to infiltrate radical societies and a barrage of comment and malicious rumor was spread by whatever means—in newspapers and periodicals, songs and broadsheets. It was within this atmosphere that Paine completed the manuscript of what would come to be known as Part I of *Rights of Man* and arranged for Joseph Johnson, the radical publisher, to print the text. It was scheduled for publication on February 22, 1791. Two days later, on February 24, the *Morning Chronicle* announced that Paine's text was unavailable: "There is not now a copy to be had."[25] The same paper on March 7 announced the imminent reappearance of the book along with Paine's own return to London.[26] What happened around these early months of 1791? The story that has been told and retold goes like this.

Johnson, a friend to many of the most visible dissenters in the capital and known to Paine, agreed to print the book. But sometime before February 22 he got cold feet, fearing that he would run afoul of the law.[27] Some

23. The Test and Corporation Acts, passed in the seventeenth century, prevented non-Anglicans from holding public office. Bills to rescind these acts were proposed in Parliament in 1787, 1789, 1790, and 1791 and on each occasion defeated.

24. See J. C. D. Clark, ed., *Edmund Burke: Reflections on the Revolution in France* (Stanford, Calif.: Stanford University Press, 2001), 146–47n9 and n10.

25. Cited in Alfred Owen Aldridge, *Man of Reason: The Life of Thomas Paine* (London: Cresset Press, 1960), 134.

26. W. T. Sherwin, an early biographer, noted that it appeared on March 13. See W. T. Sherwin, *Memoirs of the Life of Thomas Paine* (London: R. Carlisle, 1819), 101.

27. It is said that Johnson was intimidated by government agents who repeatedly visited his premises. See, among others, John Keane, *Tom Paine: A Political Life* (London: Bloomsbury, 1995), 305. I have found no substantiation for this story.

early collected sheets of the complete text were bound or sewn since we
know for certain that there are some copies with Johnson's name on the
title page (see fig. 1).[28]

It has been suggested that the number of copies of this Johnson im-
print is exceedingly small, essentially early copies that were given away.[29]
Paine then agreed with J. S. Jordan that he could take over the sheets that
Johnson had printed and continue with the publication. We do not know
if Jordan had to complete the printing or, alternatively, simply bind or sew
the sheets that Johnson had printed. In any case, the book was advertised
for sale on March 16.[30] Over the next nine months Jordan was to bring
to sale a further eight editions, although calling them editions is slightly
misleading. It is certainly possible that early biographers of Paine, noticing
the many "editions" produced by Jordan, calculated that the book must
have circulated in tens of thousands of copies, but this seems likely to be a
misapprehension.[31] Until relatively recently it has been assumed that numbers of editions of a text provide direct evidence for the size of circulation
and, more opaquely, as indices to the significance or importance a text had
in its immediate reception culture. Recent scholarship in the history of the
book has suggested that this assumption is at best a guess. This is to say,
we can no longer assume that further so-called editions necessarily indicate

28. This is the title page of the British Library copy, entered into ECCO as document number CB3327177054.

29. Alfred Owen Aldridge, *Man of Reason: The Life of Thomas Paine* (London: Cresset
Press, 1960), 134.

30. *General Evening Post*, March 5, 1791.

31. Unfortunately such misapprehensions continue to the present day. One of the
recent and well regarded biographies of Paine, John Keane's *Tom Paine: A Political Life*
(London: Bloomsbury, 1995), tells the story in the following way: "Alarmed by the
prospect that the work would be stillborn, Paine reacted fast. He agreed to a deal with
another publisher, J. S. Jordan on Fleet Street, and with the help of friends and a horse
and cart delivered to him Johnson's printed, unbound sheets. Paine scurried around for
money to pay for the work. He managed to borrow forty pounds from George Lewis
Scott, an old friend from excise days. . . . Two centuries later, it is hard to imagine the
public fuss whipped up by Jordan's three shilling edition of this small book, which appeared on March 13th, 1791, three weeks later than Paine had originally intended"
(305). This is certainly a lively account, but as far as I can determine there is no evidence
for the detail in the story—the cart, friends, delivery of the sheets, and so forth, but
perhaps most misleading is the inference that Paine needed the £40 to pay for the print-
ing/publishing of the first copies supplied by Jordan and published on March 13. Since
Godwin's diary entry is for May 14, the date on which the loan is recorded, this cannot
be correct.

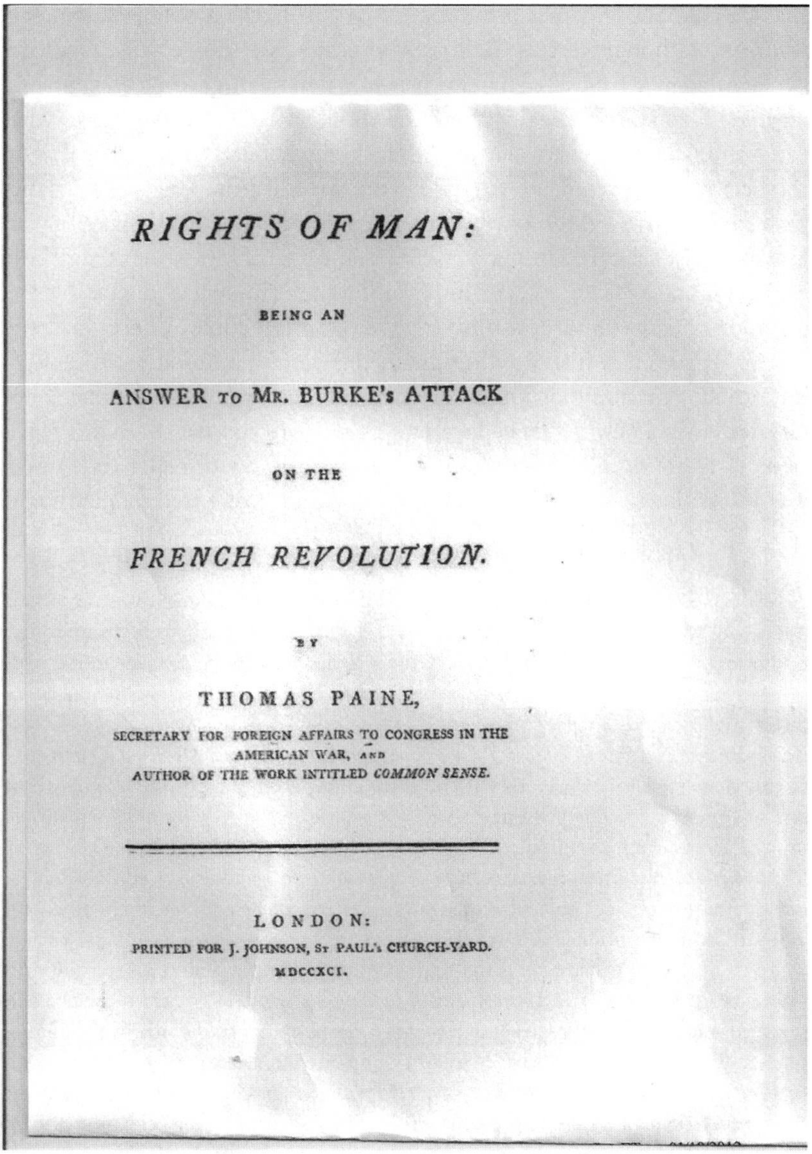

RIGHTS OF MAN:

BEING AN

ANSWER TO MR. BURKE's ATTACK

ON THE

FRENCH REVOLUTION.

BY

THOMAS PAINE,

SECRETARY FOR FOREIGN AFFAIRS TO CONGRESS IN THE AMERICAN WAR, AND AUTHOR OF THE WORK INTITLED *COMMON SENSE.*

LONDON:

PRINTED FOR J. JOHNSON, ST PAUL's CHURCH-YARD.

MDCCXCI.

Figure 1. Title page to the first edition of Part I of Thomas Paine's *Rights of Man* (1791), printed by J. Johnson, price sixpence.

that the number of copies printed increased from the first (or subsequent) printing. Although further "editions" do, in some simple sense, indicate further demand from the market, it is not possible to estimate accurately what such increases actually represented numerically. Furthermore, what constituted an edition was far from standardly applied or accepted during the period and, even more troubling, the sizes of print runs are very difficult to establish.[32] Moreover, demand could easily be manipulated by an industry that operated in many senses as a cartel. Notwithstanding these impediments, it is nevertheless important to determine if at all possible the distinction between a reprinting (that is, printing copies in excess of the first print run) and further editions. In this case it seems at least likely, if not probable, that either Jordan or Paine, or perhaps both in concert, decided to print a new first page for each "edition" of the text through 1791.[33] If, as William St. Clair outlines, the standard supply of paper to printers was at least half a ream (since taxation regulations prevented smaller quantities being viable), this meant that a minimum print run would have been

32. For a very detailed account of the complexities of the eighteenth-century book trade, see William St. Clair, *The Reading Nation in the Romantic Period* (Cambridge: Cambridge University Press, 2004). St. Clair attaches extreme importance to the 1774 act altering the terms of copyright, essentially arguing that the "reading nation" was a direct consequence of that act. Richard B. Sher, in his *The Enlightenment and the Book* (Chicago: University of Chicago Press, 2006), presents a vigorously argued corrective to this view. He also makes a very useful distinction between a reprint, a book whose text was recast from one printing to another, and a reissue, a book using the unsold printed sheets from a printing. It is most likely that in the case of Jordan's bringing *Rights of Man, Part I* to the market in 1791 he was not reprinting new editions but reissuing the first edition, only with each successive reissue he attached a new title page indicating a "new edition."

33. This seems to have been the practice of Daniel Isaac Eaton as well since his "editions" of Paine's *The Decline and Fall of the English System of Finance*—thirteen editions through 1796—are unlikely to have been *reprintings* since the title page indicates that the text was printed by Hartley, Adlard, and Son, rue Neuve de Berry in Paris. Adlard seems to have been the preferred printer for Paine's works outside Britain, a tactic presumably aimed at avoiding prosecution. See, for example, Thomas Paine, *Agrarian Justice Opposed to Agrarian Law, and to Agrarian Monopoly; Being a Plan for Meliorating the Condition of Man* whose title page reads: "W. Adlard, rue Menilmontant. London Re-Printed and sold by the Booksellers of London and Westminster." I have been unable to ascertain if these two addresses for Adlard indicate a family operating as printers/booksellers in Paris from two different addresses or, alternatively, that Adlard and son moved premises. See also Thomas Paine, *The Age of Reason: Being an Investigation of True and Fabulous Theology* (1794), which reads on its title page "Printed in Paris. Sold by D. I. Eaton at the Cock and Swine, 74 Newgate Street."

two hundred fifty copies or thereabouts.[34] We do not know how large the Johnson/Jordan first print run might have been, but since there is evidence that Paine needed to raise money to pay for copies in May (see below) it seems unlikely that the number of copies put into circulation by Jordan was very substantial. At best, if we take the figure indicated by Paine himself in a letter to George Washington on July 21, 1791, the total run was 16,000 copies. If, as I suspect, Jordan had a new title page printed each time he had further batches of the text sewn or bound, thereby suggesting that new "editions" were being called for very rapidly, that initial print run was not augmented. But on this matter we simply do not know the facts.[35]

There is, however, evidence that in 1792 other printers/booksellers entered the market with further printings of the text. Jordan himself sold a text in 1792 at a cost of sixpence and the same price appears on copies printed and sold by Parsons, Symonds, and "The Booksellers," all of them in the same year, 1792.

One should be careful not to jump to the conclusion that these editions and printings were in direct competition with each other since there is good evidence to suggest that booksellers operated within very constrained local—geographical, social, and political—markets.[36] Furthermore, the

34. See William St. Clair, *The Reading Nation in the Romantic Period* (Cambridge: Cambridge University Press, 2004), 178.

35. It seems unlikely, however, that the version given by John Keane is accurate. He writes: "No book had ever sold like it. Jordan published a new edition three days after his first. It sold out within several hours. On March 30th, a third edition appeared, followed by a fourth edition on April 14, then a fifth and sixth during the month of May, by which time 50,000 copies had been sold." See *Tom Paine: A Political Life* (London: Bloomsbury, 1995), 307. As I note below, however, William Godwin recorded in his journal on May 14 that publication had been "suspended" for want of cash. It seems more likely, then, that Paine was scraping together what he could to pay in installments. This leaves hanging, of course, the question over the size of an initial or any subsequent print runs.

36. The localization of a market could easily have been very tight or specific when one considers the geographical distribution of booksellers in the capital: Different territories for the establishment of markets for books may have been as loco-specific as a single street. Paternoster Row and St. Paul's Churchyard were so close together as to almost comprise a single street, and both combined may have given specificity to one market. The Strand, which was a bare five minutes walk away, may well have constituted a rather different market. Evidence for this observation is provided by the occupants of particular addresses over the period. It is noteworthy, for example, that booksellers around St. James's Palace tended to be associated with a specific political allegiance and published books that by and large coincided with that political filiation. The political association of publishers is discussed below.

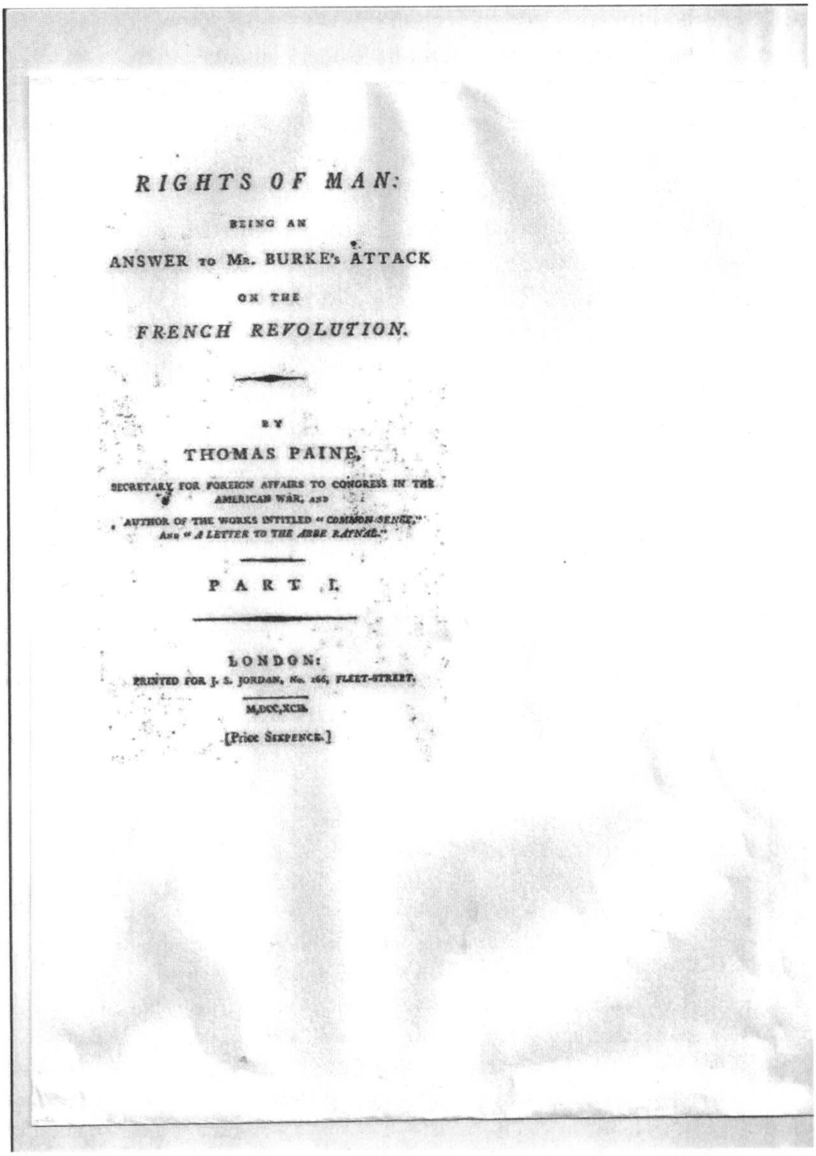

RIGHTS OF MAN:

BEING AN

ANSWER TO MR. BURKE's ATTACK

ON THE

FRENCH REVOLUTION.

BY

THOMAS PAINE,

SECRETARY FOR FOREIGN AFFAIRS TO CONGRESS IN THE
AMERICAN WAR, AND
AUTHOR OF THE WORKS INTITLED " COMMON SENSE,"
AND " A LETTER TO THE ABBE RAYNAL."

PART I.

LONDON:
PRINTED FOR J. S. JORDAN, No. 166, FLEET-STREET.

M,DCC,XCII.

[Price Sixpence.]

Figure 2. Title page to the first edition of Part I of *Rights of Man* (1792), printed and sold by J. Jordan, price sixpence.

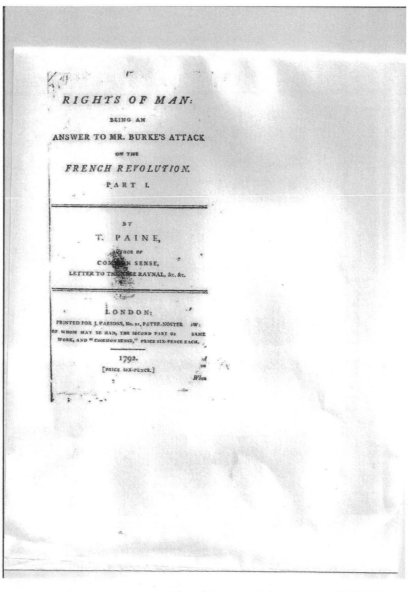

Figure 3. Title page to Part I of *Rights of Man* (1792), printed and sold by J. Parsons, price sixpence.

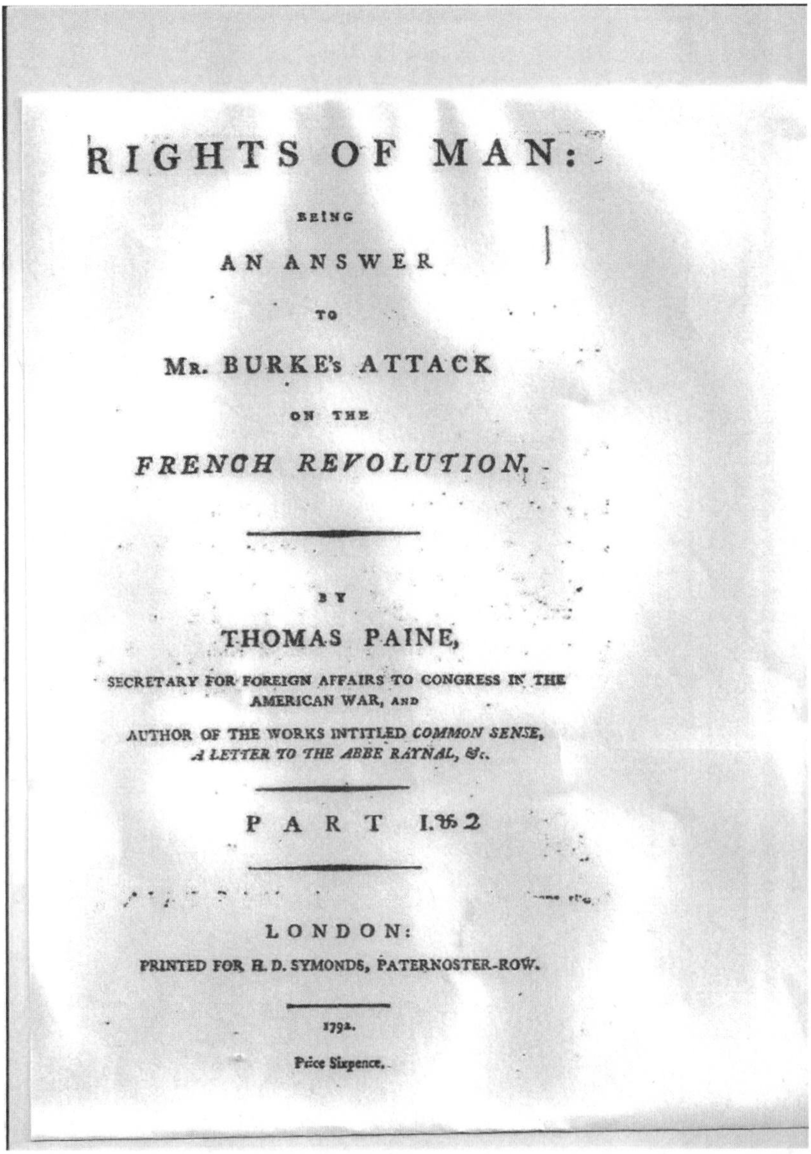

RIGHTS OF MAN:

BEING

AN ANSWER

TO

MR. BURKE's ATTACK

ON THE

FRENCH REVOLUTION.

BY

THOMAS PAINE,

SECRETARY FOR FOREIGN AFFAIRS TO CONGRESS IN THE AMERICAN WAR, AND

AUTHOR OF THE WORKS INTITLED *COMMON SENSE, A LETTER TO THE ABBE RAYNAL, &c.*

PART I.&2

LONDON:

PRINTED FOR H. D. SYMONDS, PATERNOSTER-ROW.

1792.

Price Sixpence.

Figure 4. Title page to Parts I and II of *Rights of Man* (1792), printed by H. D. Symonds, price sixpence.

eighteenth-century trade in books was highly sensitized to ways in which cooperative or cartel behavior could increase profits.[37] It is also the case that this market in books was price sensitive, but we do not know the extent to which such pricing was determined by production costs. One does well to remember that the market for books during the period was highly segmented: Cheap paper, boards in place of leather bindings, and very narrow margins were features of those books aimed at an emerging readership that had its roots in the laboring class. At the other end of the price spectrum, hand-tooled leatherbound books on high-quality paper were often requirements set by gentleman and aristocratic collectors.[38] The fact that these booksellers brought to the market copies of Paine's work priced at sixpence, then, indicates that there was perceived to be a potentially large readership within that emerging literate culture. Whether or not these printings and editions did in fact find that readership must be left hanging for the moment.

There may have been another reason for the simultaneous multiple bookseller publication of Paine's text that is more narrowly connected to the political and legal climate in which the printing, sale, and distribution of *Rights of Man* took place. These activities were fraught with danger since the government was attempting to censor the freedom of the press. It is certainly possible that a number of booksellers either sought or imagined there to be safety in numbers: Prosecutions would perhaps be less likely if the circulation of the text was so substantial as to make any attempt at restricting it useless. If this was a calculation, it clearly also played into the *claim* for very widespread circulation and readership. In any event, since there are copies of the text that provide the cover of anonymity

37. Post-1774, it was also common practice for booksellers to "rig" the market for their product by keeping a semiprivate ledger into which participating booksellers entered the detail of their publications. The market was rigged by the fact that booksellers agreed, in gentlemanly fashion, not to encroach upon each other's property even though in technical legal terms they no longer held exclusive copyright. This practice was known as honorary copyright, and the ledger was held at the Chapter Coffee House. On this see Richard B. Sher, *The Enlightenment and the Book* (Chicago: University of Chicago Press, 2006), 26.

38. For a good account of these desiderata in respect to the market for books, see James Raven, *The Business of Books: Booksellers and English Book Trade* (New Haven, Conn.: Yale University Press, 2007), esp. ch. 9; for the case of the colonies, see Elizabeth Carroll Reilly and David D. Hall, "Customers and the Market for Books," in *A History of the Book in America*, ed. Hugh Armory and David D. Hall (Chapel Hill: University of North Carolina Press, 2007), 1:387–99.

for the bookseller—the title pages of these editions state "Printed for the Booksellers"—the government witch hunt would seem to have been taken seriously.[39] It must also be the case, of course, that these booksellers were likely to have been driven by the motive for profit: They knew a good thing when they saw one. It is nevertheless difficult to find solid ground upon which to base an informed and reasonably accurate inference, even if some facts might seem to push the argument in one direction or the other.

It is known, for example, from the evidence of an entry in William Godwin's journal for 1791 that Paine did not have the resources to pay for his book.[40] He wrote on May 14, "Scott a believer in spiritual intercourses lends Paine £40 to aid the publication of his pamphlet suspended for want of money (Lewis) H. Tooke states to the Const. Soc. Paine's offer of £300 (B. Hollis)."[41] This, written in 1791, must refer to Jordan's printing, and since it is dated in May it suggests that Jordan's print runs were cautious. It is also a matter of historical record that some "editions" of both "Part I" and "Part II" of *Rights of Man* have different indications of price on the title pages, and there are some, notably Eaton's 1795 edition of *The Rights of Man*, priced at three shillings, which would seem to corroborate the observations made above in respect to the heterogeneity of the book market. Given that by 1792 there were already at least three "editions" of both Parts I and II offered for sale at sixpence, Eaton's 1795 edition must have been targeted at the "luxury" market.[42] Unfortunately, records from the period about the size of print run have not survived so it is difficult to ascertain with any precision how booksellers financed such distinctively marketed editions. Nevertheless it must be assumed that the market for Paine's book was not price insensitive, and that therefore a six-penny edi-

---

39. See, *Rights of Man, Part the Second* (1792), price 6d, and *Rights of Man* (Part I) 1792, Eighteenth Century Collections Online (Gale doc. CB130902661).

40. It was common at the time for printers to simply print the text and demand upfront payment for their materials and services. Only in those cases where copyright was held or bought by the printer/publisher (or a collective of them) would an author not have to find the wherewithal to pay for his or her book being published. See on this William St. Clair, *The Reading Nation in the Romantic Period* (Cambridge: Cambridge University Press, 2004), ch. 9.

41. Cited in Alfred Owen Aldridge, *Man of Reason: The Life of Thomas Paine* (London: Cresset Press, 1960), 135.

42. The title page of Paine's *Common Sense: addressed to the inhabitants of America* offered for sale in 1792 and sold by J. Parsons in Paternoster Row has the following information: "Sold by J Parsons, Of whom may be had Rights of Man Parts I and II. Price 6d each." See copy held in National Library of Wales (Gale doc. CB126851007).

tion would have attracted many more purchasers than one offered at three shillings. Price, however, provides only the crudest means for guessing at circulation and this is further complicated by the fact that other claims were made, both by Paine and contemporary commentators, about possibly cheaper editions still.

Within the tradition of telling the story of the publication of *Rights of Man*, Paine himself is understood to have been very eager to see a cheap edition that would enable the laboring class to have access to his text. It is not known, however, if this wish was realized, and since so much was to hang on the question of size of circulation in the subsequent government prosecution of Paine, caution is required here. It is certainly the case that Paine *claimed* he had organized a cheap edition since this is what he wrote in the text *Letter Addressed to the Addressers on a Late Proclamation*, the long pamphlet he wrote in response to the government's proclamation of May 21, 1792, against seditious writings.[43] The same day a summons was issued to Paine to appear in court on charges of sedition. The government had been nervously watching the activities of the pro-reform movement for some time and had, in fact, some seven days earlier, on May 14, issued Jordan with a summons to appear in court. As it happened, that very day Paine was visiting him and noted that no charge had been formally indicated in the summons. Both men, however, could hardly have been under any illusion: Even before the Royal Proclamation, the government had been bullying those perceived to be its enemies and was far from reluctant to use whatever means, legal or otherwise, it had at its disposal. Both Paine and Jordan assumed that the case was to be made on the fact that the bookseller had put into circulation a seditious libel in the form of Part II of *Rights of Man*.[44] Paine, taking his responsibilities seriously, suggested the two men meet the next day with Paine's lawyers present. Jordan, however,

43. The same uncertainty about whether or not Paine succeeded in bringing a very cheap edition to the market surrounds the information provided by a letter Paine sent to the Society for Constitutional Information that was read on May 18, 1792. This is included in *The Reports of the Committee of Secrecy of the House of Commons, on the papers belonging to the Society for Constitutional Information* (Edinburgh: Bell and Bradfute, et al., 1794), 26: "Read the following letter from Mr Paine, acquainting the Society that he is proceeding to bring out a cheap edition of the First and Second Parts of the Rights of Man."

44. The complexities of the law at the time and of the specific case make it difficult to summarize with accuracy. One might, for example, find it less obfuscating to say that Jordan was indicted for "publishing" Part II of *Rights of Man*, which in fact he was and to which he pleaded guilty, but more than nuance hung on what it might mean to "publish"

decided that he would employ his own legal defense and to plead guilty
to publishing the text. This left open whether or not he was liable for the
meaning of the words therein.[45] Paine, in his *Letter*, which must have been
written after May 21, 1792, since he refers to the Royal Proclamation and
the various schemes promoted by the government to give public addresses
on the glories of the constitution, notes, "I had already sent a cheap edition to Scotland" and, in an effort to satisfy demands from "Rotherham,
from Leicester, from Chester" all for a similar cheap edition, "I concluded
that the best method of complying therewith [requests for a cheaper edi-
tion] would be to print a very numerous edition in London, under my own
direction." This, he thought, would make the work "more perfect, and the
price be reduced lower than it could be by *printing* small editions in the
country of only a few thousands each."[46] It is clear that his declared intention was to print a large edition, but he does not say if he delivered on it.

The following paragraph begins, "The cheap edition of the First Part
was begun about the Middle of last April," and he notes that from that point
on he "expected a prosecution."[47] The effect of this summons, however, as
Paine was very quick to point out, was a great deal of free publicity. This
could only have provoked a significant increase in the dissemination of the
phrase "rights of man," while at the same time, perhaps, generating wider
circulation of his book. May there have been some crafty tactics here on the
part of Paine? Knowing that his book was not reaching as many people as
he wanted (or fantasized), did he make it widely known that he was about to
launch a very cheap edition in the expectation that the government would
attempt to censor it? It seems strange, for example, that in the published
Letter as we have seen, Paine claims that he determined on the plan for a
cheap edition "about the middle of last April" (i.e., April 1792 since the
government proclamation was in May), but in a letter to George Wash-

such a text. For a detailed account of these cases, see John Barrell and Jon Mee, *Trials for
Treason and Sedition, 1791–1794* (London: Pickering & Chatto, 2006), 1:xiii–xxii.

45. In fact this prosecution collapsed, but this did not prevent further indictments
of publishers/booksellers being issued. The publisher of both the second part of *Rights
of Man* and of the *Letter Addressed to the Addressers on a Late Proclamation*, Daniel Isaac
Eaton was indicted for seditious libel. He was prosecuted twice in the summer of 1793
and on both occasions the jury returned an ambiguous verdict. On this, see John Barrell, *Imagining the King's Death: Figurative Treason, Fantasies of Regicide, 1793–1796* (Oxford: Oxford University Press, 2000).

46. Thomas Paine, *Letter Addressed to the Addressers on a Late Proclamation* (London:
Daniel I. Eaton, 1792), 24.

47. Ibid. April 1792 is meant.

ington dated July 21, 1791, Paine had already indicated that he intended to "make a cheap edition, just sufficient to bring in the price of the printing and paper, as I did by *Common Sense*."[48] The reception history has always assumed that this very cheap edition (by which are we to assume cheaper than sixpence, since as we know Symonds, Parsons, and "The Booksellers" all printed editions of both parts I and II, sold separately, for that price?) provided the means for the widespread dissemination of Paine's ideas. But perhaps these editions printed and sold by Symonds, Parsons, and "The Booksellers" are those to which Paine refers. Since the tactic of not naming the bookseller/publisher appears on one of these title pages, one can assume that the threat of prosecution was felt to such a degree that protection in anonymity was sought.[49]

This would then date the "booksellers" cheap, six-penny edition as appearing in the market after May 21, 1792. It certainly makes some sense to see things this way since if Paine was referring to a different cheap edition (i.e., not any of those three above), how come not a single copy of such a work seems to have survived? Further evidence that such a discounted publication did not see the light of day is provided by a "Free Born Englishman" who published *Paine's Political and Moral Maxims; Selected from the Fifth Edition of Rights of Man, Part I and II* in 1792. The necessity for publishing this digest, the author claimed, lay precisely in the fact that at that juncture no cheap edition was available: "Your Rights of Man," he states in his introductory letter to Paine, are "at too high a price to be purchased by those, whose interests are most deeply concerned in the information they communicate."[50] He then goes on to amplify: "Many months, however, have elapsed without any appearance of such a digest of your

48. Thomas Paine, *The Complete Writings of Thomas Paine*, ed. Philip S. Foner (New York: Citadel Press, 1945), 2:1318. Does this mean that Paine was already, in April 1791, thinking of the cheap edition? If so, it was very premature since the book had hardly been put on sale (only since March 16). If one reads the comment in the *Letter* as indicating that Paine had resolved to bring a cheap edition to the market in April 1791, why did it take over a year to get books to the market?

49. The same tactic was used in publishing *Common Sense* in 1792; some copies indicate "Sold by all the Booksellers." See Gale doc. CB3330902600 and Paine's *A Letter Addressed to the Addressers, on the late Proclamation*, Gale doc. CW104573269; also *Paine's Political and Moral Maxims; Selected from the Fifth Edition of Rights of Man, Part I and II*, Gale doc. CW3306049486.

50. *Paine's Political and Moral Maxims; Selected from the Fifth Edition of Rights of Man, Part I and II* (London: printed for the booksellers, 1792), 4.

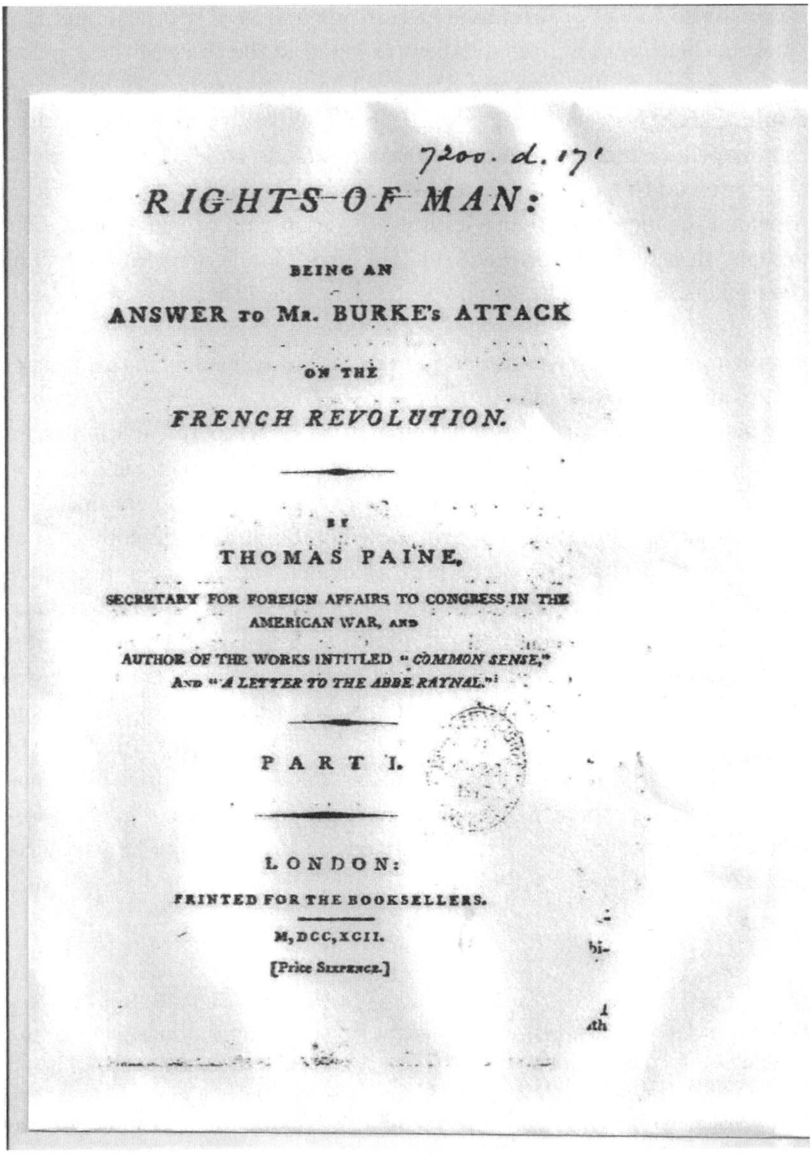

7200. d. 17

RIGHTS OF MAN:

BEING AN

ANSWER TO MR. BURKE's ATTACK

ON THE

FRENCH REVOLUTION.

———

BY

THOMAS PAINE,

SECRETARY FOR FOREIGN AFFAIRS TO CONGRESS IN THE
AMERICAN WAR, AND

AUTHOR OF THE WORKS INTITLED " *COMMON SENSE*,"
AND " *A LETTER TO THE ABBE RAYNAL*."

———

PART I.

———

LONDON:

PRINTED FOR THE BOOKSELLERS.

———

M,DCC,XCII.

[Price Sixpence.]

Figure 5. Title page to Part I of *Rights of Man* (1792), printed for the booksellers, price sixpence.

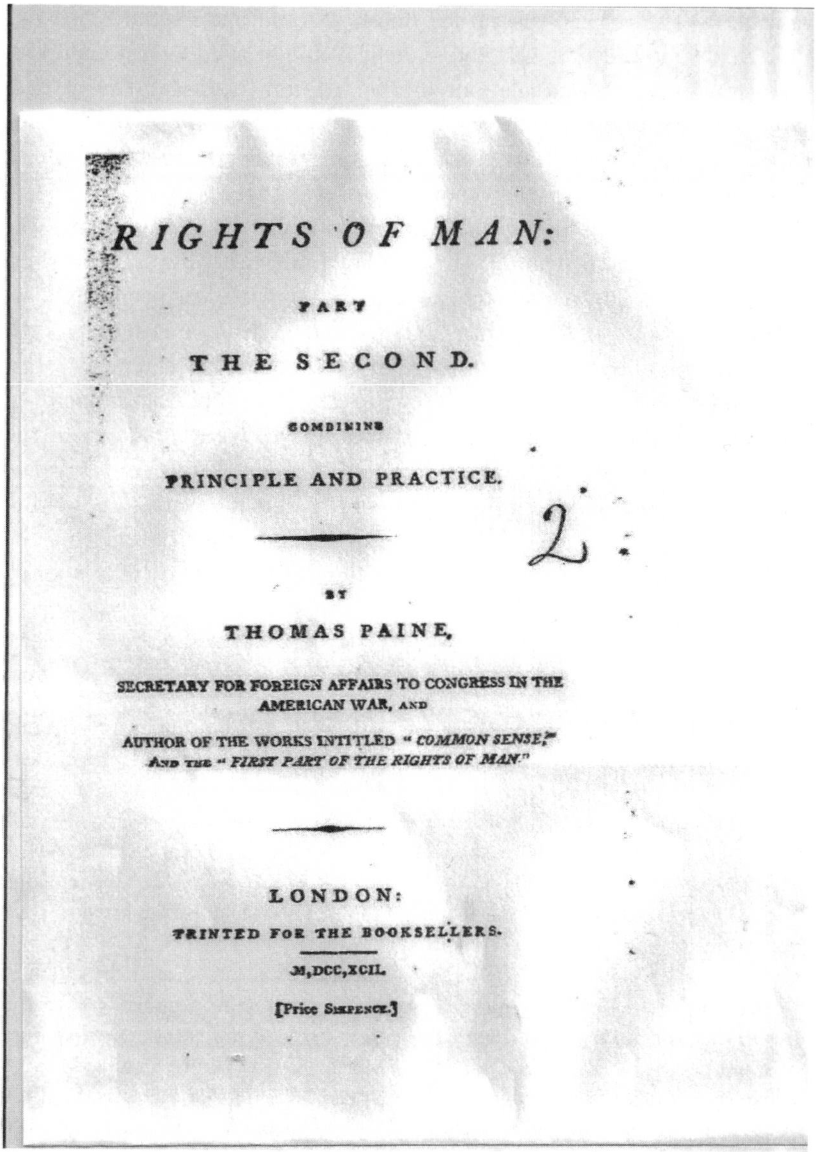

RIGHTS OF MAN:

PART

THE SECOND.

COMBINING

PRINCIPLE AND PRACTICE.

BY

THOMAS PAINE,

SECRETARY FOR FOREIGN AFFAIRS TO CONGRESS IN THE
AMERICAN WAR, AND

AUTHOR OF THE WORKS INTITLED " *COMMON SENSE,*"
AND THE " *FIRST PART OF THE RIGHTS OF MAN.*"

LONDON:

PRINTED FOR THE BOOKSELLERS.

M,DCC,XCII.

[Price Sixpence.]

Figure 6. Title page to Part II of *Rights of Man* (1792), printed for the booksellers, price sixpence.

valuable work."[51] This, the author notes, is somewhat strange since Dr. Price had followed precisely the strategy Paine seemed keen to adopt— "to print for general circulation, another edition [of Price's *Observations on Civil Liberty*] on coarse paper, at so small a price as *three pence*."[52] Our author comments that "this precedent, as nearly as possible, should have been followed with respect to your more useful tracts."[53]

In any event, even before the publication of Part II in 1792 Paine was claiming vast sales for Part I, as he compared sales with Burke. He writes: "If Mr Burke, or any person on his side of the question, will produce an answer to the 'Rights of Man,' that shall extend to an half, or even to a fourth part of the number of copies to which the 'Rights of Man' extended," then he would give Burke's *Reflections* the courtesy of a reply. And he goes on to state: "I suppose the number of copies to which the first part of the 'Rights of Man' extended, taking England, Scotland, and Ireland, is not less than between forty and fifty thousand."[54] But when this was written (in late 1791 since the manuscript for Part II was at the printers from the end of October that year) the cheap, six-penny edition had yet to appear.

51. Ibid.

52. Ibid.

53. Ibid. This tract also notes that "resolutions of the Constitutional Society, to print a cheaper edition of your treatises (referring to *Rights of Man*)" had been taken; see 4–5. Matters here are very murky; Brooke Boothby, for example, notes the rumor: "The republican landed and monied gentry of the north of Ireland, have, it is said, circulated 20,000 *Rights of Man* at two pence a-piece." Sir Brooke Boothby, *Observations on the Appeal from the New to the Old Whigs, and on Mr Paine's Rights of Man* (London: John Stockdale, 1792), 185. Given that no copies of this edition would seem to have survived, it seems likely that this was just a rumor.

54. Thomas Paine, *Rights of Man*, with a biographical introduction by Philip S. Foner (New Jersey: Citadel Press, 1974), 154. This estimate corresponds with that in *An Impartial Sketch of the Life of Thomas Paine, Author of "Common Sense," "Rights of Man" &c. &c.* (London: D. Symonds, 1792), 9: "When the Second part of *Rights of Man* appeared, the number of copies to which the First Part had extended, including England, Scotland, and Ireland, was not less than between forty and fifty thousand: and when it is recollected that, exclusive of the Second, the First Part of the work has now been eight months longer on sale, and that cheap editions of each have been published, many thousands of which have been sold, the number purchased cannot be supposed to fall short of, if indeed it does not exceed, one hundred thousand copies." This has the mark of Paine all over it—yet another instance of boosterism. I suspect that this is the source of the unverifiable figure for the circulation of *Rights of Man* and that very early on this fell into the literature on its author as an indisputable fact. It was just a short step away to the claim that "perhaps two million copies" were in circulation. See note 1 above.

One must assume, then, that Paine is referring to the editions that went on sale at three shillings. Since we know that he claimed 16,000 copies were initially printed in England, the remaining copies must have been printed in Scotland and Ireland. This corresponds with his estimate of the circulation made in a letter to John Hall, of November 25, 1791, where he claims that *"Rights of Man* has had the greatest run of anything ever published in this country, at least of later years—almost sixteen thousand has gone off—and in Ireland above forty thousand—besides the above numbers one thousand printed cheap are now gone to Scotland . . . "[55] Of the copies extant, it appears that the first six-penny editions of Part I appeared in 1792 and were almost certainly offered for sale after April that year if we take Paine's account in the *Letter to the Addressers* as accurate (and note by that time the second part was already on sale, since it was published on February 16, 1792).[56] Further evidence that the cheap, and we must assume very widely circulated, edition was not available until after, at the very least, May 18, 1792, is provided by the minute of the Society for Constitutional Information.[57] The point here, and it is perhaps compelling, is that Paine invested a great deal in giving the impression that his book was read by (or to) the entire (or at least a very substantial part) reading (or read-to) population. He was boasting.[58] But this boast was not without a purpose.

55. Thomas Paine, *The Complete Writings of Thomas Paine*, ed. Philip S. Foner, 2 vols. (New York: The Citadel Press, 1945), 2:1322. But note that in an earlier letter, July 21, he notes that in a letter from Dublin of May 10 he learned that "the fourth edition was then on sale. I know not what number of copies were printed at each edition, except the second, which was ten thousand" (2:1318–19). Was he extrapolating from this print run for the second edition and simply assuming that each edition put another ten thousand copies into circulation?

56. Paine's dedication to "M de La Fayette" in Part II is dated "London, Feb 9, 1792." See *Rights of Man, Part the Second* (London: J. S .Jordan, 1982), vi. W. T. Sherwin noted in his biography that "The *Rights of Man*, part the second, combining principle and practice, was published by Mr Jordan, of Fleet Street, on the 16th February, 1792." See *Memoirs of the Life of Thomas Paine* (London: R. Carlile, 1819), 109.

57. It reads: "The principles on which this design is founded are strongly and unequivocally proved, from resolutions formed as early as the 18th May 1792, in which the society applaud the intention of publishing a cheap edition of the first and second parts of The Rights of Man." See *An Account of the Treason and Sedition, Committed by the London Corresponding Society, the Society for Constitutional Information, the Other . . .* (London: J. Downes, 1794).

58. The same point is made by a contemporary opponent, John Bowles, who notes that "In the Advertisement to the Second Part of 'The Rights of Man,' [note the use of the definite article in the cited title] the vain Author makes his boast of the extensive

The detail surrounding the publication of Part II also bears some scrutiny. Paine is said to have offered it to both Johnson and Jordan, and both declined for fear of prosecution. Then, through an intermediary, Thomas Christie, Paine offered the manuscript to a printer Thomas Chapman.[59] Chapman began typesetting the manuscript around the end of October 1791, and Paine planned to have the book on sale in time for the opening of the new Parliament on the last day of the year. But he was unable to complete the final pages of the text in time for this schedule. Chapman, it is said, sensing that the book would prove to be a sensation, attempted to buy the copyright from Paine, first offering a hundred guineas, then five hundred and finally one thousand.[60] Paine refused to sell, but, strangely, Chapman at some point changed his mind once he realized how dangerous it would be to publish the book. It is perhaps significant that this detail is provided by Chapman's affidavit at Paine's trial.[61] As Chapman tells the story, since he and Paine were supposed friends, he found all this rather

---

and numerous distribution of the copies of the First Part . . ." John Bowles, *A Protest against T. Paine's "Rights of Man;" Addressed to the Members of a Book Society, in Consequence of the Vote of Their Committee for Including the Above Work in a List of New Publications to be Purchased for the Use of the Society.* 2nd ed. (London: Society for Preserving Liberty and Property against Republicans and Levellers, 1792), v. Bowles claimed that the large number of copies in circulation had no direct connection to the value of Paine's arguments and, furthermore, that the only reason for such a large printing was the patronage of "those benevolent coadjutors in the same cause, whose liberality and exertions have chiefly contributed to the boasted multiplication of his copies, and who, by generous and pressing *donations*, have procured the acceptance thereof by numbers who could never have been persuaded to make the acquisition on any other terms" (vi–vii). Bowles also insinuates that, even if large numbers had been printed, the pages were most likely to have been used for wrapping goods, a view that seems to have had some circulation at the time. He puts it: "the generous circulation therefore of the far greater part of our Author's copies is probably of *immediate* convenience in divers retail branches of trade" (vii). The same claim was made by the prosecution at Paine's trial; on this occasion the pages were said to have been used for wrapping children's sweets.

59. At Paine's trial, Chapman claimed that he had printed the first edition of Part I of *Rights of Man*. See *The Whole Proceedings on the Trial of an Information Exhibited Ex Officio by the King's Attorney-General against Thomas Paine* (London: Martha Gurney, 1793), 84.

60. The retail price calculators provided by Economic History Services (http://eh.net/hmit) gives a conversion of £1 in 1790 as £69 in 2006—Paine, then, was being offered the equivalent of over £70,000.

61. Chapman told the court that he had printed up to page 112 before noticing that "there was a part, which, in my weak judgment, appeared of a dangerous tendency; I therefore immediately concluded in my mind not to proceed any farther in the work."

awkward and was not at all confident that he could easily impart this news to Paine. The story continues: The two men dine one night and fall into a dispute. Paine, according to Chapman, became "abusive" (under the influence of drink) and instructed Chapman to "go no further in his work," that is, cease the printing of his text. Chapman took this as a golden opportunity to walk away from publishing the text, so when an apologetic Paine turned up at his premises the next day Chapman refused to take the apology or to continue with the book. Paine had no alternative but to find another publisher, supposedly aghast and dumbfounded that someone who had recently offered to buy the copyright from him for a thousand guineas would now walk away.[62] But there is another strand to the story: Chapman, who had printed the scurrilous *Life* of Paine by Chalmers, may have been put up to the scheme for purchasing the copyright by government agents. Since he would have been able to alter the text or even suppress it entirely, a view that Paine himself arrived at, it is possible that the government was behind these negotiations.[63]

There is more darkness than light in what can be accurately stated about the intricate publication of *Rights of Man* for reasons that have been explored above. While the juggernaut that is the story of "the most widely read book of all time, in any language" continues to roll along, a more measured assessment opens up some intriguing possibilities.[64] Although

---

The Whole Proceedings on the Trial of an Information Exhibited Ex Officio by the King's Attorney-General against Thomas Paine (London: Martha Gurney, 1793), 85–86.

62. In an early nineteenth-century "life" of Paine, the *principle* is explained in the following manner: Mr. Paine told Chapman that "he would never put it in the power of any printer or publisher to suppress or alter a work of his, by making him master of the copy, or give him the right of selling it to any minister, or to any other person, or to treat as a mere matter of traffic that which he intended should operate as a principle." See W. T. Sherwin, *Memoirs of the Life of Thomas Paine* (London: R. Carlile, 1819), 108.

63. In a letter to Henry Dundas, Paine writes, "And I am now more convinced than ever before, that the offer that was made to me of a Thousand Pounds, for the copyright of the Second Part of the *Rights of Man*, together with the remaining copy-right of the First Part, was to have effected, by a quick suppression, what is now attempted to be done by a Prosecution." *Two Letters to Lord Onslow, Lord Lieutenant of the County of Surrey, and One to Mr Henry Dundas, Secretary of State, on the Subject of the Late Excellent Proclamation*, 4th ed. (London: James Ridgway, 1792), 14.

64. This extravagant claim as to readership is made by John Keane in his *Tom Paine: A Political Life* (London: Bloomsbury, 1995), 307. Keane cites E. P. Thompson, who himself noted that sales for the second part of *Rights of Man* "totalled 200,000" by 1793, a claim that, he writes, "has been widely accepted." See E. P. Thompson, *The Making of the English Working Class* (Harmondsworth: Penguin Books, 1963), 117.

Paine was no more disposed to give up his rights in intellectual property than anyone else, his experience of publishing *Common Sense* in the colonies may have shown him how to exploit the increasing mania for print. At the time of publication in 1776 no copyright law in the colonies allowed printers and booksellers to plunder Paine's text and bring to the market unauthorized editions. This almost certainly generated the unprecedented circulation of the pamphlet, a matter that Paine found irksome since it provided no royalties for the author.[65] After the appearance of Part II of *Rights of Man* it is clear that Paine received requests from booksellers to reprint his text. In his *Letter Addressed to the Addressers on the Late Proclamation* Paine states that "many applications were made to me from various parts of the country to print the work in a cheaper manner."[66] One such request "from the people of Sheffield" to print two thousand copies was immediately granted. Although Paine does not say how many other such requests he complied with, nor does he spell out that in these cases he was happy to forego royalties, indeed he goes on to note that, given the volume of such requests, he determined that it would be better to organize a cheap edition himself; if these "editions" were brought to the market he was doing something quite unusual and important in respect to the concept of rights. Essentially he was giving up any claim or title to the work, thereby allowing any printer or bookseller to bring out its own edition of *Rights of Man*.[67] Although this had not been his design or intention with *Common Sense*, that is effectively what happened. If we are to assume that this bears some connection to fact and that this was indeed the mechanism that led to the wide-scale circulation of *Rights of Man*, then his book on rights worked

65. On the printing and publishing history of *Common Sense*, see James. N Green, "English Books and Printing in the Age of Franklin," in *A History of the Book in America*, ed. Hugh Armory and David D. Hall (Chapel Hill: University of North Carolina Press, 2007), 1:248–98, esp. 295–96. For Paine's arguments with Robert Bell, the original publisher in Philadelphia, see John Keane, *Tom Paine: A Political Life* (London: Bloomsbury, 1995), 108–10.

66. Thomas Paine, *Letter Addressed to the Addressers on the Late Proclamation* (London: printed by the booksellers, 1792), 24.

67. This is how his early biographer, W. T. Sherwin told the story: "It is difficult to form an exact estimate of the number of copies which were circulated of the first and second parts of the *Rights of Man*, but at a very moderate calculation there was at least an hundred thousand of each. When Mr Paine saw the great interest which it excited, he thought the best mode of promulgating its principles, would be to give up the copyright in favour of the public, which he did, about two months after the appearance of the second part." *Memoirs of the Life of Thomas Paine* (London: R. Carlile, 1819), 112.

its way into the culture at large on account of the fact that he renounced his rights, his claim or title to his intellectual property. Paine was literally putting into practice a different concept of rights. Turning his back on the concept of "right" as title, he embraced a concept of "rights" as both singular and plural, belonging to both one and all, to the "whole." What is meant by such a common property and the "rights" that underpin it is more fully explored in the text of the first part of Paine's book, to which I now turn.

Principles and Rights

The initial hostile reactions to *Rights of Man*, in some cases certainly prompted by the government, focused on the modes of argument Paine used and, most attentively, on the language of the text.[68] In the scurrilous *The Life of Thomas Pain, the Author of Rights of Man. With a Defence of his Writings by Francis Oldys, A.M. of the University of Pennsylvania*, published under the pseudonym Oldys but in fact written by George Chalmers, a fierce loyalist to the crown who had been commissioned by the government,[69] the list of grammatical or syntactical errors in Paine's text is substantial.[70] Chalmers carped that Paine's text was full of "barbarism,"

68. See *A Defence of the Constitution of England against the Libels That Have Been Lately Published on It; Particularly in Paine's Pamphlet on the Rights of Man* (London: R. Baldwin, 1791), 48: "'*Rights of Man*' [section title]. This at present is a cant phrase, which we have borrowed from the French. . . . Mr Thomas Paine, who is neither a Mirabeau nor a Virgil, deals only in coarse and imprudent assertions."

69. "Francis Oldys" was "outed" almost immediately—see the title page of *Paine's Political and Moral Maxims* (London: The Booksellers, 1792): Commenting on the publication "said in the title [*The Life of Thomas Paine*] to be by Francis Oldys, A.M. of whom there is no such person; and the real Author is a clerk in office at Whitehall." Chalmers was quite a well-published author with John Stockdale, having brought out four titles in 1786, a two-volume *Collection of Treaties between Great Britain and Other Powers* in 1790. Chalmers was friends with Pitt, took government commissions for writing pro-government tracts and was erstwhile employed as the chief clerk at the Office of Trade. These details can be found in Eric Stockdale, *'Tis Treason, My Good Man! Four Revolutionary Presidents and a Piccadilly Bookshop* (New Castle, Del.: Oak Knoll Press, 2005), 265, 296.

70. The title of this text went through some variations; it was, of course, no defense at all. The first three editions/printings have "with a defence of his writings"; the fifth edition has "with a review of his writings, particularly of Rights of Man, parts first and second"; the sixth edition has it *"The Life of Thomas Paine, the Author of the Seditious*

"solecism," "impropriety," and "nonsense."[71] It was not only Chalmers, however, who took the view that someone whose English was so faulty could only have faulty political opinions.[72] This was the line taken by many hostile reviewers and down to our own era has prompted some careful and illuminating accounts of the politics of grammar in the period.[73] But in Paine's own time the bottom line, seen from the angle of the language police, was that a vulgar tongue could only serve the interests of a vulgar people.[74] This is why the pro-reformers picked up on Burke's phrase *the*

Writings, Entitled Rights of Man," and this title seems to have persisted through the tenth edition. All these editions were published by John Stockdale between 1791 and 1793. The seeming inconsistency that the first publication in 1791 of this "Life" contains comment on Part II of *Rights of Man* (which was not published until 1792) may be accounted for in two ways. On the one hand, it has been claimed that Chalmers got sight of the manuscript of Paine's Part II while it was in press, while, on the other, it may be the case that the dates given on title pages are not absolutely accurate. There is also a London edition with title *The Life of Thomas Paine, the Author of Rights of Men. With a Defence of His Writings. By Francis Oldys, A.M. of the University of Pennsylvania* (London: J Stockdale, 1791) and this copy seems to have provided the title for Dublin editions in 1791 and 1795.

71. *The Life of Thomas Paine, the Author of Rights of Man. With a Defence of His Writings* by Francis Oldys of the University of Pennsylvania (London: John Stockdale, 1791), 28.

72. See *A British Freeholder's Address to His Countrymen, on Thomas Paine's Rights of Man* (London: B. White and Son, 1791), 9: "One thing indeed Paine has plainly shewn, viz. that there is in the world a more paltry blurrer of sheets than the Penman of the National Assembly; he writes such grammar as '*himself fled*,' uses such words as '*prior-ily*,' such phrases as '*very unacquainted*,' and such expressions as '*acts persuasion upon itself to suffocate its judgment*.'" Charles Harrington Elliot, *The Republican Refuted; In a Series of Biographical, Critical and Political Strictures on Thomas Paine's Rights of Man* (London: W. Richardson, 1791), 91: "If he understood grammar. . . ." *The Monthly Review* (May 1791) complained that Paine's style was "desultory, uncouth, and inelegant," continuing, "his wit is coarse, and sometimes disgraced by wretched puns; and his language, though energetic, is awkward, ungrammatical, and often debased by vulgar phraseology." Horace Walpole rather haughtily commented that Paine's style "is so coarse, that you would think he means to degrade the language as much as the government." See *Horace Walpole's Correspondence*, W. S. Lewis, ed. (New Haven, Conn.: Yale University Press, 1973), 11, 239.

73. See John Barrell, *English Literature in History 1730–80: An Equal, Wide Survey* (London: Hutcheson, 1983); Olivia Smith, *The Politics of Language* (Oxford: Clarendon Press, 1984).

74. See Charles Hawtrey, *Various Opinions of the Philosophical Reformers Considered; Particularly Pain's Rights of Man* (London: John Stockdale, 1792), 2: "The author of a publication, entitled, 'The Rights of Man,' has given us pretty much in detail the opinions of modern philosophers, and he has given them in a language which is sufficiently

swinish multitude (in their own case used with a great deal of irony) in order
to point up the politics of class and rank. Burke and his ilk were, according to these less well-connected people, merely reproducing the political
repression promulgated for centuries by the aristocracy on the laboring
classes. Here it is useful to remember that the reform movement in the
1790s, although far from exclusively a grassroots phenomenon, was very
sensitive to issues of entitlement. The working men who met in taverns
and the like to discuss republicanism did not do so entirely upon theoretical grounds, nor for anything like theoretical objectives.

It would equally be inaccurate to portray Paine as an intellectual, or
someone well versed in the political theory and history of political thought
of the Western tradition. It is unlikely that he would have lasted long in
debate over the conceptual refinements of political theory, still less that
he would have had at his fingertips the works of John Locke or Niccolò
Machiavelli. Paine was a hugely successful pamphleteer who wrote in an
idiom he deemed appropriate to his real and desired audience. Even so, it
is useful to also note that Paine's most important antagonist over *Rights
of Man*—at least the person named on its title page as the prompt for his
remarks—shied away from the high rhetoric and complex argument of
theory.[75] Burke also explicitly wrote in an idiom that distanced itself from
the language of political philosophy.[76] There is clearly an issue here over
the nature of the public sphere, its composition and perhaps enlargement,
toward the end of the eighteenth century in Britain.[77] But I want to leave

vulgar, virulent, and scurrilous." Sir Brooke Boothby, *Observations on the Appeal from
the New to the Old Whigs, and on Mr Paine's Rights of Man. In Two Parts* (London: John
Stockdale, 1792), 273–74: "If I were to precognize "Rights of Man," in a few words I
should say, that it is the work of a shrewd empiric, written in a kind of specious jargon,
well enough calculated to impose upon the vulgar. . . ."

75. This is in part a reaction to the "Frenchness" of the republican revolution of
1789. For a powerful account of the valencies of Englishness and its difference from
Frenchness, see David Simpson, *Romanticism, Nationalism, and the Revolt against Theory*
(Chicago: University of Chicago Press, 1993), esp. chs. 2 and 3.

76. On this, see Steven Blakemore, *Burke and the Fall of Language: The French Revolution as Linguistic Event* (Hanover, N.H.: University Press of New England, 1988);
James T. Boulton, *The Language of Politics in the Age of Wilkes and Burke* (London: Routledge & Keegan Paul, 1963).

77. It is no longer possible to speak of "a" public sphere with confidence since
the detailed exhumation of local contexts within which political, religious, social, and
familial life expressed itself indicates a heterogenous cultural field. The by now well-
worn Habermasian picture of coffee houses and print culture provides but an outline
of the different publics and different spheres into which eighteenth-century actors

this albeit important issue to one side in order to make another point: Grammar is at stake in more than one way. Paine's critics were, in fact, almost certainly unknown to themselves, or, to put that another way, only subconsciously aware of the difference in conceptual grammar between "right(s)" and "rights of man."[78] Thus, both Paine and Burke, whether or not such a characterization would have convinced either, were staging a battle over the grammar of a concept.

The argument I wish to pursue here needs to be seen in all its subtleties. I am not suggesting, for example, that Paine either invented or consciously invoked the concept of "rights of man" as I have been developing it over the last three chapters. Nor do I want to suggest that Paine had no use for the counterconcept of "right(s)." In fact, following the French Declaration of the Rights of Man and Citizen, which explicitly treats the rights of man as countable and specifiable, as structured through the element of the deposit, based upon the concept "right(s)," discussion of the topic of rights in Britain regularly invoked the trinity of life, liberty, and property.[79] And in doing so it was, of course, fully immersed in a very long-standing tradition in which rights were understood to have a legal basis, precisely in a claim or a title. As has been noted in previous chapters, this tradition was developed

---

were inserted (variously and incoherently). One should call to mind here not only the "dispossessed"—women, minors, the poor, and so forth—but also the multiple agencies that might have coalesced in a single individual. We need, then, to take account of a very large range of enclaves before arriving at even an approximate picture of the public spheres in the period. I have in mind here pioneering work of the following kind: Iain McCalman, *Radical Underworld: Prophets, Revolutionaries and Pornographers in London, 1795–1840* (Cambridge: Cambridge University Press, 1988); John Barrell, *The Spirit of Despotism: Invasions of Privacy in the 1790s* (Oxford: Oxford University Press, 2006); *Women, Writing and the Public Sphere, 1700–1830*, ed. Elizabeth Eger, Charlotte Grant, Clíona Ó Gallachoir, and Penny Warburton (Cambridge: Cambridge University Press, 2001); Andrew McCann, *Cultural Politics in the 1790s: Literature, Radicalism, and the Public Sphere* (London: Macmillan, 1999).

78. The critical attack launched by Charles Harrington Elliot provides a good example: Elliot takes pains in his text to disarticulate "the rights of man" from "rights of man" by using scare quotes when referring not only to the title of Paine's book but also to the rights he—Paine—claimed to be defending, thereby unwittingly highlighting the issue of a difference in grammar. See Charles Harrington Elliot, *The Republican Refuted; In a Series of Biographical, Critical and Political Strictures on Thomas Paine's Rights of Man* (London: W. Richardson, 1791), 37.

79. The dissemination of the text of the French Declaration was extremely widespread in Britain, pushed along by associations like the SCI but also in review journals and through ephemeral publications.

to a considerable degree in the ethical project of natural law and conceived of such claims as having corresponding obligations: Rights always come hand in hand with duties. By the time Paine came to pen his defense of the French, the hinged concept "rights-duty" was in the descendant; like many British writers after 1789, he intoned the mantra-like second codicil of the French declaration that was built upon the architectural element of the deposit: "The end of all political associations, is, the preservation of the natural and imprescriptible rights of man; and these rights are liberty, property, security, and resistance of oppression."[80] Thus in some places he explicitly refers to a distinction between "natural" and "civil" rights.[81] And he also thinks of natural rights as falling within different kinds or classes: "It will be easy to distinguish between that class of natural rights which man retains after entering into society, and those which he throws into common stock as a member of society."[82] Here Paine is simply invoking the standard line on those natural rights which are conceptualized as operative in a "state of nature" that must be relinquished on our entry into the collectivities of the social. While some of his contemporaries wished to emphasize that such a "state of nature" could only be a fiction and that, therefore, those rights which pertained in that state were merely conjectural, Paine was not overly concerned with the "realism" of the argument. But when, after having cited the codicils of the French declaration, Paine begins his commentary and exposition, we find play at work within his invocation of the concept of "right(s)," a play that I think indicates an embrace of a different way of thinking rights. And if one reads carefully, one can find this same play at work much earlier in the text where Paine is setting out his stall.

Already on page 12 of the first edition, Paine's text opens up the reading I am going to press. He is here commenting on Burke's assertion that at the revolution in 1688 a "body of men" made a law that no one has the power

80. Thomas Paine, *Rights of Man* (London: J. Johnson, 1791), 118. See also Samuel Sterns, *Dr Stearns's Tour from London to Paris* (London: C. Dilly, 1790), 83: ". . . the natural, imprescriptible, inalienable, and sacred rights of man"; William Belsham, *Essays, Philosophical, Historical, and Literary. In four Volumes* (Dublin: J. Moore, 1791), 3:157; Sir James Mackintosh, *Vindiciae Gallicae*, 2nd ed. (London, G. G. J. and J. Robinson, 1791), 220; and the many translations and digests of the French Declaration. See, for example, Christopher Frederic Triebner, *A Key to the French Revolution* (London: printed for the author, 1794).

81. "Hitherto we have spoken only (and that but in part) of the natural rights of man. We have now to consider the civil rights of man, and to shew how the one originates out of the other," Thomas Paine, *Rights of Man* (London: J. Johnson, 1791), 79.

82. Thomas Paine, *Rights of Man* (London: J. Johnson, 1791), 80.

to alter. This point is one of the hotly contested arguments between the two writers and indeed it spread quickly into the contemporary reactions to the text. Paine insists that no agent has the power to tie the hands of posterity and that, therefore, it is legitimate for any person or group of persons to challenge the current arrangements vis-à-vis government. Burke, conservative that he was, could not allow for such a destabilizing force within the polis. Paine gently makes fun of Burke's position—"Mr Burke has done some service, not to his cause, but to his country"[83]—before entering his own forensic analysis. That the offence for which James II was expelled, "setting up power by *assumption,*" was replicated by the Parliament that expelled him ". . . shews, that the rights of man were but imperfectly understood at the revolution."[84] There are two ways of taking this comment. On the one hand, it can mean that in 1688 the content of the rights of man were not completely understood, which is to say that binding the future must always be an infringement of liberty if one of those rights is the right to elect a government. On the other hand, it can mean that the concept "rights of man" was imperfectly understood *as a concept.* Those historical actors did not grasp the fact that there are differences in kind in respect to the concepts of rights. This second reading is to some extent a latency within the text, but when we become alerted to that second sense, further passages stand out as playfully allowing this different concept of rights, "rights of man," to emerge.

Thus, some eight pages later, Paine wishes to underscore a point that will become far more telling, namely Burke's resistance to "principles," by noting that "in the instance of France, we see a revolution generated in the rational contemplation of the rights of man," and this "rational" approach makes a distinction between "persons and principles." It is easy to see how this comment plays into the critical reception of both texts.[85] In the case of Burke, his seductive and in places sentimental account, self-confessedly written without regard for the niceties of political philosophy, puts great stress on the actions of the revolutionaries and their consequences for the hapless individuals who bore the brunt of their anger and frustration at the system of government they wished to overturn. His attention was firmly fixed on "persons." Down to our own day, this is how Burke's reaction to

83. Ibid., 12.

84. Ibid.

85. One of the immediate responses to Paine's text picks up precisely this point. See *Cursory Remarks on Dr Priestley's Letters to Mr Burke and Strictures on Mr Paine's "Rights of Man"* (London: R. Faulder, 1791), 62.

the revolution has been remembered, frequently, if not obsessively em-
blematized in the account of Marie Antoinette's suffering at the hands of
the revolutionaries as she was accosted in her bed at Versailles.[86] The passage is no doubt justly renowned for its high rhetoric—"A band of cruel
ruffians and assassins, reeking with his blood, rushed into the chamber of
the queen, and pierced with an hundred strokes of bayonets and poniards
the bed, from when this persecuted woman had but just time to fly almost naked . . ."[87]—but behind the sentimental language the attachment
to "person" is also doing something else.[88] In contrast those who criticized
Paine, then and now, wish to see him as extolling the theory of republican
government with its stress on "principles" without the faintest regard for
the consequences of holding to the beliefs he recommends.[89] Hindsight,
here, allows us to temper our assessment of Paine's politics in the knowledge that revolution in France had its dark side, the terror.

86. The immediate reception of Burke's text latched on to these few paragraphs,
sometimes to the detriment of Marie Antoinette's reputation. For these and other uses
made of Burke's sentimental prose, see F. P. Lock, *Burke's Reflections on the Revolution in
France* (London: Allen & Unwin, 1985), 138–43; Tom Furniss, *Edmund Burke's Aesthetic
Ideology: Language, Gender and Political Economy in Revolution* (Cambridge: Cambridge
University Press, 1993), esp. ch 6.

87. Edmund Burke, *Reflections on the Revolution in France, and on the Proceedings in
Certain Societies in London Relative to that Event* (London: J. Dodsley, 1790), 105–6.

88. J. G. A. Pocock in his introduction to the text sees a purpose behind the "emo-
tionally extravagant and historically sophisticated" prose of these passages. He argues
that Burke was advocating the importance of manners to a well-functioning commercial
society. See J. G. A. Pocock, ed. *Reflections on the Revolution in France* (Indianapolis,
Ind.: Hackett, 1987), see xxi, xxxii–xxxiii. Tom Furniss wishes to see Burke's account
in relation to his aesthetics, most especially the "sublime resources of language" and its
"*arbitrary* relation to ideas/or reality." Furniss argues that this leads to Burke's being unable to control the effects of his theatrical account of Marie Antoinette's suffering. See
Tom Furniss, *Edmund Burke's Aesthetic Ideology: Language, Gender and Political Economy
in Revolution* (Cambridge: Cambridge University Press, 1993), ch. 6, 163. If one reads
both Burke's account and his letters at the time; however, it is difficult to see how he
loses control of his language, or indeed that he was not fully cognizant of its (desired)
effects.

89. In a critical attack on Paine, John Bowles accuses him precisely of mistaking the
difference between "theory" and "practice" and of being a man "who has never had any
reputation either for principle or prudence." See John Bowles, *Dialogues on the Rights
of Britons, between a Farmer, a Sailor, and a Manufacturer* (London: T. Longman et al.,
1792), 15, 22. See also the pro-Paine text that characterizes the attacks on "the *natural*
Rights of Man" as having "no existence but in the imagination of Theorists." See *The
Political Crisis: or, a Dissertation on the Rights of Man* (London: J. S. Jordan, 1791), 75.

No doubt this armature around "principle" and "person" accurately lo-
cates a set of differences in both the aims and objectives the two writers
had and the character of their respective descriptions of the Revolution.
Paine, after all, determined to write his counterblast to Burke because he
thought his erstwhile friend had traduced the revolution and the achieve-
ments of the revolutionaries. But there is another way of reading this armature "principle/person" in order to make a slightly different point. If we
take the statement that in France there was a "revolution" in the "rational
contemplation of the rights of man" to mean that *how* rights were conceived underwent a revolution—that there was a *conceptual* revolution, and
that alteration was between "persons" and "principles"—then I think it is
possible to see how the second concept of rights, that of "rights of man"
begins to emerge in Paine's text.[90]

Paine is opening the thought that "right(s)" based upon persons, that is,
rights conceptualized as a title or claim that a person may have on another,
is to be distinguished from "rights of man," where rights are understood
not as to something or on behalf of someone but as a nonspecifiable aspiration, "rights of man" held as a self-evident belief by a collectivity, by what
he calls "the *whole.*" The distinction he is allowing to come into focus is
between rights conceived as title, claim, that is, rights conceived as quasi-
material, things, which may be held by an individual, as if one's own property or due and, in contrast, rights as incapable of singular possession, declared on behalf of persons, of individuals, by the collective category man.
"Rights of Man" are, under this description, only available, as it were, to
the whole and not to the individual. This is precisely the point Paine made
in the letter he sent to the court on the occasion of his trial: Paine, writing from France, notes, "My necessary absence from your country now,
in consequence of my duty here, affords me the opportunity of knowing
whether the prosecution was intended against Thomas Paine," or, rather,
"against the Rights of the People of England." Reasoning along these lines,
Paine suggests that he could not be the object of the prosecution and that
"something else was the object, and that something else can be no other
than the people of England." Thus the government was in fact bringing

90. This is precisely the point at issue in the following critical account of Paine's argument: "We learn also that the elections in France were not of men, but of principles;
that is, in fact, of *prejudices*; or I know not in this case how to comprehend Mr Paine's
distinction between a man and his principles." *Cursory Remarks on Dr Priestley's Letters to Mr Burke, and Strictures on Mr Paine's "Rights of Man"* (London: R. Faulder,
1791), 63.

a case against *"their rights."*[91] The distinction, then, between "principles" and "persons" is far more conceptually decisive than is often seen to be the case. This is why an account of "human rights" that sees its invention as dependent upon something like "sympathy" is so wide of the mark, at least if one is to argue that the concept of "rights of man" as it began to be circulated in the 1790s in Britain is identical to or the historical precedent for what we have learned to call "human rights."[92]

This way of understanding "principle" was embedded in the radical culture within which Paine moved. One can find it explicitly outlined in the Society for Constitutional Information's digest of a treatise by Major Cartwright, *The People's Barrier against Undue Influence*.[93] In that text a "principle" is defined as "a manifest and simple proposition comprehending a certain truth." The standard reading of Paine's characterization of Burke has him (Burke) running scared of "principle" in the sense of theory, that is, failing to take on Paine's argument in its own terms as a set of propositions in the abstract about the nature and forms of government (certainly a reading that has purchase), but this alternative that I am now suggesting, a kind of viral activity within the text, points somewhere else: to the conceptual architecture of "rights of man." For not only does Cartwright describe a "principle" as a 'simple proposition," he also states that "principles are the proof of everything; but are not capable of external proof, being self-evident." If the concept of "rights of man" is to be understood as a "principle," then, it is self-evident and does not require proof. Its architectural element is the platform and the modality of thinking it prompts is axiomatic. Furthermore, the basis for holding to this belief is not the oft-invoked sense of what it is to be human, that is, an individual being—precisely the assumed basis for holding human rights in our own time—but our sense of belonging to something larger than self, the individual, to the collective community howsoever described. This is the point that Paine makes in the very opening of his text, where, in citing Burke's criticism of Price, he

91. *The Whole Proceedings on the Trial of an Information Exhibited Ex Officio by the King's Attorney-General against Thomas Paine* (London: Martha Gurney, 1793), 93–94.

92. This is the argument proposed by Lynn Hunt in *Inventing Human Rights* (New York: W. W. Norton and Company, 2007).

93. One of the most significant activities of the SCI was its redaction of radical texts, circulated for free in the pamphlets published by the Society. As Jon Mee points out, the radical corresponding societies were more "devoted to putting ideas into circulation" than in "stabilising a particular programme." "Popular Radical Culture," in *The Cambridge Companion to British Literature of the French Revolution in the 1790s*, ed. Pamela Clemit (Cambridge: Cambridge University Press, 2011), 118.

notes, "Dr Price does not say that the right to do these things exists in this or that person, or in this or that description of persons, but that it exists in the *whole*."[94] And for Price in his own text that larger collective is imagined as "the nation." Exactly the same point was made in a declaration penned by Paine and agreed at the select meeting of the Friends of Universal Peace and Liberty, held at the Thatched House Tavern, St. James Street, on August 20, 1791. In that document the "French nation" was congratulated for having "laid the axe to the root of tyranny, and for erecting government on the sacred *hereditary rights of man*." These rights are said to "appertain to ALL, and not to any one more than to another," but, contra the more common understanding of the basis or authority of that claim, the sanctity of our each being human, our individuality, Paine states that "we know of no human authority superior to that of a whole nation." And, in making clear the consequence of the rights of man being derived from the legitimacy of the nation, he uses the language that was more commonly attached to the promotion of subjective rights: "And we profess and proclaim it as our principle that every nation has at all times an inherent and indefeasible right to constitute and establish such government for itself as best accords with its disposition, interest, and happiness."[95] My point, then, is that the force of the subjective or individual is tempered by its being corralled into the larger category of the whole. Men, the persons that we are, have rights in a legal sense, which are codified by the long-standing European tradition of the discourse on rights, but "rights of man" are held by no one in particular, indeed cannot be held *by* the individual, even if all individuals aspire *to* them. Such rights are conjugated in the tense of the future-present.

"Man" as the Singular Universal

There is good evidence to suggest that the radical British culture of the last decades of the eighteenth century was developing precisely such a nonsubjective account of rights. Richard Price's *Discourse on the Love of Our Country*, the prompt of course for Burke's attack on the radical culture of his time, explicitly raises the notion that a politics of mutual respect, what today we might think under the rubric of communitarianism, must throw away any dependence on the singularity of person. Price illustrates this

94. Thomas Paine, *Rights of Man* (London: J. Johnson, 1791), 7.

95. Thomas Paine, *The Complete Writings of Thomas Paine*, ed. Philip S. Foner, 2 vols. (New York: Citadel Press, 1945), 2:534–35.

point in his caution against promoting one's own nation to the detriment of others. In the case of our own country, he observes, "that love of it which is our duty, does not imply any conviction of the superior value of it to other countries, or any particular preference of its laws and constitution of government."[96] If that were the case, he notes, then only a few people of the world would be required to honor the duty he says is common to humankind, precisely those citizens within any one nation, state, or country who imagine themselves to be the most enlightened. On the contrary, "to found, there, this duty on such a preference, would be to found it on error and delusion."[97] Rather sardonically he notes in passing that "It is, however, a common delusion," and then, the point I want to underscore, he makes the move from nation to person in order to highlight the same difficulty with basing one's sense of how to act correctly on the self: "There is the same partiality in countries, to themselves, as there is in individuals."[98] Both, of course, are said to be an error or a delusion. The problem, as he points out, is that "we are too apt to confine wisdom and virtue within the circle of our own acquaintance and party,"[99] which read within the context of the development of a nonsubjective accounts of common rights, "rights of man," implies that the last place we ought to look for the basis of holding to those rights is our selves. It is because of this that "a wise man," Price says, "will guard himself against this delusion"; he will "study to think of all things as they are, and not suffer any partial affections to blind his understanding."[100] This is as far away from an account of "human rights" based on sympathy for our fellow men as one could get. That, Price suggests, is delusion. And of course it is just that sense of sympathy that Burke, in his rhetorical ramping up of the treatment of Marie Antoinette, sought to evoke.[101]

96. Richard Price, *A Discourse on the Love of Our Country* (London: T. Cadell, 1789), 3.

97. Ibid.

98. Ibid., 3–4.

99. Ibid., 4.

100. Ibid.

101. David Duff makes an extremely useful point about the hybridity of both Burke's and Paine's texts, noting that the *Reflections* contain "a huge range of expressive modes including biblical prophecy, Miltonic epic, Scriblerian satire, chivalric romance, elegy, georgic, aphorism and tragedy." "Burke and Paine: Contrasts," in *The Cambridge Companion to British Literature of the French Revolution in the 1790s*, ed. Pamela Clemit (Cambridge: Cambridge University Press, 2011), 68.

In order to understand how the radical culture of the 1790s began to develop a nonsubjective account of rights, it is necessary to reconstruct the conceptual networks that held in suspension the key terms. In this regard the edges that enabled connections between the concepts of "right(s)," "rights of man," and "man" or the "human" are of the utmost significance. Thus, although "right(s)" was commonly articulated through a connection with "man" in the long train of the natural-rights tradition (since that tra-dition sees rights as claims, which must be made on behalf of individuals), the edge was not exclusively lined up with "rights-man," and the network relation between "rights" and "man" was not exclusively dependent. Given this, the concept of "rights" allowed one to think of them as capable of being assigned to others, to animals certainly, but also in some strange cases to things.[102] In contrast, the concept "rights of man" was linked in a dependent relation to the concept of "man," where that functioned in a load-bearing capacity: It was this that made it possible to operate a concept of universal rights axiomatically.

Paine, for example, allows one to see the lineaments of the network connection when he cites Burke's critique of the French Declaration as having no content (a critique that will become far more pointed in late twentieth-century philosophical discussions of human rights), as "paltry and blurred sheets of paper about the rights of man," because as far as Paine was concerned the real issue between him and his opponent lay in the conceptualization of the human. "Man," in Paine's activation of the con-ceptual network, is a noetic concept operating with an axiomatic modality in respect to rights. This difference between Burke and Paine around the employment of conceptual forms can be seen in the former's characteriza-tion of the French Declaration as a paltry sheet of paper *about* the rights of man. That is, his conceptualization of "rights" assumes that they must have a content. The alternative architecture that supports "rights of man" cannot entertain a transitive inflection. "Right(s)" is transitive, "rights of man" is intransitive. Paine gets to the nub of this point when he chides his opponent: "Does Mr Burke mean to deny that *man* has any rights?"[103] I take this to mean that a singular man, an individual or agent, might well have "right(s)," where the concept of rights is to be understood as a claim

<hr/>

102. See Thomas Young, *An Essay on Humanity to Animals* (London: T. Cadell et al., 1798). The argument of this tract is that since animals are capable of both pain and pleasure they also possess rights. This, the author notes, is "the same sort of argument as that on which Moralists found the Rights of Mankind" (8).

103. Thomas Paine, *Rights of Man* (London: J. Johnson, 1791), 44.

or a title, but "*man*" in general stakes no claim upon anyone: Its conceptual architecture, the platform, is derived from the distinction between persons and principles. Read the alternative way I am proposing, "*man*," explicitly italicized, refers to the "principle" or noetic concept of the human that requires no proof. And since, according to Paine, it is self-evident that there are men in the world, there must also therefore be "rights of man." This is not the same thing as saying there must be "right(s)" or that there must be rights of *men*. Thus when he quizzes, "if Mr Burke means to admit that man has rights, the question then will be, what are those rights,"[104] he is not only asking if the content of "rights" can be made explicit; he is not only posing a question to which the answer might be "the rights to elect governments, to security of life and to property"—all of which Paine will defend under a different rubric. The alternative that lies within this first question is, what is the conceptual structure of "rights of man"? What (is) are *rights of man*?

In a very important passage that comes two pages later, Paine outlines his concept of the human as the singular universal. The "divine principle of the equal rights of man"—there again the principle as self-evident truth— "relates not only to the living individuals, but to generations of men succeeding each other."[105] At first sight this looks like an about-face in his argument with Burke, who had, according to Paine, attempted to tie the hands of the future illegitimately, against a universal right, against "rights of man." But in fact his comment is actually a corrective to Burke's misunderstanding of the hereditary ties that bind us to our forefathers and our descendants. That vertical integration is not made binding by the fact that the content of rights remains stable: Put simply, Paine is not saying that humankind has the same rights through time. Rather, as he puts it: "Every generation is equal in rights to the generations which preceded it."[106] The equality of rights is not held as a possession; he claims not that every generation has identical rights but that generations are "equal in rights," that is, they have the same basis for invoking "*rights of man*." And the reason for this is because when we are born we join all those before us and those who will come in the future *as men*, as humans. In this way, he accounts for the fact that every generation is equal in rights "by the same rule that every individual is born equal in rights with his contemporary."[107] Every person has

104. Ibid.
105. Ibid., 46.
106. Ibid.
107. Ibid.

the same relation to the concept "rights of man," a principle that flows from the fact that such a noetic concept operates in the modality of the axiomatic: It is self-evident truth. This is because being human is to be both singular, a person, and universal, man. As he writes, "all agree in establishing one point, *the unity of man*; by which I mean that man is all of *one degree*, and consequently that all men are born equal, and with equal natural rights."[108] I want to insist here that Paine is not drawing on a concept of man whose architecture enables one to understand the singularity of person or, to put that in more modern terms, that makes sense of the concept "identity." He is precisely refusing the subjective account of human being, personhood. In its place he invokes the plural or general concept of man, whose form is adaptive. While personhood may be intelligible under a different architecture for the concept of man, precisely the conceptual declension Burke holds fast to, man constructed upon the element of the deposit, Paine is happy to let this go just as he gives away the copyright of his text.

   In a critical response to Paine's text published in its immediate wake, Charles Elliot's *The Republican Refuted*, one can see how a contemporary reader picked up the niceties of the point I am making, albeit with a different purpose in view and using a slightly different forensics. Elliot takes Paine to task for his "vulgar" language and inability to control his "overheated mind."[109] He comments that around page 46 of Paine's text he finds "little or nothing occurs but unmeaning rant, to amaze and confound the ignorant."[110] Although it "disgusts the intelligent reader," Paine has, he notes, fortuitously provided a glossary which, according to Elliot, enables one to understand how "the *unity* of man" is the same thing as "the *equality* of man." This sets Elliot off on a point of grammar: "I thought till now he might have travelled through the accidence at the grammar school in *Thetford*, as far as old *unus, una, unum*, the root from which this *branching* cyon of *unity* springs."[111] At first sight one seems to have wandered into the carping of those critics who tried to disarm Paine's text on account of its weak grip on standard English grammar, but the point Elliot develops actually reveals something rather more interesting: It identifies precisely what was at stake in how one operated the conceptual architecture of "man," as to whether

---

   108. Ibid.
   109. Charles Harrington Elliot, *The Republican Refuted: In a Series of biographical, Critical and Political Strictures on Thomas Paine's Rights of Man* (London: W. Richardson, 1791), 1.
   110. Ibid., 34.
   111. Ibid.

its modality was schematic or axiomatic. Thus, he notes that "*Unity* is the quality of being *one*," something that we attribute to God, for example, as there is "but *one* God," though, as he further notes, "with submission to the *Old Jewry*, there may be *three persons.*" While one might correctly speak of the unity of a drama with respect to the handling of time and place, for example, or the unity of friendship that conveys how friends can be of "one mind," it is an error to speak of "the *unity of man*, if applied in this its only sense to an *individual* of the human race."[112] This, Elliot claims, is "a most absurd *pleonasm*," and "if to *mankind* in general, its application is still more absurd." "Man," according to this way of seeing things, cannot be a unity if that means there is only one man, which is to note that the concept could not operate with a schematic modality. Yet, and this is the point Elliot is making, for Paine the singular universal must operate with a schematic modality: What is true in the case of one man applies to all men. Even more problematically, the absurdity also arises if the unity is to be applied to the general, to mankind, since in this case the concept has nothing to provide a schema for: There is only a single entity "mankind."

Elliot was not the only contemporary critic who picked up on this conceptual architectonics. A similar point was made in another critical response that began by outlining the pitfalls of transforming a "civil government" into a republican one. If this were to happen, the country would be without a constitution to which one might refer in order to secure one's liberty. This, the author maintains, would involve connecting "an idea of relation to the word *unity*, which appears totally inapplicable to any thing but its opposite, that is *plurality*."[113] Such cockeyed reasoning has only one terminus, the inevitable descent into absurdity created by the disintegration of meaning.[114] As the author explains, "if I can attach no sense whatever to a word commonly in use in my own language," then in little or no time I expect "not to understand my own language at all."[115] What both

---

112. Ibid.

113. *Cursory Remarks on Dr Priestley's Letters to Mr Burke, and Strictures on Mt Paine's "Rights of Man"* (London: R. Faulder, 1791), 58–59.

114. Critics of Paine were quick to make this charge. For another version, see *Defence of the Rights of Man; Being a Discussion of the Conclusions Drawn from Those Rights by Mr Paine* (London: T. Evans, 1791), 16: "Most of his [Paine's] reasoning, if sifted and discussed in the same manner, would produce nothing but such absurdities, and would only be a subject of laughter, did not his specious language and sophistry impose upon such readers as are not at the trouble to examine him."

115. *Cursory Remarks on Dr Priestley's Letters to Mr Burke, and Strictures on Mt Paine's "Rights of Man"* (London: Parsons, 1791), 59.

these critics miss is the effort Paine is undertaking to parse the concept "man" in such a way that its edge—its connective ports that enable it to be joined to other concepts in the nexus—allows one to decline a concept of universal rights that makes the unity of man, man as the singular universal, intelligible. It was only by holding the two concepts "man" and "rights" in mutual tension, linked in a network that allowed the one to support the other, that the concept "rights of man" became a resource within the political culture of the 1790s.[116]

If one returns to Burke's argument, the contours of the conceptual distinction I have been drawing attention to can be seen quite clearly. Burke and Paine did not only, or simply, differ in their view of government and of the right of the governed to choose those who govern them; they worked with different modalities of the concept of the human. Their argument was not so much over *the* rights of man, but over rights of *man*. Here is Burke outlining the argument—commonly invoked and well embedded in the political theory of the day—over the distances and differences between the state of nature and civil society: "One of the first motives to civil society . . . is *that no man should be judge in his own cause* . . . He abdicates all right to be his own governor."[117] And, at the same time as he loses this power he also "in great measure" abandons "the right of self-defence." You cannot, says Burke, "enjoy the rights of an uncivil and of a civil state together."[118] Dressed up in the rhetoric of common sense, Burke was playing out the line that distinguished rights as to kind. Some kinds of right, those all civilized nations live by, constrict absolute freedom in the belief that a just society

---

116. This exfoliation of a new architecture for rights can be seen in texts opposing Paine's ideas as well those supporting. On this, see the discussion of the critical reactions to *Rights of Man* below. The most vigorous attack, for example, penned by the government *agent provocateur* "Francis Oldys," a.k.a. George Chalmers, sets in motion the very conceptual virus it seeks to neuter. ". . . with regard to RIGHTS OF MAN. By thus suppressing designedly the article *the*," Chalmers remarks, Paine "shews his intention . . . not to treat of the whole rights of mankind, but of particular rights." This, Chalmers opines, is fine, but somehow Paine lost the plot, departing from his original design and "now wished that *the* rights of man might become as universal as Washington's benevolence." And then the crucial characterization emerges: "They doubted the propriety of our author's sentiment; because *the* rights of man must be as universal as the residence of mankind." See [George Chalmers], *The Life of Thomas Paine, the Author of Rights of Man. With a Defence of his Writings* (London: John Stockdale, 1791), 107–8.

117. Edmund Burke, *Reflections on the Revolution in France, and on the Proceedings in Certain Societies in London Relative to That Event* (London: J. Dodsley, 1790), 88.

118. Ibid.

must have some way of accounting for the fact that my freedom is someone else's constraint. But others, which "may and do exist in total independence" of the government, are in "a much greater degree of abstract perfection." These are the rights we have in the state of nature, but they have no practical extension: "Their abstract perfection is their practical defect."[119] It is precisely this abstract quality that deems such rights beyond the purview of man as he is, as a citizen in civil society. "What is the use." Burke says, "of discussing a man's abstract right to food or to medicine?"[120]; these and other "rights in principle" are labeled by him "metaphysic rights."[121] And, as such, they are fictions; they can never be realized in the world of competing desires and scarce resources. They are abstractions that were never put into practice: "The pretended rights" of the revolutionary thinkers in France, called by Burke "theorists," are "all extremes; and in proportion as they are metaphysically true, they are morally and politically false."[122] On account of this—here Burke strikes to the heart of the matter, the emergence of a different conceptual architecture for "rights of man"—"The rights of men are in a sort of *middle*, incapable of definition, but not impossible to be discerned."[123] This is precisely the point that Paine went on to develop under the aegis of *Rights of Man*: Such rights are not susceptible of quantification or qualification. They are aspirational in effect all the way down, always held for futurity, supported by a concept that enables one to think in the tense of the historic continuous present.

Burke had no time for such "abstractions" and "metaphysical truths."[124] His was a world in which *real politik* required one's full attention. The distraction of "theory," he thought, could only lead to barbarism. As he

119. Ibid.

120. Ibid., 89.

121. Ibid., 90.

122. Ibid., 91. Making the same point, the author of *An Answer to the Second Part of Rights of Man. In Two Letters to the Author*: "I have never, I confess, thoroughly understood the ground of rights. It appears to me, to be a mere theoretical one, on which no nation ever builds its practice." (London: F and C Rivington, 1792), 34.

123. Edmund Burke, *Reflections on the Revolution in France, and on the Proceedings in Certain Societies in London Relative to that Event* (London: J. Dodsley, 1790), 92.

124. He was not alone in this. Hildebrand Freeman observed in 1792 "I was now convinced the *rights of man*, as laid down in the abstract manner of modern philosophers, are a mere pedantic abuse of elementary principles, which, in the attempt, must loosen the bands of government, and be destructive of all social freedom." See Hildebrand Freeman, *Memoirs of Hildebrand Freeman, Esq.; or a Sketch of "The Rights of Man." A Recent Story Founded upon Facts, and Written by Himself* (London: R. Edwards, 1792), 54.

writes of the revolutionaries, "this sort of people are so taken up with their theories about the rights of man, that they have totally forgot his nature."[125] So here, once again, one can see the extent to which the argument between the two writers was continuously circling back to the shape, modality, and functions of the concept "man." The same point is made by Burke's characterization of Richard Price as the "archpontiff of the *rights of men*," precisely exposing Burke's attachment to the concept of right(s), which he takes Price to be conceiving as held identically by each and every man. Price, as has been outlined above and as Paine makes explicit, held to a different view. Such general rights, the "rights of mankind," could only be held in a collectivity and not by singular individuals: "Person" could not be declined through this concept. This, as will become clear, sounds the death knell for its radical force, as can be seen all too easily in the contemporary discourse of identity rights.

During the months of writing the *Reflections*, Burke and Paine were pacing around each other, each suspecting that they knew the other's mind. In his letters of this time, Burke made it clear that his reaction to the revolution was not as a political theorist, but *as a man*, as if that in itself were enough to clinch the distinction he held to in principle. In a very revealing letter to William Cusac Smith dated July 22, 1791, he explicitly admitted that his approach to telling the story of the revolution was designed to avoid theory. Smith had sent him a copy of his own refutation of Paine, entitled *The Rights of Citizens*,[126] in which he sought to address head on Paine's "principles." Burke was admiring of the pamphlet: "Your work is indeed a very satisfactory refutation of that specious folly of the rights of men."[127] And he continues, referring to his own as-yet-unpublished rejoinder to *Rights of Man*, the *Appeal from the New to the Old Whigs*, "The points in which we happen to coinside you have certainly handled much more fully, and much better." This was because Burke "only touched upon them" since it "was not my plan to go deeply into the abstract subject."[128] And then, in closing the letter he attempts to justify his approach in the *Reflections*: "You think that my way of treating these subjects is too much in the *concrete* in which

125. Edmund Burke, *Reflections on the Revolution in France, and on the Proceedings in Certain Societies in London Relative to That Event* (London: J. Dodsley, 1790), 95.

126. *The Rights of Citizens. Being an Examination of Mr Paine's Principles Touching Government. By a Barrister* (Dublin: Henry Watts, 1791).

127. Edmund Burke, *The Correspondence of Edmund Burke*, ed. Thomas W. Copeland (Cambridge: Cambridge University Press, 1958–1978), 5:303.

128. Ibid.

I *ramble* in too large a share of circumstances, feelings &c, &c"—certainly a characterization that had some bite both at the time and, as noted above, within the long history of reception of the text—but, he says, "I console myself in this, because I think before you have done—you condemn the abstract mode as much as I do." And, to clinch it, he says: "But surely you forget, that I was throwing out reflexions upon a political event, and not reading a lecture upon theorism and principles of Government."[129]

Burke's distaste for principle, theory, and abstraction was undoubtedly cultivated by his lifelong commitment to the pragmatics of Whiggism. Commercial society could only survive, according to Burke, if it organically responded to its immediate contexts, be they constraining or enabling. A similar, conservative in the sense of conservation, commitment to the inherited unwritten constitution underpinned his refusal to embrace the radical proposal (as yet far from realized or even realizable) that all men are equal. Paine, in contrast, intuitively saw that a new conceptual grammar of rights would help transform the relations between citizens and government. The enfranchisement of the laboring classes, with their differences in language and custom, would alter for good the lines of patronage and deference that characterized the society Burke sought to defend. At the end of the day their argument was grammatical, in one case rear looking and conservative, deeply committed to the English language "properly so-called."[130] In the other case, it was forward looking, aspirational, even utopian, and deeply committed to human progress and to language's potential for imagining otherwise.

I want to insist that this emergent architecture for the "singular universal" category of "man" and its attendant networked concept of "rights of man" cannot be traced to a specific text or writer. It is a cultural phenomenon that, as I have already argued, can first be identified as having some widespread purchase on how historical actors thought about their worlds in the debates of the First Continental Congress. Furthermore, as I have also already had occasion to remark, it would be stretching a point too far were one to claim that Tom Paine set himself the task of either shaping or idiosyncratically adopting this noetic concept. For one thing, as has also been made apparent, the concept was at least *in potentia* in circulation before Paine published his own text. Catherine Macaulay, for example, in her

129. Ibid., 5:304.

130. The most useful discussion of the period's mobilization of this idea is in John Barrell, *English Literature in History 1730–80: An Equal, Wide Survey* (London: Hutchinson, 1983), 110–75.

response to Burke's *Reflections* has use for the concept in her *Observations on the Reflections of the Right Hon. Edmund Burke, on the Revolution in France. In a Letter to the Right Hon. The Earl of Stanhope*, published in 1790. She criticizes Burke for having been drawn into the "question of *right*" before going on to note that "once we *give up* the point, that there is an *inherent* right to make laws for the community, we cannot fix on any other principle that will stand the test of argument, but the *native* and *unalienable* rights of man."[131] This is because, according to Macaulay, Burke's argument that a prior generation can tie the hands of future generations will inevitably fail the test of the source for legitimacy: If governments derive their authority from the assent of the people, "how came the people . . . to exert such an authority at *one* period of society, and not at *another*"?[132] If, as Macaulay argues, a vicious circle emerges in respect to the derivation of authority—it always returns to the people—there are only two ways of understanding Burke's position. Either "an individual, or some privileged persons, have an inherent and indefeasible right to make laws for the community," or—and here one needs to be sensitive to the distinction between "right" and "rights"—"this authority rests in the unalienable and indefeasible rights of man."[133] Once more, the difference is one of conceptual architecture. Macaulay, like Paine, instinctively recognizes that distinction and embraces its aspirational equality. *Man* has rights by dint of there being *being*. As Macaulay notes, right *"exists in the very constitution of things."*

It nevertheless remains the case that the most explicit interrogation of the difference in architecture I have been at pains to identify was prompted by the publication of *Rights of Man* and can be found in the various critical accounts of Paine's text. Sir Brooke Boothby, in his *Observations on the Appeal from the New to the Old Whigs, and on Mr Paine's Rights of Man*, for example, sets out his stall by indicating that he is neither a "Burkite" not "Painite" but a Whig.[134] Indeed, he finds as much to be concerned about in Burke's text as he does in Paine's, preferring to find comfort in the age-old certainties of the settled constitution. The French, he contends, in their much celebrated "Declaration of Rights," had merely abstracted (and thus made

131. Catherine Macaulay, *Observations on the Reflections of the Right Hon. Edmund Burke, on the Revolution in France. In a Letter to the Right Hon. The Earl of Stanhope* (London: C. Dilly, 1790), 93–94.

132. Ibid., 94.

133. Ibid.

134. Sir Brooke Boothby, *Observations on the Appeal from the New to the Old Whigs, and on Mr Paine's Rights of Man* (London: John Stockdale, 1792), 5.

less useful) what "we have long been in full possession of under the English government."[135] In common with many of Paine's detractors, Boothby has no time for abstractions or what he calls "theorems." This does not prevent him, however, from making a very telling theoretical observation that drives to the heart of the issue of the shape or form for the concept of rights. "When *liberty*," he writes, "is declared in one place, to be *a natural imprescriptible right of man*" and in another to be "*a power limited by law*, two different sorts of liberty must be meaned [*sic*]."[136] The distinction, he goes on to explain, is to be found in the difference between "natural" and "civil" liberty. "To make the same thing the origin and principle of law," as one must do according to Boothby if one takes liberty to be a singular concept, would be to construct a "vicious circle." Thus, when it is asserted that "*men are born, and always continue, free, and equal in respect of rights*," one cannot find the legitimacy for this view in the concept of liberty. As Boothby points out, "natural liberty" cannot provide the superstructure because "under every government natural liberty must have been already given in exchange for the benefits of society," but equally it cannot be "civil liberty" because "civil liberty, depending upon the laws, cannot exist before the laws."[137]

In terms of the methodology I have been developing in this book, Boothby is here parsing the grammar of the concept of liberty. He is pointing to the fact that thinking liberty in the modality of the schema would mean that a vicious circle would be created. In fact, "liberty" cannot get one to "equality" because the concept operates with an isogetic modality, comparing "civil" and "natural" kinds. What is needed, then, is a noetic concept operating with an axiomatic modality: In this case, "liberty" would be self-evident and declined in the historic continuous present. According to Boothby, precisely the same problem occurs when thinking about rights: "The *equality* of the rights of man," he notes, "is subject to the same difficulties."[138] Such argumentation, he notes, is based in the same kind of incoherence: "If this equality is asserted to be a natural right, *previous to the institution of society*," he opines, then the contrary assertion is "still more probable"[139] because in a "pure state of nature, right and power seem to be perfectly equivalent terms," thereby producing "a system of inequality rather than of equality." And if equality is applied to the state

135. Ibid., 156.
136. Ibid., 159.
137. Ibid.
138. Ibid.
139. Ibid., 159–60.

of society rather than a state of nature, "civil distinctions must be founded not on natural rights but on *'public utility.'"*[140] Boothby puts his finger on the fault line that runs through eighteenth-century conceptualizations of universal rights and exposes the distinctive architecture of the concept "right(s)." Paine's embrace—albeit inconsistent and sometimes partially understood—of a different architecture and a different noetic concept, "rights of man," gave to the campaign for constitutional reform its most potent weapon and represents its most distinctive contribution to a history of the formation of the concept of human rights. Too bad, then, that it was so quickly dropped.

The Reception of "Rights of Man"

If one were to take the long view in respect to the conceptual history I have been sketching, one must conclude that the fate of this distinctive way of thinking universal rights was to be ignored or rejected. Even within the shorter time span of the long eighteenth century, its exposure was lumpy. There was no consistent operation of a network of concepts that enabled one to understand the self-evidence of putative universal rights even if, during the imperial crisis, the colonists discovered the utility of the noetic concept "rights of man." These selfsame former colonists, once the republic had been established and secured its firm footing, found little use for this concept in their deliberations about citizenship and its relations to the state. One must also take account of the fact that the concept I call "right(s)" was itself under pressure, as the longer view indicates: For most of the nineteenth century, no one sought to challenge the prevailing Benthamite consensus that rights could only make sense in terms of positive law. The architectural element of the deposit did sterling work, supporting the containing function of the concept "right(s)." It is also worth remarking that conceptual forms can be extremely slow to change, conforming to geological rather than computational temporality. Over the longer term it is clear, moreover, that the architecture of the concept "right(s)" is remarkably stable and durable: That is why the codification and policing of specific human rights became a worldwide political program in 1948. But there was a moment in the early 1790s when it may not have worked out that way. The data in table 23 indicate that from around the 1780s there was a growing incidence in use of the phrase *rights of man.*

140. Ibid., 160.

Table 23. Number of texts containing *rights* and *rights of man*, 1780–1799

	1780	1781	1782	1783	1784	1785	1786	1787	1788	1789	1790	1791	1792	1793	1794	1795	1796	1797	1798	1799
rights	1,453	1,431	1,626	1,782	1,908	1,882	1,921	2,182	2,280	2,631	2,966	3,263	3,673	3,470	3,381	3,386	3,200	3,242	3,287	3,328
rights of man	68	87	116	137	135	109	140	173	168	253	455	786	985	874	771	734	642	588	573	503

Source: Eighteenth Century Collections Online (ECCO), http://galenet.galegroup.com/servlet/ECCO.

The presence of the phrase, of course, merely signifies the use of a form of words. In order to establish the extent to which a distinctive architecture to "rights of man" may have been available, one can begin by seeking to ascertain where a difference in grammar pertained between *the* rights of man and "rights of man."[141] As will become clear, even if that difference was marked, the overwhelming preference was to operate with the established and deeply entrenched conceptual network that linked rights with duties and obligations.[142] In a text published in 1793 in Edinburgh, for example, the author sets out his stall in the following way: "In this inquiry the object shall be, not so much to ascertain what are the *Rights* of man, as what are his *Interests*: not what a man *may* do, but what, *for his own sake*, he *ought* to do."[143] If this author attempts to return the discussion of rights to an earlier and different set of arguments about ethical behavior, there are many others who simply intone the standard line about the differences between an actual social and political environment within which agents operate and the hypothetical "state of nature," which could never be recovered—if it ever, in fact, existed. For these writers, Paine was seen to merely deal in ineffectual abstractions.[144] Thus, in the *Remarks on Mr Paine's Pamphlet, Called the Rights of Man. In a Letter to a Friend* there is an insistence on "right(s)" as divisible into kind or type, the common distinction between "natural and political rights" which runs through the long tradition of rights discourse. If only Paine, the author claims, had noticed this, his objection to Burke over whether or not man has any rights at all would have been easily defeated: "There is no sophism more common or more successful than this, of laying down a position which you can-

141. This is to make the distinction between "right" and "rights." The incidence of *declarationW5rights* in the twenty-year period 1760–1780 is 271; in the final twenty years of the century, that has risen to 1,115. Over the same time spans, *declarationW5right* has an incidence of 40 for the period 1760–780, and 197 for 1780–1800.

142. See *The Duties of Man in Connexion with His Rights; or, Rights and Duties Inseparable* (London: Mssrs Rivington, 1793), 5: "I shall beg leave to lead my countrymen to consider that there are *Duties* as well as *Rights* . . ." The author of this pamphlet seeks to discredit Paine as someone promoting self interest; as he opines in order to "preserve their *rights*" men must "fulfil their *duties*" (51).

143. *The Interests of Man in Opposition to The Rights of Man: or, An Inquiry into the Consequence of Certain Political Doctrines Lately Disseminated* (Edinburgh: James Watson et al., 1793), 2.

144. Said to be the "metaphysical rights of our modern reformers." See John Jones, *The Reason of Man: With Strictures on Paine's Rights of Man, and some of his other writings*, 2nd ed. (Canterbury: John Jones, 1792), 11.

not or do not wish to deny."[145] But even in a hostile response such as this, the conceptual difference between "*the* rights of man" and "rights of man" emerges: As the author notes, Paine's use of Genesis to ground his conception of rights is merely a "declaration" because "it says nothing about them [rights]."[146] This is, of course, precisely the point: the conceptual architecture of "rights of man" does not require rights to have a content or an object. Its purpose is to provide the grammar for understanding the commonality of the singular universal that is the human. Moreover, the modality of thinking the concept employs is axiomatic: It allows or enables one to "declare" the rights of man without specifying entirely what they are or might be; it legitimizes holding to a belief in the universality of man.[147]

My earlier characterization of the argument between Burke and Paine over the usefulness of abstractions began to open up the issue of whether an alternative architecture for the concept "rights of man" was available to the 1790s debates around constitutional reform. The same issue arises in a series of letters to Paine published in 1791 which casts its argument very interestingly in terms of grammar. The author, quoting the French declaration that Paine himself cites, "Men are born, and always continue free, and equal in respect of their rights," notes that "by this you mean abstract freedom, and equality," which are "merely ideal, and exist only in the sickness of weak minds."[148] This, according to the author, must mean that "if man can possess rights abstractedly, it must be allowed that those rights are limited" since if not the absurd notion would arise that "man might be said

145. *Remarks on Mr Paine's Pamphlet, Called The Rights of Man. In a Letter to a Friend* (Dublin: Byrne, 1791), 9.

146. Ibid., 15. The same distinction is noted by Chalmers and to the same effect. Paine's critic gets it precisely wrong: "This is a disquisition, said they, with regard to RIGHTS OF MAN. By thus suppressing designedly the article *the*, he shews his intention to be, not to treat of the whole rights of mankind, but of particular rights." See [George Chalmers], *The Life of Thomas Paine, the Author of Rights of Man. With a Defence of His Writings* (London: John Stockdale, 1791), 29.

147. Chalmers also gets this point even if he misunderstands it. Paine, Chalmers claims, lost the plot, departing from his original design and "now wished that *the* rights of man might become as universal as Washington's benevolence." And then the crucial characterization emerges: "They doubted the propriety of our author's sentiment; because *the* rights of man must be as universal as the residence of mankind." See [George Chalmers], *The Life of Thomas Paine, the Author of Rights of Man. With a Defence of His Writings* (London: John Stockdale, 1791), 107–8.

148. *Letters to Thomas Paine; in Answer to His Late Publication on The Rights of Man; Shewing his Errors on That Subject; and Proving the Fallacy of His Principles as Applied to the Government of this Country*, 2nd ed. (London: W. Miller, 1791), 19.

to possess the *right* of doing *wrong*" which, he observes, "is nonsense."[149] The debating point turns on the linguistic congruence of "right" in the sense of claim or title and its alternative meaning as the converse of wrong, but there is more than just wordplay behind this critique and it is worth following in detail.

The next move in the argument is to invoke the beginning of human time: The rights of Adam are said to be uniform or, put more pointedly in respect to the commentaries already noted above, singular all the way through. This then allows the author to observe that since Adam was alone "it was impossible that he could have received a wrong from any other person."[150] This being so, and since he could also not wrong himself, he must have had no rights because the grammar of the concept requires its balancing antithesis: "There being no wrong, in this case, we cannot say there could be a right either physical or moral; for if you admit of either, you must admit of both." Moreover, as the author notes, "it is every way absurd to suppose Adam to have been both right and wrong."[151] Although this might at first glance look like mere scholasticism, a clever debating point that turns on the double meaning of the word *right* there is a far deeper theoretical point underlying the argument. That point concerns the coherence of the architecture of the concept "man." Our author notes, then, in conclusion to his sketch of the absurdity of abstract rights: "Individual man is, therefore, naturally speaking, an impossible thing, a sort of noun adjective."[152]

What might it mean for a concept to be articulated through a different kind of grammar in which a term can be both substantive, a noun, and qualifying, an adjective? How can "man" be a "unity" in Paine's formulation, both individual rights bearer and collective place holder for an aspiration? What is needed in order to square these circles in an alternative architecture for rights? The author of this critical attack on Paine's tract gets it completely right: Far from being an absurdity, Paine's concept of "man" embraces both the singular universal, upholds individuals as rights claim-

149. Ibid., 20. Many attacks on Paine sought to portray him as having a poor grip on reasoning. See *Defence of the Rights of Man; Being a Discussion of the Conclusions Drawn from Those Rights by Mr Paine* (London: T. Evans, 1791), 16: "Most of his reasoning . . . would produce nothing but such absurdities."

150. *Letters to Thomas Paine; in Answer to His Late Publication on The Rights of Man; Shewing His Errors on That Subject; and Proving the Fallacy of His Principles as Applied to the Government of This Country*, 2nd ed. (London: W. Miller, 1791), 20.

151. Ibid., 21.

152. Ibid.

ants, and the generality of mankind at the same time. Thus, when Paine notes that "all men are born equal," he does not understand that equality as applying to "man" as the singular universal. Men are born equal into their difference. All men throughout human history, according to Paine, are equal with respect to their right to claim rights, but that does not mean that they hold the same rights through time, nor, it implies, does one man necessarily hold identical rights to another man. The issue here is precisely the conceptual network within which "man," "rights," and "the universal" are suspended; that is to say, the geometries which allow these concepts to connect to each other, the edges which may or may not touch. Paine, I am suggesting, is working—albeit inconsistently—with a different grammar for both the concept "man" and the concept "rights."

The author of these letters to Paine cannot live with the departure from standard grammar. This is why he balks at what he perceives to be Paine's sloppy or vulgar use of language. When Paine notes, for example, that "the end of all political associations is the preservation of the *natural* and *imprescriptible* rights of man," those rights being liberty, property, security, and resistance to oppression, our author complains "this, at the best, has a very indefinite meaning."[153] Such rights, he notes, cannot be natural and should be more correctly understood as social. The reason for this turns on the sequence of thinking that our author takes to be hard wired in to an understanding of the argument. Step one is the claim that a "natural right" is one belonging to man in a state of nature, before he enters society. Step two is to recognize that such a being and such a state are both "abstract" in the sense that they are fictions. There never was such a state, or, if there was it can never be recovered. Therefore these rights that Paine claims to be "natural" can only be social, and as such they cannot be intelligible to man in a state of nature since the first man, Adam, lived as a unique and sole inhabitant of the world. Consequently, "abstract man," as the author terms him, "must be ignorant" of the meaning of these rights: "He can know nothing of liberty, property, security, and resistance to oppression."[154] "Abstract man" could have no rights to these things. The problem comes down to abstraction: Paine is working with a concept of rights whose architecture allows the singular universal—the noun adjective—its playful shifting between planes or around connective edges. The concept has a complex geometry that allows multiple connections to be made within and across networks. Our critical author identified the problem even if he did

153. Ibid., 23.
154. Ibid.

not put it in the same way: "You think nothing more easy than to draw a line between natural and civil rights," he says to his interlocutor, because Paine's notion of natural rights comprises "those that appertain to man, in right of his existence."[155] This, the author notes, is "another proof of your abstract idea of right," and he is right! Paine's version of "rights of man," those that derive their legitimacy from being "natural" are not the same kind of right as civil rights.[156] They are not derived from anything, being axiomatically generated by the fact of there being mankind. Furthermore, the claim to universality is not refracted through rights but through man, the human: As outlined above, Paine argued that the claim to rights was held by man, by the singular universal, but did not propose that individual rights were universally applicable to all men.

I have given space to these two critical rebuttals to Paine's text because they so clearly open out the issue of conceptual architecture. Both of them are in some sense exemplary since they bring into focus the fault line between different conceptual forms for rights, but it is also important to note that the vast majority of those texts attacking Paine—many of course prompted by political expediency—catch hold of similar and sometimes identical concerns. It is possible, therefore, to compile a set of stock responses and objections: First, Paine was said to be out to destroy the Constitution, which, the critics maintained, was the most perfect ever devised, and all the more so for being "unwritten." Second, the assertion that man, in the state of nature, had perfect rights was deemed to be merely an assertion or hypothesis: No such state ever existed. Man, from his creation, is set into society. Third, and rather more interestingly for the purposes of my larger argument, there was no objection to the notion that rights could be specified in a list that was taken from the French declaration— liberty, security, property—since it was precisely these rights that had been defended and protected at least since the glorious revolution and perhaps as far back as the Magna Carta. In this manner, the language of the revolutionaries in France whereby the rights of man were deemed to be "natural, imprescriptible, inalienable" was continuously recycled as a way of neutering the potentially destabilizing and radical force of an alternative conceptual architecture that inhered in "rights of man." For Paine's crit-

155. Ibid., 24.

156. The same point is made, albeit in a critical vein, by another critic: "But Thomas saw confusedly a sort of antithesis between *rights* and *not rights*. . . ." See William Fox, *An Examination of Mr Paine's Rights of Man* (London: T. Whiledon and Butterworth, 1793), 114.

ics, there was only one conceptual form for rights, and it was based on the architectural element of the deposit, thereby making sense of rights as a set of specific, prescriptible items: security, property, and so forth. It should be pointed out that the author of *Rights of Man* from time to time fell into precisely the same habits of locution.[157] To some degree, Paine's wavering with regard to a consistent use of the alternative conceptual form, "rights of man," explains its failure of widespread adoption. But one should also be careful to note that there was no interdiction on using both conceptual forms as the occasion demanded. As far as the Pitt government was concerned, the circulation of all rights talk was potentially destabilizing, whether or not the experimental environment the reformers were creating succeeded in establishing the currency of the noetic concept. And in this regard Paine's switching between conceptual structures was perhaps more dangerous than a consistent adoption of the concept "rights of man" since it opened up the prospect of radical new networks of connectivity that were completely unpredictable. The texts published in support of Paine provide good-enough evidence for some of the potential effects of that unpredictability. Take, for example, a work that appeared quickly on the heels of the first part of *Rights of Man* and also published by Jordan, entitled *The Political Crisis; or, A Dissertation on the Rights of Man*. In many ways this text demonstrates the power of Paine's manner of thinking, of his "ungrammatical" declension of concepts, for transforming an understanding of universal rights into the defining aspiration of being human. Seen this way, the "human" in human rights gives shape and form to our futurity, our yet-to-be-achieved universal equality. No wonder, then, that Paine and his coconspirators in liberty failed. It is, nevertheless, instructive to follow the lineaments of the radical intervention texts such as this made.

The author begins by asking "whether man has any natural rights— what they are—and how they might be distinguished from his political and other rights."[158] Rights, to begin with, are rendered intelligible by the concept of "right(s)": Its element is the deposit, and it functions as containing. The second move is to explore the tense of the concept of "right(s)." Some might believe that there never was a time when man had pure natural rights since, the author notes, "man is naturally a *social being*," thereby ren-

157. At Paine's trial, Erskine quotes his client: "The end of all political associations is the preservation of the rights of man, which rights are liberty, property, and security . . ." See *The Genuine Trial of Thomas Paine* (London: J. S. Jordan), 45.

158. *The Political Crisis: or, a Dissertation on the Rights of Man* (London: J. S. Jordan, 1791), 5.

dering the notion of the rights of man "wholly unphilosophical,"[159] but he begs to differ. On entering society, he claims, the rights of man "were not *reduced*—they were only *exchanged*";[160] he goes on to explain that "the obligations of the law of Nature do not *cease* in society; they are only in many cases *drawn* closer."[161] The move from the hypothesized state of nature to society does not entail a shift in tense; there is no "before" and "after," no prehistory to our lived present. As far as rights are concerned, they exist in the historic continuous present. Thus, according to our author, on entering society man gives up those rights formally held in his own right, own person, so that they can be held by the commonality, by what he calls the "common stock of society."[162] In effect, he notes, this turns the particular into the general, creating "one soul in the republic."[163] And the rights deposited in this common stock are "political," perhaps the most important of them being the right of security. But, in a passage that is crucial for understanding how the dual functionality of the concept of rights operates in this case, he notes that these political rights "grow out of the *natural* Rights of Man."[164] Here the concept of "right(s)" also functions in a load-bearing capacity, enabling one to understand how rights such as political liberty are legitimated. So it transpires that "civil rights stand in the same relation to political rights, as political rights do to natural rights, each springing out of the other."[165] "Right(s)" operates at one moment as containing and at the next as load bearing.

A similar way of operating a dual functionality for "imprescriptible" rights is outlined in Citizen Randol's *A Political Catechism of Man. Wherein His Natural Rights are Familiarly Explained*, a text published by the radical bookseller Daniel Isaac Eaton, who styled himself "printer and bookseller to the supreme majesty of the people."[166] In this case the author asks, "What is man?" and provides the following answer: He is "a rational Being" who has been "endowed by his creator, with the precious faculty

159. Ibid., 6.

160. Ibid., 11.

161. Ibid.

162. This way of conceptualizing the move from a state of nature into society is clearly congruent with both Price's and Paine's notion of the "singular many."

163. *The Political Crisis: or, A Dissertation on the Rights of Man* (London: J. S. Jordan, 1791), 12.

164. Ibid., 21.

165. Ibid., 22.

166. Eaton began to use this self-description on the title pages of works he printed and sold in 1795.

of judging right from wrong." He is, moreover, "a free agent, possessing rights imprescriptible" that have been bestowed on him at his creation and, he adds, "unalienable to any other power."[167] In answer to the question "And what are those rights?" he replies: "Liberty of Body—Freedom of Mind—Security of Property—and Resistance of Oppression."[168] So far, so standard within the republican or radical tradition, but the following move by which those "trump" rights are attenuated is more a feature of the 1790s. He notes that "as an individual man" he possesses "those rights un-limited, and uncontrouled," but when he enters society "I deposit a part of those rights in the social fund."[169] Once in this safety deposit they are "in trust for the joint use and benefit of myself, and society."[170] What I want to draw out of these texts that circulated within the radical culture Paine did so much to energize is the difficulty of thinking exclusively through a noetic concept of "rights of man." If, as the radical mode of expression had it after 1789, the rights of man are (in any combination and order) "natu-ral," "unalienable," and "imprescriptible," does this mean that all rights are so?[171] Or, rather, does it mean that "rights of man" are, unlike rights to act in any way one pleases, say, not fungible: They cannot be left at the door on entry into society or cashiered for prescriptive rules that enable the polis to function in harmony. What is at stake, then, is a way of having it both ways, of declaring an aspiration to universal equal rights, rights that can never be fully delimited, while at the same time preventing the dilution of those

167. Citizen Randol, *A Political Catechism of Man. Wherein His Natural Rights are Familiarly Explained*, 3rd ed. (London: Daniel Isaac Eaton, 1798), 12.

168. Ibid.

169. It is important to note the difference between giving us a portion of one's rights as one enters society and giving away part of one's liberty. Although, as outlined in the second chapter, the conceptual armature between rights and liberties is one of the most enduring hinges across the century, there is nevertheless a significant alteration in emphasis in moving from the one to other. Thus, in a critical account of *Rights of Man*, the move from a state of nature to society is described as a loss of a "portion of that Liberty which would belong to a State of Nature." See John Bowles, *Dialogues on the Rights of Britons, between a Farmer, a Sailor, and a Manufacturer* (London: T. Longman et al., 1792), 18.

170. Citizen Randol, *A Political Catechism of Man. Wherein His Natural Rights Are Familiarly Explained*, 3rd ed. (London: Daniel Isaac Eaton, 1798), 12.

171. This is the formulation that began to be taken up in English radical discussion of rights after the French had issued their declaration of the rights of man and citizen. It appears, for example, in the discourse of the treason trials of 1794. See *The Trials at Large of Thomas Hardy, and Others; for High Treason, Which Began on Saturday, October 25, 1794* (Nottingham: C. Sutton, 1794), 57.

aspirations in the protection of those positive rights—liberty, property, security—one deems to be essential for civil society.[172] The substitution of "rights of man" for "right(s)" turned out to be much more difficult and problematic than expected.

While it may have appeared to the colonists that they had found a way through this in 1776, some of their contemporaries understood the difficulties of negotiating the path between absolute rights and political rights. "It will serve to show that the Representatives of the United States of America were well acquainted with the real rights of mankind," a pamphlet of 1793 notes, and that "they knew with what a cautious and religious hand it was their duty to relax those other rights, and to tear those bonds and connexions which unite men together in society."[173] Their great wisdom, the author maintains, lay in the fact that the Americans acknowledged "the abstract existence of these original rights" while at the same time holding that it was not "lawful to dissolve society." Our author here is extremely acute since what the colonists effectively did was cashier an axiomatic modality for a schematic: They discarded the noetic concept of universal rights in favor of the politically more easily applied ideational concept of natural rights. The removal from the state of nature, it turned out, was no big deal with respect to "rights," even if it was so with respect to the institutions that supported and guaranteed those rights. Government, the collective "we," simply named its own kind of "natural" claims and entitlements. No wonder that the deep seam of debate over the extent and reach of government in the new republic refuses to go away.

The "Real History" of "Rights of Man"

As I have been at pains to argue, the distinction between the concept "rights of man" and the phrase needs to be marked if one is to understand the intervention made by Paine and the pro-reformers to the long history

172. The Society for Constitutional Information tried to conceptualize this knotty problem in the following manner: "That in entering into civil society, men give up no more of their natural rights, than what may be necessary for the good government of society; and that there are rights, which remain undelegated, that neither the violence of the times, nor the power of magistrates, nor decrees or judgments, nor Acts of Parliament, nor the authority of the whole People, which in civil things is supreme, can subvert or repair." See Society of Constitutional Information, *Tracts*, (broadsheet) I.

173. *The Expediency of a Revolution Considered: In Which the Advantages Held Out to the People Are Examined and Refuted* (London: J. Debrett, 1793), 54–55.

of human rights. Although there can be little doubt that the publication of *Rights of Man* increased the circulation of the phrase *the rights of man*, it is not so clear that Paine's text prompted, encouraged or effected widespread use of the noetic concept "rights of man." One needs to tread cautiously here. While it is true that Paine was extremely interested in boosting the circulation of his arguments in the culture at large, one should not take the contemporary estimations of the ubiquity of his "radical" ideas at face value, or at least without considering the part the government and its supporters played in talking up Paine's influence. The more Paine and the reform movement claimed the widespread embrace of the principles set out in *Rights of Man*, the more Pitt and his government claimed a revolution was on the doorstep.[174] It is nevertheless incontrovertible that, in the immediate aftermath of the appearance of Paine's text, the book market became excited: Following the publication of Part II of *Rights of Man* at least forty pamphlets and books entered the debate and commentary in periodicals and newspapers was also plentiful.[175] Many of those publications contributed to a government campaign (and some were undoubtedly prompted by government agencies) to discredit Paine, and this was certainly successful.[176] These texts along with those that were more clearly pro Paine's position undoubtedly contributed to the period's articulation of rights discourse, and as such they employed concepts that were net-

174. Ironically referring to the celebrity Paine achieved, John Bowles in his critical attack has his sailor comment: "Pray who is this TOM PAINE, who makes such a noise? I think I have not heard of any one talked of so much since the time of *John the Painter*." John Bowles, *Dialogues on the Rights of Britons, between a Farmer, a Sailor, and a Manufacturer* (London: T. Longman et al., 1792), 22.

175. Paine in his letter to Onslow Cranley gives the estimate: "Not less than forty pamphlets, as intended as answers thereto, have appeared," but he also notes that they "as suddenly disappeared: scarcely are the titles of any of them remembered . . ." *Miscellaneous Articles by Thomas Paine* (London: J. Ridgway, 1791), 27. See note 4 above for the book market. The incidence of use for the phrase *rights of man* in newspapers following the publication exploded. See below, p. 271.

176. The literature poking fun at Paine was substantial, including prints, songs, and so forth. See David Duff, "Burke and Paine: Contrasts," in *The Cambridge Companion to British Literature of the French Revolution in the 1790s*, ed. Pamela Clemit (Cambridge: Cambridge University Press, 2011), 47–70. A contemporary collection of songs was published in 1798; see R. Thompson, *A Tribute to Liberty; or, A Collection of Select Songs: Together with a Collection of Toasts and Sentiments. Sacred to the Rights of Man* (London: n.p., 1798). A satirical pamphlet that seeks to make the proposition that all men are born naked as telling as all men are born equal was published in 1792. See *Buff; or, A Dissertation on Nakedness: A Parody on Paine's Rights of Man* (London: J. Mathews, 1792).

Table 24. Number of texts containing *rights of man*

	1700–1720	1720–1740	1740–1760	1760–1780	1780–1800
total texts with *rights*	8,949	8,934	11,395	16,820	26,184
rights of man	409	400	467	678	1,088

Source: Eighteenth Century Collections Online (ECCO), http://galenet.galegroup.com/servlet/ECCO.

worked in various ways in the distinct and divergent political, social, and legal cultures of the era. But this cacophony of voice and opinions was, at least according to one feted political theorist, not necessarily conducive to a coherent use or understanding of the concept of rights.[177] In order to gauge the measure of that, one can first track the rising incidence of the use of the phrase *rights of man*. As the run of figures in table 24 indicates, the phrase *rights of man* only began to be used with any significant frequency in the last twenty years of the century. The data from contemporary newspapers are even more emphatic, as table 25 shows.

One can also note that, although the data indicate very clearly that the phrase became more commonly used in the 1790s, analysis of the orbital drag for the term *rights* suggests that the network within which the concept of "right(s)" was suspended changed little over the course of the century.[178] Moreover, as the following table demonstrates, although the publication

177. Writing in 1793, Godwin observed that "there is nothing that has been of greater disservice to the cause of truth, than the hasty and unguarded manner in which its [the rights of man] advocates have sometimes defended it." And he goes on to note that "whatever is meant by the term right" can only be evidence for the fact that the term "has never been clearly understood." In support of this view he outlines how rights and duties are connected before noting the absurdity of claiming that one man may claim a right to be free at the same time as another stakes a claim to making him a slave. Similarly, "if my neighbour have a right to a sum of money in my possession, I cannot have a right to retain it in my pocket." This leads him to conclude that "it inevitably follows that men have no rights." William Godwin, *An Enquiry concerning Political Justice, and Its Influence in General Virtue and Happiness* (Dublin: Luke White, 1793), 1:10–103.

178. See table 2. In this respect Godwin's insistence on the hinged concepts of "rights" and "duties" would not have troubled the conservative churchmen of the 1720s.

Table 25. Number of times *rights of man* appears in British newspapers

	1700–1720	1720–1740	1740–1760	1760–1780	1780–1800
total texts with *rights*	8,949	8,934	11,395	16,820	26,184
rights of man	3	8	2	84	2,980

Source: Burney Collection, http://www.jisc.ac.uk/news/stories/2009/01/burney.aspx.

Table 26. Number of texts containing *rights of man*, 1789–1799

	1789	1790	1791	1792	1793	1794	1795	1796	1797	1798	1799
rights of man	183	382	712	908	792	679	641	566	529	512	433

Source: Eighteenth Century Collections Online (ECCO), http://galenet.galegroup.com/servlet/ECCO.

of both parts of *Rights of Man* generated a notable upswing in usage of the phrase *rights of man*, this was very short lived (table 26).

The most obvious explanation for this curve must be the effectiveness of the Pitt government's measures to stifle the reform movement. The traces of that policy of censorship and intimidation are all too evident in these bare, chilly raw numbers. Although one should not blithely elevate Paine and his tract to a position of preeminence in that movement it is nevertheless incontrovertible that between 1791 and 1794, the period when *Rights of Man* most insistently caught the public's imagination, saw a spike in the usage of the phrase *the rights of man*. Here I mean to call to mind the other reformers, more than one of whom were imprisoned for their antigovernment opinions or role in disseminating them.[179] One must suppose, then,

179. At the distance of some two hundred years, it is relatively easy to underestimate the courage of these men in the book trades, all of whom risked fine or imprisonment. Although by the end of the eighteenth century it was possible to earn a comfortable income by selling books, and indeed some booksellers fancied themselves as better than mere tradesmen, the threat of a fine for publishing seditious material was enough to dissuade many who could easily have been bankrupted by the government's prosecution. It is, perhaps, too easy to assume that the acquittals of the prominent men or the collapsed cases in the treason trials of 1794 indicated that the climate of fear and intimidation was not particularly savage, or the government's bullying and attempts to close down the freedom to publish not particularly effective. Here one does well to remember a good

that the gagging acts of 1793 and the suspension of habeas corpus in 1794, the Treasonable Practices Bill and the Seditious Meetings Bill of 1795 cumulatively succeeded in reducing the print circulation of the phrase *rights of man*. Evidence for the cultural dispersal of the noetic concept "rights of man," however, is rather thin on the ground.

If, for example, one of the consequences of operating the noetic concept were an unspecifiability for rights, as the preceding has argued, one would expect to see an increasing incidence for the use of a qualifier such as *impresciptible*. But the extraordinary fact is that no text used the phrase *imprescriptible rights* until 1789. And even at the height of the Paine-prompted riot of "rights talk" in 1791–1794, its use was almost negligible (see below).[180] Furthermore, the other important qualifiers of rights that declare their self-evidence and invulnerability, *inalienable* and *indefeasible*, have a similar miserable presence in the print culture of the period. Table 27 presents a rather depressing and bleak picture: The fate of Paine's efforts and those

---

number of men were successfully prosecuted and imprisoned. These included William Holland (one year's imprisonment and £100 fine) for publishing Paine's *Letter Addressed to the Addressers on a Late Proclamation*; W. D. Symonds (two years' imprisonment and £20 fine for publishing *Rights of Man* and a second sentence of one year and £100 fine for publishing *Letter addressed to the Addressers*); Richard Phillips, a printer in Leicester (eighteen months for printing *Rights of Man*); and J. Ridgway (one year's imprisonment and £100 fine for publishing *Rights of Man*, a further one year and £100 for *Letter addressed to the Addressers*). The harshest punishment, however, was meted out to Daniel Holt, a bookseller in Newark, who was sentenced to four years' imprisonment and a fine of £500. Given this, the departure from the "norm" identified above not only provides evidence for the different architecture for a concept of rights circulating in the radical culture of the period; it also underlines the bravery of those men who fought for the freedom to express political views that a repressive government did all it could to suppress. These details are taken from W. T. Sherwin, *Memoirs of the Life of Thomas Paine* (London: R. Carlisle, 1819), 137–38.

180. Perhaps one should not be surprised at the start date: the term was introduced into English following the French Declaration of the Rights of Man and Citizen. It is noteworthy, however, that only a handful of writers in the 1790s took to using it. The formula varied to some extent, but Samuel Stearns's version gives an accurate sense of the novelty: "The representatives of the people of France . . . have resolved to explain, in a solemn declaration, the natural imprescriptible, inalienable, and sacred rights of man . . ." See Samuel Stearns, *Dr Stearns's Tour from London to Paris* (London: C. Dilly, 1790), 83; but also William Belsham, *Essays, Philosophical, Historical, and Literary* (Dublin: J. Moore, 1791), 4:157; Sir James Mackintosh, *Vindiciae Gallicae* (London: G. G. J. & J. Robinson, 1791), 220; *Paine's Political and Moral Maxims; Selected from the Fifth Edition of Rights of Man, Part I and Part II. With Explanatory Notes and Elucidations* (London: printed for the booksellers, 1792), 25.

Table 27. Number of texts in which *rights* appears within five words of search term and where *rights of man* appears, 1789–1799; peaks for each search highlighted

	1789	1790	1791	1792	1793	1794	1795	1796	1797	1798	1799
rights N5↓											
imprescriptible	13	41	58	55	77	77	45	40	52	47	25
inalienable	17	25	28	39	40	36	41	53	21	20	23
unalienable	68	103	135	134	127	131	120	94	83	87	76
indefeasible	23	56	68	40	28	26	22	17	14	14	16
rights of man	183	382	712	908	792	679	641	566	529	512	433
equal	119	214	284	286	270	326	301	213	193	185	187
natural	352	467	552	568	500	469	415	337	315	319	326

Source: Eighteenth Century Collections Online (ECCO), http://galenet.galegroup.com/servlet/ECCO.

of his pro-reform colleagues was to dazzle in the firmament for no more than the blink of an eye.

As can be seen from table 27, the bell curve is consistent, and not only with regard to the first four search items in the list. It suggests that any claim for the ubiquity, solid formation, acceptance, or even widespread understanding of the concept of universal equal human rights by the end of the eighteenth century must be wrong. Unequal, subjective, and contestatory rights claims were in evidence at the century's opening. On at least two occasions over the course of the century, a new and transformative way of thinking rights had been proposed, but by century's end one must conclude that not much had changed. And as it turns out, the persistence and durability of the architecture of the concept "right(s)" have been impregnable. The conclusion suggests some ways in which that might not be the end of the story.

CHAPTER 5

The Futures of Human Rights

Throughout this book I have been primarily engaged in an effort to think conceptuality in ways that might significantly enhance our understanding how the world comes to seem to us as it does. No doubt this is an ambitious objective, and it would perhaps be hubristic to assume that it could deliver on its ambition all at once or in just one book. Throughout I have kept firmly in view what I thought to be, before I started, a single concept, or conceptual network. It turns out that the story about rights during the Anglophone eighteenth century is rather more complicated than I had imagined, but the history of the formation of this singular conceptual form does not exhaust the reach and purpose of my argument. Although it has intermittently fallen into the background, I hope that my attempt to create a new way of conceiving conceptual forms in general has not faded too far from view. My intention has been to develop some exemplary analytic procedures in the hope that other scholars will take them up, argue with them, and refine them as different concepts and conceptual networks are moved into view. With respect to the example I have taken, my attention has primarily been theoretical and historical; notwithstanding this narrow focus, it remains the case that I have not written this book on a desert island or in an isolation chamber. Consequently, in thinking about *this* concept I have been continuously aware of the vast literature on human rights that has exploded in the period after the Second World War. To be so aware of course entails calling to mind the fact that injustice and violations of human rights continue to bring shame upon our elected and unelected representatives, to bring shame on all of us, the citizenry of the world, for as long as that situation continues. Although I have no expertise or credentials when it comes to the praxis of contemporary international relations, still less any credible means of persuading those who do, I nevertheless hope that others will engage with the arguments I have set out and find in them provocations that might help us collectively advance the aim and aspiration of universal "rights of man."

Although this is not a book of political theory, it does wish to prompt thinking along the following lines: What use are "human rights" to us today? Is the conceptual architecture of this concept structured in such a way as to allow or enable states, nations and supra-national institutions to implement programs and oversee judicial instruments that might deliver "human rights" for all the citizens of the world? If, as I have argued, the dominant architectural support for rights commits us to understanding rights as claims, does that architecture also delimit or constrain the network within which the concept operates, and thus determine what can be understood under its rubric? Does this account for the shortcomings of the concept when applied to the category of the universal? My suggestion, then, is that our commitment to or adoption of such an architecture—perhaps it would be better to say our inattention to the consequence of having such a rudimentary understanding of what concepts are, what they do and how they operate—condemns the project of universal human rights to failure. Thus, the frustration that many people today feel with respect to our ability to deliver on those universal aspirations can be best understood as being *caused* by the fact that we are trapped within a conceptual architecture that will not do the work we demand of it. We have simply inherited an early modern formulation of "right(s)" and are unable to do anything about it. In response to that observation, this book asks the following: Might it be possible to move beyond the increasingly forceful contemporary critiques of "human rights" not, perhaps, by abandoning them altogether, as some has have suggested, but by rethinking and reconceptualizing the category?[1]

---

1. Slavoj Žižek, in his inimitable fashion, seems to argue that if the concept were coherent, we would not want it and should be against it while at the same time proposing a way of understanding what might be at the heart of the concept (renamed? as *ega-liberty*)

And, as by now must be very obvious, I think that could only become achievable once we understand better how concepts work at the conceptual level, how they become adopted by our modes of thinking or do that thinking for us, how our habits of making sense are silently coopted as commitments to particular ways of seeing the world. What is needed here, as I see it, is a better understanding of the means and processes by which we might begin to build a new, different architecture for a concept of universal rights. This book proposes a history of the formation of the concept of "rights of man" as a first step toward that understanding.

Here in conclusion I offer a summary. The preceding chapters have outlined a way of understanding the historical formation of concepts considered as cultural entities. My aim has been to cast a light on the architecture of the concept of "right(s)" as it was deployed during the eighteenth century in English. In brief, my analysis has demonstrated that the early modern concept of rights as a claim by and large determined how eighteenth-century persons came to think with a network of related concepts: rights, liberties, privileges, and so forth. Or, to put that more strongly in terms of the kind of conceptual analysis I have been developing over the course of this book, "right(s)" were tied into a conceptual network linking these and other concepts that determined the range, shape, and structure of understanding available to eighteenth century persons in the Anglophone world. The concept "Rights" in its largest and most indiscriminate sense, of course, contributed to only a small part of that understanding, but, in common with many political concepts, the networks within which it was suspended connected it to most of the other crucial conceptual forms that were necessary for making sense of the world and our places within it: person, polity; subject, society; identity, ideology; personality, property; law, liberty; citizen, civility; government, goodness; religion, rationality; the human. As I have argued, the narrower sense of rights that was embedded in the natural-law tradition, "right(s)," needs to be distinguished from a different conceptual architecture that was, at the very least, available to and operated by the colonists in the 1770s and British constitutional reformers in the decade of the 1790s. That alternative, the concept "rights of man," failed to gain much purchase in the culture at large so that, by the early nineteenth century, talk of aspirational universal rights was very thin on the ground. Indeed, as Samuel Moyn has pointed out, it was not until the aftermath of the Second World War and the proposals to formulate a Uni-

---

as essential to progressive politics. See Slavoj Žižek, "Against Human Rights," *New Left Review* 34 (July–August 2005): 130.

versal Declaration of Human Rights that talk of rights in this particular fashion began once again in earnest.[2] This lumpy history seems accurate to me when seen in terms of discourse, but the emphasis I wish to make concerns the difference between "rights talk" and a conceptual history. As I have argued, the long history of natural rights continues to inflect our own parsings of the concept of "rights" as we seek to apply and work with contemporary universal "human rights." In this sense the 1948 initiative, while being "lumpy" in respect to a continuity between the late eighteenth century and mid-twentieth (essentially, rights talk faded from public discourse in the intervening one hundred fifty or so years) also constructed a bridge that can (and often has) be seen to connect our contemporary uses of human rights with a legitimating past set of uses. If that connection is understood to link "right(s)" as I describe the concept in the Anglophone eighteenth century to human "right(s)" today, then the bridge accurately conveys a continuity between our past and now. But this is not the common way of seeing things: When claiming that historical lineage, a legitimating move for sure, the bridge that is assumed to be made is between what I call "rights of man" and contemporary human rights. Such a claim cannot be compellingly defended since, as this book has agued in detail, the noetic concept "rights of man" even in the heyday of the radical 1790s never fully became a cultural conceptual resource. If one were to locate a single cause for the problems we currently experience in our attempts to operate the concept "human rights," it would be our failure to recognize that the architecture of "right(s)" ties our hands in ways that are obstructive to thinking universal human rights in the appropriate tense.

One can see the force of this observation by attending to the explosion of rights talk that occurred in the late twentieth century, since within that discourse rights were (and are) consistently conceived in terms as a set of entitlements held by individuals.[3] As Article 2 of the Universal Declaration

2. See Samuel Moyn, *The Last Utopia: Human Rights in History* (Cambridge, Mass.: Belknap Press of Harvard University Press, 2010). His point is even more startling, since he claims that even in the 1940s there was not much interest: "The 1940s later turned out to be crucial, not least for the Universal Declaration they left behind, but it is essential to ask why human rights failed to interest many people—including international lawyers—at the time or for decades." (7). He goes on to substantiate this claim and to propose that the real spike in interest has to wait until the civil rights movement in the United States.

3. Here I would slightly temper the point that Moyn makes by suggesting that the most significant *recent* event with respect to how human rights are conceptualized is the post-1945 hegemonic emergence of rights as entitlements. He writes, "the central event

of Human Rights states: "Everyone is entitled to all the rights and freedoms set forth in this Declaration." The architecture of this concept conforms to what I have described in the foregoing as an ideational concept whose function is both containing and load bearing and operating in a dual phase. The Universal Declaration is founded on the concept of "right(s)." That concept, as the preceding has argued, gained coherence over the *longue durée* of the European natural-law tradition that networked rights, duties, and claims. Given this lineage it is, perhaps, unsurprising that some commentators since the Universal Declaration was made in 1948 have been quick to point out the protoimperialism that is implied by its articles.[4] As Anthony Pagden, among others, has cogently argued, "'rights' are cultural artefacts masquerading as universal, immutable values."[5] And, as he goes

---

in human rights history is the recasting of rights as entitlements that might contradict the sovereign nation-state from above and outside rather than serve as its foundation." *The Last Utopia: Human Rights in History* (Cambridge, Mass.: Belknap Press of Harvard University Press, 2010), 13. As this book has argued, another way of conceptualizing rights emerged over the course of the eighteenth century, which I certainly think of as "central" to the formation of the concept. Of course, as I have also pointed out, it failed to gain purchase, so in that sense it was, and has remained, marginal. I do not mean to score a trivial debating point here (in fact in those terms I'm sure my point would be lost) but to insist on the usefulness of a careful and detailed *historical* account of conceptual forms. In my view it is only through an understanding of how concepts are structured that we might come to some proposals for how to change them or evolve new ones that might better do the tasks we ask of them.

4. Many anthropologists take the view that talk of universals nearly always covers over cultural relativism, a failure of imagination that is difficult to rectify since such views are based upon a misguided conception of culture. For a good overview of this kind of critique, see Richard A. Wilson, "Human Rights, Culture and Context: An Introduction," in *Human Rights, Culture and Context: Anthropological Perspectives*, ed. Richard A. Wilson (London: Pluto Press, 1997), 1–27. Kwame Antony Appiah dissents from this view: "simply put, the spread of human rights culture and the growth of human rights NGOs all around the world does not amount to the diffusion of a metaphysics of Enlightenment liberalism. To the extent that that is right, we do not have to defend it against the charge of ethnocentrism." See Kwame Anthony Appiah, "Grounding Human Rights," in *Human Rights as Politics and Idolatry*, ed. Michael Ignatieff (Princeton, N.J.: Princeton University Press, 2001), 109. Jack Donnelly argues more vociferously for a "soft" universalism that does not imply "or justify cultural imperialism. Quite the contrary, (relatively) universal human rights protect people from imposed conceptions of the good life where those visions are imposed by local or foreign actors." See *International Human Rights*, 3rd ed. (Boulder, Colo.: Westview Press, 2007), 51.

5. Anthony Pagden, "Human Rights, Natural Rights, and Europe's Imperial Legacy," *Political Theory* 31, no. 2 (April 2003): 172. The same point is made in a recent

on to note, these rights are the "creation of a specific legal tradition—that of ancient Rome, and in particular that of the great Roman jurists from the second to the sixth centuries."[6] Thus the current format for identifying rights that are said to be universally applicable derives from what he calls a "secularized transvaluation of the Christian ethic, at least as it applies to the concept of rights."[7] Such an argument finds support if one considers those rights the Declaration upholds that are social in character, or that are derived significantly from specific cultural assumptions. These would include Articles 15, the right to a nationality, where it is assumed that a particular form of supra-individual, community, or regional and geographical entity is "natural" or universally desired or applicable; 16, the right to marriage; 19, the right to freedom of opinion and expression—this doubtless more contentious as a questionable contender for universality; 22, the right to social security—where whatever that might comprise is far from settled or perhaps indeterminable universally; 23, the right to work—again contentious, but if based on a particular contemporary Western conception of "work," its universality might prove to be difficult to achieve; 24, the right to rest and leisure—where the same problem occurs; 25, the right to a standard of living adequate for the health and well-being of himself and of his family—where the comparative nature of a "standard" of living causes friction; 27, the right to participate in the cultural life of the community— where what is taken to be "the arts" may be culturally specific.

Such observations have caused some commentators to note that, as Michael Ignatieff puts it, human rights activists often fail to understand that "these ends—liberty and equality, freedom and security, private property and distributive justice—conflict."[8] And that conflict, according to him, drives all the way down to the rights that define these entitlements. Consequently, he argues, "If rights conflict and there is no unarguable order of moral priority in rights claims, we cannot speak of rights as trumps."[9]

Amnesty lecture by Seyla Benhabib; see "Cosmopolitanism after Kant: Claiming Rights across Borders in a New Century," in *Self-Evident Truths? Human Rights and the Enlightenment*, ed. Kate E. Tunstall (New York: Continuum, 2012), 73–99. I am grateful to the editor for letting me see a proof copy of this outstanding collection in advance of its publication.

6. Anthony Pagden, "Human Rights, Natural Rights, and Europe's Imperial Legacy," *Political Theory* 31, no. 2 (April 2003): 172.

7. Ibid., 173.

8. See Michael Ignatieff, *Human Rights as Politics and Idolatry* (Princeton, N.J.: Princeton University Press, 2001), 20.

9. Ibid.

If universal human rights in the contemporary geopolitics of our time are necessarily tainted with this imperialist agenda, it has led others to conclude that they are, in the words of Raymond Geuss, "a kind of puffery or white magic" because a "human right" is "an inherently vacuous conception."[10] He is thinking of the contemporary discourse of human rights and its attendant politics whereby one government might, for example, upbraid another for its abuse of so-called human rights. His example is Indonesia: "To say that all humans have a natural or human right to self-determination, although the Indonesian government effectively prevents various groups in the archipelago from determining how they wish to live" means, he says, "that we think the Indonesians *ought* to allow some groups to determine their own political life and we *wish* there were a mechanism which could be invoked to ensure this outcome."[11] The general form in which we invoke human rights, Geuss thinks, is this: Group X has a natural right to Y, which is code for noting that group X does not "have a (legal) right to Y but we think they ought to."[12]

Geuss is one critic among a perhaps growing number who, after the International Declaration in 1948, have pointed out the unstable platform upon which those rights were declared.[13] As much recent history of international relations has shown, we have yet to create a sufficiently robust and universally acceptable mechanism for imposing one set of moral beliefs on the world as a whole. And of course such an imposition would only be acceptable if we did in fact believe that one set of moral imperatives could and should be universal.[14] Even good Kantians have to concede on this

10. Raymond Geuss, *History and Illusion in Politics* (Cambridge: Cambridge University Press, 2001), 144.

11. Ibid.

12. Ibid.

13. As Ignatieff notes, "The Universal Declaration enunciates rights; it does not explain why people have them." And he goes on to describe this as a "silence" at the very core of international human rights culture—the failure to agree upon the metaphysical and general philosophical bases of rights: "Instead of a substantive set of justifications explaining why human rights are universal, instead of reasons that go back to first principles—as in Thomas Jefferson's unforgettable preamble to the American Declaration of Independence—the Universal Declaration of Human Rights simply takes the existence of rights for granted and proceeds to their elaboration." Michael Ignatieff, *Human Rights as Politics and Idolatry* (Princeton, N.J.: Princeton University Press, 2001), 78.

14. As Diane F. Orentlicher notes in her commentary to Ignatieff's Tanner lectures, answers to the questions "Why do human beings have rights in the first place" and "What is it about the human species and the human individual that entitles them to rights?"—here she is quoting from Ignatieff's second lecture—remain "elusive more

point that if one does not accept the argument over moral imperatives, it is hard to see how the cosmopolitanism he proposed would ever emerge.[15] The skepticism over universalism is, of course, far from recent. Bentham pointed out the self-interest, as it were, of any rights claim in his insistence that "*real* law" upholds "*real* rights," in contrast to the French Declaration of "imaginary" universal rights. Marx thought that universal claims were in fact camouflaged techniques for the continuation of oppression and the bourgeois order. More recently, skepticism about the claim to universality has come from those who see the danger of supposing that all cultures can be understood by the same lights—insisting that moral judgments are always sited in particular cultures and traditions—as well as feminists who wish to highlight the fact that so-called "universal rights" are far from gender blind.[16]

The most common defense of contemporary human rights seeks to put a different spin on the concept's genealogy, tracing its roots to the natural-rights tradition, as if that heritage alone provides prestige for an unexaminable linkage between the fact of being human and the universality of equality. But this nonnegotiable belief—in our *being* human—has also proved to be a shaky platform upon which to construct the mechanisms for the delivery and monitoring of a universally applicable code of behavior. Even when "natural rights" are shunted to the position occupied by Kantian moral imperatives, arguments over the legitimacy of universal human rights continue unabated. This leads someone like Geuss to note that there's not much difference between "natural rights" and "human rights": As he notes sarcastically, "perhaps if we repeat claims about natural rights long enough and loudly enough . . . people will stop doing various horrible things to each other," and in another moment he states that "the point . . .

than a half century into the international human rights movement . . ." "Relativism and Religion," in *Human Rights as Politics and Idolatry*, ed. Michael Ignatieff (Princeton, N.J.: Princeton University Press, 2001), 147.

15. For a good account of the complexities of the Kantian argument, see Martha Nussbaum, "Kant and Cosmopolitanism," in *Perpetual Peace: Essays on Kant's Cosmopolitan Ideal*, ed. James Bohman and Mathias Luz-Bachmann (Cambridge, Mass.: MIT Press, 1997). A brief overview of the critical reception of Kant's notion of the cosmopolitan can be found in Seyla Benhabib, "Cosmpolitanism after Kant: Claiming Rights across Borders in a New Century," in *Self-Evident Truths? Human Rights and the Enlightenment*, ed. Kate E. Tunstall (New York: Continuum Press, 2012), 75–83.

16. For a good account of how these different critiques have operated in the domain of recent legal disputes, see Marie-Benedicte Dembour, *Who Believes in Human Rights? Reflections on the European Convention* (Cambridge: Cambridge University Press, 2006).

of appeal to 'natural or human rights' was to be that they were not supposed to be something we made to exist, but something we discovered."[17] Like Pagden, Guess sees the continuities between the early modern conception of rights as claims and contemporary universal human rights—and he is doubtless correct in suspecting that under such a conceptual regime we are unlikely to make much progress in this area since, echoing Hobbes, the covenants of the Universal Declaration are likely to be and remain mere words without swords. The argument of this book, however, has been to demonstrate that there was—and is—more than one way of building a concept of rights that may do the work we want it to.[18] Although I would agree that "human rights" as we operate the concept under the rubric of the 1948 Declaration and its subsequent outworking in international law and politics, is shackled to the concept of "right(s)," I also believe it possible to conceive of rights differently. Or, to put that more pointedly, to build a different architecture for a different concept: What Paine and others were building as "rights of man."

I find similarities in thinking this way with James Griffin, for example, who in his recent book *On Human Rights* argues that the problem with human rights is that the concept is poorly formed or "incomplete." He thinks that even today we still work with "what can reasonably be called the Enlightenment notion" that derives a human right from the fact of being human: "The idea is still that of a right we have simply in virtue of being human, with no further explanation of what 'human' means here."[19] This is a good place to begin since it puts far greater pressure on the hinge: *human-rights*. We need to think far harder about both sides of this hinged concept as well as the conjunction it makes. In the first place it would be useful to have a far more developed account of what a claim to the "human" might entail, how it might be upheld or legitimated, and on whose behalf it might be made. In the second, the role that rights play in any such claim to the human needs to be opened out for closer inspection. This book has argued that the second objective gains focus through the lens of history—and the first, through the particular form of conceptual analysis developed herein.

17. Raymond Geuss, *History and Illusion in Politics* (Cambridge: Cambridge University Press, 2001), 145.

18. This, of course, takes for granted that one might see the benefit to universalist aspirations with respect to rights. This is not the view of Sonu Bedi, who argues that rights are "*inadequate* to secure freedom and equality." *Rejecting Rights* (Cambridge: Cambridge University Press, 2009), 5.

19. James Griffin, *On Human Rights* (Oxford: Oxford University Press, 2008), 13.

Another useful recent account, Charles R. Beitz's *The Idea of Human Rights*, proposes a practical model for understanding and realizing the political doctrine enshrined in our contemporary version of universal rights. Beitz's analysis of the problems we face is very close to mine since he thinks there is a *conceptual* disjunction at the heart of much contemporary human-rights discourse. "The human rights of international doctrine," he writes, "appear to convey a different conceptual space than that defined by the natural rights model."[20] Beitz argues that the naturalistic account for the basis of human rights—those rights we have by dint of being human—could never form an adequate basis for grounding international human rights because those rights are supra-personal: "International human rights" he notes, "are primarily claims on institutions and other social agents—one's own government, in the first instance, and other states and international actors, when one's own government defaults."[21] Naturalistic views about human rights could never be robust enough, he thinks, to help us understand or justify why outside agents might be sanctioned to interfere in the affairs of a particular state. They may "put into philosophical form the beneficiary-centeredness of much popular thought about human rights,"[22] but when we look at the actual content of international discourse within the framework of rights it becomes clear that another model is required. For Beitz the solution is to take a pragmatic approach to the ongoing development of human rights law and discourse and to hold fast to a distinction between rights as applied to individuals and rights applied to institutions. "Human rights," he notes, are "standards that apply in the first instance to institutions" and we ought to "distinguish this view from individualistic conceptions."[23] It seems to me that there is great merit in this pragmatic solution, which, if my own forensic analysis of the eighteenth-century debates is correct, might gain traction through the establishment of our contemporary universal human rights on the platform of the concept "rights of man." This is because the concept "rights of man" is intransitive. Its syntax and grammar do not give coherence to a list of specifiable claims or entitlements: "rights of man" are not *the* rights of man. The consequences of this need to be properly understood. Constructing contemporary human rights upon this conceptual architecture would doubtlessly lead to their being, in Geuss's terms, con-

20. Charles R. Beitz, *The Idea of Human Rights* (Oxford: Oxford University Press, 2009), 58.
21. Ibid., 65.
22. Ibid.
23. Ibid., 115.

tentless. This does not, however, mean that they would also by necessity be "inherently vacuous." Here the mood of the concept needs to be called to mind. The concept "Rights of Man" proposes a future, or more correctly, an aspiration for a future in which the singular universal "man" will have applied equally to all; its tense is the historic continuous present. But that future "man" in its universal application does not render all "men" identical. In contrast to the imperializing tendency of the machinery of international human rights, which seeks to make every individual not only equal before the law but identical as a subject within human society, thereby collapsing the difference of the human into the similarity of the universal rights holder, the declaration of "rights of man" would seek to speak in the name of the singular universal. I take this to be close to what Ignatieff characterizes as the purpose and significance of human rights, that is, to "protect agency." As he writes, "To protect human agency necessarily requires us to protect all individuals' right to chose the life they see fit to lead."[24] The problem, however, with this formulation is the conceptual architecture of "agency." In Ignatieff's account, that concept is compounded with the "individual," or, to put that in terms that his critics would use, the bourgeois liberal subject (the individual) is the prerequisite for agency.[25] Only individuals have the power to act, intend, persuade, coerce others. Some might rightly object that this is too restricted a version of the agent. Collectivities, communities are also agents, but, in the cultural domain in which concepts as cultural entities circulate, so are traditions, habits, beliefs.

It seems both inevitable and important that the contemporary debate around human rights asks some basic questions: Are there human rights? If so, what is their content? If there are distinct human rights what is their status vis-à-vis each other? Does one trump another?[26] My point is that answers to these questions are determined to a great extent by the internal wiring and external connections of the concept we reach to for making sense in this case. We will only make progress, then, if we have a better

24. Michael Ignatieff, *Human Rights as Politics and Idolatry* (Princeton, N.J.: Princeton University Press, 2001), 57.

25. He writes: "The usual criticism of this sort of individualism is that it imposes a Western conception of the individual on other cultures. My claim is the reverse: that moral individualism protects cultural diversity, for an individualist position must respect the diverse ways individuals choose to live their lives." Michael Ignatieff, *Human Rights as Politics and Idolatry* (Princeton, N.J.: Princeton University Press, 2001), 57.

26. These are the kinds of question raised by Alan Gerwith in his "The Basis and Content of Human Rights," in *Human Rights*, ed. J. R. Pennock and J. W. Chapman (New York: New York University Press, 1981), 121–47.

sense of how the concept of rights (or concept*s*) operates according to its specific grammar and syntax. That is, how concepts prevent our understanding as well as enable it. If one wishes to explore how rights can be something other than contestable claims, and thus how "human rights" might be understood as nonconflictual, it will be necessary to find a different architecture. The concept of "right(s)" as it has been articulated and networked through the European natural-law tradition will not allow us to open out that new terrain. This is because the ideational concept of rights, operating with a dual functionality, containing and load bearing, constructs rights as a set of claims that have content. These claims will always be on behalf of claimants and therefore antagonistic to those upon whom the claims are made. As Ignatieff recognizes, "right(s)" are inherently conflictual.[27] We need to recognize, then, that rights as claims cannot be universal in the sense of always and everywhere simultaneously applied equally. Under the rubric of contemporary human rights as formulated in the 1948 Universal Declaration, an incoherence will always need to be negotiated because the concept of "right(s)" that it uses is required to function simultaneously as load bearing and containing, simultaneously invoking the support of both the platform and the deposit.[28] If the mood of this concept had been restricted to the declarative, it could have operated in the historic continuous present, but the program instituted in the wake of that historical declaration shifted the mood decisively. Almost immediately it began to operate under the regimen of the legislative. But perhaps that

27. In his commentary on Michael Ignatieff's Tanner Lectures, Thomas W. Laqueur wonders if, in fact, thinking about rights as a universal category, or as universally applicable, is the most efficacious way of ensuring that abuses under the rubric of the Universal Declaration are prevented. He notes: "But perhaps we do not need a universalistic notion of rights at all to protect the individual; historically rooted, or other so-called traditional liberties and restraints, might do." See Thomas W. Laqueur, "The Moral Imagination and Human Rights" in Michael Ignatieff, *Human Rights as Politics and Idolatry* (Princeton, N.J.: Princeton University Press, 2001), 137.

28. This is to note that the Universal Declaration has not only to delineate or identify those rights it wishes to claim are universal but also, at the same time, to provide a justification for why they should be so thought of. This task was beyond the framers of the Declaration not because they did not try but because the concept "right(s)" would not allow them to provide both. This was recognized at the time by Jacques Maritain, who was prepared to live with the fact that practical agreement about what universal human rights should be included in the articles need not be supported by theoretical agreement about the basis for holding to these claims. See J. Maritain, introduction to *Human Rights: Comments and Interpretations*, ed. Jacques Maritain (Westport, Conn.: Greenwood Press, 1949), 9–17.

move was made too precipitately; it jettisoned a resource that had been developed during the eighteenth century, the differently networked noetic concept, "rights of man," operating in a tense and with a single-phase modality that preserved the futurity of an aspiration. I am suggesting, then, that one way out of our current impasse would be to recover, or reinvent a conceptual architecture that would allow us to think universal human rights differently. This recovery need not come in the guise of fatuous nostalgia; rather, it would seek to place at the center of our politics of universal human rights the senses of futurity. It would help us understand and develop a politics of aspiration for the singular universal, get closer to achieving the common unshareable humanity that is the aspirational heart beating in Jefferson's declaration of self-evident rights.

What would it mean for contemporary human rights if one were to utilize this resource, perhaps even develop its architecture? In the terms I have been working throughout this book, this would be to ask, among other things, whether one can construct a politics with and through a conceptual architecture that does not operate as a deposit and that therefore cannot easily be used to designate or identify specific rights. If "rights of man" are at the end of the day unspecifiable, simply those rights that are aspirational, those that can be declared as a bundle, as singular general, but not necessarily be realized as specific claims, then how could this conceptual architecture be used in a realpolitik seeking to address the situation of citizens across the world, many of whom live under conditions that do not reach anywhere close to the minimum standards promoted by the Universal Declaration of 1948? Here the question of who defines and polices these "minimum standards" immediately rears its head. Those standards are, of course, the "content" of international human rights, and as such even if they are "declared" to be held in common, agreed by all those who are signatories to the Declaration and its subsequent codicils, they nevertheless remain claims that will always be susceptible of the accusation of being human constructions made by and on behalf of particular interests.[29] No matter how one legitimates those claims, in, say, the proposal that a

29. This is the kind of argument many anthropologists are quick to make. See Marie-Benedicte Dembour, *Who Believes in Human Rights? Reflections on the European Convention* (Cambridge: Cambridge University Press, 2006), 3: "The idea that human rights are universal flies in the face of societies which are based on social, political and ethical premises completely foreign to the liberal—and possibly market—logic of human rights. In other words, the concept of human rights rests on a peculiarly short-sighted view of humanity."

universal moral code is both achievable and applicable to human society (a legitimating strategy that falls at the first hurdle with respect to cultural difference), they will always be prey to the charge that rights-claims are always already levers of power. They seek to police or adjudicate the relations between individuals whose practices of daily social, political, cultural, and economic life take place under the aegis of supra-individual institutions: states, nations, faiths, global corporations.[30]

The way out of this seeming impasse is to make greater use of the declaratory mood. That is what the colonists discovered, and Paine and the pro-reformers after them. In this respect "rights of man," operating as a single-phase noetic concept, can provide the platform for understanding the political heft of an act of declaration on behalf of an aspiration. To be clear about the specifics of that aspiration, it is to realize "the human" as the singular universal. The performative structure of the declaratory mood and its tense, the historic continuous present, implies and entails its reiteration. Declaring "rights of man" cannot be done with, finished, and over. It is an ongoing, even continuous action, endlessly recaptured and reformulated in each successive performance. And it is made by the one on behalf of the many, or by the individual in the mode of aspiration to become the collective, by the citizen in the voice of universal citizenship. Compare this to the sequential temporality of the Universal Declaration: Its articles codify a series of protocols that now and in the future are supposed to govern how states and nations act with respect to their citizens. It has the shape and form of the event, a single finished declaratory act that sets in stone (or at least hopes, expects, or aspires to) the codicils by which all states, nations and supra-national institutions will be called to account. And having been made, it implies and entails the construction of a machinery that will hold all its signatories to account into an indefinite future. Its universality does not find coherence in the common unshareable but in the transferability of what is mine to what can and must be yours. Its conception of human rights, "those *rights* that one has simply because one is *human*,"[31] sees them as necessarily always and everywhere available. What requires our attention, then, is merely their universal application.

---

30. As Ignatieff correctly points out: "Rights are inescapably political because they tacitly imply a conflict between a rights holder and a rights 'withholder,' some authority against which the rights holder can make justified claims." See Michael Ignatieff, *Human Rights as Politics and Idolatry* (Princeton, N.J.: Princeton University Press, 2001), 67.

31. This is the standard formulation. See Jack Donnelly, *International Human Rights*, 3rd ed. (Boulder, Colo.: Westview Press, 2007), 21.

And it makes its declaration of the will to achieve this in the tense of the present-future, binding all future generations to its declaratory act. Paine would have recognized Burke's resistance to a truly aspirational politics of and for the one as the many.

The politics of aspiration for the singular universal require us to understand the peculiar signature of an "aspiration," to effectively work with its conceptual architecture. Aspirations are articulated in a very distinctive mood, part hopeful, part willful, part on behalf of a future that is deaf to our voice. But, when their expression moves from the individual, private, and singular to the political, public, and collective, something very powerful takes place. We begin to appropriate the impossible on behalf of the realizable, give the power of enactment to what can only remain at the horizon of the imagined. The public declaration of an aspiration is not a will to utopia but the collective possession of the present as an imagined future. This is why "rights of man" can only be declared in the mood or tense of an aspiration thereby preserving the architecture of its thinking: a singular universal humanity for the future-present.

What would universal human rights look like if the citizens of the world committed themselves to future-present "rights of man"? Would this mean that one would have to give up on the specific rights encoded in the Universal Declaration? Perhaps not, since one way of understanding those specific rights-as-claims would be to see them as steps along the way to another kind of "right," "rights of man," that did not come tied to the Western interpretation of moral value. Since the tense of the concept "rights of man" is the historic continuous present, and because it functions axiomatically in a single phase, there could never be a moment when those rights would be fully enunciable. They must be at once and always declarable in prospect. Human rights, then, rather than being defined as those we hold by dint of being human, may come to be understood in a different tense and with a different conceptual architecture, as our collective aspiration on behalf of humanity. Such a conceptual structure, it seems to me, would deliver on the aspiration of universality and equality while respecting the difference of the singular. It would enable us to think "rights of man" now in the future tense, as good a way of delivering on the aspiration to perpetual peace as I can think of.